PENGUIN BOOKS
READ ALL ABOUT IT!

Jim Trelease is the author of both *T*  (Penguin) and an anthology of read-aloud selections for children from kindergarten to fourth grade, *Hey! Listen to This* (Viking/ Penguin). His long-standing interest in reading to children stemmed from his experiences of being read to by his own father, from reading to his own children, and from serving frequently as a school volunteer.

Observing that children who are read to are children who love to read themselves, Trelease unearthed a wealth of information on the subject and self-published a thirty-page booklet in 1979. Penguin published the first of three expanded editions of *The Read-Aloud Handbook* in 1982. That edition spent seventeen weeks on the *New York Times* best-seller list and was published in Great Britain, Australia, and Japan. To date, more than one and a half million copies have been sold.

A former newspaper journalist, Jim Trelease today works full-time addressing parents, teachers, and professional groups on the subjects of children, literature, and television, and he is still a regular visitor to classrooms in his home community of Springfield, Massachusetts. He and his wife are the parents of two grown children.

Jim Trelease's lectures are available on 16mm film video, and on a ninety-minute audiocassette. For information, write Reading Tree Productions, Dept. B, 51 Arvesta Street, Springfield, MA 01118-1239.

Read All About It!

Great Read-Aloud Stories,
Poems, and Newspaper Pieces
for Preteens and Teens

EDITED BY JIM TRELEASE

PENGUIN BOOKS

PENGUIN BOOKS
Published by the Penguin Group
Penguin Books USA Inc., 375 Hudson Street,
New York, New York 10014, U.S.A.
Penguin Books Ltd, 27 Wrights Lane, London W8 5TZ, England
Penguin Books Australia Ltd, Ringwood, Victoria, Australia
Penguin Books Canada Ltd, 10 Alcorn Avenue,
Toronto, Ontario, Canada M4V 3B2
Penguin Books (N.Z.) Ltd, 182–190 Wairau Road,
Auckland 10, New Zealand

Penguin Books Ltd, Registered Offices:
Harmondsworth, Middlesex, England

First published in Penguin Books 1993

10 9 8 7 6 5 4 3 2 1

Copyright © Jim Trelease, 1993
All rights reserved

Pages 491–493 constitute an extension of this copyright page.

Library of Congress Cataloging in Publication Data
Read all about it!: great read-aloud stories, poems, and newspaper
pieces for preteens and teens / edited by Jim Trelease.
p.   cm.
Summary: Presents a collection of fictional stories,
autobiographical pieces, and newspaper columns, arranged for reading aloud.
ISBN 0 14 01.4655 5
1. Children's literature.   [1. Literature—Collections.]
I. Trelease, Jim.
PZ5.R19835   1993
[Fic]—dc20   93-21781

Printed in the United States of America
Set in Bembo
Designed by Ann Gold

For Susan

CONTENTS

INTRODUCTION

Hal Moore, currently teaching reading at the federal prison camp in Duluth, Minnesota, recalls his first teaching assignment back in 1986: "It was at a Chicago Catholic high school in the middle of gang territory. Most of the students weren't gang members, though a few were, but they were all pretty streetwise. The school rule was to begin every class with a prayer." At this point in his story, Moore rolls his eyes. "It just didn't work—at least not for me as a first-year teacher."

Sensing the futility in this approach, Moore, the son of a Presbyterian minister, hit upon an alternative idea that still fell within the letter of the law. "I began to read aloud stories from the Old Testament. These proved so successful that whenever I forgot to do it, the students would remind me, 'Don't forget to read from the Bible today, Mr. Moore!'"

Moore's solution to his classroom dilemma coincided with one of the primary recommendations the Commission on Reading had just made in its national report—that parents and teachers should be reading aloud to students "throughout the grades," and not just in early primary classes.

Upon its creation in 1983, the commission acknowledged a curious conundrum. In the process of achieving an education miracle—reversing the national school dropout rate (from 76 percent in 1940 to 30 percent in the 1980s) and increasing to nearly 50 percent the number of students seeking advanced degrees (the highest in the world) while assimilating 150 million more people (of very diverse cultures) into the population—America appeared to have created successive generations who read only for a diploma, not for pleasure.

By focusing exclusively on drill and skill in the reading process, we had created schooltime readers instead of lifetime readers. Indeed, research by the American Publishers Association showed that, during the year 1990, 60 percent of American households did not buy a single book—hardcover or paperback—and most did not subscribe to a newspaper.

Indicative of the problem was a visit I made in the fall of 1991 to a kindergarten class at Connecticut Farms Elementary School in Union, New Jersey. Forty-five years earlier I had begun my school years in that very room, playing with what looked like the same blocks and walking home by way of the same tree-shaded streets these children did.

Sitting as an adult now among these bright-eyed, shining faces, I asked them, "How many of you want to learn to read this year?" Without a moment's hesitation, 100 percent of the hands shot into the air, some children even boasting, "I *already* know how to read!" That same fall, the National Assessment of Educational Progress released what is called the nation's "Reading Report Card." Among its findings were these: among fourth-grade students, 45 percent read for pleasure daily; by twelfth grade, only 24 percent read anything—book, magazine, or newspaper—for pleasure on a daily basis. Somewhere between kindergarten and twelfth grade, we are losing 75 percent of our potential readers, learners, and thinkers.

In an attempt to solve this problem, the Commission on Reading examined more than ten thousand reading research projects that had been done in the last quarter century. In 1985 it issued a landmark report called *Becoming a Nation of Readers*, a compendium of findings, ideas, and recommendations that has been the basis for major changes in the way many of the nation's schools teach reading.

The commission's most immediate recommendation was this: "The single most important activity for building the knowledge required for eventual success in reading is reading aloud to children." Reading to children was more important than textbooks, workbooks, and homework. While this came as a shock to most parents, many teachers and librarians were not surprised. What surprised even them, however, was the commission's recommendation that the practice of reading aloud "should continue throughout the grades."

There are many reasons for this recommendation. To begin with, research shows that it is not until eighth grade that a student's reading level catches up to his or her listening level. Until that time, most students are capable of hearing, understanding, and enjoying material that is more complicated than what they can read.

This listening experience boosts the student's listening comprehension and listening vocabulary—both of which directly feed reading comprehension and writing skills. Moreover, the person reading aloud serves as an important role model, and the material being read serves as a commercial for the pleasures of print. The "pleasure" connection is essential in creating lifetime readers and of paramount importance during the difficult teenage years, when the greatest reading attrition is likely to take place. Two factors make up what might be called a "lifetime reader" formula:

1) Human beings—be they five-year-olds or fifty-five-year-olds—will only do over and over what brings them pleasure.

2) Like driving a car or swimming, reading is an accrued skill. That is, in order to get better at it, one must do it as much as possible. The only way to improve from a fourth-grade reading level (achieved by 90 percent of American students) to an eighth-grade level (75 percent) to a twelfth-grade level (25 percent) is by reading. And the more you read, the better you get at it. The better you get at it, the more you like it. And the more you like it, the more you do it, *ad infinitum*.

Thus we are back to the concept of reading aloud to students in order to make the pleasure connection. That was part of the reason Cambridge University teachers read aloud to my daughter's college classes on the novels of Charles Dickens when she attended summer courses there six years ago. When I mentioned this to a convocation in Kansas, a teacher who had just returned from her second straight summer of study at Oxford University told me her instructors regularly read aloud to classes there as well.

The impact such practice has on adolescent reading attitudes and appetites is witnessed by the Solomon Lewenberg Middle School (grades six, seven, and eight) in the Mattapan section of Boston, Massachusetts. As I described in *The New Read-Aloud Handbook*, the Lewenberg was an inner-city school drawing students from some of the most socioeconomically deprived corners of the city, and its reading scores ranked last among the twenty-two middle schools in the school system. Four years after it instituted daily sessions of reading aloud to students, along with sustained silent reading (SSR), the school's reading scores rose from last place to first in the district.

Since the Commission on Reading's recommendations for reading aloud, parents and teachers have besieged librarians and publishers for appropriate material, resulting in a wave of read-aloud publications. Little or nothing, however, has been done for the middle- and upper-grade students. Each year as I lectured throughout North America, increasing numbers of parents and teachers would ask me, "What can I read to teens? Is there any kind of collection available?"

With that in mind when I planned my first read-aloud anthology,

I decided to create two separate volumes: one for elementary students (*Hey! Listen to This*) and this collection for older students. The anthology format is especially suited to this latter group for three reasons: (1) the frantic life-style of both the parent and the adolescent, (2) the brevity of the classroom period, and (3) the sometimes shallow nature of the adult's own reading background.

In making the selections for this collection, I used a simple tool: hindsight. First, I asked lifetime readers, "What did you like to read when you were a teenager?" Then I asked myself, "What did my own children like me to read to them when they were adolescents?"

There was also the strong, lingering memory of two teenage boys (my brother Brian and me) sharing both a bedroom and a 396-page anthology called *The Fireside Book of Baseball.* Author and editor Charlie Einstein has compiled three more *Fireside* baseball books since that first one, all of them excellent, but none can compare in our minds with that first one.

We loved the idea of its variety. It had fiction and nonfiction, humor, satire, tragedy, biography, reportage, short pieces, long pieces, articles about yesterday and today, about all-stars and also-rans. It may not have been Einstein's purpose, but that collection also served as a nonthreatening introduction for two teenagers to some of the great writers of the century—Zane Grey, Ring Lardner, H. L. Mencken, Ogden Nash, James Thurber, P. G. Wodehouse, and Thomas Wolfe. As if these attributes were not enough, the collection had one more: It was completely portable. We read it in bed, in the bathroom, in the car, the kitchen, and on the porch.

With all of that in mind, my goal was to create an anthology that would please and interest both the reader and the listener. Because the selections would be heard rather than read silently, the material would have to be direct and not overly descriptive. The style and sentence structure could not be so convoluted that they tripped up the reader or lost the listener in a maze of parenthetical thoughts.

I also recalled what I used to read when my children, Jamie and Elizabeth, were teens. While they cleaned up the dinner dishes, I would read aloud newspaper columns, magazine articles, sometimes portions of a novel that I was reading for myself. Lifetime readers swim in a sea of print from many different sources—not just books.

The newspaper selections included here are human-interest columns from some of America's best journalists, along with a number of short but powerful op-ed essays. The nonfiction selections range from the origins of teenagers' favorite snack foods (potato chips, pretzels, popcorn, and peanuts) to what I think is the greatest sports fan story of all time, and the locales vary from a filthy Soviet prison camp to the immaculate bedside of a brother who remained in bed for nearly thirty-three years.

Of course, we should not assume the "pleasure" connection with print need always be amusing or entertaining. It can also be associated with anything that is moving or intriguing. As they grow older, students become increasingly interested in real people. With that in mind, I chose selections from five autobiographies, each describing how literacy enabled the subject to escape dire circumstances.

In addition to numerous short stories, there are excerpts from novels, including Newbery award winners and a Pulitzer Prize winner that is read in high school and used in law school ethics courses. I also chose to include (Lord, help me!) the opening chapter from a beautiful love story about a father and son—a book that is listed annually among the teen novels most frequently protested by book banners.

With each selection I have attempted to rectify what I have long felt was a mistake on the part of publishers. They go to great expense publishing the work of an author, but devote only an inch of copy in the book or on its jacket to biographical information. And what they give you is usually as bland as "He lives in New Jersey with his wife, Susan, and their two dogs." Meanwhile, there are four empty pages at the beginning or end of the book that could have been used for a personal profile of the author. Books are written by people, not machines; they are created by men and women with fascinating personal stories of how they came to be writers or how they created a particular story.

With that in mind, each selection is preceded by an introduction or author profile. Along with personal interviews, the research for these author profiles often took on the trappings of detective work as I pored over ancient newspaper obituaries, magazine profiles, and dozens of biographies. Every day I thanked the Lord for those wonderful encyclopedic library reference resources, the *Something About the Author* and *Current Biography* yearbooks.

But even diligence and determination are not always enough. Sometimes you need Lady Luck to smile on you. Like the time I was giving a luncheon speech in Evansville, Indiana, and casually mentioned the difficulties I was encountering in researching one particular author. After lunch, the woman whose retired husband had volunteered to drive me to the airport whispered to me as we walked to the car, "Chuck is too shy to tell you this himself, so I will. When he was in law school, he dated that author for four months." That serendipitous connection eventually led to the University of Alabama Library, from which I obtained the photograph on page 67.

And lastly, in constructing the book I kept in mind the notion of a front porch. Novelist Josephine Humphreys once explained the success of southern writers by noting that so many of them got their start sitting on front porches and watching the town go by. "From a porch," she said, "other people's lives look interesting." In a sense, the listeners to these stories will be sitting on their adolescent porches, watching and listening to the parade of characters in this book. My hope is that they will be interesting enough to somehow lure the passive observer off the porch and into their pages for the lifetime ahead.

FOR THEIR TENACIOUS ATTENTION to the hundreds of details involved in a book like this, to say nothing of their bountiful patience with my endless requests for information, I thank my wonderful staff at Reading Tree Productions—Susan Trelease, Linda Long, Kathy and Kelli Botta, and Carma Sorcinelli. (It should be kept in mind, however, that any errors in the book should be credited entirely to the author!) In addition, my appreciation is extended to the excellent reference staffs of my home library, the City Library of Springfield, Massachusetts, as well as the Boston (Massachusetts) Public Library, the Jones Library in Amherst, Massachusetts, and the Pasadena (California) Public Library.

Growing Pains

Eight stories about growing up—
its pains, fears, loves,
failures, discoveries, crimes,
and misdemeanors.

from **M**ANIAC MAGEE
by Jerry Spinelli

The Author Who Beat the Odds

Each year, more than one thousand novels are published for young readers in the United States. And each year since 1922, a team of fifteen librarians and children's-book experts spends twelve eye-wearying months reading, analyzing, and discussing them to determine which will win the Newbery Medal, the oldest and most prestigious of children's book awards.

If Las Vegas posted odds for such things, most novelists would start out as greater than thousand-to-one shots. But for Jerry Spinelli, the odds would have been among the longest. After all, he had at least six strikes against him.

Strike one was the fact that his previous books were funnier than they were serious. The past Newbery winners are not known for their laugh tracks. With a few exceptions, such as Beverly Cleary and Betsy Byars, Newbery authors specialize in seriousness, with story lines running from somber to tragic.

Strike two was the fact that the characters in his previous six novels (with one exception) were seldom involved in the courageously noble David-and-Goliath endeavors some adults think all young people should be doing. They were the same people you meet in any junior or senior high school cafeteria.

Strike three was the fact that his characters talked and acted like adolescents. That is, instead of discussing ways to solve society's monstrous social ills, they sometimes discussed pimples, body parts, food, dates, parents, teachers, each other, and themselves. Some adults think it's OK for children to act like children—except in children's books. Then they must act like Nobel Peace Prize winners (or Newbery prize winners). To give Spinelli's characters their due, they also did warm, generous, and innocent things as well, but too often adults' blinders prevent them from seeing these.

Strike four was the fact that the language Spinelli's characters used in such discussions often bordered on "gross" or crude, in the opinion of some critics and teachers. While the offending words or topics weren't dirty, some described them as sexist, racist, or just plain disgusting. Critics, of course, keep forgetting that fourteen-year-olds are neither finished products nor completely civilized. They grow to such status through at least twenty years of painful mistakes.

Strike five was the fact that Spinelli's *new* novel focused on racism (both white and black), and its protagonist was white. Since 1970, three distinguished and popular Newbery winners had addressed racism in America and, though two of the three authors were white, all approached it through the lives of black subjects: *Sounder* by William Armstrong, *The Slave Dancer* by Paula Fox, and *Roll of Thunder, Hear My Cry* by Mildred Taylor.

Strike six was the fact that the same novel also seemed to have too large an agenda, addressing homelessness, runaways, adult illiteracy, violence, and truancy, all with (horror of horrors) a dollop of *humor* thrown in to relieve the tension.

And in spite of these strikes and the long odds, Spinelli, the dead-end kid from Norristown, Pennsylvania, where every kid had a nickname and the woods and ball fields were filled with legends, the same Spinelli who worked twenty-two years as an editor for a business magazine so he could feed his growing family and wrote four unpublished novels during sixteen years of lunch hours before his first one was published, finally pulled it off, hit the grand slam with two out in the bottom of the ninth, and won the 1991 Newbery Medal for *Maniac Magee*.

He won it with a story that some critics call a parable, others call a morality play, and kids just call a terrific book. Sure they like it because of the unpreachy plot, the humor, and the characters. They like it because every neighborhood has legendary kids like the ones in the book. But they also like it for reasons they don't quite understand—because it addresses one of the most persistent worries of childhood: the fear of helplessness. What would happen to me if my parents died or abandoned me? How would I survive? In trying to cope with such fears, children frequently fantasize about a world without parents, and then gravitate to stories like "Hänsel and Gretel," *Oliver Twist, The Little Princess, Huckleberry Finn, Tarzan of the Apes, The Jungle Books, Island of the Blue Dolphins*, and even Bible stories

such as "Joseph and His Brothers" and "Moses in the Bulrushes."
They love Maniac for the same reasons.

Before you officially meet Maniac, allow me to address a mis-
conception that appears at the very beginning of the book. You will
find the same statement in many books of fiction and, though once
in a while it is true, more often it is not. In my hardcover copy, right
below the notice of copyright and the words "FIRST EDITION," there
is this declaration: "The characters and events in this book are fictitious. Any similarity to real persons, living or dead, is coincidental
and not intended by the author." The publisher's legal department
requires this sort of statement, but *I* know, and *Jerry Spinelli* knows,
and pretty soon *you* will know, it's not always true.

Each year, when the Newbery and Caldecott medals are pre-
sented to their respective winners, about a thousand librarians, authors, and editors gather for the banquet and awards. The best part
of the evening is when the winners give their acceptance speeches.
These have been written and practiced well in advance; in fact, they
have been recorded ahead of time by Weston Woods Studios, and an
audiocassette of the speeches rests at each dinner plate at the start of
the banquet.

On June 30, 1991, in Atlanta, Georgia, Jerry Spinelli gave his
acceptance speech, and it was just like his books—funny, poignant,
daring, and original. And in front of all those people he admitted he
didn't "make up" the people or events in *Maniac Magee*. He *stole* them,
the way many authors do. He stole them from his childhood, from
his seven children, and from the readers he meets or corresponds with.

Part of Maniac himself was loosely based on an old friend of
Spinelli's who was abandoned on a judge's doorstep at nine months
of age and raised in an orphanage. The place was called a "home" and
the children in it were "homies." As Spinelli explained, "Around the
age of seven or eight, my friend found himself among a busload of
fellow homies streaming and chattering toward a swimming pool.
There was a turnstile—only one child admitted at a time. When my
friend's turn came, a brawny hand clamped the metal pipe and held
it still. It would not move. And my friend, who until then had known
merely that he was black, discovered now that it made a difference.

"He does not know if the running began that day. He recalls
only that he ran everywhere he went. He ran the three miles to Tony
and Pete's Hoagie Hut, because if you were a homie, your hoagie
from Tony and Pete's was free. He made that trip two or three times
a week."

And Amanda is just as real, too, stolen from a school in New York State where a teacher introduced Spinelli to the sixth-grader who brought her entire home library of books to school each day in a suitcase. Spinelli gave her his address and asked her to write to him. She never did, so he's written to her—through the pages of his book.

So here are the first four chapters from *Maniac Magee*. Whether his legend lasts as long as Huck's or Mowgli's will be determined by future young readers. But I wouldn't bet against Spinelli. He's got much better odds this time.

• • • •

CHAPTER 1

MANIAC MAGEE was not born in a dump. He was born in a house, a pretty ordinary house, right across the river from here, in Bridgeport. And he had regular parents, a mother and a father.

But not for long.

One day his parents left him with a sitter and took the P & W high-speed trolley into the city. On the way back home, they were on board when the P & W had its famous crash, when the motorman was drunk and took the high trestle over the Schuylkill River at sixty miles an hour, and the whole kaboodle took a swan dive into the water.

And just like that, Maniac was an orphan. He was three years old.

Of course, to be accurate, he wasn't really Maniac then. He was Jeffrey. Jeffrey Lionel Magee.

LITTLE JEFFREY WAS SHIPPED off to his nearest relatives, Aunt Dot and Uncle Dan. They lived in Hollidaysburg, in the western part of Pennsylvania.

Aunt Dot and Uncle Dan hated each other, but because they were strict Catholics, they wouldn't get a divorce. Around the time Jeffrey arrived, they stopped talking to each other. Then they stopped sharing.

Pretty soon there were two of everything in the house. Two bathrooms. Two TVs. Two refrigerators. Two toasters. If it were possible, they would have had two Jeffreys. As it was, they split him up as best they could. For instance, he would eat dinner with Aunt Dot on Monday, with Uncle Dan on Tuesday, and so on.

Eight years of that.

Then came the night of the spring musicale at Jeffrey's school. He was in the chorus. There was only one show, and one auditorium, so Aunt Dot and Uncle Dan were forced to share at least that much. Aunt Dot sat on one side, Uncle Dan on the other.

Jeffrey probably started screaming from the start of the song, which was "Talk to the Animals," but nobody knew it because he was drowned out by all the other voices. Then the music ended, and Jeffrey went right on screaming, his face bright red by now, his neck bulging. The music director faced the singers, frozen with his arms still raised. In the audience faces began to change. There was a quick smatter of giggling by some people who figured the screaming kid was some part of the show, some funny animal maybe. Then the giggling stopped, and eyes started to shift and heads started to turn, because now everybody could see that this wasn't part of the show at all, that little Jeffrey Magee wasn't supposed to be up there on the risers, pointing to his aunt and uncle, bellowing out from the midst of the chorus: "Talk! Talk, will ya! Talk! Talk! Talk!"

No one knew it then, but it was the birth scream of a legend.

And that's when the running started. Three springy steps down from the risers—girls in pastel dresses screaming, the music director lunging—a leap from the stage, out the side door and into the starry, sweet, onion-grass-smelling night.

Never again to return to the house of two toasters. Never again to return to school.

• • • •

CHAPTER 2

EVERYBODY KNOWS that Maniac Magee (then Jeffrey) started out in Hollidaysburg and wound up in Two Mills. The question is: What took him so long? And what did he do along the way?

Sure, two hundred miles is a long way, especially on foot, but the year that it took him to cover it was about fifty-one weeks more than he needed—figuring the way he could run, even then.

The legend doesn't have the answer. That's why this period is known as The Lost Year.

And another question: Why did he stay here? Why Two Mills?

Of course, there's the obvious answer that sitting right across the Schuylkill is Bridgeport, where he was born. Yet there are other theories. Some say he just got tired of running. Some say it was the butterscotch Krimpets. And some say he only intended to pause here but that he stayed because he was so happy to make a friend.

If you listen to everybody who claims to have seen Jeffrey-Maniac Magee that first day, there must have been ten thousand people and a parade of fire trucks waiting for him at the town limits. Don't believe it. A couple of people truly remember, and here's what they saw: a scraggly little kid jogging toward them, the soles of both sneakers hanging by their hinges and flopping open like dog tongues each time they came up from the pavement.

But it was something they heard that made him stick in their minds all these years. As he passed them, he said, "Hi." Just that— "Hi"—and he was gone. They stopped, they blinked, they turned, they stared after him, they wondered: *Do I know that kid?* Because people just didn't say that to strangers, out of the blue.

• • • •

CHAPTER 3

A S FOR THE FIRST PERSON to actually stop and talk with Maniac, that would be Amanda Beale. And it happened because of a mistake.

It was around eight in the morning, and Amanda was heading for grade school, like hundreds of other kids all over town. What made Amanda different was that she was carrying a suitcase, and that's what caught Maniac's eye. He figured she was like him, running away, so he stopped and said, "Hi."

Amanda was suspicious. Who was this white stranger kid? And what was he doing in the East End, where almost all the kids were black? And why was he saying that?

But Amanda Beale was also friendly. So she stopped and said "Hi" back.

"Are you running away?" Jeffrey asked her.

"Huh?" said Amanda.

Jeffrey pointed at the suitcase.

Amanda frowned, then thought, then laughed. She laughed so

hard she began to lose her balance, so she set the suitcase down and sat on it so she could laugh more safely. When at last she could speak, she said, "I'm not running away. I'm going to school."

She saw the puzzlement on his face. She got off the suitcase and opened it up right there on the sidewalk.

Jeffrey gasped. "Books!"

Books, all right. Both sides of the suitcase crammed with them. Dozens more than anyone would ever need for homework.

Jeffrey fell to his knees. He and Amanda and the suitcase were like a rock in a stream; the school goers just flowed to the left and right around them. He turned his head this way and that to read the titles. He lifted the books on top to see the ones beneath. There were fiction books and nonfiction books, who-did-it books and let's-be-friends books and what-is-it books and how-to books and how-not-to books and just-regular-kid books. On the bottom was a single volume from an encyclopedia. It was the letter A.

"My library," Amanda Beale said proudly.

Somebody called, "Gonna be late for school, girl!"

Amanda looked up. The street was almost deserted. She slammed the suitcase shut and started hauling it along. Jeffrey took the suitcase from her. "I'll carry it for you."

Amanda's eyes shot wide. She hesitated; then she snatched it back. "Who *are* you?" she said.

"Jeffrey Magee."

"Where are you from? West End?"

"No."

She stared at him, at the flap-soled sneakers. Back in those days the town was pretty much divided. The East End was blacks, the West End was whites. "I know you're not from the East End."

"I'm from Bridgeport."

"Bridgeport? Over there? *That* Bridgeport?"

"Yep."

"Well, why aren't you there?"

"It's where I'm from, not where I am."

"Great. So where do you *live*?"

Jeffrey looked around. "I don't know . . . maybe . . . here?"

"*Maybe?*" Amanda shook her head and chuckled. "*Maybe* you better go ask your mother and father if you live here or not."

She speeded up. Jeffrey dropped back for a second, then caught up with her. "Why are you taking all these books to school?"

Amanda told him. She told him about her little brother and sister at home, who loved to crayon every piece of paper they could find, whether or not it already had type all over it. And about the dog, Bow Wow, who chewed everything he could get his teeth on. And that, she said, was why she carried her whole library to and from school every day.

First bell was ringing; the school was still a block away. Amanda ran. Jeffrey ran.

"Can I have a book?" he said.

"They're mine," she said.

"Just to read. To borrow."

"No."

"Please. What's your name?"

"Amanda."

"Please, Amanda. Any one. Your shortest one."

"I'm late now and I'm not gonna stop and open up this thing again. Forget it."

He stopped. "Amanda!"

She kept running, then stopped, turned, glared. What kind of kid was this, anyway? All grungy. Ripped shirt. Why didn't he go back to Bridgeport or the West End, where he belonged? Bother some white girl up there? And why was she still standing here?

"So what if I loaned you one, huh? How am I gonna get it back?"

"I'll bring it back. Honest! If it's the last thing I do. What's your address?"

"Seven twenty–eight Sycamore. But *you* can't come there. You can't even be *here*."

Second bell rang. Amanda screamed, whirled, ran.

"Amanda!"

She stopped, turned. "*Ohhh*," she squeaked. She tore a book from the suitcase, hurled it at him—"*Here!*"—and dashed into school.

The book came flapping like a wounded duck and fell at Jeffrey's feet. It was a story of the Children's Crusade. Jeffrey picked it up, and Amanda Beale was late to school for the only time in her life.

• • • •

CHAPTER 4

JEFFREY MADE three other appearances that first day.

The first came at one of the high school fields, during

eleventh-grade gym class. Most of the students were playing soccer. But about a dozen were playing football, because they were on the varsity, and the gym teacher happened to be the football coach. The star quarterback, Brian Denehy, wound up and threw a sixty-yarder to his favorite receiver, James "Hands" Down, who was streaking a fly pattern down the sideline.

But the ball never quite reached Hands. Just as he was about to cradle it in his big brown loving mitts, it vanished. By the time he recovered from the shock, a little kid was weaving upfield through the varsity football players. Nobody laid a paw on him. When the kid got down to the soccer field, he turned and punted the ball. It sailed back over the up-looking gym-classers, spiraling more perfectly than anything Brian Denehy had ever thrown, and landed in the outstretched hands of still stunned Hands Down. Then the kid ran off.

There was one other thing, something that all of them saw but no one believed until they compared notes after school that day: up until the punt, the kid had done everything with one hand. He had to, because in his other hand was a book.

• • • •

A s Maniac runs from one end of town to the other, he encounters a fierce tide of racism, among whites and blacks alike. What can one homeless twelve-year-old legend do against such ingrained ignorance?

Jerry Spinelli's other young adult novels include *Space Station Seventh Grade*; its sequel, *Jason and Marceline*; *Night of the Whale*; and *There's a Girl in My Hammerlock*.

Fans of Jerry Spinelli will also enjoy *Baseball in April and Other Stories* by Gary Soto (page 29), *Four Miles to Pinecone* by Jon Hassler (page 40), *Good Old Boy* by Willie Morris (page 105), *Miracle at Clement's Pond* by Patricia Pendergraft (page 45), and *S.O.R. Losers* and *Romeo and Juliet Together (and Alive!) at Last*, both by Avi.

AUNT MILLICENT
by Mary Steele

Dreaming Up an Aunt from Down Under

One evening in 1991, at a lecture I was giving in Tennessee, a woman approached me and asked with some delight in her voice, "Have you read 'Aunt Millicent' in the *Dream Time* anthology?" I must confess, I was too surprised at first to respond. The book was so new and so obscure, I couldn't believe someone else not only had read it, but had singled out my favorite story from the collection.

Other than textbook editions, anthologies usually are not big sellers and consequently have a short life span in print (excepting, I pray, the book you are holding in your hands). Thus, as an anthology, *Dream Time* was up against it from the start. Furthermore, it was originally published in Australia and *all* its writers were Australian. The nuances of language and customs of other cultures don't always translate well—even when the language is English.

I suppose, for all these reasons, *Dream Time* (edited by Toss Gascoigne, Jo Goodman, and Margot Tyrrel) did not receive more than a token amount of attention and promotion upon publication here. It was but one of two dozen books produced by its U.S. publisher that season. You would think that nothing about it, not even the cover, was extraordinary—until you begin to read the stories.

The idea of the book originated with members of the Children's Book Council of Australia who suggested a collection of stories by authors who had won that country's prestigious Book of the Year award. As an organizing structure, the council asked the sixteen authors to address the general topic of "dream time." Their approaches were as diverse as the authors themselves, and the tales ranged from the present to the future, from school to outer space, and from eerie to comic.

Glancing through the contents, I recognized some familiar international names, such as Ivan Southall and Patricia Wrightson, but most were new to me. All the stories were excellent but, in the end, the one that stayed with me (as well as with the woman in Tennessee) the longest was the whimsical "Aunt Millicent" by Mary Steele.

This Mary Steele is not to be confused with the American author Mary Q. Steele who wrote the Newbery-honored book *Journey Outside*. *This* Mary Steele grew up in Australia before television and computer games. In their absence, there was plenty of time for reading things such as Kipling's *Jungle Books* and Frances Hodgson Burnett's *The Secret Garden*. There was also time for listening—listening to parents and teachers read stories aloud and listening to stories being acted out as radio dramas.

"Aunt Millicent" is a grand and comic testimonial to the art of storytelling and story writing. It is also a tribute to the creative spirit of childhood, to inspired teaching, and to future aunts like Millicent. I should also add, it is an excellent example of what Sir Walter Scott might have had in mind when he wrote, "O what a tangled web we weave, when first we practise to deceive!"

Editor's note: In this story, the word "pram" refers to what Americans commonly call a baby carriage, and "surgery" is the dentist's office.

• • • •

"I," said ANGELICA TONKS, grandly, "have eight uncles and eleven aunts."

Angelica Tonks had more of most things than anyone else. She held the class record for pairs of fashion sneakers and Derwent pencil sets, and her pocket-money supply was endless. Now, it seemed, she also had the largest uncle-and-aunt collection in town. Her classmates squirmed and made faces at each other. *Awful* Angelica Tonks.

Mr. Wilfred Starling dusted the chalk from his bony hands and sighed. "Well, Angelica, aren't you a lucky one to have nineteen uncles and aunts. You'll just have to choose the most interesting one to write about, won't you?"

"But they're *all* interesting," objected Angelica. "The Tonks family is a wonderfully interesting family, you know. It will be terribly hard to choose just one.''

There were more squirms. The class was fed up with the wonderfully interesting Tonks family. In fact, Mr. Wilfred Starling nearly screamed. He just managed to swallow his exasperation, which sank down to form a hard bubble in his stomach. Straightening his thin shoulders, he said, ''Right, everyone, copy down this week's homework assignment from the board. And remember, Angelica, a pen-portrait of just *one* aunt or uncle is all I want. Just *one*.'' *Please not a whole gallery of tedious and terrible Tonkses*, he thought to himself.

The class began to write. Jamie Nutbeam, sitting behind Angelica, leaned forward and hissed, ''If the rest of your family is so *wonderfully interesting*, they must be a big improvement on you, Honky! And, anyway, I bet the aunt I write about will beat any of yours!''

''I bet she won't,'' Angelica hissed back. ''She'll be so *boring*. What's her name, this boring aunt?''

Jamie finished copying and put down his pen. ''Aunt Millicent, and she's pretty special.''

''Millicent!'' scoffed Angelica. ''What a name! No one's called Millicent these days!''

''QUIET, you two!'' barked Mr. Starling, massaging his stomach, ''and start tidying up, everyone—it's time for the bell.'' *Oh bliss*, he thought.

As the classroom emptied, Jamie lingered behind.

''What is it, Jamie?'' asked Mr. Starling wearily, piling his books and papers together and trying not to burp.

''Well, the trouble is I haven't any aunts or uncles to do a portrait of,'' said Jamie, turning rather red, ''so is it all right if I make one up? An aunt?''

''Oh, I see! Well, in that case . . . yes, perfectly all right,'' replied Mr. Starling. He gazed rather sadly out the window. ''The most interesting characters in the world are usually the made-up ones, you know, Jamie. Think of Sherlock Holmes and Alice and Dr. Who and Indiana Jones . . .''

Jamie interrupted. ''Does anyone need to know I've made her up? This aunt?''

''Well, *I* won't say anything,'' promised Mr. Starling. ''It's for you to make her seem real so we all believe in her. You go home and see what you can dream up.''

"She has a name already," Jamie called back as he left the room. "She's Aunt Millicent."

Aunt Millicent Nutbeam! The hard bubble in Mr. Starling's stomach began to melt away.

THAT EVENING, Jamie Nutbeam said to his family at large, "Did you know that awful Angelica Tonks has eight uncles and eleven aunts?"

"Well, everybody knows that they're a big family," replied his mother.

"Prolific, I'd call it," grunted Jamie's father from behind his newspaper.

"Yes, dear—prolific. Now, Mrs. Tonks was a Miss Blizzard," continued Mrs. Nutbeam, "and there are lots of Blizzards around here as well as Tonkses, all related, no doubt. But fancy nineteen! Who told you there were nineteen, Jamie?"

"She did—old Honky Tonks herself. She told the whole class *and* Mr. Starling—boasting away as usual. She's a *pill*." Jamie was jotting things on paper as he talked. "We have to write a pen-portrait of an aunt or uncle for homework, and Honky can't decide which one to do because they're all so *wonderfully interesting*, she says. Urk!" He paused and then added, "I'm doing Aunt Millicent."

Jamie's father peered over the top of his newspaper. "Aunt who?"

"Who's Aunt Millicent?" demanded Jamie's sister, Nerissa.

"You haven't got an Aunt Millicent," said his mother. "You haven't any aunts at all, *or* uncles, for that matter."

"I *know* I haven't," Jamie snapped. "It's *hopeless* belonging to a nuclear family! It's unfair—I mean, awful Honky has nineteen aunts and uncles and Nerissa and I haven't got any, not one." Jamie ground the pencil between his teeth.

"You won't have any teeth either, if you munch pencils like that," remarked his father, who was a dentist.

Jamie glowered, spitting out wet splinters.

"Anyway, he's right," announced Nerissa. "It would be great to have even one aunt or uncle. Then we might have some cousins, too. Everyone else has cousins. Angelica Tonks probably has about a hundred-and-twenty-seven."

"Well, I'm sorry," sighed Mrs. Nutbeam, "but your father and I are both 'onlys' and there's nothing we can do about that, is there? Not a thing! Now, what's all this about an Aunt Millicent?"

"Oh, it's okay," grumbled her son. "Mr. Starling said to write about *an* aunt or uncle, not exactly *my* aunt or uncle. He says I can invent one."

"Will you explain that she's not real?" asked Nerissa, doubtfully.

"Mr. Starling says I don't have to, and he's not going to tell. He says I have to make people believe that she *is* real. Anyway, I don't want Honky Tonks to know that she's made up, because Aunt Millicent is going to be amazing—much better than any of those boring Tonkses. It's time Honky was taken down a peg or two."

Dr. Nutbeam quite understood how Jamie felt. From time to time Angelica Tonks visited his dentist's chair. She would brag about her "perfect" teeth if there was nothing to be fixed, but if she needed a filling her shrieks of "agony" would upset everyone in the waiting room and Mrs. Tonks would call Dr. Nutbeam a *brute*. He was often tempted to give Angelica a general anesthetic and post her home in a large jiffy bag.

Now he folded his newspaper; Jamie's project sounded rather fun. "Right, Jamie," he said, "tell us about Aunt Millicent and let us get some facts straight. Is she my sister, or Mum's? We must get that settled to start with."

"I can't decide," frowned Jamie. "What do you think?"

"She'd better be your sister, dear," said Mrs. Nutbeam calmly to her husband. "I grew up here and everyone knows I was an only child, but you came from another town. You're more mysterious."

Dr. Nutbeam looked pleased. 'Mm . . . mm. That's nice . . . having a sister, I mean. Is she younger than me?"

"No, older," said Jamie.

"Where does she live?" asked Nerissa. "Has she a family of her own? Lots of cousins for us?"

"No way—she hasn't time for all that sort of thing. And she doesn't live anywhere in particular."

Mrs. Nutbeam looked puzzled. "What *do* you mean, dear? What does Auntie Millicent do, exactly?"

"She's an explorer," said Jamie, proudly. "She works for foreign governments, and she's terribly busy—flat out."

There was something of a pause. Then Dr. Nutbeam said, "Ah," and stroked his bald patch. "That explains why we haven't seen her for so long."

"What does she explore?" demanded Nerissa. "Is there anything left in the world to look for?"

Jamie was beginning to feel a bit rushed. "Well, I'm not sure yet, but foreign governments need people like her to search for water

in deserts and rich mineral deposits and endangered species and things
. . . you know.''

Nerissa lay on the floor with her eyes closed and began to imagine
her new aunt slashing a path through tangled jungle vines, searching
for a rare species of dark blue frog. The mosquitoes were savage. The
leeches were huge and bloated. Aunt Millicent's machete was razor
sharp . . .

"This is all very unexpected," murmured Mrs. Nutbeam, "to
have a sister-in-law who is an explorer, I mean. I wonder how you
get started in that sort of career?" Her own job as an assistant in an
antique and curio shop suddenly seemed rather drab.

Dr. Nutbeam was staring at the wall. In his mind's eye he clearly
saw his sister on a swaying rope suspension bridge above a terrifying
ravine. She was leading a band of native bearers to the other side.
How much more adventurous, he thought, than drilling little holes
in people's teeth. He wrenched his gaze back to Jamie and asked, "Do
we know what Millie is actually exploring at present?"

Jamie munched his pencil for a moment and then said, "She's in
Africa, somewhere near the middle, but I'm not sure where, exactly."

"In the middle of Africa, is she?" echoed Dr. Nutbeam. "Mm
. . . then it wouldn't surprise me if she were in the Cameroons. There's
a lot of dense forest in the Cameroons, you know."

"I thought Cameroons were things to eat," frowned Nerissa.
"Sort of coconut biscuits."

"No, no, dear, those are macaroons," said her mother.

"*They're* bad for your teeth, too," remarked her father, absently,
"like eating pencils."

Jamie fetched the atlas and found a map of Africa. His father
stood behind him, peering at it. "There it is, in the middle on the
left-hand side, just under the bump."

"It's called Cameroon here," Jamie said. "Just one of them."

"Well, there's East Cameroon and West Cameroon, see," pointed
his father, "and sometimes you lump them together and call them
Cameroons. Look—here's the equator just to the south, so it must
be pretty hot and steamy at sea level."

"Poor Millicent," sighed Mrs. Nutbeam. "I do hope her feet
don't swell in the heat, with all that walking."

Jamie examined the map closely. "That's peculiar—the north
border of the Cameroons seems to be floating in a big lake . . . um,
Lake Chad . . . it looks all swampy, with funny dotted lines and
things. I bet that bit needs exploring. They've probably lost their

border in the mud and Aunt Millicent could be on an expedition to find it."

"Is she all by herself?" asked Nerissa. "I'd be scared in a place like that."

"Of course she's not by herself," snorted Jamie. "She works for a foreign government, don't forget, and she'd have a whole support team of porters and cooks and scientists and things."

"She must be an expert at something herself, don't you think?" suggested Mrs. Nutbeam. "I would imagine that she's a surveyor."

"Yes, she'd use one of those instruments you look through, on legs," added Nerissa.

"You mean a theodolite, dimwit," answered her brother.

"She'd certainly need one of those, if she's measuring angles and distances and drawing maps," agreed Dr. Nutbeam. "My word, what a clever old sister I have!"

"I wonder if she was good at Geography at school?" said Nerissa.

"Well, you'll be able to ask Grandma tomorrow. She's coming for her winter visit, remember?"

"Oh help! What'll Grandma *say*?" gasped Jamie. "Do you think she'll mind? I mean—we've invented a daughter for her without asking!"

"I shouldn't think she'd mind," said his mother. "We'll break the news to her carefully and see how she takes it."

GRANDMA NUTBEAM, as it turned out, was delighted.

"How exciting!" she exclaimed. "I always wanted a daughter, and it's been very lonely since Grandpa died. Now I'll have a new interest! Just show me on the map where Millicent is at the moment, please dear."

Jamie pointed to the dotted lines in swampy Lake Chad near the top end of the Cameroons, and Grandma stared in astonishment.

"Gracious heaven! What an extraordinary place to go to, the silly girl! I hope she's remembered her quinine tablets. Millicent was never very good at looking after herself, you know. Let me see—I think I'll get some wool tomorrow and knit her some good stout hiking socks."

Jamie blinked. "There's no need to do that, Grandma. She's not really real, you know."

"Well, she'll be more real to me if I make her some socks," Grandma declared.

"Wouldn't they be rather hot in the Cameroons?" objected Nerissa. "It's awfully near the equator, don't forget."

"Woolen socks are best in any climate," said Grandma firmly. "They breathe."

"Now, Mother," interrupted Dr. Nutbeam, "you can tell us what Millicent was like as a girl. I can't remember her very well, as she was so much older than me, but I have a feeling that she ran away from home a lot."

Grandma pondered a moment. "Now that you mention it, she did. She did indeed. I thought we'd have to chain her up sometimes! We lived near the edge of town, you'll remember, and Millie would look out towards the paddocks and hills and say that she wanted to know what was over the horizon, or where the birds were flying to, or where the clouds came from behind the hills. We never knew where she'd be off to next—but she certainly ended up in the right job! I'm so glad she became an explorer. If I were a bit younger and had better feet, I might even go and join her. It would be most interesting to see the Cameroons. It's full of monkeys, I believe."

"Was Aunt Millicent good at Geography at school?" Nerissa remembered to ask.

"Let me think—yes, she must have been because one year she won a prize for it, and the prize was a book called *Lives of the Great Explorers*."

"Well, there you are," remarked Mrs. Nutbeam. "That's probably how it all started."

Next day, Grandma Nutbeam began to knit a pair of explorer's socks. She decided on khaki with dark blue stripes round the top.

ANGELICA TONKS had found it so difficult to select one of the nineteen aunts and uncles, that her pen-portrait was left until the very last minute and then scrawled out in a great hurry. She had finally chosen Aunt Daisy Blizzard, Mrs. Tonks's eldest sister.

Mr. Wilfred Starling asked Angelica to read her portrait to the class first, to get it over with. As he had expected and as Jamie Nutbeam had hoped, Angelica's aunt sounded anything but wonderfully interesting. She had always lived in the same street, her favorite color was deep purple and she grew African violets on the bathroom shelf, but that was about all.

Many of the other portraits weren't much better, although there was one uncle who had fallen into Lake Burley Griffin and been rescued by a passing Member of Parliament. Someone else's aunt had competed in a penny-farthing bicycle race in Northern Tasmania, only to capsize and sprain both her knees; and there was a great-uncle who had been present at the opening of the Sydney Harbor Bridge in 1932, but couldn't remember it at all as he'd been asleep in his pram at the time.

Mr. Starling saved Jamie's portrait until last, hoping for the best. Jamie cleared his throat nervously and began:

"I have never met Aunt Millicent and no one in my family knows her very well, as she hasn't been in Australia for a long time. This is because Aunt Millicent is an explorer . . ."

Mr. Wilfred Starling had been hoping for a bright spot in his day, and Aunt Millicent Nutbeam was it. He smiled happily when Jamie explained how Millicent had gained her early training as an explorer by regularly running away from home. He sighed with pleasure as Jamie described the swampy region of Lake Chad, where Millicent was searching through the mud and papyrus for the northern border of the Cameroons. He positively beamed when he heard that Grandma Nutbeam was knitting explorer's socks for her daughter.

The rest of the class sat spellbound as Jamie read on, except for Angelica Tonks, whose scowl grew darker by the minute. Jamie had barely finished his portrait when her hand was waving furiously.

Mr. Starling's beam faded. "What *is* it, Angelica?"

"I don't believe it. Women don't go exploring! I think Jamie's made it all up! He's a cheat!"

Mr. Starling's stomach lurched, but before he had time to say anything the other girls in the class rose up in a passion and rounded on Angelica.

"Who *says* women don't go exploring?"

"Women can do anything they want to these days, Angelica Tonks! Don't you know that?"

"*I'd* really like to be an explorer or something—maybe a test pilot."

"Well, *I'd* like to be a diver and explore the ocean floor and have a good look at the *Titanic*."

"What does your aunt wear when she's at work?"

"What color are her new socks?"

The boys began to join in.

"Can your aunt really use a machete?"

"How many languages can she speak?"

"Does she always carry a gun? I bet she's a crack shot!"

"How does a theodolite work?"

The clamor was so great that hardly anyone heard the bell. Angelica Tonks heard it and vanished in a sulk. Mr. Starling heard it and happily gathered up his books. He gave Jamie a secret wink as he left the room.

THE END OF THE ASSIGNMENT was not the end of Aunt Millicent. At school, the careers teacher ran some special sessions on "Challenging Occupations for Women" after he had been stormed by the girls from Jamie's class for information about becoming test pilots, mobile-crane drivers, buffalo hunters and ocean-floor mappers. The Science teacher was asked to explain the workings of a theodolite to the class.

At home, Aunt Millicent settled happily into the Nutbeam family, who all followed her adventures with great interest. Dr. Nutbeam brought home library books about the Cameroons and Central Africa. Jamie roared his way through one called *The Bafut Beagles*. Mrs. Nutbeam rummaged through an old storeroom at the curio shop and began to collect exotic objects. She brought home a brace of hunting spears from Kenya, which she hung on the family-room wall.

"Just the sort of souvenir Millicent could have sent us," she explained. "See—those marks on the blades are very probably dried bloodstains."

Another time she unwrapped a stuffed mongoose, announcing that Auntie had sent this from India on one of her earlier trips.

Jamie and Nerissa stroked it. "What a funny animal," said Nerissa. "Like a weasel."

Grandma was knitting her way down the second sock leg. "That funny animal is a very brave creature," she admonished, tapping the mongoose with her knitting needle. "I'll always remember Kipling's story of Rikki-tikki-tavi and how he fought that dreadful king cobra. Brrr!"

"Who won?" asked Jamie.

"You could read it yourself and find out, young man," said Grandma, starting to knit a new row. "I expect Millicent has met a few cobras in her time."

Nerissa had splendid dreams nearly every night. Aunt Millicent strode through most of them, wielding her machete or shouldering her theodolite. Sometimes Nerissa found herself wading through swirling rivers or swinging on jungle vines like a gibbon. Jamie was often there, too, or some of her school friends, or Grandma followed by a mongoose on a lead. Once, Mrs. Nutbeam speared a giant toad, which exploded and woke Nerissa up. In another dream, Nerissa's father was polishing the fangs of a grinning crocodile, which lay back in the dentist's chair with its long tail tucked neatly under the sterilizer. It looked slightly like Mrs. Tonks.

Mrs. Nutbeam brought home still more curios: a bamboo flute and a small tom-tom which Jamie and Nerissa soon learnt to play. Mysterious drumbeats and thin flutey tunes drifted along the street from the Nutbeams' house. School friends came to beat the tom-tom and to stroke the mongoose and to see how the explorer's socks were growing.

"Will you be sending them off soon, to the Cameroons?" they asked Grandma, who was turning the heel of the second sock.

"I think I'll make another pair, perhaps even three pairs," replied Grandma. "I might just as well send a large parcel as a small one."

"Yes, and then Aunt Millie will have spare pairs of socks she can wash," said Nerissa. "Socks must get very smelly near the equator."

Word of Millicent Nutbeam, intrepid explorer, began to spread through the town. Children told their families about the spears, the tom-tom, the mongoose and the khaki socks. Not every small town could claim to be connected to a famous international explorer—it was exciting news.

Angelica Tonks, however, told her mother that she didn't believe Jamie's aunt was an explorer at all. "I bet he just invented that to make his aunt seem more interesting than all the rest," she scoffed.

Mrs. Tonks sniffed a good deal and then decided it was time to have a dental check-up. "I'll get to the bottom of that Millicent Nutbeam, you mark my words," she told Angelica, as she telephoned Dr. Nutbeam's surgery for an appointment.

"WELL, WELL—good morning Mrs. Tonks," said Dr. Nutbeam, a few days later. "We haven't seen you for a while! Just lie right back in the chair please, and relax!"

Mrs. Tonks lay back, but she didn't relax one bit. Her eyes were sharp and suspicious. "Good morning, Dr. Nutbeam. How is the family?" she enquired. "And how is your sister?"

Dr. Nutbeam pulled on his rubber gloves. "My sister? Which one? . . . Er, probe, please nurse."

Before he could say "Open wide," Mrs. Tonks snapped, "Your sister the so-called explorer. Huh! The one in the Cameroons."

"Ah, *that* sister. You mean Millicent . . . now, just open wider and turn this way a little. Yes, our Millie, she does work so hard . . . oops, there's a beaut cavity! A real crater!" He crammed six plugs of cotton wool around Mrs. Tonks's gums. "My word, what a lot of saliva! We'll have some suction please nurse, and just wipe that dribble from the patient's chin." He continued to poke and scrape Mrs. Tonks's molars, none too gently. "Ah, here's another trouble spot. Mm . . . have you ever been to the Cameroons, Mrs. Tonks?"

Mrs. Tonks's eyes glared. She tried to shake her head, but could only gurgle, "Arggg . . ."

"No, I didn't think you had. Such a fascinating place!" Dr. Nutbeam turned on the squealing high-speed drill and bored into her decaying tooth, spraying water all over her chin.

When he had told his family about this encounter with Mrs. Tonks, his wife complained, "It's all very well for you. *You* can just cram people's mouths full of wadding and metal contraptions and suction tubes if they start asking awkward questions, but what am I supposed to do?"

The truth was that increasing numbers of townsfolk were calling at the antique shop where Mrs. Nutbeam worked. They were eager to know more about Millicent Nutbeam and her adventurous life. They felt proud of her.

"It's getting quite tricky," Mrs. Nutbeam explained. "People are asking to see photos of Millicent and wanting us to talk at the elderly citizens' club about her. This aunt is becoming an embarrassment. I wish people weren't so curious. Sometimes I don't know what to say!"

Grandma found herself on slippery ground, too, when she met the postman at the gate.

"Morning," he said, sorting through his mailbag. "You must be Jamie's grandmother, then."

"Yes, I am," Grandma replied, rather surprised.

"Mother of the explorer, eh?"

"Gracious!" exclaimed Grandma. "Fancy you knowing about that!"

"Oh, my girl Julie has told us all about it. She's in Jamie's class at school. Funny thing—Julie's gone round the twist since she heard about all that exploring business. Says she wants to buy a camel and ride it round Australia, and one of her friends is going to apply for a job on an oil rig. I ask you!"

"Well, that's nice," said Grandma, soothingly. "Girls are so enterprising these days."

"Huh! Mad, I call it." The postman held out a bundle of letters. "Here you are. Now, that's *another* funny thing—the Nutbeams don't get much foreign mail, come to think of it. You'd think the explorer would write to them more often, her being in the traveling line."

Grandma breathed deeply. "Oh, it's not easy, you know, writing letters when you're exploring. For one thing, there's never a decent light in the tent at night—and besides, there's hardly ever a post office to hand when you need it." She glanced through the letters. "Goodness! There's one from South America . . . Peru."

"That's what made me wonder. Is it from her?" asked the postman, eagerly.

"Her? Ah . . . Millicent. I don't know. It's for Dr. Nutbeam, my son, and it's typed. Anyway, as far as we know, Millicent is still in the Cameroons, although we've not had word for some time."

"She could have moved on, couldn't she?" suggested the postman, "Peru, eh? Oh well, I'd better move on, too. G'day to you!"

AT SCHOOL, Julie the postman's daughter said to Jamie, "Why has your auntie gone to South America? What's she exploring now?"

"Who said she's gone to South America?" demanded Jamie. He felt he was losing control of Aunt Millicent.

"My dad said there was a letter from her in Peru," replied Julie.

"Well, no one told *me*," growled Jamie.

At home he announced, "Julie is telling everybody that our Aunt Millicent is in Peru! What's she talking about? What's happening?"

Grandma stopped knitting. "Julie. Is that the name of the postman's girl?"

"Yes—her dad said there was a letter for us from Auntie in Peru, or somewhere mad."

"Oh, I remember—he asked me about it," said Grandma.

"Well . . . what did you *say*?" wailed Jamie.

"I just said I didn't know who the letter was from and that I thought Millicent was still in the Cameroons, but that we hadn't heard for a while where she was. That's all."

"The letter from Peru," chuckled Dr. Nutbeam, "is about the World Dental Conference on plaque, which is being held next year in Lima. It has nothing to do with Millicent."

"Well of *course* it hasn't," spluttered Jamie. "She doesn't exist!"

"But Jamie, in a funny sort of way she *does* exist," said Mrs. Nutbeam.

His father grinned. "My sister is quite a girl! She's begun to live a life of her own!"

"That's the trouble," said Jamie. "She seems to be doing things we don't know about."

While they were talking, the telephone rang. Dr. Nutbeam was no longer grinning when he came back from answering it. "That was Frank Figgis from the local paper."

"Frank, the editor?" asked Mrs. Nutbeam. "What did he want?"

"He wants to do a full-page feature on our Millicent," groaned her husband. "He's heard that she's about to set out on a climbing expedition in the Andes! Up some peak that has never yet been conquered!"

"What nonsense!" snapped Grandma. "She's too old for that sort of thing."

"It's just a rumor!" shouted Jamie. "Who said she's going to the Andes? *I* didn't say she was going there. She's still in the Cameroons!"

"Calm down, dear," said his mother, "and let's hear what Dad said to Frank Figgis."

Dr. Nutbeam was rubbing his head. "I stalled for time—I said we'd not heard she was in the Andes, but that we'd make enquiries and let him know. Whatever happens, Millicent mustn't get into print. We'll all be up on a charge of false pretenses or something!"

Jamie snorted. "Well, if she's climbing an Ande, it might be best if she fell off and was never seen again."

Nerissa shrieked, "*No!* She mustn't—she's our only aunt and we've only just got her!"

Mrs. Nutbeam sighed. "Listen, Jamie, perhaps the time has come to own up that Aunt Millicent is not real."

"We can't do that!" wailed Jamie. "Everyone would think we're loony . . . and that Grandma's absolutely bonkers, knitting socks for an aunt who isn't there. And what about the mongoose? Anyway, I *can't* let Honky Tonks find out now—she'd never stop crowing and she'd be more awful than ever."

Jamie decided to lay the whole problem of Aunt Millicent Nutbeam before Mr. Starling, right up to her unexpected expedition to the Andes and Mr Figgis's plan to write a full-page feature about her for the local paper. He finished by saying, "I think I might have to kill her off."

"That'd be a shame," sighed Mr. Starling. "She's quite a lady, your aunt!"

"It would be pretty easy to get rid of her," Jamie went on. "In her sort of job she could sink into a quicksand, or be trampled by a herd of elephants, or something."

Mr. Starling shook his head violently. "No, no—it would only make things worse if she died a bloodcurdling death like that. No one would be likely to forget her if she was squashed flat by a stampeding elephant. She'd become more interesting than ever!"

"Well, she could die of something boring, like pneumonia," said Jamie. "Or . . . will I have to own up that she isn't real?"

"Do you want to own up?"

"Not really. I'd feel stupid, and I specially don't want Angelica Tonks to know I invented an aunt."

Mr. Starling quite understood. "I see! Anyway, a lot of people would be sad to discover that Millicent Nutbeam was a hoax. The girls in your class, for example—she means a lot to them."

"What'll I do then?"

"If you want people to lose interest in her, you'll just have to make her less interesting. I think she should retire from exploring, for a start."

"Aw, gee!" Jamie felt very disappointed. "I suppose so. I'll see what they think at home."

"WHAT HE MEANS," said Dr. Nutbeam, when Jamie had repeated Mr. Starling's advice, "is that it's time my dear sister Millicent settled down."

"I quite agree with that," remarked Grandma, who was up to the sixth sock foot. "She's not as young as she was, and it's high time she had some normal home life. I think she should get married, even though she's getting on a bit. Perhaps to a widower."

"That sounds terribly boring," yawned Nerissa.

"Well, that's what we need," said Jamie, "something terribly boring to make people lose interest."

Grandma sniffed. "In my day it would have been called a happy ending."

"Well, I suppose it's a happier ending than being squashed by an elephant," conceded Jamie.

"How about marrying her to a retired accountant who used to work for a cardboard box company?" suggested his father. "That sounds pretty dull."

"Good heavens, it's all rather sudden!" said Mrs. Nutbeam. "Last time we heard of her she was climbing the Andes!"

"No, she *wasn't*." At last Jamie felt he had hold of Aunt Millicent again. "That South American stuff was just a rumor. The postman started it because of the letter from Peru, and then the story just grew!"

Dr. Nutbeam nodded. "Stories seem to have a habit of doing that, and so do rumors! But we can easily squash this one about the Andes. I'll just explain about the World Dental Conference on plaque. I even have the letter to prove it."

Dr. Nutbeam called Frank Figgis on the phone. He explained about the letter from Peru and about the ridiculous rumor which the postman had started. "In your profession, Frank," he added sternly, "you should be much more careful than to listen to baseless rumor. It could get you into all sorts of trouble! In any case, Millicent is giving up exploring to marry a retired accountant. She's had enough."

Frank Figgis was fast losing interest. "I see—well, sometime when she's in Australia, we could do an interview about her former life . . . maybe."

"Maybe, although she has no immediate plans to return here. I believe she and her husband are going to settle down in England— somewhere on the seafront, like Bognor."

Jamie passed on the same information to his classmates. The girls were shocked.

"She's what?"

"Getting married to an *accountant*?"

"She can't be!"

"How boring for her!"

"Where in the world is Bognor? Is there really such a place?"

Angelica Tonks smiled like a smug pussycat. "See! Your Aunt Millicent is just like any other old aunt, after all!"

Jamie caught Mr. Starling's eye. It winked.

AUNT MILLICENT NUTBEAM RETIRED, not to Bognor but to live quietly with her family. Nerissa still had wonderful dreams. Dr. Nutbeam still brought home books about far-off places. The blood-stained spears remained on the wall and the mongoose on the shelf. Jamie and Nerissa still played the tom-tom and the bamboo flute.

Grandma Nutbeam's holiday came to an end and she packed up to return home. She left a parcel for Jamie. When he opened it, he found three pairs of khaki socks with dark blue stripes, and a card which said:

Dear Jamie,
Aunt Millicent won't have any use for these now that she
has settled down, so you might as well have them for school
camps. Isn't it lucky that they are just your size!

With love from Grandma.

BROKEN CHAIN

by Gary Soto

When the Fighter on the Block Turns Author

The *Best Christmas Pageant Ever* is a modern children's classic by Barbara Robinson about the Herdmans, "the worst kids in the history of the world." What makes the book immediately recognizable is that every neighborhood and every school has its own particular tribe of Herdmans—that raggedy, cursing, fighting, thieving bunch of kids you are told by your mother "never to bring into this house again!" The author of this next selection, Gary Soto, was a Herdman, at least figuratively.

As of this writing, Soto also holds a singular distinction in American children's literature. The fact that he grew up poor isn't extraordinary. So did lots of authors—including some in this collection. Nor is he unusual for being a nonachiever in school, or for fighting on the playground. What sets him apart is that he is one of the few Mexican-Americans or Latinos—maybe the only one—currently earning a living as an author for children.

Soto grew up in the middle of industrial Fresno, California, during the 1950s and 1960s—across the street from a pickle factory, next door to a junkyard, and down the street from a raisin factory. His days outside school were spent fighting with his brother and sister, and then alongside them against neighbor kids. When that got boring, they took to fighting in original ways—with sacks filled with cats. Boredom was another of their enemies, and the extremes to which they went to avoid it ranged from hysterical to frightening. Once Soto's older brother told him that peanut butter could also be used as shoe polish. So he "buffed his loafers with it and went off to school smelling like a sandwich." Another time, after seeing a television show about fire fighting, they gleefully set fire to the inside of their house and played fire fighters with the garden hose.

Soto sat with the "stupids" at his Catholic school, where the nuns threw chalk at him and squeezed him into coat closets. Asked what he would like to be when he grew up, he alternated between "a priest" and "a hobo." When he transferred to public school for fifth grade, they asked him the name of the last book he read. "*The Story of the United States Marines*," he replied, striking immediate fear into the heart of his teacher.

Junior and senior high schools were hardly an improvement, and at seventeen he ran away from home to work in a tire factory, sleeping in cars and church balconies at night. But somewhere in the dust and dirt, there arose in Soto the dream to be more than he was. When he drew a high lottery number in the Vietnam draft, he decided to take advantage of the reprieve and go to college. Two years at Fresno City College were followed by California State University at Fresno, and then a masters program in writing at the University of California— Irvine.

At Fresno State a writing teacher named Philip Levine took a particular interest in Soto's writing. Using a nuts-and-bolts approach, he showed Soto how bad his writing was, line by line, image by image. Once Soto knew how *not* to write, he could begin to write successfully. By then his heart was set on writing poetry, but his eye was on teaching—largely because he didn't know anyone who earned a living by writing, especially a Latino.

After graduation, he continued his writing, submitting poetry to various journals and magazines. Recognizing the limited income from poetry, he expanded his writing into essays about growing up poor and Mexican-American. A small Northern California publisher, Strawberry Hill Press, took both his poetry and essays and printed collections of both, which word of mouth began to carry into class-rooms. Hundreds of college and high school students immediately saw themselves in the dirty Latino kid sweating out the hundred-degree summers in Fresno and began to write fan letters to the author.

Soto, who was by now teaching in the English department at the University of California—Berkeley and seeing his poetry printed in such prestigious publications as *The New Yorker* magazine and *The Norton Anthology of Modern Poetry*, had never thought about writing for a youth audience until the letters began to arrive. At that point, he began to translate his adult essays into a book of similar stories for young adults.

Although the collection was rejected by eight publishers over a two-year period, Soto had become convinced there was an audience for the book. The problem was, the audience was invisible. "Mexican-Americans are the invisible culture in America," he explained. Everyone accepts they're out there but no one acknowledges it. Their tranquil ways and muted skin tones leave them in a kind of "no-man's-land," from which they are routinely expected to cross over into the Anglo culture. Latinos will soon constitute one-third of the population in the United States, yet hardly anyone makes movies or builds sitcoms around them, or publishes books about them.

Soto finally convinced an editor at Harcourt Brace Jovanovich of the book's uniqueness. "If you don't take this book," he said, "you won't see another one like it for ten years." The book was published in 1990 as *Baseball in April and Other Stories*, and its critical reception and sales record stunned everyone. Among other citations, it won *Parenting* magazine's "Reading Magic" award and the Patricia Beatty Award for the year's best children's book on California history.

The eleven stories ring immediate bells with its readers—Latino or otherwise. The same unreasonable, outrageous, and illogical hopes and fears tease every kid, regardless of race or neighborhood. Here is the first story from that collection.

• • • •

ALFONSO SAT ON THE PORCH trying to push his crooked teeth to where he thought they belonged. He hated the way he looked. Last week he did a hundred sit-ups a day, thinking that he would burn those already apparent ripples on his stomach to even deeper ripples, dark ones, so when he went swimming at the canal next summer, girls in cutoffs would notice. And the guys would think he was tough, someone who could take a punch and give it back. He wanted "cuts" like those he had seen on a calendar of an Aztec warrior standing on a pyramid with a woman in his arms (even she had "cuts" he could see beneath her thin dress). The calendar hung above the cash register at La Plaza. Orsua, the owner, said he could have the calendar at the end of year if the waitress, Yolanda, didn't take it first.

Alfonso studied the magazine pictures of rock stars for a hairstyle. He liked the way Prince looked—and the bass player from Los Lobos. Alfonso thought he would look cool with his hair razored into a V in the back and streaked purple. But he knew his mother wouldn't go for it. And his father, who was *puro Mexicano*, would sit in his chair after work, sullen as a toad, and call him "sissy."

Alfonso didn't dare color his hair. But he had it butched on the top, like in the magazine. His father came home that evening from a softball game, happy that his team had drilled four homers in a 13-to-5 bashing of Color Tile. He swaggered into the living room, but stopped cold when he saw Alfonso and asked, not joking, but with real concern, "Did you hurt your head at school? *¿Qué pasó?*"

Alfonso pretended not to hear his father and went to his room, where he studied his hair from all angles in the mirror. He liked what he saw until he smiled and realized, as if for the first time, that his teeth were crooked, like a pile of wrecked cars. He grew depressed and turned away from the mirror. He sat on his bed and leafed through the rock magazine until he came to the rock star with the butched top. His mouth was closed, but Alfonso was sure his teeth weren't crooked.

Alfonso didn't want to be the handsomest kid at school, but he was determined to be better-looking than average. The next day he spent his lawn-mowing money on a new shirt, and, with a pocket knife, scooped moons of dirt from under his fingernails.

He spent hours in front of the mirror trying to herd his teeth into place with his thumb. He asked his mother if he could have braces, like Frankie Molina, her godson, but he asked at the wrong time. She was at the kitchen table licking the envelope to the house payment. She glared up at him. "Do you think money grows on trees?"

His mother clipped coupons from magazines and newspapers, kept a vegetable garden in the summer, and shopped at J. C. Penney's and K mart. Their family ate a lot of *frijoles*, which was okay because nothing else tasted so good, although one time Alfonso had had Chinese pot stickers and thought they were the next best food in the world.

He didn't ask his mother for braces again, even when she was in a better mood, and decided to fix his teeth by pushing on them with his thumbs. After breakfast that Saturday he went to his room, closed the door quietly, turned the radio on, and pushed for three hours straight.

He pushed for ten minutes, rested for five, and every half hour, during a radio commercial, checked to see if his smile had improved. It hadn't.

Eventually he grew bored and went outside with an old gym sock to wipe down his bike, a ten-speed from Montgomery Ward.

His thumbs were tired and wrinkled and pink, the way they got when he stayed in the bathtub too long.

Alfonso's older brother, Ernie, rode up on *his* Montgomery Ward bicycle looking depressed. He parked his bike against the peach tree and sat on the back steps, keeping his head down and stepping on ants that came too close.

Alfonso knew better than to say anything when Ernie looked mad. He turned his bike over, balancing it on the handlebars and seat, and flossed the spokes with the sock. When he was finished, he pressed a knuckle to his teeth until they tingled.

Ernie groaned and said, "Ah, man."

Alfonso waited a few minutes before asking, "What's the matter?" He pretended not to be too interested. He picked up a wad of steel wool and continued cleaning the spokes.

Ernie hesitated, not sure if Alfonso would laugh. But it came out. "Those girls didn't show up. And you better not laugh."

"What girls?"

Then Alfonso remembered his brother bragging about how he and Frostie met two girls from Kings Canyon Junior High last week on Halloween night. They were dressed as gypsies, the costume for all poor Chicanas—they just had to borrow scarves and gaudy-red lipstick from their *abuelitas*.

Alfonso walked over to his brother. He compared their two bikes: His gleamed like a handful of dimes while Ernie's looked dirty.

"They said we were supposed to wait at the corner. But they didn't show up. Me and Frostie waited and waited like *pendejos*. They were playing games with us."

Alfonso thought that was a pretty dirty trick but sort of funny too. He would have to try that someday.

"Were they cute?" Alfonso asked.

"I guess so."

"Do you think you could recognize them?"

"If they were wearing red lipstick, maybe."

Alfonso sat with his brother in silence, both of them smearing ants with their floppy high tops. Girls could sure act weird, especially the ones you met on Halloween.

Later that day, Alfonso sat on the porch pressing on his teeth. Press, relax; press, relax. His portable radio was on, but not loud enough to make Mr. Rojas come down the steps and wave his cane at him.

Alfonso's father drove up. Alfonso could tell by the way he sat in his truck, a Datsun with a different-colored front fender, that his team had lost their softball game. Alfonso got off the porch in a hurry because he knew his father would be in a bad mood. He went to the backyard, where he unlocked his bike, sat on it with the kickstand down, and pressed on his teeth. He punched himself in the stomach, and growled, "Cuts." Then he patted his butch and whispered, "Fresh."

After a while Alfonso pedaled up the street, hands in his pockets, toward Foster Freeze, where he was chased by a ratlike chihuahua. At his old school, John Burroughs Elementary, he found a kid hanging upside down on the top of a barbed wire fence with a girl looking up at him. Alfonso skidded to a stop and helped the kid untangle his pants from the barbed wire. The kid was grateful. He had been afraid he would have to stay up there all night. His sister, who was Alfonso's age, was also grateful. If she had to go home and tell her mother that Frankie was stuck on a fence and couldn't get down, she would get scolded.

"Thanks," she said. "What's your name?"

Alfonso remembered her from his school and noticed that she was kind of cute, with ponytails and straight teeth. "Alfonso. You go to my school, huh?"

"Yeah. I've seen you around. You live nearby?"

"Over on Madison."

"My uncle used to live on that street, but he moved to Stockton."

"Stockton's near Sacramento, isn't it?"

"You been there?"

"No." Alfonso looked down at his shoes. He wanted to say something clever the way people do on TV. But the only thing he could think to say was that the governor lived in Sacramento. As soon as he shared this observation, he winced inside.

Alfonso walked with the girl and the boy as they started for home. They didn't talk much. Every few steps, the girl, whose name was Sandra, would look at him out of the corner of her eye, and Alfonso would look away. He learned that she was in seventh grade, just like him, and that she had a pet terrier named Queenie. Her father was a mechanic at Rudy's Speedy Repair, and her mother was a teacher's aide at Jefferson Elementary.

When they came to the street, Alfonso and Sandra stopped at the corner, but her brother ran home. Alfonso watched him stop on the front yard to talk to a lady he guessed was their mother. She was raking leaves into a pile.

"I live over there," she said, pointing.

Alfonso looked over her shoulder for a long time, trying to muster enough nerve to ask her if she'd like to go bike riding tomorrow.

Shyly, he asked: "You wanna go bike riding?"

"Maybe." She played with a ponytail and crossed one leg in front of the other. "But my bike has a flat."

"I can get my brother's bike He won't mind."

She thought a moment before she said, "Okay. But not tomorrow. I have to go to my aunt's."

"How about after school on Monday?"

"I have to take care of my brother until my mom comes home from work. How 'bout four thirty?"

"Okay," he said. "Four thirty." Instead of parting immediately, they talked for a while, asking questions like: "Who's your favorite group?" "Have you ever been on the Big Dipper at Santa Cruz?" and "Have you ever tasted pot stickers?" But the question-and-answer period ended when Sandra's mother called her home.

Alfonso took off as fast he could on his bike, jumped the curb, and cool as he could be, raced away with his hands stuffed in his pockets. But when he looked back over his shoulder, the wind raking through his butch, Sandra wasn't even looking. She was already on her lawn, heading for the porch.

That night he took a bath, pampered his hair into place, and did more than his usual set of exercises. In bed, in between the push-and-rest on his teeth, he pestered his brother to let him borrow his bike.

"Come on, Ernie," he whined. "Just for an hour."

"*Chale*, I might want to use it."

"Come on, man, I'll let you have my trick-or-treat candy."

"What you got?"

"Three baby Milky Ways and some Skittles."

"Who's going to use it?"

Alfonso hesitated, then risked the truth. "I met this girl. She doesn't live too far."

Ernie rolled over on his stomach and stared at the outline of his brother, whose head was resting on his elbow. "*You* got a girlfriend?"

"She ain't my girlfriend, just a girl."

"What does she look like?"

"Like a girl."

"Come on, what does she look like?"

"She's got ponytails and a little brother."

"Ponytails! Those girls who messed with Frostie and me had ponytails. Is she cool?"

"I think so."

Ernie sat up in bed. "I bet you that's her."

Alfonso felt his stomach knot up. "She's going to be my girl-friend, not yours!"

"I'm going to get even with her!"

"You better not touch her," Alfonso snarled, throwing a wadded Kleenex at him. "I'll run you over with my bike."

For the next hour, until their mother threatened them from the living room to be quiet or else, they argued whether it was the same girl who had stood Ernie up. Alfonso said over and over that she was too nice to pull a stunt like that. But Ernie argued that she lived only two blocks from where those girls had told them to wait, that she was in the same grade, and, the clincher, that she had ponytails. Secretly, however, Ernie was jealous that his brother, two years younger than himself, might have found a girlfriend.

Sunday morning, Ernie and Alfonso stayed away from each other, though over breakfast they fought over the last tortilla. Their mother, sewing at the kitchen table, let her eyes grow big and warned them to knock it off. At church they made faces at one another when the priest, Father Jerry, wasn't looking. Ernie punched Alfonso in the arm, and Alfonso, his eyes wide with anger, punched back.

Monday morning they hurried to school on their bikes, neither saying a word though they rode side by side. In first period, Alfonso worried himself sick. How would he borrow a bike for her? He considered asking his second best friend, Raul, for his bike. But Alfonso knew Raul, a paper boy with dollar signs in his eyes, would charge him, and he had less than sixty cents, counting the soda bottles he could cash.

Between history and math, Alfonso saw Sandra and her girl friend huddling at their lockers. He hurried by without being seen.

During lunch Alfonso hid in metal shop so he wouldn't run into Sandra. What would he say to her? If he weren't mad at his brother, he could ask Ernie what girls and guys talk about. But he *was* mad, and anyway, Ernie was pitching nickels with his friends.

Alfonso hurried home after school. He did the morning dishes as his mother had asked and raked the leaves. After finishing his chores, he did a hundred sit-ups, pushed on his teeth until they hurt, showered, and combed his hair into a perfect butch. He then stepped out to the patio to clean his bike. On an impulse, he removed the chain to wipe off the gritty oil. But while he was unhooking it from the back sprocket, it snapped. The chain lay in his hand like a dead snake.

Alfonso couldn't believe his luck. Now, not only did he not have an extra bike for Sandra, he had no bike for himself. What a mess. Frustrated, and on the verge of tears, he flung the chain as far as he could. It landed with a hard slap against the back fence and spooked his sleeping cat, Benny. Benny looked around, blinking his soft gray eyes, and went back to sleep.

Alfonso retrieved the chain, which was hopelessly broken. He cursed himself for being stupid, yelled at his bike for being cheap, and slammed the chain onto the cement. The chain snapped in another place and hit him when it popped up, slicing his hand like a snake's fang.

"Ow!" he cried, his mouth immediately going to his hand to suck on the wound.

After a dab of iodine, which only made his cut hurt more, and a lot of thought, he went to the bedroom to plead to Ernie, who was changing to his after-school clothes.

"Come on, man, let me use it," Alfonso pleaded. "Please, Ernie, I'll do anything."

Although Ernie could see Alfonso's desperation, he had plans with his friend Raymundo. They were going to catch frogs at the Mayfair Canal. Ernie felt sorry for his brother, and gave him a stick of gum to make him feel better, but there was nothing he could do. The canal was three miles away, and the frogs were waiting.

Alfonso took the stick of gum, placed it in his shirt pocket, and left the bedroom with his head down. He went outside, slamming the screen door behind him, and sat in the alley behind his house. A sparrow landed in the weeds, and when it tried to come close, Alfonso screamed for it to scram. The sparrow responded with a squeaky chirp and flew away.

At four, he decided to get it over with and started walking to Sandra's house, trudging slowly, as if he were waist deep in water. Shame colored his face. How could he disappoint his first date? She would probably laugh. She might even call him *menso*!

He stopped at the corner where they were supposed to meet and watched her house. But there was no one outside, only a rake leaning against the steps.

Why did he have to take the chain off, he scolded himself. He always messed things up when he tried to take them apart, like the time he tried to repad his baseball mitt. He had unlaced the mitt and filled the pocket with bird feathers. But when he tried to put it back together, he had forgotten how it laced up.

Everything became tangled like kite string. When he showed the mess to his mother, who was at the stove cooking dinner, she scolded him but put it back together and didn't tell his father what a dumb thing he had done.

Now he had to face Sandra and say, "I broke my bike, and my stingy brother took off on his."

He waited at the corner a few minutes, hiding behind a hedge for what seemed like forever. Just as he was starting to think about going home, he heard footsteps and knew it was too late. His hands, moist from worry, hung at his sides, and a thread of sweat raced down his armpit.

He peeked through the hedge. She was wearing a sweater with a checkerboard pattern. A red purse was slung over her shoulder. He could see her looking for him, almost tiptoeing to see if he was coming around the corner.

What have I done? Alfonso thought. He bit his lip, called himself *menso*, and pounded his palm against his forehead. Someone slapped the back of his head. He turned around and saw Ernie.

"We got the frogs, Alfonso," he said, holding up a wiggling plastic bag. "I'll show you later."

Ernie looked through the hedge, with one eye closed, at the girl. "She's not the one who messed with Frostie and me," he said finally. "You still wanna borrow my bike?"

Alfonso couldn't believe his luck. What a brother! What a pal! He promised to take Ernie's turn next time it was his turn to do the dishes. Ernie hopped on Raymundo's handlebars and said he would remember that promise. Then he was gone as they took off without looking back.

Free of worry now that his brother had come through, Alfonso emerged from behind the hedge with Ernie's bike, which was mud-splashed but better than nothing. Sandra waved.

"Hi," she said.

"Hi," he said back.

She looked cheerful. Alfondo told her his bike was broken and asked if she wanted to ride with him.

"Sounds good," she said, and jumped on the crossbar.

It took all of Alfonso's strength to steady the bike. He started off slowly, gritting his teeth, because she was heavier than he thought. But once he got going, it got easier. He pedaled smoothly, sometimes with only one hand on the handlebars, as they sped up one street and down another. Whenever he ran over a pothole, which was often, she screamed with delight, and once, when it looked like they were going to crash, she placed her hand over his, and it felt like love.

• • • •

OFTEN, IT ONLY TAKES ONE BOOK or one award to wake up the publishing industry to a writer it has been ignoring for years. Gary Paulsen had written nearly fifty books before he wrote his first Newbery Honor book, but few had ever heard of him. Two years after *Baseball in April* appeared, Dell published Soto's two "underground" essay collections in mass-market paperback editions—*Living Up the Street* and *A Summer Life*—and Harcourt was preparing to publish two more Soto novels, *Taking Sides* and *Pacific Crossing*, as well as a poetry collection, *Neighborhood Odes*.

A more harrowing view of the Mexican-American experience can be found in *Lupita Mañana* by Patricia Beatty, which explores the pain borne by a thirteen-year-old girl smuggled into the United States from Mexico.

from FOUR MILES TO PINECONE

by Jon Hassler

A Novel to Learn On

Today, fifteen years after writing a young-adult novel entitled *Four Miles to Pinecone*, Jon Hassler sees his adult novels regularly reviewed in places like *The New York Times* with words such as "[He] is a writer good enough to restore your faith in fiction. . . . It makes you want to keep on reading just to remain in the company of such a wise man." Hassler has come a long way from the days of *Pinecone*, the book he says he "learned on."

Ever since he listened to his parents reading aloud from A. A. Milne's *When We Were Very Young*, and later, as a teenager, read the John R. Tunis sports books, Hassler knew he would be a writer someday. It just took him thirty-seven years to get around to sitting down to the task—which means he has more than a passing acquaintance with Tommy, the central character in this selection from *Four Miles to Pinecone*. Hassler was busy teaching high school English and raising a family before he began his writing. Two straight years of rejection slips followed, then five more years during which he wrote and rewrote *Pinecone* five times. When he couldn't get it published, he wrote an adult novel (*Staggerford*), which was accepted for publication, and that positive response convinced another publisher to take a chance on *Pinecone*.

Drawing upon a lifetime of small Minnesota towns and his experiences as both a teacher and parent of adolescents as well as working in his father's grocery store, Hassler set the book in a small town with a high school sophomore as its central character.

The opening scene has always been one of my favorites in young-adult literature. It reflects an age-old condition within the classroom and faculty. Every classroom has a Tommy in it, a student capable of accomplishing much but doing too little. And on every faculty there resides a Mr. Singleton, a crusty teacher who resists the tide of the times and refuses to reward mediocrity. At one time or another, most of us have known these two characters. We may have even *been* one of them.

When Hassler was asked if he had once been a Tommy, he replied, "No, as a student I always did my assignments. But quite frankly, I never liked school very much." How, then, did he arrive at a teaching career, both in high school and now as a writing teacher at St. John's University in Minnesota? "I like school a lot more now," he explained with a chuckle, "from the other side of the desk. As a student I don't think I ever had a real conversation with a teacher. I tried to change that when I became a teacher. First, I like my students. And second, I talk with them. It makes a difference."

The conversation between Tommy and Mr. Singleton will also make a difference—one that will help put a traumatic summer into perspective.

• • • •

CHAPTER 1

SUMMER IS OVER.
    I hope I never have to live through another one like it.

First, I flunked English. Then there was the break-in at the grocery store that put Mr. Kerr in the hospital and me out of work. And finally, a three-hundred-pound goon tried to run me over with a truck.

I'm not the scholarly type, so you may be wondering why I'm sitting here in the public library with a ballpoint pen and a notebook.

It all started back in June, on the last day of school. Mouse Brown and I stood by our lockers comparing report cards. I had an F in sophomore English and so did Mouse. I knew my parents would have a fit, and I asked Mouse to go with me to see Mr. Singleton. I thought we might talk him into changing our grades.

But Mouse said no. He said flunking English didn't make any difference to him. He said he was thinking about quitting school now that he had turned sixteen. He said he'd had a fantastic job offer, and if he liked the work his school days would be over for good. I tried to picture Mouse working, but I couldn't do it. He's like his dad. I've never known him to shovel snow or mow a lawn or set out the garbage. His mother does it all.

So I went alone to see Mr. Singleton. I found him sitting in his classroom, cleaning his glasses with his tie, and squinting at thirty empty desks. Without his glasses he looked ten years older, and very tired. The sound of city traffic drifted up through the open windows. The room was hot.

"Thomas," he said, "I know why you're here. You are less than satisfied with your grade."

"I'm in a state of shock," I said.

"All is not lost, Thomas. Pull up a desk and be seated. We shall talk. Nothing is hopeless."

"That's what I came to hear," I said. I sat down.

"Hope is a thing with feathers that perches in the soul." Mr. Singleton is forever quoting dead poets. He put on his glasses and gave me the same repulsive smile he always gives students who talk out of turn or carve on desks. It's the only smile he's got, and he shows a lot of crooked gray teeth. He's the only teacher I know who can discipline a student simply by smiling at him. You'd rather behave yourself than look at those teeth a second time.

"Mr. Singleton," I said, "I deserve better than an F in English. I did great on all your tests. I know everything you teach, and here you flunk me. How can you get away with that?"

I was coming on strong. His smile faded.

"Please do not question my judgment," he said. "Now it's true that you know a great deal about what I teach, but you have one great weakness—one vast flaw—in an otherwise adequate mentality."

"What's that?"

"You lack perseverance, my good young man."

"What's that?"

"Perseverance is another word for handing in assignments. Would you care to estimate the number of written assignments you failed to hand in during the year?"

"I know I skipped a few. Ten or twelve."

"Guess again."

"Maybe more. Maybe twenty. But I had a job, Mr. Singleton. I couldn't always find time to do the assignments."

"Guess again."

"Twenty-five?"

He opened his grade book and said, "Look at this," and pushed it across his desk. "Forty-seven," he said.

"Forty-seven?" I said. I pretended to be surprised, but I knew he was right. I had decided early in the year that I wouldn't trouble myself with English assignments, because English always came pretty easy for me, and I figured I could get by with at least a C by simply showing up for class and taking the tests. English assignments, if you take them seriously, can really cut into your free time.

He insisted I look at his grade book. With a dirty fingernail, he was pointing to my name. Sure enough, except for the A's and B's I got on tests, every little square after my name was blank. Forty-seven of them.

"Those A's and B's don't average out to F," I said. I wasn't about to give up.

"Those forty-seven empty squares stand for forty-seven F's. A very low average, indeed. Perhaps the lowest average in the history of Donnelly High School. Perhaps the lowest in the city of St. Paul. For all I know, it may be the lowest of any sophomore in the western hemisphere."

He was getting nasty now, so I decided to quit reasoning and play on his sympathy—even tell a lie or two if I had to. I told him my father would come after me with a leather strap. I told him I might lose my job at the grocery store. My mother might die of grief. I told him I might have to drop out of high school because I couldn't afford the extra time it would take to make up his course.

When I got to the part about my mother, he realized I was spreading it pretty thick. That's when he gave me a big horrible smile.

"Thomas," he said, "I have a plan. That F can be changed to the B you're capable of earning—if you will write one long story in a mature style and free of mechanical errors. I will give you the whole summer to finish it. If you bring it to me on the first day of school next fall I will change your grade."

"But in the summer I work full time in the grocery store. I'm not sure I'd have the time to work on English."

"If you wish to pass the course you will find the time. It will be up to you. It is your one chance."

"Well, maybe I can work it out. Just tell a story in writing—is that it?"

"Yes. A story of some length."

"What length?"

"Forty-seven pages," he said. And smiled.

• • • •

TOMMY DOES WRITE THE PAPER. In fact, *Four Miles to Pinecone* is that paper. In it, he describes the events of his summer vacation. His grocery store job turns out to be short lived when his elderly boss is beaten and hospitalized after a robbery attempt. Even worse for Tommy, however, are the haunting thoughts that follow the robbery: (1) He witnessed the event and wonders if he might have done more to save the old man from harm, and (2) he recognized one of the robbers as his friend Mouse, yet cannot bring himself to report the crime to the police.

Fans of *Four Miles to Pinecone* might turn to the following selections: *A Day No Pigs Would Die* by Robert Newton Peck (page 99) and *Miracle at Clement's Pond* by Patricia Pendergraft (page 45). They might also enjoy *The Duplicate* by William Sleator.

from **M**IRACLE AT CLEMENT'S POND

by Patricia Pendergraft

Climbing Out of Poverty's Grasp

"**T**he only way I can explain it, and I know this sounds corny—I was a born writer!" declares Patricia Pendergraft, high school dropout and author of six novels.

Growing up in a dirt-poor broken home in the Central Valley of California, Pendergraft had no reason to believe she'd ever become a writer. She wasn't sure where her next meal was coming from, never mind a typewriter and paper. She did become a reader, though, when she realized each book could be an escape hatch from the unhappiness around her. The feeling was so good, she soon began to think about writing her own books. Fourth grade found her writing stories and stapling them together so they would look like books.

Outside of the books she wrote for herself, the closest she came to owning books was when she was in sixth grade and her father came to visit one day when her mother was working. He was accompanied by his girlfriend, who had brought along a box of books, which she left behind. Most of them were by adult authors—such as Oscar Wilde and Guy de Maupassant—but Pendergraft waded through them, ignoring what she couldn't understand and absorbing the rest.

Because of her family's desperate finances, she dropped out of high school to work. For the next few years she worked in people's homes, either cleaning them or taking care of their children and aging relatives. At nineteen, she began the first of three regrettable marriages. And with each year, her urge to write increased. Finally, against the wishes of a husband who attempted to cut off any further means of escape by limiting her reading and writing to two hours a morning, she wrote an adult novel that went out of print almost as fast as it was published.

Undeterred, she divorced the husband, wrote a young-adult novel called *Miracle at Clement's Pond*, and sent it to an agent. The agent took it but confided that it would never sell, and it sat for a year on the agent's desk. In desperation, Pendergraft took a copy of the manuscript and sent it to a publisher herself. Fortunately, a new editor had just come aboard at Philomel and the story struck the right chord with her. In 1987, the book was published in hardcover, followed by a Scholastic paperback in 1988 and an NBC movie version in 1993, which starred Cloris Leachman.

In this opening chapter from that novel, we meet three original and colorful teenagers from rural America, embarking on a seemingly innocent escapade that will turn a small community upside down and change many lives before it is finished.

• • • •

CHAPTER 1
We Find More Than Bullfrogs
at Clement's Pond

WELL, IF YOU WANT TO KNOW THE TRUTH, and I guess you do, I mean, what would be the point of lying about it now? You'd be sure to run into someone in Clement's Pond who knows the whole story and find out I'd lied, so I'm going to tell the whole truth and nothing but, just like my Aunt Ester said I should. She said if I told the truth, I'd get some mighty big blessings in life, but if I didn't tell the truth, the way she said it was, for sure and for certain, I'd get a plague of damnation on me. So this is the way it all happened—cross my heart and stick a thousand needles in my eyes, if it ain't.

When we put the baby on Adeline Newberry's front porch, we thought it would make her joyful and happy, just like the way she was always telling everyone in Clement's Pond she'd be if she had a little baby to take care of. Being the only old maid in Clement's Pond was a pretty hard cross to bear. She was childless and all alone and all she had to love was the chickens that pecked around in the dust in her yard and a stray dog or two whenever one wandered onto her property. She had been jilted by Ferdie Hughs when she was young and no one else in town ever looked at her twice. Leastways, not with marriage on their minds. Except maybe old man Oscar Bebee, who flirts with all the women in church and out, and he ain't exactly a good catch for any woman. He lumbers around town on a cane and spits tobaccer juice all over wherever he happens to be. Aunt Ester said it ain't likely any woman, even Adeline Newberry, would want to spend the rest of her life washing tobaccer stains off her shoes.

I couldn't rightly put my finger on why no one wanted Adeline Newberry. It wasn't that Adeline was ugly. There are lots of old ladies in Clement's Pond uglier and fatter and even skinnier than Adeline. And it wasn't that she had a physical deformity neither, like the hunchback Gypsy who lives in the woods and only comes out once in a blue moon and, when she does, goes up and down the road looking for lost change.

"Maybe it's because Adeline has false teeth," Sylvie Bogart said once. Sylvie is Justin Bogart's sister, and Justin is my best friend in all the world.

"That's stupid," I told Sylvie. "My Aunt Ester has got false teeth. I seen them in a cup of water lots of times. That didn't keep her from getting married to Uncle Clayborn."

"Maybe she didn't have them false teeth when your Uncle Clayborn married her," Sylvie said sarcastically.

But it wasn't the teeth and it wasn't the way Adeline looked. She had a right fine cushion of fat on her and plenty of what Aunt Ester called "get up and go." Her eyes was dark and kind, and according to Aunt Ester, any gent in his right mind ought to be glad to get a good woman like Adeline Newberry. But they weren't and it just seemed Adeline was the loneliest person in all of Clement's Pond. Just about every time she come to visit Aunt Ester, she'd start in telling how lonely she was.

"If I had me a little baby . . ." she'd start out, until Aunt Ester would cut right in and tell her, "You're too old for a baby, Adeline Newberry!"

"But, if I had one . . ."

"You won't have one!" Aunt Ester would tell her flatly.

"But, if I did . . ."

"All right, what would you do with a baby *if* you had one?" Aunt Ester would stare over the top of her glasses at Adeline with eyes so sharp they could bore a hole through a plank of wood.

But Adeline didn't pay no attention to that. She'd get a look on her face and fix a stare on some far-off place and say, "Oh, I'd hold it and love it and take grand care of it. I'd dress it up every day just like as if I was taking it to church and I'd make it cute little clothes and order some, too, out of the Sears and Roebuck catalog. And I'd curl its hair and teach it all kinds of fine manners. I'd never let it cry or be afraid . . ."

"You'd spoil it rotten!" Aunt Ester would snort with a loud smack of her lips.

"Yes, Ester, I would. I'd spoil it like a little baby ought to be spoiled. With all the love and tenderness I got inside me," Adeline would say, pulling her eyes back from the far-off place and fixing them on Aunt Ester.

"Well, you may as well get them notions out of your head, Adeline. You ain't married and you're too old to have a baby even if you was," Aunt Ester would tell her like she was an authority on the subject.

A brave, sunny look would appear on Adeline's face; then suddenly a curtain, like the heavy fog that hangs over the pond in winter, would take its place. She'd sigh and look down at her ringless wedding-band finger and say in a low voice, "Well, I reckon you're right, Ester."

So I reckon you can see why we wanted to make Adeline Newberry happy. But the way we got the baby was, Sylvie and Justin and me went down to the pond one evening late to go froggin'. There was a chill coming up in the wind by the time we got halfway there but we just kept trudging along, hoping to lose Sylvie along the way. Seemed like there was times when we just couldn't shake her off us. Just as we got near enough to see the water in the pond, we heard a strange sniffling noise like a girl was crying and a man's voice saying in a short, gruff way, "Aw, come on, Fleur. It won't do no good to cry. You know someone will come along. Any minute, too. This place is thick with all kinds of people, day and night."

That just seemed to make the girl cry harder and the man said in an angry, impatient voice, "You hadn't got no money to take care of it no way! Come on now!"

The girl sniffled again and said something real quiet and soft that we couldn't understand and, right after that, we heard a rustle in the underbrush and the movement of the tree limbs that hang low over the pond, and soon after that, the sound of a car door slamming shut and someone driving away in it real fast. We could hear the pebbles and dirt kick up under the wheels of the car as it spun away.

"What do you suppose they left over there?" Justin asked.

"Maybe they robbed a bank over to Tylersville and are hiding the money until they can come back for it. Maybe J. Edgar Hoover is on their trail—"

"Aw, shoot," Justin snorted, cutting Sylvie off just as she got going good. "You listen to the radio too much."

"J. Edgar Hoover is the busiest man in the whole world!" I spoke up. "Ain't he the head of the FBI? He wouldn't go after plain old robbers. Besides, you heard what the man said, Sylvie. He said they ain't got no money to take care of whatever it is."

"Maybe it's a hurt puppy," Sylvie said. "Or a cat in a gunnysack. Folks is always dropping kittens off around here."

"Aw, shoot!" Justin snorted disgustedly.

Me and Sylvie follered Justin to where the sniffling and talking come from and pushed the low branches and vines out of our way. Up in the darkness of one of the trees a whippoorwill set up a fuss.

"Holy pinchin' earwigs!" Justin shouted, looking down.

Me and Sylvie leaned close and looked down too. "A baby!" Sylvie cried. "It's a baby!"

"Why would anyone leave a baby here?" Justin asked, frowning hard.

"I don't know, but I know one thing—it will die, sure as a frog has legs, if we leave it here," I said, staring hard at that little baby. It was sound asleep. We could see its little face in the moonlight that was slowly creeping up over the pond. It was wrapped up in a heavy blanket like as if the person who left it there wanted it to stay nice and warm.

"I guess we ought to take it to the police station—" Justin started, and Sylvie cut him off quick.

"No!" she cried. "The police will only put it in a place with some old mangy folks who might not even want it," Sylvie rushed on.

"How do you know what the police'll do?" I asked her.

"I heard tell. And sometimes them mangy folks lock the babies up in a room and tie them to a bed and let them starve."

"We could take the baby to your Aunt Ester, Lyon," Justin said.

"We can't do that! Aunt Ester would take it to the police for sure."

"Well, maybe we should just leave it here," Justin said, staring down at the baby again. "There's bound to be people around here tomorrow."

"Justin Bogart! How can you even think about leaving this little baby here all night long?" Sylvie cried. "It might rain so hard the water would rise and this baby would float right into it and get drowned."

"And what if old man Lyman's half-starved red hound come along?" I said. "Or Oscar Bebee's bull got out of the pasture or a snake come crawling up . . ." I shuddered, just thinking about all the things that could happen to that baby. And I guess I sounded like Sylvie, because Justin give me a disgusted look.

"Well, what are we going to do?" Justin asked impatiently.

Sylvie squatted down and her hand moved gently over the blanket to make sure it covered the baby good and snug.

"I want to keep it, that's what I want to do. I want to keep it and play with it," Sylvie said softly.

Justin laughed, then snorted and threw his head up to the sky and laughed again. "Listen to her! She thinks it's an old doll!"

"You shut up, Justin! I'm a mind to take this baby home and put it in my playhouse in the backyard that Daddy built for me and play with it every day."

"What would you do when Mama and Daddy found out?" Justin asked, still laughing.

"I'd . . . well, I'd say . . . I'd say it was Taffy's little cousin from over to Tylersville or something."

"Taffy don't have no cousin. Taffy don't even have a sister ner brother. All Taffy's got is her mean old mama and a big wall-eyed cat her mama kicks the wind out of nine times a day and twice on Sunday," Justin snarled.

"You be quiet about Taffy! Taffy Marshall is my best friend!"

"You got to feed a baby, Sylvie," I told her. "You got to have milk and mashed pertaters and gravy too."

"And you know Mama ain't going to buy no extry milk ner nothing else for no baby," Justin said.

Sylvie picked the baby up gently and gathered it close into her arms and we all stared down into its little face. "Ain't no way I'm going to leave this baby here," she said like she was filled with fire. The baby didn't make a move or a sound, and just about then the wind started chattering in the trees and little sprinkles of rain started dripping down through the branches. We stood a little closer and watched its face.

"I ain't never been this close to a baby before," I said.

"Me neither," Justin said.

"Well, they're just persons," Sylvie told us softly. "They're just little persons and there ain't no reason to be afraid of them."

The wind started whipping at the baby's blanket and we watched its little nose twitch like it was getting ready to wake up. Sylvie held it a little closer, and we started walking, with me and Justin pushing the low branches and tangled vines out of the way so Sylvie could carry the baby without stumbling or having a twig hit the baby.

"We better head for the police station," Justin said, pulling his collar up close to his neck.

"Maybe Justin is right," I said, and Sylvie turned eyes of fury on me.

"Whose side are you on, Lyon Savage? I thought you was my boyfriend! I thought you was my true love that would do anything I asked of you, that would be on my side, no matter what. I thought—"

"I *am* your boyfriend, Sylvie. I *am* your true love," I told her dismally. "But I don't know about doing just anything you ask of me."

Sylvie stopped walking and her eyes went through me like the prongs on a pitchfork. "Didn't we prick our palms with your Aunt Ester's sewing needle and didn't we hold hands and let our blood run together and make a true-love vow?"

I thought I'd get a headache for sure, just thinking about that time. It was all Sylvie's idea. She said if the blood of two people run together, that meant they was true loves forever and ever. Even after I did it, I wondered how much "ever and ever" I wanted of Sylvie.

Me and Justin stopped walking and I looked straight into Sylvie's eyes that sometimes looked so transparent, it seemed I could look right through them to her soul. "We did that. But we didn't vow nothing about no baby," I told her.

"A true-love vow takes in all dimensions of life," Sylvie stated with a toss of her head.

There was a quick, bright flash and we looked up. Smoky-colored clouds was racing across the sky, blotting out the moon. It was an eerie look. Just like the end of the world might come. And, all at once, through the pine trees, we heard the rumble of thunder. We started running, heading away from the pond as fast as we could go. Sylvie carried the baby hugged up close to her, careful to see that its head was covered by the blanket and protected from the wind and rain. The rain started coming down harder, making a loud tap-tap noise as it hit the tangles of vines and branches along the road that led away from the pond.

"Where are we going?" Justin asked as we ran.

"Uncle Jack Spicer's house is just around the corner where that clump of tall elm trees is. We'd better stop there," I panted.

"Uncle Jack's house don't even protect all them fleas he's got in it!" Justin said through heavy breaths. "It's got so many holes in the roof that the rain floods the place every winter!"

"We can sit on the porch," I said. "Uncle Jack will never know."

Sylvie slowed down and looked up into the sky. "I guess we'd better stop there. It's liable to come a flood that'll drowned every old bullfrog around the pond. We can't let Uncle Jack know about the baby, though. No matter what happens!"

• • • •

THE LONGER SYLVIE HOLDS THE BABY, the more attached to it she becomes, until she believes she can raise it herself. The two boys immediately see the lunacy of such an idea and, against the backdrop of an approaching electrical storm, propose a religious solution: Why not place the baby on the doorstop of the one person who has prayed to God for a baby more than anyone in Clement's Pond—Miss Adeline Newberry? Thus when Miss Adeline discovers the child on her doorstep, she and everyone in the community think of it as nothing short of a "miracle" from the Lord. As word spreads, the three conspirators discover that their generosity has turned into a guilt-ridden headache.

Patricia Pendergraft's other books include: *As Far as Mill Springs*; *Brushy Mountain*; *Hear the Wind Blow*; and *The Legend of Daisy Flowerdew*.

You might also enjoy *A Blue-Eyed Daisy* by Cynthia Rylant (page 92); *A Day No Pigs Would Die* by Robert Newton Peck (page 99); *Pinch* by Larry Callen, and *Where the Red Fern Grows* by Wilson Rawls.

OBJECT LESSON
by Ellery Queen

The Two-Headed Mystery Author

Here is a mystery question: I am the best-selling American detective of all time; I was born at the age of twelve and, in a manner of speaking, my father was the most famous detective in the world; I am also a twin. Who am I?

Two clues: Frederic Dannay and Manfred B. Lee, two Brooklyn-born cousins.

If you are an expert mystery fan, that may have been all you needed. Those two cousins wrote under one name, the name they gave both to themselves as authors and to their detective ("If we mention him twice as much—as author and central character—people will remember him better"): Ellery Queen. Their forty-two-year career together as the most successful writing team in publishing history resulted in the sale of 150 million books. They collaborated on thirty-five novels, more than one hundred anthologies, one radio and three television series, comic books, and the best-selling mystery magazine in the world.

According to Dannay on one of the rare occasions when he wrote outside of the character of Ellery, Queen was "born" one cold winter day when Dannay was twelve years old and lying in bed at his grandfather's house, ill with an abscessed ear. Up to this point, his recreational reading had consisted of the day's popular formula fiction, adventure series for boys such as the works of Horatio Alger, the Frank Merriwell books, the Tarzan series, the works of Jules Verne, as well as the Oz books.

All of that would change to past tense after his aunt handed him a library book that day. Years later he described the birth process this way: "I opened the book with no knowledge that I stood—rather, I sat—on the brink of my fate. I had no inkling, no premonition that in another minute my life's work would be born. My first glance was disquieting—I saw a rather innocuous man in dress coat and striped trousers, holding the arm of a young woman in bridal gown. *A love story*, I said to myself."

It wasn't an inspiring start, so he turned to the table of contents and the first story, "A Scandal in Bohemia," didn't set off any alarms either. "But," said Dannay, "the next story was, and always will be, a milestone.

"A strange rushing thrill challenged the pain in my ear. 'The Red-headed League'! What a combination of single words to skewer themselves into the brain of a hungry boy. I glanced down quickly —'The Man with the Twisted Lip'—'The Adventure of the Speckled Band'—and I was lost! Ecstatically, everlastingly lost!"

What the future Ellery Queen held in his hand was Arthur Conan Doyle's *The Adventures of Sherlock Holmes*. The next morning found the boy pleading with an elderly New York librarian. He was staying temporarily at his grandfather's house and his entreaties were for her to dispense with the customary three-day waiting period and let him have a library card *that very minute*. It must have been something in his honest face or eyes—surely she could not have known she was helping to launch a writing career of worldwide proportions—but she gave him the card and showed him where the Doyle books were shelved. From that day on, Dannay was a mystery addict.

Eleven years later, in 1928, Dannay took time from writing advertising copy to join forces with his cousin Manfred, who was writing movie publicity. Together they created a dapper fictional detective named Ellery Queen for a story they called *The Roman Hat Mystery*, and they entered the manuscript in a mystery novel contest sponsored by a national magazine. Their delight in winning first prize quickly turned to disappointment, however, when the magazine's publisher was bought out and the new publishers reversed the decision and awarded the prize to another novel.

Their frustration was short lived as well. One of the cosponsors of the contest had been a book publisher who was impressed enough with Ellery Queen to publish the book the following year. The rest is history. Though their books and stories have been translated into nearly all of the world's major languages (excepting Russian and Chinese), their longest-lasting contribution to the mystery field was creating and editing *Ellery Queen's Mystery Magazine*, which they founded in 1941. In subsequent years, as other magazines published less short fiction and fewer mysteries, and as more mystery writers turned to mystery novels, Queen's magazine became a sanctuary for that endangered species known as the mystery short story. Manfred Lee died in 1971 and Frederic Dannay in 1982.

Because of our natural curiosity, we humans have always gravitated to "whodunit" stories—from early mysteries such as "Who ate the apple in the Garden of Eden?" to crime stories such as "Cain rose up against Abel his brother, and slew him." It would take a while, though, before the detective arrived. As Queen pointed out in the introduction to his anthology *101 Years' Entertainment: The Great Detective Stories 1841–1941*, the detective story had to wait until man created a police force—in 1829. Since this occurred in London, one would assume the first literary detective would appear in that locale soon thereafter—someone like Sherlock Holmes. Wrong assumption.

The truth is, the Baker Street master was forty-six years late showing up at the scene of the crime. Instead, the first recorded detective story appeared in 1841 in Philadelphia, where an unknown editor-writer, wrestling with poor circulation figures for his magazine, decided to create a new kind of story figure. The magazine, *Graham's*, is long gone, but the name of the editor-writer is still around more than a century later—Edgar Allan Poe.

In the years since, some of the most famous names in literature have tried their hands at the genre—Mark Twain, Fyodor Dostoyevski, Charles Dickens, G. K. Chesterton, Agatha Christie, Dashiell Hammett, Pearl S. Buck, W. Somerset Maugham, Aldous Huxley, Graham Greene, P. D. James, Raymond Chandler, and Ray Bradbury. Through their efforts, the detective figure has taken on larger-than-life proportions in characters such as Charlie Chan, Miss Marple, Hercule Poirot, Nero Wolfe, Nick and Nora Charles, Perry Mason, Nancy Drew, Spenser, and, stretching a point, Sergeant Joe Friday and Jim Rockford.

The Queen adventure that follows originally appeared in *Ellery Queen's Mystery Magazine* in 1955—not long after the sensational appearance of a book and film called *The Blackboard Jungle*, written by a future crime and mystery writer named Evan Hunter. Hunter's story and film heightened public awareness of a new buzzword, *juvenile delinquent*, as well as the deteriorating condition of American inner-city schools.

A quarter century later, it would appear on the surface that the problems Queen encounters in this story are pretty tame when compared to school problems in the 1990s. There are no drugs or guns in this story. But on another level, the basic ingredients of the 1955 Queen story are still operating today: peer pressure, poverty, delinquency, a teacher who cares, and citizens who want to make things better. And that age-old classroom question hasn't changed a syllable with the years: "All right, class, who did it?"

• • • •

E LLERY HURRIED DOWN West 92nd Street toward the main entrance of Henry Hudson High School stealing guilty glances at his watch. Miss Carpenter had been crisply specific about place, date, and time: her homeroom, 109; Friday morning, April 22nd; first period ("Bell at 8:40, Mr. Queen"). Miss Carpenter, who had come to him with an unusual request, had struck him as the sort of dedicated young person who would not take kindly to a hitch in her crusade.

Ellery broke into an undignified lope.

The project for which she had enlisted his aid was formidable even for a crusading young teacher of Social Studies on the 9th Grade Junior High level. For two months merchants of the neighborhood had been reporting stores broken into by a teen-age gang. Beyond establishing that the crimes were the work of the same boys, who were probably students at Henry Hudson High School, the police had got nowhere.

Miss Carpenter, walking home from a movie late the previous Monday night, had seen three boys dive out of a smashed bakery window and vanish into an alley. She had recognized them as Howard Ruffo, David Strager, and Joey Buell, all fifteen-year-old homeroom students of hers. The juvenile crime problem was solved.

But not for Miss Carpenter. Instead of going to the police, Miss Carpenter had gone to Ellery, who lived on West 87th Street and was a hero to the youth of the neighborhood. Howard, David, and Joey were *not* hardened delinquents, she had told him, and she could *not* see their arrest, trial, and imprisonment as the solution to anything. True, they had substituted gang loyalty for the love and security they were denied in their unhappy slum homes, but boys who worked at after-school jobs and turned every cent in at home were hardly beyond recall, were they? And she had told him just where each boy worked, and at what.

"They're only patterning their behavior after criminals because they think criminals are strong, successful, and glamorous," Miss

Carpenter had said; and what she would like him to do was visit her class and, under the pretext of giving a talk on the subject of Notorious Criminals I Have Known, paint such a picture of weak, ratting, empty, and violently ending criminality that David and Joey and Howard would see the error of their ways.

It had seemed to Ellery that this placed a rather hefty burden on his oratorical powers. Did Miss Carpenter have her principal's permission for this project?

No, Miss Carpenter had replied bravely, she did *not* have Mr. Hinsdale's permission, and she might very well lose her job when he heard about it. "But I'm *not* going to be the one who gives those boys the first shove toward reform school and maybe eventually the electric chair!" And besides, what did Mr. Queen have to lose but an hour of his time?

So Mr. Queen had feebly said yes, he would come; and here he was, at the door of the determined young woman's classroom . . . seven minutes *late*.

Ellery braced himself and opened the door.

THE MOMENT HE SET FOOT in the room he knew he had walked in on a catastrophe.

Louise Carpenter stood tensely straight at her desk, her pretty face almost as white as the envelope she was clutching. And she was glaring at a mass of boy and girl faces so blankly, so furtively quiet that the silence sizzled.

The first thing she said to him was, "I've been robbed."

The terrible mass of boy and girl eyes followed him to her desk. In his nose was the pungent smell of ink, glue, paper, chalk, musty wardrobe closets; surrounding him were discolored walls, peeling paint, tarnished fixtures, warped window poles, and mutilated desks.

"Robbed in my own classroom," Miss Carpenter choked.

He laid his coat and hat gently on her desk. "A practical joke?" He smiled at the class.

"Hardly. They didn't know you were coming." They had betrayed her, the sick shock in her voice said. "Class, this is Ellery Queen. I don't have to tell you who Mr. Queen is, and how honored we are to have him visit us." There was a g sp, a buzz, a spatter of applause. "Mr. Queen was kind enough to come here today to give us a talk on crime. I didn't know he was going to walk in on one."

"You're sure there has been a crime, Miss Carpenter?"

"An envelope with seven one-dollar bills in it was stolen, and from the way it happened the thief can only be someone in this room."

"I'm sorry to hear that."

He deliberately looked them over, wondering which of the forty-one pairs of eyes staring back at his belonged to Joey Buell, Howard Ruffo, and David Strager. He should have asked Louise Carpenter to describe them. Now it was too late.

Or was it?

It seemed to Ellery that three of the twenty-odd boy faces were rather too elaborately blank. One of them was set on husky shoulders; this boy was blond, handsome, and dead-white about the nostrils. The second was a sharp-nosed, jet-haired boy with Mediterranean coloring who was perfectly still except for his fingers, and they kept turning a pencil over and over almost ritually. The third, thin and red-haired, showed no life anywhere except in a frightened artery in his temple.

Ellery made up his mind.

"Well, if it's a real live crime," he said, turning to Louise, "I don't imagine anyone wants to hear me ramble on about crimes that are dead and buried. In fact, I think it would be more interesting if I gave the class a demonstration of how a crime is actually solved. What do you think, Miss Carpenter?"

Understanding leaped into her eyes, along with hope.

"I think," she said grimly, "it would be *lots* more interesting."

"Suppose we begin by finding out about the seven dollars. They were yours, Miss Carpenter?"

"One dollar was mine. Miss McDoud, an English teacher, is being married next month. A group of us are chipping in to buy her a wedding present, with me as banker. All this week teachers have been dropping in to leave their dollars in an envelope I've had on my desk. This morning—"

"That's fine for background, Miss Carpenter. Suppose we hear testimony from the class." Ellery surveyed them, and there was a ripple of tittering. Suddenly he pointed to a little lipsticked girl with an Italian haircut. "Would you like to tell us what happened this morning?"

"I don't know anything about the money!"

"Chicken." A boy's jeering voice.

"The boy who said that." Ellery kept his tone friendly. It was one of the three he had spotted, the husky blond one. "What's your name, son?"

"David Strager." His sneer said, *You don't scare me.* But his nostrils remained dead-white. He was the boy Miss Carpenter had said worked after school as a stock boy at the Hi-Kwality Supermarket on Amsterdam Avenue.

"All right, Dave. You tell us about this morning."

The boy glanced scornfully at the girl with the Italian haircut. "We all knew the money was in the envelope. This morning before the bell rings Mrs. Morell comes in with her buck and Miss Carpenter puts it with the other money and lays the envelope on her desk. So afterward the bell rings, Mrs. Morell beats it out, Miss Carpenter picks up the envelope and takes a look inside, and she hollers, 'I been robbed.' "

The thin boy with the red hair called out. "So what are we supposed to do, drop dead?" and winked at David Strager, who had already sat down. The big blond boy winked back.

"And your name?" Ellery asked the redhead.

"Joseph Buell," the boy answered defiantly. He was the one who worked at Kaplan's, the big cigar, candy, and stationery store on 89th Street. "Who wants their old seven bucks?"

"Somebody not only wants it, Joey, somebody's got it."

"Aaa, for all we know she took it herself." And this was the third of the trio, the sharp-faced dark boy. If Ellery was right, he was the one who delivered part-time for O'Donnel's Dry Cleaning on Columbus Avenue.

"And you are—?"

"Howard Ruffo."

The Three Musketeers, rushing to one another's support.

"You mean, Howard, you're charging Miss Carpenter with having stolen the teachers' money?" Ellery asked with a smile.

The boy's dark glance wavered. "I mean maybe she took it like by mistake. Mislaid it or somepin'."

"As a matter of fact," came Louise's quiet voice, "when I saw the money wasn't in the envelope, my first thought was exactly that, Mr. Queen. So I searched myself thoroughly."

"May I see the envelope?"

"This isn't the one I was keeping the seven dollars in—" she handed him the envelope—"though it looks the same. I have a box of them in my locker there. The lock hasn't worked for ages. This one must have been stolen from my locker yesterday, or earlier this week."

"It's a blank envelope, Miss Carpenter. How do you know it isn't the one that contained the money?"

"Because the original had a notation in ink on the flap—*Gift Fund for Helen McDoud*." She looked about and glances fell in windrows. "So this theft was planned, Mr. Queen. Someone came to class this morning armed with this duplicate envelope, previously stolen and filled with worthless paper, prepared to make a quick exchange if the opportunity arose. And it did. The class was milling around while Mrs. Morell and I chatted."

The paper in the substitute envelope consisted of a sheaf of rectangular strips cut to the size of dollar bills.

"At the time you placed Mrs. Morell's dollar among the others in the original envelope, was everybody here?"

"Yes. The door opened and closed only once after that—when Mrs. Morell left. I was facing the door the whole time."

"Could Mrs. Morell, as a practical joke, have made the switch?"

"She wasn't anywhere near my desk after I laid the envelope on it."

"Then you're right, Miss Carpenter. The theft was planned in advance by one of the boys or girls in this room, and the thief—and money—are both still here."

The tension was building beautifully. The boy must be in a sweat. He hadn't expected his theft to be found out so soon, before he got a chance to sneak the money out of the room.

"What time does the first period end, Miss Carpenter?"

"At 9:35."

Every head turned toward the clock on the wall.

"And it's only 8:56," Ellery said cheerfully. "That gives us thirty-nine minutes—more than enough time. Unless the boy or girl who planned this crime wants to return the loot to Miss Carpenter here and now?"

This time he stared directly from David to Howard to Joey. His stare said, *I hate to do this, boys, but of course I'll have to if you think you can get away with it.*

The Strager boy's full lips were twisted. The skinny redhead, Joey Buell, stared back sullenly. Howard Ruffo's pencil twirled faster. *It's one of those three, all right.*

"I see we'll have to do it the hard way," Ellery said. "Sorry I can't produce the thief with a flick of my wrist, the way it's done in books, but in real life, detection—like crime—is pretty unexciting stuff. We'll begin with a body search. It's voluntary, by the way. Anybody rather not chance a search? Raise your hand."

Not a muscle moved.

"I'll search the boys, Miss Carpenter. You roll those two bulletin boards over to that corner and search the girls."

The next few minutes were noisy. As each boy was searched and released he was sent to the blackboard at the front of the room. The girls were sent to the rear.

"Rose Perez has a single dollar bill. The other girls either have small change or no money at all."

"No sign of the original envelope?"

"No."

"I found two boys with bills—in each case a single, too. David Strager and Joey Buell. No envelope."

Louise's brows met.

Ellery glanced up at the clock. 9:07.

He strolled over to her. "Don't show them you're worried. There's nothing to worry about. We have twenty-eight minutes." He raised his voice, smiling. "Naturally the thief has ditched the money, hoping to recover it when the coast is clear. It's therefore hidden somewhere in the classroom. All right, Miss Carpenter, we'll take the desks and seats first. Look under them, too—chewing gum makes a handy adhesive. Eh, class?"

Four minutes later they looked at each other, then up at the clock. 9:11.

Exactly twenty-four minutes remaining.

"Well," said Ellery.

He began to ransack the room. Books, radiators, closets, lunchbags, schoolbags. Bulletin boards, wall maps, the terrestrial globe. The UN poster, the steel engravings of Washington and Lincoln. He even emptied Louise's three pots of geraniums and sifted the earth.

His eyes kept returning to the clock more and more often.

Ellery searched everything in the room, from the socket of the American flag to the insect-filled bowls of the old light fixtures, reached by standing on desks.

Everything.

"It's not here!" whispered Louise in his ear.

The Buell, Ruffo, and Strager boys were nudging one another, grinning.

"Well, well," Ellery said.

Interesting. Something of a problem at that.

Of course! He got up and checked two things he had missed— the cup of the pencil sharpener and the grid covering the loudspeaker of the PA system. No envelope. No money.

He took out a handkerchief and wiped his neck.

Really, it's a little silly. A schoolboy!

Ellery glanced at the clock.

9:29.

Six minutes left in which not only to find the money but identify the thief!

He leaned against Louise's desk, forcing himself to relax.

It was these "simple" problems. Nothing big and important like murder, blackmail, bank robbery. A miserable seven dollars lifted by a teen-age delinquent in an overcrowded classroom . . .

He thought furiously.

Let the bell ring at 9:35 and the boy strut out of Miss Carpenter's room undetected, with his loot, and he would send up a howl like a wolf cub over his first kill. *Who says these big-shot law jerks ain't monkeys? The biggest! He's a lot of nothin'. Wind. See me stand him on his ear? And this is just for openers. Wait till I get goin' for real, not any of this kid stuff . . .*

No, nothing big and important like murder. Just seven dollars, and a big shot to laugh at. Not important? Ellery nibbled his lip. It was probably the most important case of his career.

9:30½.

Only four and a half minutes left!

Louise Carpenter was gripping a desk, her knuckles white. Waiting to be let down.

Ellery pushed away from the desk and reached into the patch pocket of his tweed jacket for his pipe and tobacco, thinking harder about Helen McDoud's seven-dollar gift fund than he had ever thought about anything in his life.

And as he thought . . .

At 9:32 he was intently examining the rectangles of paper the thief had put into the substitute envelope. The paper was ordinary cheap newsprint, scissored to dollar-bill size out of a colored comics section. He shuffled through the dummy dollars one by one, hunting for something. Anything!

The forty-one boys and girls were buzzing and giggling now.

Ellery pounced. Clinging to one of the rectangles was a needle-thin sliver of paper about an inch long, a sort of paper shaving. He fingered it, held it up to the light. It was not newsprint. Too full-bodied, too tough-textured . . .

Then he knew what it must be.

Less than two minutes left.

Feverishly he went through the remaining dollar-sized strips of comic paper.

And there it was. There it was!

This strip had been cut from the top of the comic sheet. On the margin appeared the name of a New York newspaper and the date *April 24, 1955.*

Think it over. Take your time. Lots of seconds in a minute.

The buzzing and giggling had died. Louise Carpenter was on her feet, looking at him imploringly.

A bell began clanging in the corridor.

First period over.

9:35.

Ellery rose and said solemnly, "The case is solved."

WITH THE ROOM CLEARED and the door locked, the three boys stood backed against the blackboard as if facing a firing squad. The bloom was gone from David Strager's cheeks. The blood vessel in Joey Buell's temple was trying to wriggle into his red hair. And Howard Ruffo's eyes were liquid with panic.

It's hard to be fifteen years old and trapped.

But harder not to be.

"Wha'd I do?" whimpered Howard Ruffo. "I didn't do nothin'."

"We didn't take Miss Carpenter's seven dollars," said David Strager, stiff-lipped.

"Can you say the same about Mr. Mueller's baked goods last Monday night, Dave?" Ellery paused gently. "Or any of the other things you boys have been stealing in the past two months?"

He thought they were going to faint.

"But this morning's little job," Ellery turned suddenly to the red-haired boy, "you pulled by yourself, Joey."

The thin boy quivered. "Who, me?"

"Yes, Joey, you."

"You got rocks in your skull," Joey whispered. "Not me!"

"I'll prove it, Joey. Hand me the dollar bill I found in your jeans when I searched you."

"That's my dollar!"

"I know it, Joey. I'll give you another for it. Hand it over . . . Miss Carpenter."

"Yes, Mr. Queen!"

"To cut these strips of newspaper to the same size as dollar bills, the thief must have used a real bill as a pattern. If he cut too close, the scissors would shave off a sliver of the bill." Ellery handed her Joey's dollar. "See if this bill shows a slight indentation along one edge."

"It does."

"And I found this sliver clinging to one of the dummies. Fit the sliver to the indented edge of Joey's bill. If Joey is guilty, it should fit exactly. Does it?"

Louise looked at the boy. "Joey, it does fit."

David and Howard were gaping at Ellery.

"What a break," Joey choked.

"Criminals make their own bad breaks, Joey. The thing inside you that told you you were doing wrong made your hand shake as you cut. But even if your hand hadn't slipped, I'd have known you were the one who substituted the strips of paper for the money."

"How? How could you?" It was a cry of bewilderment.

Ellery showed him the rectangular strip with the white margin. "See this, Joey? Here's the name of the newspaper, and the date is *April 24, 1955*. What date is today?"

"Friday the 22nd . . ."

"Friday, April 22nd. But these strips of colored comics come from the newspaper of April 24th, Joey—*this coming Sunday's paper*. Who gets advance copies of the Sunday comics? Stores that sell newspapers in quantity. Getting the bulldog editions in advance gives them a jump on the Sunday morning rush, when they have to insert the news sections.

"Nothing to it, Joey. Which of you three boys had access before this morning to next Sunday's bulldog editions? Not David—he works in a supermarket. Not Howard—he works for a dry cleaner. But you work in a big cigar and stationery store, Joey, where newspapers must be one of the stock items."

Joey Buell's eyes glassed over.

"We think we're strong, Joey, and then we run into somebody stronger," Ellery said. "We think we're the smartest, and someone comes along to outsmart us. We beat the rap a dozen times, but the thirteenth time the rap beats us. You can't win, Joey."

Joey burst into tears.

Louise Carpenter made an instinctive gesture toward him. Ellery's head-shake warned her back. He went close to the boy and tousled the red head, murmuring something the others could not hear. And after a while Joey's tears sniffled to an end and he wiped his eyes on his sleeve in a puzzled way.

"Because I think this is going to work out all right, Joey," Ellery said, continuing their curious colloquy aloud. "We'll have a session with Mr. Hinsdale, and then with some pretty right guys I happen to know at Police Headquarters. After that it will be up to you."

Joey Buell gulped. "Okay, Mr. Queen." He did not look at his two friends.

David and Howard communicated silently. Then David turned to Ellery. "Where do we stand, Mr. Queen?"

"You and Howard are coming along."

The blond boy bit his lip. Then he nodded, and after a moment the dark boy nodded, too.

"Oh, I almost forgot." Ellery dipped briskly into the jacket pocket that held his pipe and tobacco. His hand reappeared with a wrinkled envelope, its flap written over. From the envelope protruded the corners of some one-dollar bills. "Your Helen McDoud wedding gift fund, Miss Carpenter. With Joey's compliments."

"I did forget!" gasped Louise. "Where did you find it?"

"Where Joey in desperation slipped it as I was frisking the other boys. The only thing in the room I didn't think of searching—my own pocket. Coming, fellas?"

• • • •

FOR MORE MYSTERY STORIES, I recommend *Tales from Ellery Queen's Mystery Magazine*, selected by Eleanor Sullivan and Cynthia Manson. If your public library is like most, it contains a shelf of Ellery Queen novels and anthologies. And your local bookstore has one large section devoted to nothing but mysteries.

The following Queen titles are also available on audiocassette: *Calendar of Crime, Vols. 1 and 2*, short-story collections, six hours each volume (Dercum Press); *The Chinese Orange Mystery*, novel, eight hours (Books on Tape); *The Siamese Twin Mystery*, novel, eight hours (Books on Tape); and *The Spanish Cape Mystery*, novel, eight hours (Books on Tape).

Sherlock Holmes, of course, is still readily available in hardcover and paperback, with a 1992 hardcover edition of *The Adventures of Sherlock Holmes* published by Morrow and lavishly illustrated by Barry Moser. I also highly recommend the following young-adult Gothic mystery titles: Leon Garfield's *The December Rose*, Joan Aiken's *Midnight Is a Place*, and Robert Newman's books (*The Case of the Baker*

Street Irregular, The Case of the Murdered Players, The Case of the Vanishing Corpse, and *The Case of the Watching Boy*).

Consider also the following mystery titles by award-winning young-adult author Jay Bennett: *The Birthday Murderer, The Coverup, The Dark Corridor, Deathman: Do Not Follow Me,* and *Say Hello to the Hitman.*

For an excellent overview of mystery stories and their changes through the years, see: *Crime Classics: The Mystery Story from Poe to the Present,* edited by Rex Burns and Mary Rose Sullivan; and *Great Tales of Detection: 19 Stories,* chosen by Dorothy L. Sayers.

from TO KILL A MOCKINGBIRD

by Harper Lee

The Long-Lost Writer of a Modern Classic, *or* Whatever Happened to Harper Lee?

It was her first novel and it won the top American literary award, the Pulitzer Prize. From there it went to the top of the best-seller charts and then on to Hollywood to become a classic film that won three Academy Awards. Today, more than thirty years later and with more than twelve million copies in print, it is arguably the most widely used—and best loved—novel in American junior and senior high schools. It is also used in law school ethics classes from Notre Dame to the University of Mississippi.

The book is *To Kill a Mockingbird* by Harper Lee. That's the easy part. The challenging part—the part that 99.99 percent of its readers and teachers cannot answer—is this: Whatever happened to Harper Lee?

If this were baseball, we'd be saying, "Her first time at the plate and she hits not just a home run, but a grand slam! And then . . . nothing! For all intents and purposes, she never comes to bat again."

More times than I can count in the last twenty years, I have asked educators and editors, "Whatever happened to Harper Lee?" The majority of their responses have ranged from "Oh, she must be dead" and "I think she became some kind of vagrant down South someplace" to "Why—I never thought of that. Whatever *did* happen to her?"

But a few have provided both clues and answers. Those, combined with some standard research, give us an intriguing portrait of a literary mystery figure, the southern equivalent of J. D. Salinger.

She was born Harper "Nelle" Lee in 1925, the youngest child of Amasa and Frances Lee, in Monroeville, Alabama. Amasa, her father and the model for Atticus Finch, the stalwart lawyer-father in her novel, was a lawyer and a descendant of Robert E. Lee. Her mother was a housewife who was obsessed with crossword puzzles. Neighbors report that she would sit on the front porch for hours, filling in the tiny square boxes.

Monroeville in those days was a tiny farm town of about twelve hundred people, most of whom lived off the cotton or corn fields. It was rural enough to have not one paved street and was the model for Maycomb in Harper Lee's novel. She grew up on Alabama Street but, more important, she lived next door to a small, fair-haired boy who had been left by his eccentric parents to live with his three bickering aunts and a reclusive uncle. The boy was Truman Capote, and he would go on to become one of the most famous, eccentric, and bestselling authors of the 1950s and 1960s. Lee would use him as the model for the boy Dill in *Mockingbird*.

The narrator of the novel is "Scout" Finch, the six- to eight-year-old daughter of Atticus, and she is based on Harper Lee herself. Which leaves Lee's mother unaccounted for—other than the fact that she quietly dies of a heart attack on the fourth page of the book. The truth, however, is not only stranger than fiction, in this case it is also more painful. In his biography, *Capote*, Gerald Clarke describes the mother Lee left out of her book: "Her mind was not altogether right, however. She wandered up and down the street saying strange things to neighbors and passersby, and twice she tried to drown Harper . . . in the bathtub." Both times older sisters saved the child.

"Harper survived the dunkings to become the tomboy of the block, a girl who . . . could beat the steam out of most boys her age, or even a year or so older, as Truman was," Clarke notes. "Indeed, he was one of her favorite targets. But that did not stop them from becoming constant companions, and a treehouse in the Lees' chinaberry tree became their fortress against the world, a leafy refuge where they read and acted out scenes from their favorite books."

Eventually their acting out moved from the treehouse to the typewriter, as Capote explained many years later: "When we were children, I had a typewriter and worked every day in a little room I used as an office. I convinced her [Lee] she ought to write, too, so we would work there each day for two or three hours. She didn't really want to, but I held her to it. We kept up that routine for quite a long time."

Their friendship would last a lifetime, even after young Capote moved away to New York and private schools, sold his first story at age sixteen, and became a jet-set celebrity. Lee stayed in Monroeville and went to the University of Alabama Law School but dropped out one week short of completing her degree. Nonetheless, law became one of the major focal points of her one novel. Finally, she too moved to New York City, where she took a job as an airline reservations clerk and wrote in her spare time.

The writing consisted of several unpublished short stories and essays when she showed it to an agent, who suggested that it had the makings of a novel. So she quit the airline job and wrote full-time to produce the novel. An editor read it and explained that it was not a novel yet, but only connected short stories. For the next two years she wrote and rewrote until it was finished in 1959 and published in 1960.

In November of 1959, however, with her own *Mockingbird* done and awaiting publication, she saw that her childhood chum had reached an impasse in his life. Truman Capote had run out of ideas for stories. The glamorous Fifth Avenue crowd was no longer an inspiration. In desperation he turned to nonfiction for help, reading every newspaper he could lay his hands on until finally, on November 16, he found a *New York Times* story about a wealthy farm family in Kansas who had been brutally killed in their home. He would write the story of a crime—its commission, its solving, and its punishment—and he would write it with all the drama of a novel, a modern, nonfiction *Crime and Punishment*.

Capote must have known instinctively that his mouselike appearance, which had charmed the social world's upper crust, would never work with the Kansas villagers. Harper Lee, on the other hand, could get *anyone* to talk, and she could keep him on an even keel if things got messy. Within a month, Capote and his treehouse companion arrived at the scene of the crime and began their chase.

No one in that county in Kansas had ever heard of Capote, never mind read his books. To the locals, this New York writer with the high-pitched voice was "like someone coming off the moon," as Lee said later. So she set to making friends with every farmer's wife in sight, and they in turn got their husbands to relax with the "outsiders." More than once, Capote was overcome with discouragement and Lee convinced him to stay the course—reversing the roles they'd once played at the typewriter on Alabama Street.

Ultimately the townsfolk became so enamored of Capote and Lee that they were besieged with dinner invitations. Capote's book (*In Cold Blood*) required six thousand pages of interviews and five years to write, but it became a huge best-seller. Unfortunately, the fame and fortune that followed would put him on a downward spiral, and not even his old playmate could save him from the drugs and alcohol that eventually killed him at age fifty-nine.

Shortly after Lee played this "girl Friday" role in Kansas, *To Kill a Mockingbird* was published and won the 1961 Pulitzer Prize for fiction. When the fanfare abated, Lee returned to the quiet solitude of Monroeville to write her next book. The writing process had always been painfully slow for her and she usually produced only a page or two each day. In 1965 she wrote a small but lovely piece for *McCall's* magazine entitled "When Children Discover America." And then— there was nothing. Gregory Peck, the actor who won his only Academy Award playing Atticus, begged her to write something else, promising to star in the movie if that would persuade her.

Had she hit an impenetrable writer's block, or had she changed her mind at the last minute—as she had done with law school?

In the ensuing years, Harper Lee lived a life-style that was the opposite of Capote's. He spent the last twenty-five years of his life chasing the public eye. She continued to live, shop, and worship in Monroeville, outside the scrutiny of the media. Her telephone was unlisted and she accepted no interviews. None. In direct proportion to her reclusiveness, relatives, neighbors, library clerks, and police officers became extremely protective of her. If you were a teenager in Monroeville and happened to have your copy of *Mockingbird* on your person when you bumped into Miss Lee at the grocery checkout counter, she'd be happy to sign it for you. But if you were a reporter looking for a two-minute interview, you would experience the opposite of southern hospitality. Once a reporter traveled all the way from London to do a feature story on "the long-lost Harper Lee," only to return bitter and empty-handed.

There was, however, one small, largely unknown parting of the protective blinds. In 1983, some university professors and locals were planning a history and humanities festival/seminar that would celebrate the history of Alabama. What we need, they said to each other, is a "draw," a famous writer who would be willing to participate. As luck would have it, one of Lee's sisters was at the planning session and she, in turn, convinced her celebrated sister to contribute a piece about an early Alabama historian named Albert James Pickett. The essay was called "Romance and High Adventure" and was included in *Clearing in the Thicket: An Alabama Humanities Reader*, published by Mercer University Press. (The first page of *Mockingbird* testifies to Lee's longtime interest in Alabama history.)

Lee not only wrote a piece for the event, she agreed to read it publicly. Those who were present say she was magnificent. The butterflies quickly passed and she was again the winning southern woman who had charmed the Kansas farmers. The essay itself was so polished and well written that it boldly contradicts the view that writing is a skill that must be practiced regularly in order to shine. Either that or one is led to consider *other* possibilities, the things people have suggested about Salinger through the years. Suppose the reclusive Harper Lee never stopped writing. What if she's been writing all these years under a *peṅ name*? Or what if she's been filling an attic trunk with novels and short stories, manuscripts the public will not see until she dies?

It makes for fascinating speculation. But in the end it doesn't make an iota of difference, because of that magnificent first novel. In the book, a neighbor explains why it's a sin to kill a mockingbird: "Mockingbirds don't do one thing but make music for us to enjoy." Like a mockingbird, perhaps Harper Lee didn't do but one thing— she made music for us to enjoy—and if she did it only once, she did it beautifully enough to echo through the lives of everyone who has ever experienced it.

Here, then, is a selection from the first chapter of the little novel that sang the glories and pain of life in a small southern town, tranquil, segregated, and mysterious, in the 1930s.

• • • •

from CHAPTER 1

MAYCOMB WAS AN OLD TOWN, but it was a tired old town when I first knew it. In rainy weather the streets turned to red slop; grass grew on the sidewalks, the courthouse sagged in the square. Somehow, it was hotter then: a black dog suffered on a summer's day; bony mules hitched to Hoover carts flicked flies in the sweltering shade of the live oaks on the square. Men's stiff collars wilted by nine in the morning. Ladies bathed before noon, after their three-o'clock naps, and by nightfall were like soft teacakes with frostings of sweat and sweet talcum.

People moved slowly then. They ambled across the square, shuffled in and out of the stores around it, took their time about everything. A day was twenty-four hours long but seemed longer. There was no hurry, for there was nowhere to go, nothing to buy and no money to buy it with, nothing to see outside the boundaries of Maycomb County. But it was a time of vague optimism for some of the people: Maycomb County had recently been told that it had nothing to fear but fear itself.

We lived on the main residential street in town—Atticus, Jem and I, plus Calpurnia our cook. Jem and I found our father satisfactory: he played with us, read to us, and treated us with courteous detachment.

Calpurnia was something else again. She was all angles and bones; she was nearsighted; she squinted; her hand was wide as a bed slat and twice as hard. She was always ordering me out of the kitchen, asking me why I couldn't behave as well as Jem when she knew he was older, and calling me home when I wasn't ready to come. Our battles were epic and one-sided. Calpurnia always won, mainly because Atticus always took her side. She had been with us ever since Jem was born, and I had felt her tyrannical presence as long as I could remember.

Our mother died when I was two, so I never felt her absence. She was a Graham from Montgomery; Atticus met her when he was first elected to the state legislature. He was middle-aged then, she was fifteen years his junior. Jem was the product of their first year of marriage; four years later I was born, and two years later our mother died from a sudden heart attack. They said it ran in her family. I did not miss her, but I think Jem did. He remembered her clearly, and sometimes in the middle of a game he would sigh at length, then go off and play by himself behind the car-house. When he was like that, I knew better than to bother him.

When I was almost six and Jem was nearly ten, our summertime boundaries (within calling distance of Calpurnia) were Mrs. Henry Lafayette Dubose's house two doors to the north of us, and the Radley Place three doors to the south. We were never tempted to break them. The Radley Place was inhabited by an unknown entity the mere description of whom was enough to make us behave for days on end; Mrs. Dubose was plain hell.

That was the summer Dill came to us.

Early one morning as we were beginning our day's play in the back yard, Jem and I heard something next door in Miss Rachel Haverford's collard patch. We went to the wire fence to see if there was a puppy—Miss Rachel's rat terrier was expecting—instead we found someone sitting looking at us. Sitting down, he wasn't much higher than the collards. We stared at him until he spoke:

"Hey."

"Hey yourself," said Jem pleasantly.

"I'm Charles Baker Harris," he said. "I can read."

"So what?" I said.

"I just thought you'd like to know I can read. You got anything needs readin' I can do it. . . ."

"How old are you," asked Jem, "four-and-a-half?"

"Goin' on seven."

"Shoot no wonder, then," said Jem, jerking his thumb at me. "Scout yonder's been readin' ever since she was born, and she ain't even started to school yet. You look right puny for goin' on seven."

"I'm little but I'm old," he said.

Jem brushed his hair back to get a better look. "Why don't you come over, Charles Baker Harris?" he said. "Lord, what a name."

" 's not any funnier'n yours. Aunt Rachel says your name's Jeremy Atticus Finch."

Jem scowled. "I'm big enough to fit mine," he said. "Your name's longer'n you are. Bet it's a foot longer."

"Folks call me Dill," said Dill, struggling under the fence.

"Do better if you go over it instead of under it," I said. "Where'd you come from?"

Dill was from Meridian, Mississippi, was spending the summer with his aunt, Miss Rachel, and would be spending every summer in Maycomb from now on. His family was from Maycomb County originally, his mother worked for a photographer in Meridian, had entered his picture in a Beautiful Child contest and won five dollars. She gave the money to Dill, who went to the picture show twenty times on it.

"Don't have any picture shows here, except Jesus ones in the courthouse sometimes," said Jem. "Ever see anything good?"

Dill had seen *Dracula*, a revelation that moved Jem to eye him with the beginning of respect. "Tell it to us," he said.

Dill was a curiosity. He wore blue linen shorts that buttoned to his shirt, his hair was snow white and stuck to his head like duck-fluff; he was a year my senior but I towered over him. As he told us the old tale his blue eyes would lighten and darken; his laugh was sudden and happy; he habitually pulled at a cowlick in the center of his forehead.

When Dill reduced Dracula to dust, and Jem said the show sounded better than the book, I asked Dill where his father was: "You ain't said anything about him."

"I haven't got one."

"Is he dead?"

"No . . ."

"Then if he's not dead you've got one, haven't you?"

Dill blushed and Jem told me to hush, a sure sign that Dill had been studied and found acceptable. Thereafter the summer passed in routine contentment. Routine contentment was: improving our tree-house that rested between giant twin chinaberry trees in the back yard, fussing, running through our list of dramas based on the works of Oliver Optic, Victor Appleton, and Edgar Rice Burroughs. In this matter we were lucky to have Dill. He played the character parts formerly thrust upon me—the ape in *Tarzan*, Mr. Crabtree in *The Rover Boys*, Mr. Damon in *Tom Swift*. Thus we came to know Dill as a pocket Merlin, whose head teemed with eccentric plans, strange longings, and quaint fancies.

But by the end of August our repertoire was vapid from countless reproductions, and it was then that Dill gave us the idea of making Boo Radley come out.

The Radley Place fascinated Dill. In spite of our warnings and explanations it drew him as the moon draws water, but drew him no nearer than the light-pole on the corner, a safe distance from the Radley gate. There he would stand, his arm around the fat pole, staring and wondering.

The Radley Place jutted into a sharp curve beyond our house. Walking south, one faced its porch; the sidewalk turned and ran beside the lot. The house was low, was once white with a deep front porch and green shutters, but had long ago darkened to the color of the slate-gray yard around it. Rain-rotted shingles drooped over the eaves of the veranda; oak trees kept the sun away. The remains of a picket drunkenly guarded the front yard—a "swept" yard that was never swept—where johnson grass and rabbit-tobacco grew in abundance.

Inside the house lived a malevolent phantom. People said he existed, but Jem and I had never seen him. People said he went out at night when the moon was down, and peeped in windows. When people's azaleas froze in a cold snap, it was because he had breathed on them. Any stealthy small crimes committed in Maycomb were his work. Once the town was terrorized by a series of morbid nocturnal events: people's chickens and household pets were found mutilated; although the culprit was Crazy Addie, who eventually drowned himself in Barker's Eddy, people still looked at the Radley Place, unwilling to discard their initial suspicions. A Negro would not pass the Radley Place at night, he would cut across to the sidewalk opposite and whistle as he walked. The Maycomb school grounds adjoined the back of the Radley lot; from the Radley chickenyard tall pecan trees shook their fruit into the schoolyard, but the nuts lay untouched by the children: Radley pecans would kill you. A baseball hit into the Radley yard was a lost ball and no questions asked.

The misery of that house began many years before Jem and I were born. The Radleys, welcome anywhere in town, kept to themselves, a predilection unforgivable in Maycomb. They did not go to church, Maycomb's principal recreation, but worshiped at home; Mrs. Radley seldom if ever crossed the street for a mid-morning coffee break with her neighbors, and certainly never joined a missionary circle. Mr. Radley walked to town at eleven-thirty every morning and came back promptly at twelve, sometimes carrying a brown paper bag that the neighborhood assumed contained the family groceries. I never knew how old Mr. Radley made his living—Jem said he "bought cotton," a polite term for doing nothing—but Mr. Radley and his wife had lived there with their two sons as long as anybody could remember.

The shutters and doors of the Radley house were closed on Sundays, another thing alien to Maycomb's ways: closed doors meant illness and cold weather only. Of all days Sunday was the day for formal afternoon visiting: ladies wore corsets, men wore coats, children wore shoes. But to climb the Radley front steps and call, "He-y," of a Sunday afternoon was something their neighbors never did. The Radley house had no screen doors. I once asked Atticus if it ever had any; Atticus said yes, but before I was born.

According to neighborhood legend, when the younger Radley boy was in his teens he became acquainted with some of the Cunninghams from Old Sarum, an enormous and confusing tribe domiciled in the northern part of the county, and they formed the nearest thing to a gang ever seen in Maycomb. They did little, but enough to be discussed by the town and publicly warned from three pulpits: they hung around the barbershop; they rode the bus to Abbottsville on Sundays and went to the picture show; they attended dances at the county's riverside gambling hell, the Dew-Drop Inn & Fishing Camp;

they experimented with stumphole whiskey. Nobody in Maycomb had nerve enough to tell Mr. Radley that his boy was in with the wrong crowd.

One night, in an excessive spurt of high spirits, the boys backed around the square in a borrowed flivver, resisted arrest by Maycomb's ancient beadle, Mr. Conner, and locked him in the courthouse outhouse. The town decided something had to be done; Mr. Conner said he knew who each and every one of them was, and he was bound and determined they wouldn't get away with it, so the boys came before the probate judge on charges of disorderly conduct, disturbing the peace, assault and battery, and using abusive and profane language in the presence and hearing of a female. The judge asked Mr. Conner why he included the last charge; Mr. Conner said they cussed so loud he was sure every lady in Maycomb heard them. The judge decided to send the boys to the state industrial school, where boys were sometimes sent for no other reason than to provide them with food and decent shelter: it was no prison and it was no disgrace. Mr. Radley thought it was. If the judge released Arthur, Mr. Radley would see to it that Arthur gave no further trouble. Knowing that Mr. Radley's word was his bond, the judge was glad to do so.

The other boys attended the industrial school and received the best secondary education to be had in the state; one of them eventually worked his way through engineering school at Auburn. The doors of the Radley house were closed on weekdays as well as Sundays, and Mr. Radley's boy was not seen again for fifteen years.

But there came a day, barely within Jem's memory, when Boo Radley was heard from and was seen by several people, but not by Jem. He said Atticus never talked much about the Radleys: when Jem would question him Atticus's only answer was for him to mind his own business and let the Radleys mind theirs, they had a right to; but when it happened Jem said Atticus shook his head and said, "Mm, mm, mm."

So Jem received most of his information from Miss Stephanie Crawford, a neighborhood scold, who said she knew the whole thing. According to Miss Stephanie, Boo was sitting in the livingroom cutting some items from *The Maycomb Tribune* to paste in his scrapbook. His father entered the room. As Mr. Radley passed by, Boo drove the scissors into his parent's leg, pulled them out, wiped them on his pants, and resumed his activities.

Mrs. Radley ran screaming into the street that Arthur was killing them all, but when the sheriff arrived he found Boo still sitting in the livingroom, cutting up the *Tribune*. He was thirty-three years old then.

Miss Stephanie said old Mr. Radley said no Radley was going to any asylum, when it was suggested that a season in Tuscaloosa might be helpful to Boo. Boo wasn't crazy, he was high-strung at times. It was all right to shut him up, Mr. Radley conceded, but insisted that Boo not be charged with anything: he was not a criminal. The sheriff hadn't the heart to put him in jail alongside Negroes, so Boo was locked in the courthouse basement.

Boo's transition from the basement to back home was nebulous in Jem's memory. Miss Stephanie Crawford said some of the town council told Mr. Radley that if he didn't take Boo back, Boo would die of mold from the damp. Besides, Boo could not live forever on the bounty of the county.

Nobody knew what form of intimidation Mr. Radley employed to keep Boo out of sight, but Jem figured that Mr. Radley kept him chained to the bed most of the time. Atticus said no, it wasn't that sort of thing, that there were other ways of making people into ghosts.

My memory came alive to see Mrs. Radley occasionally open the front door, walk to the edge of the porch, and pour water on her cannas. But every day Jem and I would see Mr. Radley walking to and from town. He was a thin leathery man with colorless eyes, so colorless they did not reflect light. His cheekbones were sharp and his mouth was wide, with a thin upper lip and a full lower lip. Miss Stephanie Crawford said he was so upright he took the word of God as his only law, and we believed her, because Mr. Radley's posture was ramrod straight.

He never spoke to us. When he passed we would look at the ground and say, "Good morning, sir," and he would cough in reply. Mr. Radley's elder son lived in Pensacola; he came home at Christmas, and he was one of the few persons we ever saw enter or leave the place. From the day Mr. Radley took Arthur home, people said the house died.

But there came a day when Atticus told us he'd wear us out if we made any noise in the yard and commissioned Calpurnia to serve in his absence if she heard a sound out of us. Mr. Radley was dying.

He took his time about it. Wooden sawhorses blocked the road at each end of the Radley lot, straw was put down on the sidewalk, traffic was diverted to the back street. Dr. Reynolds parked his car in front of our house and walked to the Radleys' every time he called. Jem and I crept around the yard for days. At last the sawhorses were taken away, and we stood watching from the front porch when Mr. Radley made his final journey past our house.

"There goes the meanest man ever God blew breath into," murmured Calpurnia, and she spat meditatively into the yard. We looked at her in surprise, for Calpurnia rarely commented on the ways of white people.

The neighborhood thought when Mr. Radley went under Boo would come out, but it had another think coming: Boo's elder brother returned from Pensacola and took Mr. Radley's place. The only difference between him and his father was their ages. Jem said Mr. Nathan Radley "bought cotton," too. Mr. Nathan would speak to us, however, when we said good morning, and sometimes we saw him coming from town with a magazine in his hand.

The more we told Dill about the Radleys, the more he wanted to know, the longer he would stand hugging the light-pole on the corner, the more he would wonder.

"Wonder what he does in there," he would murmur. "Looks like he'd just stick his head out the door."

Jem said, "He goes out, all right, when it's pitch dark. Miss Stephanie Crawford said she woke up in the middle of the night one time and saw him looking straight through the window at her . . . said his head was like a skull lookin' at her. Ain't you ever waked up at night and heard him, Dill? He walks like this—" Jem slid his feet through the gravel. "Why do you think Miss Rachel locks up so tight at night? I've seen his tracks in our back yard many a mornin', and one night I heard him scratching on the back screen, but he was gone time Atticus got there."

"Wonder what he looks like?" said Dill.

Jem gave a reasonable description of Boo: Boo was about six-and-a-half feet tall, judging from his tracks; he dined on raw squirrels and any cats he could catch, that's why his hands were bloodstained —if you ate an animal raw, you could never wash the blood off. There was a long jagged scar that ran across his face; what teeth he had were yellow and rotten; his eyes popped, and he drooled most of the time.

"Let's try to make him come out," said Dill. "I'd like to see what he looks like."

Jem said if Dill wanted to get himself killed, all he had to do was go up and knock on the front door.

Our first raid came to pass only because Dill bet Jem *The Gray Ghost* against two Tom Swifts that Jem wouldn't get any farther than the Radley gate. In all his life, Jem had never declined a dare.

Jem thought about it for three days. I suppose he loved honor more than his head, for Dill wore him down easily: "You're scared," Dill said, the first day. "Ain't scared, just respectful," Jem said. The next day Dill said, "You're too scared even to put your big toe in the front yard." Jem said he reckoned he wasn't, he'd passed the Radley Place every school day of his life.

"Always runnin'," I said.

But Dill got him the third day, when he told Jem that folks in Meridian certainly weren't as afraid as the folks in Maycomb, that he'd never seen such scary folks as the ones in Maycomb.

This was enough to make Jem march to the corner, where he stopped and leaned against the light-pole, watching the gate hanging crazily on its homemade hinge.

"I hope you've got it through your head that he'll kill us each and every one, Dill Harris," said Jem, when we joined him. "Don't blame me when he gouges your eyes out. You started it, remember."

"You're still scared," murmured Dill patiently.

Jem wanted Dill to know once and for all that he wasn't scared of anything: "It's just that I can't think of a way to make him come out without him gettin' us." Besides, Jem had his little sister to think of.

When he said that, I knew he was afraid. Jem had his little sister to think of the time I dared him to jump off the top of the house: "If I got killed, what'd become of you?" he asked. Then he jumped, landed unhurt, and his sense of responsibility left him until confronted by the Radley Place.

"You gonna run out on a dare?" asked Dill. "If you are, then—"

"Dill, you have to think about these things," Jem said. "Lemme think a minute . . . it's sort of like making a turtle come out . . ."

"How's that?" asked Dill.

"Strike a match under him."

I told Jem if he set fire to the Radley house I was going to tell Atticus on him.

Dill said striking a match under a turtle was hateful.

"Ain't hateful, just persuades him—'s not like you'd chunk him in the fire," Jem growled.

"How do you know a match don't hurt him?"

"Turtles can't feel, stupid," said Jem.

"Were you ever a turtle, huh?"

"My stars, Dill! Now lemme think . . . reckon we can rock him. . . ."

Jem stood in thought so long that Dill made a mild concession: "I won't say you ran out on a dare an' I'll swap you *The Gray Ghost* if you just go up and touch the house."

Jem brightened. "Touch the house, that all?"

Dill nodded.

"Sure that's all, now? I don't want you hollerin' something different the minute I get back."

"Yeah, that's all," said Dill. "He'll probably come out after you when he sees you in the yard, then Scout'n'me'll jump on him and hold him down till we can tell him we ain't gonna hurt him."

We left the corner, crossed the side street that ran in front of the Radley house, and stopped at the gate.

"Well go on," said Dill, "Scout and me's right behind you."

"I'm going," said Jem, "don't hurry me."

He walked to the corner of the lot, then back again, studying the simple terrain as if deciding how best to effect an entry, frowning and scratching his head.

Then I sneered at him.

Jem threw open the gate and sped to the side of the house, slapped it with his palm and ran back past us, not waiting to see if his foray was successful. Dill and I followed on his heels. Safely on our porch, panting and out of breath, we looked back.

The old house was the same, droopy and sick, but as we stared down the street we thought we saw an inside shutter move. Flick. A tiny, almost invisible movement, and the house was still.

• • • •

To *Kill a Mockingbird* arrived on the American scene just before the American South reached the racial boiling point. It daringly predicted the cataclysm awaiting America if whites and blacks refused to heal their old wounds. In subsequent chapters, the children's father defends an innocent black man accused of raping a white girl.

For other views of southern life, see the works of Maya Angelou (page 332) and Willie Morris (page 105).

The film of *To Kill a Mockingbird* is available as a 129-minute video, starring Gregory Peck and Brock Peters, with a screenplay by Horton Foote, and there is also a fourteen-hour audiocassette of the book (Recorded Books).

THANK YOU, MA'AM

by Langston Hughes

From Grandma's Lap to "Bard of the Streets"

Over the years, as I have read about or researched the childhoods of authors, a particular figure has emerged from their backgrounds often enough to make me stop and wonder: Is there a connection between this person and the future writer? In many cases, this one person was the sole beacon of hope for the child. No, it was not a parent, a teacher, or a librarian, though often enough those people were there. It was a grandparent.

Author biographies show a remarkable number who experienced unusually warm or live-in relationships with a grandparent: Hans Christian Andersen, Roald Dahl, Dorothy Canfield Fisher, Kenneth Grahame, Alex Haley, Beatrix Potter, Wilson Rawls, and, as described in this volume, Maya Angelou, Ray Bradbury, Frederick Douglass, Loren Eiseley, Moss Hart, Willie Morris, Gary Paulsen, Cynthia Rylant, and Robert W. Service. But none was more important than the maternal grandmother who raised the most famous and most important black writer of this century—Langston Hughes.

Before he died in 1967 at age sixty-five, Hughes had achieved fame as a poet, songwriter, lecturer, playwright, short-story writer, novelist, anthologist, reporter, and columnist. All of it was touched by the issue of race, particularly the African-black-brown-Negro race. Considering his remarkable heritage, one could hardly expect otherwise.

As his biographer, Arnold Rampersad, explained in *The Life of Langston Hughes*, "Much was expected by his ancestors. They demanded, from the moment his elders recognized the boy's unusual intelligence and began to talk to him about Duty and the Race, that he had a messianic obligation to the Afro-American people, and through them to America." Rampersad notes that among these ghostly ancestors were a white Virginia planter (the poet's great-grandfather), who had defied the mores of the South to live with the black woman he loved; two of their sons—one who risked almost everything in fighting against slavery and segregation, another who had also fought for freedom but lived to serve in the U.S. Congress and represent his country in Haiti; and the poet's maternal grandfather, who was killed at Harpers Ferry in John Brown's band. For young Hughes, the proud and passionate link with his ancestors would be his story-telling grandmother.

Hughes's parents separated when he was very young, and though he would grow to know both his father and mother intimately, it was his grandmother who raised and sheltered him during his formative years. His father was an ambitious, greedy businessman who hated the fact that he was black and loathed his son for being proud of it. In his autobiography, Hughes summarized their relationship: "I hated my father." The pride instilled by his grandmother was in constant contradiction to his father's racial shame, and Hughes eventually dropped his first name, James, in favor of his middle name, Langston. He did this because James was his father's name and Langston was his grandmother's last name.

His grandmother was almost seventy-five years old when he came under her care. It was her husband who had died at Harpers Ferry, and she herself had narrowly escaped being enslaved at the age of nineteen. She was religious enough to read Bible stories regularly to her grandson, but worldly enough to read Grimms' fairy tales to him as well. More important, she shared with young Hughes a lifetime's inventory of stories about heroic black men and women who fought the yoke of slavery and racism. Though she seldom left the house during his years with her, she did make several memorable journeys with him—including a trip to hear a speech by Booker T. Washington, then the most famous black man in America, and another to Kansas ceremonies where she was honored by former president Theodore Roosevelt as the last surviving widow of the Harpers Ferry raiding party.

Whenever Hughes joined his mother in Topeka, Kansas, she also made a point of reading to him and taking him regularly to the public library. It was she who refused to allow him to be sent to an all-black first grade across town. When the principal refused her pleas, she fought the case all the way to the school board and won. Forty-two years later, the same Kansas school district would carry its argument for segregated schools to the U.S. Supreme Court. There the Court would pass down its landmark *Brown* v. *Board of Education* ruling that declared school segregation deprived African-Americans of equal opportunity to an education.

His first-grade teacher resented his presence, however, and seated him out of alphabetical order in the last seat. Making racial remarks in class, she did her best to break his spirit, but his natural intelligence and quickness to learn proved more than a match for her. The same proved true in seventh grade when another teacher put all the black students in a separate row. Hughes printed up cards reading "Jim Crow Row," put them on each desk, was expelled, and then won the support of local black leaders for his reinstatement, by which time the teacher had abandoned her segregated seating plan. Despite such incidents, his high grades and positive response to school never wavered throughout his academic years.

His junior high reading ran the gamut from the essays of the famous black thinker W. E. B. Du Bois and the sensational accounts of racial lynchings in the weekly *Chicago Defender* to Zane Grey western novels and classics such as *The Adventures of Huckleberry Finn*, one of his lifelong favorites.

Hughes went to high school in Cleveland where his mother was then living, though she moved away after one year. He then spent his sophomore, junior, and senior years living alone in boarding-houses, working after school, studying, running track, and blossoming into the star of the high school literary magazine, while his first poetry was rejected by professional magazines. Those who would wonder years later why Hughes's writings did not have a white-hot rage against all whites needed to see him in those Cleveland years, when he was often warmed and fed by the families of white classmates and his writing talents were loudly encouraged by white faculty members. They needed to see him as editor of the white school's yearbook and the unsuccessful "Jewish candidate" for class president, backed by the Jewish members of his senior class. All his life he refused to paint his racial protests with a broad brush.

By the time he finished high school, he was determined to accomplish what no other black man had yet accomplished in America—he would earn a living as an author. Not only that, he wanted to "write stories about Negroes, so true that people in faraway lands would read them—even after I was dead." The road to that goal would not be easy or short. Before he achieved it and became "the Poet Laureate of Harlem" and "the Bard of the Streets," he would know the same bleak, rolling-stone years experienced by other writers from impoverished backgrounds, white and black (see the biographies of Robert W. Service, Loren Eiseley, Gary Paulsen, Pete Hamill, and Maya Angelou in this volume). He would become a seaman, cook, laundryman, delivery boy, and busboy, all the while writing his poems. It would be these years of blue-collar labor, along with the lessons of his ancestors, that would flavor his future writing.

Slowly and painfully, his poetry won recognition among both whites and blacks with its poignant and powerful images of African-Americans as dockhands, domestics, waiters, cooks, elevator operators, factory workers, even streetwalkers, struggling to survive, to raise families, to enjoy life, to achieve with dignity. As his writings expanded into short stories, novels, and plays, so too did his commentary on racial and social justice. During World War II, his was among the loudest voices raised in protest over the treatment of African-American soldiers and Japanese-American families forced into "relocation camps." He made his points with humor and ironic satire as well as indignation and impatience, but always with the dignity his grandmother would have expected.

Though one would expect a black man with his worldwide acclaim to have his share of white critics, he also collected criticism from his own people, especially when he dared to write "too close to home," describing seamier events that affluent blacks preferred be ignored or forgotten. They also resented his use of black English. Hughes, however, ignored their criticisms and stayed with his roots.

By the time the short story that follows appeared in 1958, the black community had come to see what Hughes had seen all along— the beauty in blackness, the brotherhood and sisterhood of the struggle, the lilting quality in colloquial and ethnic speech. Also, by this time Hughes had grown increasingly concerned with the expanding underbelly of poverty in places such as Harlem. He saw it in the escalation of street crime among young boys. Where once he would have been criticized for using such material as subject matter, by now he had legions of followers who realized it would not go away if it was ignored.

In "Thank You, Ma'am," we see not just a story about moral responsibility but also Hughes's determination to depict both the strengths and the weaknesses of his people. Not surprisingly, the strength and saving grace in the tale appear in the form of a grandmother figure.

• • • •

S HE WAS A large woman with a large purse that had everything in it but a hammer and nails. It had a long strap, and she carried it slung across her shoulder. It was about eleven o'clock at night, dark, and she was walking alone, when a boy ran up behind her and tried to snatch her purse. The strap broke with the sudden single tug the boy gave it from behind. But the boy's weight and the weight of the purse combined caused him to lose his balance. Instead of taking off full blast as he had hoped, the boy fell on his back on the sidewalk and his legs flew up. The large woman simply turned around and kicked him right square in his blue-jeaned sitter. Then she reached down, picked the boy up by his shirt front, and shook him until his teeth rattled.

After that the woman said, "Pick up my pocketbook, boy, and give it here."

She still held him tightly. But she bent down enough to permit him to stoop and pick up her purse. Then she said, "Now ain't you ashamed of yourself?"

Firmly gripped by his shirt front, the boy said, "Yes'm."

The woman said, "What did you want to do it for?"

The boy said, "I didn't aim to."

She said, "You a lie!"

By that time two or three people passed, stopped, turned to look, and some stood watching.

"If I turn you loose, will you run?" asked the woman.

"Yes'm," said the boy.

"Then I won't turn you loose," said the woman. She did not release him.

"Lady, I'm sorry," whispered the boy.

"Um-hum! Your face is dirty. I got a great mind to wash your face for you. Ain't you got nobody home to tell you to wash your face?"

"No'm," said the boy.

"Then it will get washed this evening," said the large woman, starting up the street, dragging the frightened boy behind her.

He looked as if he were fourteen or fifteen, frail and willow-wild, in tennis shoes and blue jeans.

The woman said, "You ought to be my son. I would teach you right from wrong. Least I can do right now is to wash your face. Are you hungry?"

"No'm," said the being-dragged boy. "I just want you to turn me loose."

"Was I bothering *you* when I turned that corner?" asked the woman.

"No'm."

"But you put yourself in contact with *me*," said the woman. "If you think that that contact is not going to last awhile, you got another thought coming. When I get through with you, sir, you are going to remember Mrs. Luella Bates Washington Jones."

Sweat popped out on the boy's face and he began to struggle. Mrs. Jones stopped, jerked him around in front of her, put a half nelson about his neck, and continued to drag him up the street. When she got to her door, she dragged the boy inside, down a hall, and into a large kitchenette-furnished room at the rear of the house. She switched on the light and left the door open. The boy could hear other roomers laughing and talking in the large house. Some of their doors were open, too, so he knew he and the woman were not alone. The woman still had him by the neck in the middle of her room.

She said, "What is your name?"

"Roger," answered the boy.

"Then, Roger, you go to that sink and wash your face," said the woman, whereupon she turned him loose—at last. Roger looked at the door—looked at the woman—looked at the door—*and went to the sink*.

"Let the water run until it gets warm," she said. "Here's a clean towel."

"You gonna take me to jail?" asked the boy, bending over the sink.

"Not with that face, I would not take you nowhere," said the woman. "Here I am trying to get home to cook me a bite to eat, and you snatch my pocketbook! Maybe you ain't been to your supper either, late as it be. Have you?"

"There's nobody home at my house," said the boy.

"Then we'll eat," said the woman. "I believe you're hungry—or been hungry—to try to snatch my pocketbook!"

"I want a pair of blue suede shoes," said the boy.

"Well, you didn't have to snatch *my* pocketbook to get some suede shoes," said Mrs. Luella Bates Washington Jones. "You could of asked me."

"Ma'am?"

The water dripping from his face, the boy looked at her. There was a long pause. A very long pause. After he had dried his face and not knowing what else to do, dried it again, the boy turned around, wondering what next. The door was open. He could make a dash for it down the hall. He could run, run, run, *run*!

The woman was sitting on the day bed. After a while she said, "I were young once and I wanted things I could not get."

There was another long pause. The boy's mouth opened. Then he frowned, not knowing he frowned.

The woman said, "Um-hum! You thought I was going to say *but*, didn't you? You thought I was going to say, *but I didn't snatch people's pocketbooks*. Well, I wasn't going to say that." Pause. Silence. "I have done things, too, which I would not tell you, son—neither tell God, if He didn't already know. Everybody's got something in common. So you set down while I fix us something to eat. You might run that comb through your hair so you will look presentable."

In another corner of the room behind a screen was a gas plate and an icebox. Mrs. Jones got up and went behind the screen. The woman did not watch the boy to see if he was going to run now, nor did she watch her purse, which she left behind her on the day bed. But the boy took care to sit on the far side of the room, away from the purse, where he thought she could easily see him out of the corner of her eye if she wanted to. He did not trust the woman *not* to trust him. And he did not want to be mistrusted now.

"Do you need somebody to go to the store," asked the boy, "maybe to get some milk or something?"

"Don't believe I do," said the woman, "unless you just want sweet milk yourself. I was going to make cocoa out of this canned milk I got here."

"That will be fine," said the boy.

She heated some lima beans and ham she had in the icebox, made the cocoa, and set the table. The woman did not ask the boy anything about where he lived, or his folks, or anything else that would embarrass him. Instead, as they ate, she told him about her job in a hotel beauty shop that stayed open late, what the work was like, and how all kinds of women came in and out, blondes, redheads, and Spanish. Then she cut him a half of her ten-cent cake.

"Eat some more, son," she said.

When they were finished eating, she got up and said, "Now here, take this ten dollars and buy yourself some blue suede shoes. And next time, do not make the mistake of latching onto *my* pocketbook *nor nobody else's*—because shoes got by devilish ways will burn your feet. I got to get my rest now. But from here on in, son, I hope you will behave yourself."

She led him down the hall to the front door and opened it. "Good night! Behave yourself, boy!" she said, looking out into the street as he went down the steps.

The boy wanted to say something other than, "Thank you, ma'am," to Mrs. Luella Bates Washington Jones, but although his lips moved, he couldn't even say that as he turned at the foot of the barren stoop and looked up at the large woman in the door. Then she shut the door.

• • • •

Langston Hughes's books include: *Dream Keeper*; *The Langston Hughes Reader*; *Not Without Laughter*; *The Selected Poems of Langston Hughes*; *The Simple Omnibus*; and *Something in Common and Other Stories*.

Langston Hughes: A Biography by Milton Meltzer is an excellent young people's biography. The definitive adult biography is the two-volume *The Life of Langston Hughes* by Arnold Rampersad.

Hughes's work available on audiocassette includes: *The Poetry of Langston Hughes*, two cassettes, read by Ruby Dee and Ossie Davis (Harper-Caedmon); *Poetry and Reflections*, performed by Langston Hughes (Harper-Caedmon); and *Simple Stories*, about the black folk-philosopher Hughes made famous through his newspaper column and books, read by Ossie Davis (Harper-Caedmon).

Fans of Langston Hughes's stories also will enjoy these books on contemporary African-American life by two of today's outstanding black writers for young adults: by Rosa Guy: *The Disappearance*, *The Friends*, and *New Guys Around the Block*; and by Walter Dean Myers: *Fallen Angels*, *Hoops*, and *Scorpions*.

Animal Tales

Four memorable stories
about a deer, a cow, a dog,
and a nature boy.

from A BLUE-EYED DAISY
by Cynthia Rylant

The Unlikely Author
Out of Appalachia

Looking at her on her first day as a children's librarian at the Huntington, West Virginia, public library, who would have guessed her story—the one behind her and the ones to come? She was a pretty blond twenty-three-year-old with two college degrees in English. No one knew she'd never before been in the children's room of a library. She hadn't even been in a *public library* at all until she was halfway through college. This new librarian had never heard of—never mind *read*—*Make Way for Ducklings* or *Charlotte's Web*.

Cynthia Rylant doesn't fit the stereotype we create for authors —of growing up in homes surrounded by books, spending half their time being read to by their parents and the other half going to the library, and writing their first amateurish novels at age twelve. There are such authors (see Ray Bradbury, page 252), but Rylant is not one of them. She isn't even close.

To begin with, there was no happy Mom and Dad. And no books at home, or even a library in town. Rylant's parents separated when she was four, at which time she went to live with her grandparents in the rural mountains of southern West Virginia while her mother left to become a nurse.

Her grandparents' four-room house not only didn't have books in it, it didn't have running water, an indoor toilet, or any extra space. Along with Grandma and Grandpa, there was an assortment of teenage aunts and uncles still living there, along with a couple of cousins— not counting the relatives who came to visit for a weekend.

Her grandfather was a coal miner and suffered a permanently disabling injury soon after she arrived, so money wasn't abundant either. Store-bought food was such a rare treat that when Rylant once tasted Ritz crackers at a friend's house, she asked if she could bring some home. Needless to say, the television reception wasn't too good in the mountains in those days before cable, and there were no shopping malls or a library. Some folks might say Cynthia Rylant had a deprived childhood. And they would be wrong.

What she had in that house full of relatives was an abundance of love and affection that washed around her like waves. In fact, her life with her grandparents might be the only part of her story that *is* stereotypical, since a large number of authors seem to have an unusually close relationship with a grandparent (see page 82). When her grandfather stood in the dew-wet darkness each morning and waited until she safely boarded her school bus, he was silently telling her, "Even at this dark hour and in this chill, you are loved." Her school didn't have modern equipment or up-to-date textbooks, but its teachers "gave me something far more important: a feeling of being loved, a feeling of welcome. It is the best that schools can give," she says in retrospect.

She also had a best friend named Cindy and they were inseparable. What more could a child ask for? Rylant's was a lovely, warm, happy childhood, made even nicer when her mother finally graduated from nursing school and together they moved to a small town not far from her grandparents.

In a poignant autobiographical sketch for *Something About the Author*, Rylant wrote: "All this time, all these years of growing up so far, I did not read many books. I did not see many books. There was no library in our little town. No bookstore. Adults got paperbacks off the drugstore rack and kids bought comic books. I read comics by the hundreds, trading huge piles of mine for huge piles of Danny Alderman's or whoever else would swap with me. I guess most people assume that future famous authors are supposed to be reading fat hardbound books and writing poetry by age ten. But all I wanted to do was read *Archie* and play the Beatles."

Eventually she graduated from comic books to cheap paperback romances from the drugstore (high school literature was "boring"). Only when she arrived at college did she discover "real" literature, and that's when she began to fall in love with words. But they were other people's words, not her own: "I had not tried to write anything myself. I was too intimidated. There were no writers where I came from, so I believed the world of writers was a world in which I didn't belong."

After graduate school, she applied for a job with the Huntington,

West Virginia, public library. When they eventually transferred her out of the film department and into the children's room, could they ever have imagined they were igniting the creative fires of a writer— a future Newbery Medal winner?

She recalls, "My job was to check out books and shelve them. I started reading the books I was supposed to be shelving and soon I was taking children's books home by the boxful. I was enchanted. I read children's books all night long. And I knew, with a certainty like I'd never had about anything before, that I wanted to write children's books."

A year later Rylant took a pen and yellow pad to bed with her one night and wrote for an hour. She wrote about the corn bread and fried okra, about walking hand-in-hand with her grandmother to the johnny-house at night, about baths in tin tubs filled with well water, and about Sunday baptisms in the swimming hole. There was no revision—she just opened a vein in her heart and let it spill over the yellow pad. Then she typed it up, mailed it to a stranger, and two months later it was accepted. Thus was born her award-winning picture book *When I Was Young in the Mountains*.

Within ten years, drawing upon the rich fabric of those relatives, friends, and dirt roads, she became one of America's most honored and versatile children's and young-adult writers. Cynthia Rylant has written picture books, poetry, essays, short-story collections, and novels—including the 1993 Newbery Award novel, *Missing May*. How much of an achievement is that? Well, if she were a baseball player it would be the equivalent of winning the batting, home run, RBI, stolen base, and fielding titles—all in one year.

The selection here is the opening chapter from her first novel, *A Blue-Eyed Daisy*, written with the warm affection she still feels for the people of Appalachia but also with the unsugared directness of mountain folk. (The character Ellie is largely based upon her childhood best friend, Cindy.)

• • • •

The Prettiest

ELLIE'S FATHER was a drinking man. Everybody knew it. Couldn't help knowing it because when Okey Farley was drunk he always jumped in his red and white Chevy truck and made the rocks fly up and down the mountains.

He had been a coal miner. Drank then, too, but just on weekends. A lot of miners drank on the weekend to scare away the coming week.

Okey had been hurt in a slate fall, so he couldn't work anymore. Just stayed home and drank.

Ellie was his youngest daughter, the youngest of five. She didn't look anything like Okey or her mother, both of whom had shiny black hair and dark eyes.

Ellie was fair. Her hair was nearly white and her skin pale like snow cream. Ellie was a pretty girl, but her teeth were getting rotten and she always hid them with her hand when she laughed.

Ellie loved her father, but she was afraid of him. Because when he drank he usually yelled, or cried or hit her mother. At those times Ellie stayed in her room and prayed.

One day Okey did a strange thing. He brought home a beagle. Her father couldn't hunt because his right arm wasn't strong enough to manage a rifle anymore. But there he was with a beagle he called Bullet.

He made Bullet a house. Spent the whole weekend making it and didn't even stop to take a drink.

Then Bullet was tied up to his house, and he kept them all awake three nights in a row with his howling.

Okey would not explain why he'd bought a hunting dog when he couldn't hunt. He just sat on the porch with a bottle in his hand (he'd taken it up again) and looked at Bullet.

Ellie was the only one of Okey's children who took an interest in his pet. The older girls were not impressed by a dog.

But Ellie, fair and quiet, liked the beagle and was interested in her father's liking for it. And when Okey was sober, she'd sit with him on the porch and they'd talk about Bullet.

Neither of them could remember later who mentioned it first, but somehow the subject of hunting came up one day, and, hardly knowing she was saying it, Ellie announced she wanted to learn how to hunt.

Okey laughed long and hard. In fact, he had a little whiskey down his throat and nearly choked to death on it. Ellie slapped his back about fifty times.

The next time they sat together, though, she said it again. And this time more firmly, for she'd given it some thought. And Okey set down his bottle and listened.

He tested her. He set up some cans, showed her how to handle his rifle, then stepped back to watch. The first day she missed them all. The second day she hit one. The fifth day she hit four out of nine.

So when she brought up hunting again, they fixed the date.

They went out on a Saturday about five-thirty in the morning, just as the blackness was turning blue. Ellie was booted and flanneled like her father, and she had her own gun.

Okey held his rifle under his left arm. They both knew he'd never be able to shoot it. But neither said anything.

It was just getting light when they made the top of the mountains, their breaths coming fast and smoky cold. They each found a tree to lean against and the wait began.

Bullet had traveled far away from them. He was after rabbit, they knew that much, and they were after squirrel. Okey told Ellie she might have half a chance of hitting a squirrel. Rabbit was out of the question.

Ellie flexed her fingers and tried not to shiver. She was partly cold and partly scared, but mostly happy. For she was on a mountain with her father and it was dawn.

Neither Okey nor Ellie expected a deer to come along. So neither was prepared when one did. But less than twenty feet away, stamping its front hoof in warning, suddenly stood a doe. Okey and Ellie looked across the trees at each other and froze themselves into the scenery.

The doe did not catch their scent. And she could not see them unless they moved. But she sensed something was odd, for she stamped again. Then moved closer.

Ellie looked at the animal. She knew that if she shot a deer, doe or buck, her father would never stop bragging about it. "First time out and she got a deer." She knew it would be so.

The doe was nearing her tree and she knew if she were quick about it, she could get that deer. She knew it would be easier than shooting a squirrel off a tree limb. She could kill that deer.

But she did not. The doe moved nearer; it was a big one, and its large brown eyes watched for movement. They found it. Ellie raised her arm. And she waved.

The deer snorted hard and turned. It was so quickly gone that Ellie could not be sure in which direction it headed.

"Godamighty!" she heard Okey yell. She knew he might be mad enough to shoot her, if he could hold onto his rifle. She heard his crashing across the ground.

"Now wasn't that," Okey gasped as he reached her tree, "wasn't that the *prettiest* thing you ever seen?"

Ellie hesitated, wondering, and then she grinned wide.

"The *prettiest*," she answered.

And they turned together and went quickly down the mountain to find Bullet and go on home.

• • • •

IN SUCCEEDING CHAPTERS, the reader follows Ellie through the seasons of a year, tasting the joys and sorrows of rural life—sending her beloved uncle off to war, coping with her aunt "Crazy Cecile," receiving the perfect valentine, mourning the death of a classmate, finding a best friend, going to her first boy-girl party, and getting her first real kiss.

Rylant has written a variety of books to appeal to all readers, including: Picture books: *Miss Maggie*; *The Relatives Came*; *Appalachia: The Voices of Sleeping Birds*; and *An Angel for Solomon Singer*. Poetry: *Waiting to Waltz: A Childhood*; and *Soda Jerk*. Essays: *But I'll Be Back Again*. Short-story collections: *A Couple of Kooks: An Album. And Other Stories About Love*; and *Children of Christmas*. Novels: *A Fine White Dust*; and *A Kindness*.

Award-winning author Lawrence Yep's novel *The Star Fisher* also recounts a story of rural West Virginia, based upon his family's experiences in 1927 as the community's first Chinese residents. Other books relating to small-town or rural life in America: *Baseball in April and Other Stories* by Gary Soto (page 29), *A Day No Pigs Would Die* by Robert Newton Peck (page 99), and *Miracle at Clement's Pond* by Patricia Pendergraft (page 45).

See also a sixty-minute PBS video entitled *Appalachian Journey*.

from A DAY NO PIGS WOULD DIE

by Robert Newton Peck

The Love Story They Love to Protest

It is, above all else, a love story about a boy, his father, and a pig. As *The New York Times* noted, though "nobody in [the book] ever mentions the word love or any other emotion, for that matter—love nevertheless infuses every page." And the author is quick to point out, "There is not one dirty thought in the book." Yet, year after year, *A Day No Pigs Would Die* is listed among the top ten young-adult books targeted for censorship.

Soon after Robert Newton Peck was fired from an advertising job on Madison Avenue, he remembered a conversation he'd had with an editor at Alfred A. Knopf, Inc. They had met for lunch to discuss a small nature book (*Path of Hunters*) Peck was writing, and the editor casually asked about Peck's childhood. Never at a loss for words, oral or written, Peck reminisced about growing up in a rural Vermont community, one of seven children in a loving Shaker family whose illiterate father was a farmer and slaughtered pigs for a living. The editor immediately saw the story potential in what he was hearing and exclaimed, "If you ever put this on paper, it would be sensational!" Thereafter, every time they spoke the editor would ask, "When are you going to do that pig book?" Peck just laughed it off—until he lost his job.

Locked away in his suburban Connecticut home, Peck wrote nonstop for two and half weeks. "It was a book that was *mechanically* easy to write—it wrote itself! I'd been carrying it inside me since I was thirteen years old," says Peck. "But because it was the story of my childhood, of my relationship with my family, it was *emotionally* a very difficult book to write." The book semiautobiographically describes the year of Peck's coming-of-age—helping neighbors, raising a pig, exhibiting at the state fair, and absorbing the wisdom of his father's simple Shaker ways as the shadow of death invades their lives.

After writing the book longhand on yellow legal pads, Peck had it typed, and delivered it to the receptionist's desk at Knopf (the editor was at lunch). At eleven that night, Peck was awakened by the editor's call. "It is absolutely perfect," he exclaimed. "No one will ever dare try to change a word." And no one did—until community censors took offense at young Peck's occasional utterances of earth-shattering words such as *damn, ass*, and *bitch*.

The story was originally marketed as an adult book and selected as a *Reader's Digest* Condensed Book. Word of mouth, however, began to spread among adolescents and their teachers. Today, almost a quarter century after its publication, its sales show no sign of abating, thanks to both the book's quality and the censors who keep unwittingly publicizing it.

Anyone who has either lived on a farm or spent time in the wild will attest to the fact that Mother Nature can be as harsh as she is beautiful. As in this first chapter of *A Day No Pigs Would Die*, humans often try to balance these two extremes with an earthy humor. Young Peck is skipping school one day when he encounters a neighbor's cow that is calving while choking on a goiter.

• • • •

CHAPTER 1

I SHOULD OF BEEN in school that April day.

But instead I was up on the ridge near the old spar mine above our farm, whipping the gray trunk of a rock maple with a dead stick, and hating Edward Thatcher. During recess, he'd pointed at my clothes and made sport of them. Instead of tying into him, I'd turned tail and run off. And when Miss Malcolm rang the bell to call us back inside, I was halfway home.

Picking up a stone, I threw it into some bracken ferns, hard as I could. Someday that was how hard I was going to light into Edward Thatcher, and make him bleed like a stuck pig. I'd kick him from one end of Vermont to the other, and sorry him good. I'd teach him not to make fun of Shaker ways. He'd never show his face in the town of Learning, ever again. No, sir.

A painful noise made me whip my head around and jump at the same time. When I saw her, I knew she was in bad trouble.

It was the big Holstein cow, one of many, that belonged to our near neighbor, Mr. Tanner. This one he called "Apron" because she was mostly black, except for the white along her belly which went up her front and around her neck like a big clean apron. She was his biggest cow, Mr. Tanner told Papa, and his best milker. And he was fixing up to take her to Rutland Fair, come summer.

As I ran toward her, she made her dreadful noise again. I got close up and saw why. Her big body was pumping up and down, trying to have her calf. She'd fell down and there was blood on her foreleg, and her mouth was all thick and foamy with yellow-green spit. I tried to reach my hand out and pat her head; but she was wild-eyed mean, and making this breezy noise almost every breath.

Turning away from me, she showed me her swollen rump. Her tail was up and arched high, whipping through the air with every heave of her back. Sticking out of her was the head and one hoof of her calf. His head was so covered with blood and birth-sop that I had no way telling he was alive or dead. Until I heard him bawl.

Apron went crashing through the puckerbush, me right behind. I'd never caught up. But because she had to stop and strain, I got to the calf's head and got a purchase on him.

He was so covered with slime, and Apron was so wandering, there was no holding to it. Besides, being just twelve years old, I weighed a bit over a hundred pounds. Apron was comfortable over a thousand, and it wasn't much of a tug for her. As I went down, losing my grip on the calf's neck, her hoof caught my shinbone and it really smarted. The only thing that made me get up and give the whole idea another go was when he bawled again.

I'd just wound up running away from Edward Thatcher and running away from the schoolhouse. I was feathered if I was going to run away from one darn more thing.

I needed a rope. But there wasn't any, so I had to make one. It didn't have to be long, just strong.

Chasing old Apron through the next patch of prickers sure took some fun out of the whole business. I made my mistake of trying to take my trousers off as I ran. No good. So I sat down in the prickers, yanked 'em off over my boots, and caught up to Apron. After a few bad tries, I got one pantleg around her calf's head and knotted it snug.

"Calf," I said to him, "you stay up your ma's hindside and you're about to choke. So you might as well choke getting yourself born."

Whatever old Apron decided that I was doing to her back yonder, she didn't take kindly to it. So she started off again with me in the rear, hanging on to wait Christmas, and my own bare butt and privates catching a thorn with every step. And that calf never coming one inch closer to coming out. But when Apron stopped to heave again I got the other pantleg around a dogwood tree that was about thick as a fencepost.

Now only three things could happen: My trousers would rip. Apron would just uproot the tree. The calf would slide out.

But nothing happened. Apron just stood shaking and heaving and straining and never moved forward a step. I got the other pantleg knotted about the dogwood; and like Apron, I didn't know what to do next.

Her calf bawled once more, making a weaker noise than before. But all old Apron did was heave in that one place.

"You old bitch," I yelled at her, grabbing a dead blackberry cane that was as long as a bullwhip and big around as a broom handle, "you move that big black smelly ass, you hear?"

I never hit anybody, boy or beast, as I hit that cow. I beat her so hard I was crying. Where I held the big cane, the thorns were chewing up my hands real bad. But it only got me madder.

I kicked her. And stoned her. I kicked her again one last time, so hard in the udder that I thought I heard her grunt. Both her hind quarters sort of hunkered down in the brush. Then she started forward, my trousers went tight, I heard a rip and a calf bawl. And a big hunk of hot stinking stuff went all over me. Some of it was calf, some of it wasn't.

As I went down under the force and weight of it, I figured something either got dead or got born.

All I knew was that I was snarled up in a passel of wet stuff, and there was a strong cord holding me against something that was very hot and kicked a lot. I brushed some of the slop away from my eyes and looked up. And there was Apron, her big black head and her big black mouth licking first me and then her calf.

But she was far from whole. Her mouth was open and she was gasping for air. She stumbled once. I thought for sure I was going to wind up being under a very big cow. The noise in her throat came at me again, and her tongue lashed to and fro like the tail of a clock. It looked to me as if there was something in her mouth. She would start to breathe and then, like a cork in a bottle, some darn thing in there would cut it off.

Her big body swayed like she was dizzy or sick. As the front of her fell to her knees, her head hit my chest as I lay on the ground, her nose almost touching my chin. She had stopped breathing!

Her jaw was locked open so I put my hand into her mouth, but felt only her swollen tongue. I stretched my fingers up into her throat—and there it was! A hard ball, about apple-size. It was stuck in her windpipe, or her gullet. I didn't know which and didn't care. So I shut my eyes, grabbed it, and yanked.

Somebody told me once that a cow won't bite. That somebody is as wrong as sin on Sunday. I thought my arm had got sawed off part way between elbow and shoulder. She bit and bit and never let go. She got to her feet and kept on biting. That devil cow ran down off that ridge with my arm in her mouth, and dragging me half-naked with her. What she didn't do to me with her teeth, she did with her front hoofs.

It should have been broad daylight, but it was night. Black night. As black and as bloody and as bad as getting hurt again and again could ever be.

It just went on and on. It didn't quit.

• • • •

WHEN PECK REGAINS CONSCIOUSNESS, his neighbor and parents are getting ready to stitch up his bloody arm. The neighbor, Mr. Tanner, appreciates the boy's courage and determination, for if not for him, the cow probably would have lost her two bull calves. His reward is a newborn pig. And though Peck plans to raise her as a sow, Mother Nature intends otherwise. As E. B. White's *Charlotte's Web* is successful with younger readers, so is this realistic depiction of farm life equally successful with an older audience.

Since that first novel, Peck has authored more than fifty-six books, including *Arly, Justice Lion, Kirk's Law, Mr. Little*, and, for middle-grade readers, the enormously popular Soup series—*Soup, Soup and Me, Soup for President, Soup in the Saddle, Soup on Fire, Soup on Ice, Soup on Wheels, Soup's Drum, Soup's Goat, Soup's Hoop*, and *Soup's Uncle*.

Fans of *A Day No Pigs Would Die* will also enjoy *Good Old Boy: A Delta Boyhood* by Willie Morris (page 105), *Miracle at Clement's Pond* by Patricia Pendergraft (page 45), *Isaac Campion* by Janni Howker, *Old Yeller* by Fred Gipson, *Where the Red Fern Grows* by Wilson Rawls, and *Words by Heart* by Ouida Sebestyen.

from GOOD OLD BOY:
A DELTA BOYHOOD

by Willie Morris

A Good Old Boy
and His Dog

A great Russian novelist named Leo Tolstoy once observed that "happy families are all alike; every unhappy family is unhappy in its own way." I think the same thing can be said for happy childhoods. Many of the same sensations of growing up happy in Massachusetts can be found in the happy childhoods of Mississippi or Michigan. Willie Morris proves that in his warm memoir of growing up in Yazoo City on the Mississippi Delta, *Good Old Boy*.

Morris was himself a "good old boy." He did his schoolwork well enough to capture A's and said the things teachers liked to hear, but when he joined his friends outside school, he was just one of the boys, doing the wild and mischievous things kids did in those days and still do.

His family was so deeply rooted in the South that he could trace his heritage to the Harpers of Harpers Ferry and an uncle whose newspaper press was dumped in the town well by General Sherman's troops. These were stories he heard told and retold in the cool shade of his grandparents' home each time he visited. Indeed, spending lazy summer vacations with them and his eccentric aunts in Jackson, listening to shortwave baseball broadcasts from New York, and traveling to Memphis for minor-league games, Morris slowly came to realize the world was bigger than Yazoo City. Not better, just bigger. Eventually his father persuaded him to attend the University of Texas, where he edited the college newspaper and steered it into a confrontation with the board of trustees over censorship. Along the way he won one of the world's premier academic awards, a four-year Rhodes scholarship to Oxford University in England.

A few years later in New York (which he called "the Cave"),

he became the eighth and youngest editor in the history of *Harper's* magazine. And just as *Harper's* had distinguished itself a century earlier with its graphic coverage of the Civil War, under its transplanted "good old boy" it would distinguish itself again—this time shedding important and revealing light on the New South born from the civil rights movement.

In order to understand that South, however, one must also know its past. In knowing that past through the childhoods of people such as Willie Morris, Harper Lee, and Maya Angelou, we come to know the southern men and women who built the bridges there between white and black, who mended the ancient wounds of intolerance. In the end, what saved the South from the flames of conflagration and hate was the overwhelming goodness of its people—white and black. *Good Old Boy* speaks to the roots of that goodness.

Morris's success made him famous throughout the South, inspiring at least one southern scholar to stop by Morris's office at Harper's in 1969 to meet a "good old boy" who had made good in the North. The personable twenty-three-year-old from Arkansas was on his way to England on a Rhodes scholarship and wanted Morris to know how touched he was by Morris's first book, *North Toward Home* (upon which *Good Old Boy* is based). Morris must have been just as impressed with the young man because he took the time to give him a cab-ride tour of New York City and take him to lunch. All without a clue that he was escorting and feeding a man who twenty-four years later would be President of the United States—Bill Clinton.

Morris's Yazoo City was just a town of gravel streets, forty miles from the Mississippi. His father ran a gas station, taught him how to hunt, and inspired him to love the game of baseball. The America they experienced in the 1930s and 1940s was eons before shopping malls and high-speed interstates. Sometimes it seems like another planet. Morris writes, "There was something in the very atmosphere of a small town in the Deep South, something spooked-up and romantic, which did extravagant things to the imagination of its bright and resourceful boys. It had something to do with long and heavy afternoons with nothing doing, with rich slow evenings when the crickets and the frogs scratched their legs and made delta music, with plain boredom, perhaps with an inherited tradition of contriving elaborate plots or one-shot practical jokes."

But more likely his very familiar childhood behavior had less to do with the geography of his home than with the geography of his heart. Having grown up in New Jersey, I can truthfully say that happy childhoods are very much alike.

Morris's son, David, who was growing up in New York City while his father was editing *Harper's*, asked his father one day what his childhood was like. *Good Old Boy: A Delta Boyhood* is his father's answer, introduced to the reader as an open-letter response to his son's question.

In this selection, we meet Morris's beloved dog, one that is something of a rarity in children's literature. Most of the famous dog stories are ultimately sad ones—*Lassie Come-Home* by Eric Knight, *The Call of the Wild* by Jack London, and *Where the Red Fern Grows* by Wilson Rawls. Willie Morris, however, offers a respite from those tear-streaked episodes.

· · · ·

CHAPTER 4

ONE DAY DURING MY IMPRISONMENT under Miss Abbott I got Old Skip, the best dog I ever owned, shipped from a kennel all the way from Springfield, Missouri. He was a black-and-white fox terrier. I had never been without a dog for more than six months at a time; this one had been promised to me ever since I behaved myself at my first funeral.

I came across a faded photograph of him not too long ago, his black face with the long nose sniffing at something in the air, his tail straight and pointing, his eyes flashing with mischief. Looking at a photograph taken a quarter of a century before, I admit that even as a grown man I still miss him. We had had a whole string of dogs before, first big birddogs like Tony, Sam, and Jimbo, and then pure-bred English smooth-haired fox terriers like this one. I got to know all about dogs—their crazy moods, how they looked when they were sick or just bored, when they were ready to bite or when their growling meant nothing, what they might be trying to say when they moaned and made strange human noises deep in their throats.

None of those other dogs could compare with this one. You could talk to him as well as you could to some human beings, and he would understand more of what you said than some people I knew. He would look you straight in the eye, and when he knew what you were saying he would turn his head sideways, back and forth, his ears cocked to get every word. Before going to bed at night I would say, "First thing tomorrow I want you to get your leash, and then come get me up, 'cause we're gonna get in the car and go out in the woods and get us some *squirrels*." And the next morning he would wake up both my father and me, get the leash, walk nervously around the house while we ate breakfast, and then lead us out to the car. Or I could say, "Bubba Barrier and Billy Rhodes are comin' over here today, and we're gonna play some football." And his face would light up, and he would wait around in front of the house and pick up Bubba's and Billy Rhodes' scent a block down the street and come tell me they were coming. Or, "Skip, how about some catch?" and he would get up and walk into the front room, open the door in the cabinet with his long nose, and bring me the tennis ball.

Every time I shouted "*Squirrel!*" Skip would head for the nearest tree and try to climb it, sometimes getting as high as five or six feet with his spectacular leaps. This would stop traffic on the street in front of our house. People in cars would see him trying to climb a tree, and would pull up to the curb to watch. They would gaze up into the tree to see what the dog was after, and after a pause ask me, "What's he got up there?" and I would say, "Somethin' small and mean." They seldom realized that the dog was just practicing.

This exercise was nothing compared to football games, however. I cut the lace on a football and taught Skip how to carry it in his mouth, and how to hold it so he could avoid fumbling when he was tackled. I taught him how to move on a quarterback's signals, to take a snap from center on the first hop, and to follow me down the field.

Fifteen or sixteen of us would organize a game of tackle in my front yard. Our side would go into the huddle, the dog included, and we would put our arms around each other's shoulders the way they did in real huddles at Ole Miss and Tennessee, and the dog would stand on his hind legs and, with me kneeling, drape a forepaw around *my* shoulder. Then I would say, "Skip, Pattern 39, off on three." We would break out of huddle, with the dog dropping into the tailback position as I had taught him. Bubba or Ralph would be the center, and I would station myself at quarterback and say, "Ready, set, one . . . two . . . *three!*" Then the center would snap the ball on a hop to the dog, who would get it by the lace and follow me downfield, dodging would-be tacklers with no effort at all, weaving behind his blockers, spinning loose when he was trapped, sometimes balancing just inside the sidelines until he made it into the end zone. Big Boy

Wilkinson or Muttonhead Shepherd would slap him on the back and say, "Good run, boy," or, when we had an audience, "Did you see my block back there?" Sometimes he would get tackled, but he seldom lost his grip on the ball, and he would always get up from the pile of tacklers and head straight to the huddle. He was a perfect safetyman when the other side punted, and would get a grip on the second or third bounce and gallop the length of the field for a touchdown.

"Look at that ol' dog playin' football!" someone passing by would shout, and before the game was over we would have a big crowd watching from cars or sitting on the sidewalk. They would let go with great whoops of admiration: "That's *some* dog. Can he catch a pass?"

When I was going on twelve and started driving our old green DeSoto, I always took the dog on my trips around town. He rode with his nose extended far out the window, and if he caught the scent of one of the boys we knew, he would bark and point his way, and we would stop and give that person a free ride. Skip would shake hands with our mutual friend, and lick him on the face, and sit on the front seat between us listening to our conversation. Cruising toward a country crossroads, I would spot a group of old men standing around in front of the grocery store. I would get the dog to prop himself against the steering wheel, his black head peering out of the windshield, while I ducked out of sight under the dashboard. Slowing the car to ten or fifteen, I would guide the steering wheel with my hand while Skip, with his paws, kept it steady. As we drove by the grocery store, I would hear one of the men shout: *"Look at that ol' dog drivin' a car!"*

One day Skip and I were driving out in the hills. In a certain area near Highway 49 there is one tall hill after another for many miles. All these hills and the little valleys in between them are overgrown with a beautiful green creeping vine, right up to the highway itself. This vine grows in strange and wonderful shapes. Sometimes it grows onto the trees and telephone poles and makes ghostly forms. The green creeping vine protected the land and kept it from washing away during heavy rains, but when I was a boy I thought the whole world would someday be covered by it, that it would grow as fast as Jack's beanstalk, and that every person on earth would have to live forever knee-deep in its leaves.

Skip and I drove off the highway to a road right in the middle of that fantastic green vine. I stopped in a clearing to let him run. Everyone knew that the vines were crawling with snakes, so I was not surprised to see a monstrous copperhead slither out of the underbrush across the same clearing. I *was* surprised, however, to see Skip's reaction. He circled round and round the snake, barking and growling. The snake did not like its privacy disturbed, and it snapped back at the dog, making ungodly hisses to match its foe's commotion. Skip got closer and closer to the snake. He would not listen to my shouts telling him to get away. All of a sudden, in one great leap, Skip came at the copperhead from the rear, caught it by the tail and began dragging it all over the field. Every time the snake tried to bite back, the dog would simply let go of its tail, and then move back in again to give the snake a couple of brisk shakes. While I was looking around for a rock to kill the copperhead, it headed out in a flash for the vines again, wishing no doubt it had never left home. For Skip it was all in a day's work. This nerve in the face of danger, which was Old Skip's strongest quality, would hold us all in good stead during the Episode of the Clark Mansion.

He was the best retriever we ever had. I would throw a stick as far as I could, then hide in the bushes or under the house. Skip would come tearing around with the stick in his mouth and, not finding me where I had been, drop the stick and look everywhere. He would jump onto the hood of the car and look inside, or sniff at the trees, or even go into the house to see if I was there. This game backfired one day. Bubba Barrier, Rivers Applewhite, and I threw a stick for Skip and then climbed up the elm tree in the backyard, hiding far up in the branches among the leaves. It took the dog half an hour to find us, but when he did he became extremely angry. He refused to let us out of that tree. We tried everything. Every time one of us came down he snapped at our legs with his long white teeth, and since no one was around to come to our rescue, we were trapped up there for over two hours until Skip dozed off. And we missed the biggest Cub Scout baseball game of the season.

His favorite food was bologna, and we worked out a plan with my pal Bozo, the clerk who worked behind the meat counter at Goodloe's Grocery Store down the street. I made a small leather pouch and attached it to Skip's collar. I would say, "Skip, now go on down to Bozo and get yourself a pound of bologna." Then I would put a quarter in the leather pouch, and Skip would take off for the store, bringing the package back in his mouth and Bozo's change in the pouch. Bozo enjoyed entertaining his friends with this ritual. They would be standing around, talking baseball or something, and when Bozo heard the dog scratching at the front door, he would open the door and tell his friends, "Here's ol' Skip, shoppin' for a pound of his favorite food," and with a great gesture would sell him the bologna.

One summer I entered Old Skip in the local dog contest, a highly important event sponsored by the United Daughters of the Confederacy. About five hundred people were in the audience, and I felt certain that Skip would win, since the prize was to be based on good looks and on the tricks the dogs could perform. About fifty dogs were entered in the contest, including Dusty Rhodes, Billy Rhodes' dog. Skip was the thirty-fifth dog on the program, and when he was announced and I led him out on the stage of the auditorium, everyone applauded loudly, because Skip was rather well known. Then a silence fell as I got Skip to walk around the stage two or three times so the judges could get a good look at the way he carried himself. Now it was time for the tricks.

"Sit down!" I commanded. But Skip did not sit down. Instead he jumped up and barked. *"Lie down and roll over!"* I said. This time he sat down and shook hands. *"Play dead!"* I shouted, but to this order he leapt off the stage, ran up the aisle, turned around and jumped on the stage again. The audience began to laugh, and I was by this time quite embarrassed. *"Sit down!"* I repeated. He rolled over twice and then stretched out on his back with all four feet sticking in the air. I had never seen that dog acting so ornery. I led him backstage and told him he had made a fool of me. I suspect now that Skip simply did not care about winning prizes, and this was his way of making fun of them. But when the prizes were announced, he tied for first place with Super-Doop, the Hendrixes' Labrador. The judges said they were not impressed with Skip's discipline, but they gave him the prize because he was such a fine looking dog.

At night Skip would go to sleep curled up in the bend of my legs. When it was cold he would root around and scratch at me to get under the covers. First thing in the morning, after he had gone outside for a run, he would bound back into my bed and roust me out with his cold nose. If that didn't work he would make as much racket as a dog can make, and leap all over me from three feet away. Then he would walk halfway to school with me, turning back at the same spot every morning to go home. He and Dusty Rhodes spent a lot of time together during school hours, wandering all over town to pass the time and making general nuisances of themselves.

Later, when I first joined the Boy Scouts and began working on merit badges, I found out that not a single member of the Yazoo City troop had the Dog Care badge. I decided to become the first one, but

I needed to have my knowledge of dogs approved by a veterinarian. I made an appointment with the town vet, Dr. Jones. I went to his office and he said, "Since I've never been asked to do this before, I'll just ask you some questions about your dog." He asked me about his age, weight, breed, and training habits, and then said:

"What about fleas?"

"What about 'em?" I replied.

"Does your dog have fleas?"

"He's got plenty, yessir."

"How do you rid him of fleas?"

"Well, I pick 'em off him one by one and throw 'em on top of the heater."

This must have discouraged the doctor. He started in on other questions.

"Do you feed your dog a good diet?"

"Yessir, I sure do."

"How many times a day do you feed him?"

"Oh, I guess about seven or eight."

"*Seven* or *eight*?" the doctor said. "Don't you know you're not supposed to feed a dog but once a day?" Then, shaking his head, he signed my certificate, making me the first scout in Yazoo County to get Dog Care.

• • • •

IN THE CHAPTERS THAT FOLLOW, Willie Morris and his cohorts wreak their havoc on the Wednesday meeting of the Women's Society with cookies tainted with milk of magnesia and dog-worming medicine, discover unique uses for dead animals, create original radio programs via the telephone, visit cemeteries at night, and have a terrifying encounter with giant Choctaw Indians at the legendary Clark Mansion. And if all this sounds a bit familiar, a bit like something another American writer described a century earlier, perhaps it's because Tom Sawyer and Huck Finn also grew up in a village along the Mississippi River, several hundred miles north of Yazoo City.

Good Old Boy was followed by a sequel, *Good Old Boy and the Witch of Yazoo*, and Morris has also written several adult books: *Always Stand in Against the Curve*; *Terrains of the Heart and Other Essays on Home*; and *North Toward Home*, the adult version of his autobiography. Your local library should be able to obtain a copy of the December

1978 issue of *Reader's Digest*, in which Morris writes of another wonderful dog in his life, "Pete, the Mayor of Bridgehampton."

Fans of *Good Old Boy* will also enjoy: *Baseball in April and Other Stories* by Gary Soto (see page 29), *Four Miles to Pinecone* by Jon Hassler (page 40), *Maniac Magee* by Jerry Spinelli (page 3), and *Miracle at Clement's Pond* by Patricia Pendergraft (page 45).

from **I**NCIDENT AT HAWK'S HILL

by Allan Eckert

1,147 Rejections in Twelve Years!

The expression used to be "Some people don't know when to take 'No!' for an answer." The latest version is "What part of the word 'No' don't you understand?" In either case, the message would have been applied again and again to people like "Ted the advertising artist," or Allan Eckert, the author of the next selection.

Ted was the young artist from Madison Avenue who had created a silly little story about his own daydreams walking to and from school as a child in Springfield, Massachusetts. Twenty-eight publishers gave him rejection notices, until finally Vanguard Press thought it saw something in both the story, *And to Think That I Saw It on Mulberry Street*, and its author, Ted Geisel—henceforth to be known as Dr. Seuss.

Publishing people like to tell that story to demonstrate how fallible is the business of spotting talent and how important it is for authors to be persistent. But I think even the eternally optimistic Dr. Seuss would have grown discouraged, if not bitter, facing the rejections notices collected by Allan Eckert—1,147 in twelve years! Apparently, a great many editors couldn't see in his writing a future six-time Pulitzer Prize nominee and Newbery Honor Medal winner. Few saw a man who would write more than thirty books and two hundred magazine articles.

The only number that rivals his rejection slips is the number of jobs he held in the six years after high school before he began to earn a living as a writer. To name but a few, he was a postman, private detective, fireman, plastics technician, cook, dishwasher, laundryman, salesman, chemist's assistant, trapper, commercial artist, draftsman, air force sergeant, and a worker in nearly fifteen different types of factories.

Much of Eckert's writing has focused on nature or natural history, and on that score the odds were also against him. For one thing, he grew up in the slums of Chicago—not exactly field-and-stream country. His father had died when Eckert was young and his mother had a great aversion to anything that resembled an insect. Hardly a nurturing environment for someone who would grow up to write two hundred television scripts for nature shows such as "Wild Kingdom," have a Florida nature conservancy for endangered species named after him, and own an insect collection of twenty-five thousand specimens.

An excellent student, he was plagued by poverty throughout his youth. He was seventeen years old and working in a restaurant before he saw his first real "meat meal"—prime rib. Working full-time and trying to go to college at the same time left him with only four hours of sleep a day. Two years of that routine at Ohio State University was all he could absorb before dropping out to work at his various jobs and write in his spare time.

In an interview with *Contemporary Authors*, Eckert explained an incident that typifies both his persistence and the obstacles he faced: "One of the things that sticks out in my mind was the very first book I ever wrote. It was a horrible thing. I think I had titled it *Unlawful*. Anyway, it was very bad, a cops-and-robbers shoot-up type of thing." Eckert was in the service at the time and his commanding officer read the book and liked it enough to suggest sending it to a friend who was an agent and bookseller to see how he liked it. Eckert agreed and subsequently received a letter from the man: "Dear Corporal Eckert: I have to say first off that I wish you'd stop wasting your time, my time, and everybody else's time, because you are not a writer now, you will never be a writer, you do not have it." Eckert recalls that not many years after that he saw that the same man was selling his books in his store. Unlike many other authors who would have relished the opportunity, Eckert didn't remind the man of what he had written to him.

The impersonal form-letter rejection notices from hundreds of magazines eventually gave way to those with a warmer tone. "I began getting little personal notes jotted here and there on the rejection slips. And I began to realize that it was not the fault of the editors, but my own fault; I was not writing what people wanted to read. I was writing what *I* wanted to read. That's a big mistake that many new writers make," he recalls. His first sale was to an outdoor sports magazine and was entitled "Hunting Pheasant with Bow and Arrow."

Eventually Eckert's talents were honed enough to land him a job as assistant editor for the National Cash Register Company's *Factory News* in 1955. This job led to four years with a daily newspaper in Dayton, Ohio, where he had to master the same pains of writing under deadline pressure that were faced a half century earlier by one of his childhood inspirations, Rudyard Kipling, who was at eighteen a reporter on a two-man newspaper in India.

Through the years Eckert has perfected a writing style that critics call "documentary fiction." When he first suggested the idea of a historical book on the great Dayton flood, his publisher initially rejected it: "Allan, you're not a history writer. You write about bugs and birds." His persistence with the project eventually earned him his first Pulitzer Prize nomination.

His Newbery Honor Medal–winning novel, *Incident at Hawk's Hill*, uses the "documentary" style, though it was not written for or even marketed for children when first published. Indeed, when he was notified of his Newbery Honor, he asked blankly, "What's a Newbery?" Eckert begins by taking an actual incident documented in historical records, in this case in Canada, and fleshes it out with dialogue. The landscape (twenty miles north of Winnipeg and forty miles north of the Minnesota state line), people, events, and animals are authenticated with meticulous research.

Ben MacDonald, encountered in this first chapter, is not only the tiny six-year-old frontier boy who later in the story will be adopted by a wild badger, he is also the personification of both a North American Mowgli and a young Allan Eckert.

Kipling partially based his wolf-boy on reported instances of wild or feral children discovered in the jungle. Eckert followed his lead, but while filling in the missing pieces of the Ben MacDonald character and trying to imagine what would drive a child like that, he had only to envision himself as a child in Chicago, obsessed with nature: "I remember as a little boy, four or five years old, crawling between the areaways of buildings and looking under piles of junk at the mice nesting there, or sometimes seeing spiders or a rare snake, and studying the bugs that would turn up when I turned over a board."

• • • •

CHAPTER 1

Benjamin MacDonald was following a mouse.

The fact that he was doing so was nothing out of the ordinary for Ben; he often followed mice. For that matter, he followed birds, too, when they'd walk rather than fly, and ground squirrels and snowshoe rabbits and anything else if he got half a chance. He sometimes even followed insects. The odd thing about it all was not so much that he was following the mouse as that the mouse was evidently letting itself be followed without taking alarm and disappearing at once.

The little rodent moved along casually, stopping here to sniff, stopping there to pick up and nibble a grain of wheat that had fallen on the barn floor, now and then standing high on its hind legs to look around while nose and ears twitched delicately as it sniffed and listened. Incredibly, the boy was doing the same thing, emulating each movement of the mouse. He crawled on hands and knees a yard behind the mouse as the mouse walked along normally. Where the mouse dipped its muzzle to sniff something on the rough wooden flooring, so too Ben, when he came to that same spot, would bend until his nose was at floor level and he would sniff there. When the mouse would nibble a wheat grain, Ben would also, resting back on his haunches and daintily holding the single grain in his fingers and nibbling in the same manner. At the frequent pauses in its passage, when the mouse would lift its forepaws from the ground and stand there sniffing and twitching its ears, Ben would do likewise, squatting with his feet flat on the floor, knees bent, hands held limply in front of his chest, nose wrinkling as he sniffed, head cocked to one side as he listened.

At one point the mouse gave voice to a high pitched chirring sound. Immediately, and with incredibly accurate mimicry, the same sound came from Ben, hardly any louder than that which the mouse had uttered. The small rodent cocked its head and stared at him, just as it had looked at him a dozen times before this since the boy had started following it near the barn door. Ben looked back, his own head tilted in the same way.

There was no way of saying how much further this strange little game of follow-the-leader might have gone had there been no interruption. But then, annoyingly, feet clumped heavily near the doorway and the familiar sound of William MacDonald's voice carried through the dimness of the barn's interior.

"Ben? Ben! I saw you come in here, so don't try to pretend you're not there. I want you to come outside."

The boy had turned his head at the sound of his father's voice and now when he looked back, the tiny mouse was gone. He frowned and then reluctantly got to his feet and walked toward the door. He followed his father outside and squinted against the midmorning brightness until his eyes adjusted. Ben's mother was standing at a point about midway between barn and house, looking toward the east. They walked to her.

"He was in the barn," MacDonald commented as she glanced at them, "on his hands and knees, as usual." He sounded disgusted.

Esther MacDonald shook her head faintly at her husband and then squatted down and held her arms out to Ben, smiling warmly at the boy. He came to her without hesitation and put his arms around her neck when she gave him a brief hug. She kissed his cheek and smiled again, took his small hand in hers and squeezed it. She inclined her head in the direction of the rutted wagon road leading eastward from the farm. A few hundred yards away a rider was approaching with a dog trotting along beside his horse.

"Mr. Burton's coming," she said. "Your father saw him on the way back from Winnipeg last week and he said then that he'd probably come by in the forenoon today. He's our closest neighbor now and your father wanted both of us to meet him. We'd like it, Ben, if you'd start taking an interest in people as well as animals. And I'd like it if you'd shake hands with him like a little man. Will you do that for mother?"

Ben's glance shifted to the rider and then back to her. He shook his head once and then looked at the ground in front of his feet. Esther MacDonald sighed.

"What'd you expect," the boy's father said, irritation heavy in his voice, "a miracle? Nothing short of that's going to change him."

Esther frowned and again shook her head slightly as she stood and murmured, "Will, he's only a little child yet. Give him time. He'll be all right. It just takes time."

Now it was MacDonald who sighed, slapping his hands against his sides resignedly. "I know, I know. It's what you keep saying and I guess you're right. But it's hard to be patient. Well, let's see what Burton wants."

George Burton sat easily astride his walking horse as he neared the MacDonalds. The dog accompanying him was a huge, nondescript yellow-gray cur which gave no indications of friendliness. It was apparent that the horseman was keeping the animal at heel only with continued low threatening commands.

Burton was a very large man with a massive chest and huge hands. A dense, untrimmed black beard covered the lower portion of his face and his brows seemed abnormally bushy. Without the distracting influence of the beard and brows his nose might have been somewhat too big for his face and his chin too weak, but now there was a kind of unkempt ruggedness to his countenance that one might well have expected of the frontier type that this fur trader was. He was a man who caused discomfort in those around him because his eyes never really met those of the person to whom he was talking. It gave the disconcerting impression of shiftiness, insincerity.

MacDonald was not fond of Burton, though he had to keep reminding himself that it wasn't quite fair to make a judgment yet, since he'd only met the man a few months ago and had talked with him only twice before last week. Still, there was something about the man that rankled—a sort of bluff, insincere heartiness and forced joviality that was irritating.

The farmer had met Burton—with this same dog tagging along beside him—last week while on the way back to Hawk's Hill from getting supplies in Winnipeg. It was to Winnipeg that Burton had been heading and he seemed to be anxious to get there. MacDonald had reined in his team, prepared to chat for a while with the relatively new neighbor, and he had felt a bit miffed when Burton hadn't stopped but merely said he was in a hurry and had to get on. The dog showed its teeth at MacDonald as they passed and a deep growl had rumbled in its throat. Burton cursed the animal into silence but hardly slowed his horse, and it wasn't until after he passed that he had turned and called over his shoulder that he wanted to talk with the farmer about something and would drop by in the morning next week. It was another little thing that irked; Burton didn't ask MacDonald if it would be all right for him to drop by, but rather told the farmer he'd be there.

Undoubtedly part of the dislike MacDonald felt for this man was due to hearsay. The talk among other neighbors and in town was that Burton was a cowardly man and a bully; that he was something of a ne'er-do-well who had worked for years for the Hudson's Bay people until they ran him out for defrauding the company. As near as it could be pieced together, Burton had originally come from around Quebec somewhere and for many years had trapped on his own to the north and west of Winnipeg until his brutality and cruelty toward the Indians made it dangerous for him to travel alone in the more remote areas any more. It was why, so people said, he took the huge dog with him wherever he went. Tongues waggled with stories that the dog was a killer and that on at least one occasion it had torn out the throat of an Indian who had come skulking around Burton's camp late one night.

MacDonald strongly doubted the story, but he was still wary of the big unfriendly canine. Burton, so MacDonald was told, had quit his own trapping then and had taken a job as a grader of furs for the Hudson's Bay Company. He'd held that position for six or seven years until, almost by accident, it was discovered that all this time he had been undergrading furs to the seller and then reselling them to the company himself for a much higher figure. He had evidently stashed enough money away through such fraud that when the company fired him, he boasted that he was now going to become a gentleman farmer, and immediately he bought the old Cecil homestead—a farm about six miles from MacDonald's and adjoining it to the south. This made him one of MacDonald's closest neighbors now, though William MacDonald would much rather have seen the Cecil family stay on. Edgar Cecil had crippled himself up pretty badly, however, in a fall from his horse and had felt it was best for his family and himself that he sell out and go back east. MacDonald wished now that he had bought the place, as he'd been strongly tempted to. It was good land and the idea of having Burton as a neighbor did not set too well with him. But, of course, at that time he'd had no idea Burton was to be his neighbor. Well, it was too late now. MacDonald put the hearsay behind him, determined to do his part toward maintaining good relations with a new neighbor. And here at Hawk's Hill, with Burton already reining up and dismounting, William MacDonald smiled with considerably more friendliness than he really felt and shook the visitor's hand. The big dog, he noted, continued standing stiffly, alertly, beside the horse.

"This is my wife, Esther," MacDonald said, and was pleased to see that at least Burton had the decency to remove his hat as he nodded to her and said "Ma'am" in greeting.

"The older children, John, Beth and Coral," MacDonald added, "are at school over in North Corners, but this is our youngest, Benjamin."

"Benjamin, eh?" Burton said. He smiled broadly and seemed on the point of reaching out for the boy and saying more, when the dog suddenly lunged forward at Ben. It happened so quickly that everyone was taken by surprise.

"*Lobo!*" Burton snapped. He snatched at the dog as it passed him, but missed. Lobo came to a stop just in front of Ben. His lip curled back, exposing yellowed teeth, and a hair-raising growl left his throat. And then, taking them just as much by surprise, the dog's hackles abruptly lowered and the low-slung tail wagged ever so faintly as a thin, almost inaudible whining replaced the growl.

Ben had shown not the slightest trace of fear. As the dog approached him he left his mother's side and advanced to meet the animal. When Lobo stopped, Ben dropped to all fours and an identical whining sound left his own throat. In this position he was so much smaller than the dog that he had to look up to Lobo and now, completely oblivious of the people around him, he craned upward to put his own nose close to that of the dog. Lobo whined again, but this time a sound deeper in tone and of a different quality. Immediately Ben responded with the same whine.

The entire little tableau had all happened in a matter of seconds. Burton had paled, but now he reacted and strode forward, took the dog by the scruff, and virtually hurled him back toward the horse, commanding him to "Sit! Stay!" When Lobo obeyed, the bearded man turned his attention back to the MacDonalds.

"Lord A'mighty, I'd not've believed it!" he said wonderingly. "Lobo ain't never let nobody but me get so close to 'im. He's been taught to be mean. I swear, it skeered me half t'death. Thought sure to God he'd grab the boy's throat when the li'l feller stuck his head up like that." He shook his shaggy head and looked at Ben, who was standing up again but still looking at the dog. "Wouldn't've give no bets he'd've had that much sense, but I reckon Lobo must've knowed the chil' was jus' hardly no more'n a baby. How old is the boy, three?"

MacDonald, not fully recovered and a trifle pale himself, said tightly, "He's six."

"Six!" Burton was taken aback, and with reasonable cause. Physically, Ben really did look far more to be only three or four years old rather than six. Not only was he unusually short for his age—not very much over three feet tall—he was also slight. Burton strode over toward the boy and stood looking down at him, his own massiveness underlining the extreme runtiness of the child.

"Six!" he repeated, grabbing Ben up under the arms and raising him high. "By Henry, boy, you ain't nothin' but a li'l ol' stick wearin' clothes."

He bounced the boy a time or two as a man does when estimating the weight of an object and then shook his head and added, "Yessir, this young'un don't weigh much more'n most of the growed-up badgers I've h'isted an' not nigh as much as the beavers."

The stench of the big man sickened Ben and the liberties he was taking frightened him, but though he squirmed unavailingly to get free, he said nothing. The nearness and strength of this stranger, his unwashed odor and the booming resonance of his voice were terrifying to one so small. He increased his efforts and they bore a strange kinship with the desperate struggling of a wild animal. William MacDonald's expression was more strained than before and he seemed on the verge of interceding when the trapper put the boy back down on his feet and then slapped his thigh and laughed loudly as Ben raced away to disappear inside the nearby barn.

Without pause Ben scaled the ladder to the loft and partially buried himself in the hay along the front wall. He peered down at the adults outside through a wide crack in the wall planking. George Burton was still laughing, but the sound abruptly cut off as he noted that neither William nor Esther MacDonald was sharing his amusement.

" 'Pears I skeered the l'il feller some. 'Pologize for that." He didn't sound in the least sorry, but he went on, "Didn't aim t'give the boy no fright. Jus' wouldn't've believed the way he an' Lobo got together right off. By grab that chil' *talked* to Lobo. Yessir, he actually talked to 'im. Now where'd he learn that?"

Esther MacDonald spoke up. "Ben likes animals," she said. "All animals. And it seems that animals like him. He plays with all the animals around here. They seem to know he won't bother them."

"Not wild ones, too?" Burton was skeptical.

"Well, yes." Esther looked as if she wished she had said nothing at all, but she went on, "They're not afraid of him, either. He gets fairly close to them."

"Talks to 'em, does he?"

Esther was uncomfortable and though she made an attempt to sound flippant, it didn't come out that way. "Well, he imitates the sounds they make, but . . ." She let the sentence die.

Burton clucked his tongue. "Talks to critters!" he said, more to himself than to her. Then he glanced toward her husband and added,

"But six years old, y'say? Couldn't've believed it if you wasn't his own pa. No sir, he jus' ain't nowhere near big enough for six."

"He's six," MacDonald repeated shortly. His manner was less cordial than before. "He's small, but he's six. He's shy. Too shy, I'm afraid, but he doesn't get to see many other people besides the family. You said you wanted to see me about something?"

"That's right, McDougall, I was wonderin'—"

"MacDonald," the farmer said tightly, "not McDougall."

"Well bless me for a dumb Injun," Burton said, slapping his thigh again and shaking his head. "Sure looks like I started out on the wrong track here. Now I 'pologize again—to you an' the missus both. What I come for, Mr. MacDonald, I was wonderin' if you do any trappin' on your land."

Thawing only a little, MacDonald shook his head. "No," he said, "we just farm. Mostly wheat and a few vegetables. Raise some sheep, too. Why?"

"Well sir, I was wonderin', us bein' neighbors now an' all, an' you not doin' no trappin' your own self, I was wonderin' iffen you'd mind I sorta let my string of traps wander over 'cross your land from mine."

MacDonald was surprised. "I'd heard that you were going to be farming now."

"Been a-tryin' it, sort of," Burton replied, grimacing, "but it don't much seem like as how I'm cut out t'be the farmer type. Reckon I'm jus' too set in my ways. Oh, I 'spect I'll keep on tryin' a mite, but it sure ain't gonna be as much as ol' man Cecil was a-growin' there. Dunno how one ol' man could've done so much. Anyhow, I got me a misery in my back that don't much like farm workin', so I'm reckonin' I'll jus' live offen what I been lucky enough t'put away, plus whatever extry I can get offen what I trap roun' here. Won't be trappin' like when I was younger an' more able, but mebbe in a twenty-thirty-mile circle I'll get me a fair 'mount of skins. It'd sure help out iffen you won't mind my runnin' 'cross your land some."

William MacDonald did not answer at once. He considered the request carefully. He liked Burton even less now than before and his immediate reaction was to refuse him. Esther, watching him closely, said nothing. At length he gave a vague nod.

"I guess," he said, speaking slowly, "it won't make any difference to me if you run your trap line over my land. I wouldn't want you to put traps anywhere close by, though, where Ben might stumble into one and get hurt."

"Well now, that's right neighborly of you. Yessir, it truly is. Don't you fret none at all 'bout that li'l feller mebbe gettin' hisself caught in any of 'em. No sir, I 'spect I ain't gonna make no sets prob'ly nowheres nearer'n a couple miles or better from the house here. That set all right with you?"

"Yes, I suppose so, provided they're not any closer than that." MacDonald paused and then added with ill-concealed reluctance, "I'm forgetting my manners. Will you come in for something to eat and some cool water?"

"Sure did pick me a fine neighbor, I did." Burton's laughter boomed out again. "I thank you, but no, I guess me'n Lobo here'll get on. Got things t'do. It was a real pleasure meetin' you, ma'am." He dipped his head at Esther. "I sure ain't one t'forget a favor done me like this."

He bobbed his head at MacDonald, too, turned and stepped back and then raised himself smoothly into the saddle. "Lobo, come!" he commanded, then nodded a final time at the couple, yanked rather too hard on the reins to turn his mount around and cantered off down the wagon road. The big yellow-gray dog kept pace easily.

William and Esther watched him go and she spoke softly, without looking at her husband. "Do you think you should have? I mean, after all the bad things we've heard about him? I don't like him, Will. He . . . scares me."

MacDonald shot a quick look at her and shook his head. "Just the result of gossip. I never yet have condemned any man on the basis of what people say about him, and I don't intend to now. A man has a right to be judged by how he acts, not by how someone may have *told* you he acts."

Esther flushed slightly but met his gaze directly. "I'm not basing how I feel about him on gossip. I just didn't like him. Or his dog. In fact his dog scared me to death. I think that animal would tear you apart at the first opportunity. Furthermore, I certainly didn't like the way he snatched Ben up. I didn't think you would, either."

"Well you're right, I didn't. But . . . well, maybe it was a little improper for him to do it, honey, but he was just trying to be friendly. And he apologized for scaring Ben."

MacDonald sighed and shook his head. "For that matter," he continued, "I've had Ben act almost as afraid of me, so I don't see how we can hold that against Burton." He paused, but when Esther made no reply he went on. "As for letting the man trap across our property, I can't see what it'll harm. He couldn't get very much right around here. The only beaver we have are way up in the wooded north section in Wolf Creek. Maybe he'll get a marten or an otter or two over there as well, but," he indicated the surrounding prairie with a sweep of his hand, "he's not apt to get much out there. I suppose he might pick up some wolves or some coyotes and foxes around the prairie dog towns, and he's apt to get some badger there, too, but I don't see that that's any loss. As a matter of fact, I wouldn't mind seeing him get rid of some of the badger. You know as well as I that we've lost two horses since we've been here because they broke their legs in badger holes."

"That's true," Esther admitted. "Oh, I suppose I'm just being silly, but somehow I took a very strong dislike to that man. And his dog."

"Can't say I'm particularly fond of him or the dog either, but he wasn't asking much, Esther, and the least we can do is to start off being good neighbors. He may be living here a long time and there wouldn't be much sense in commencing an unfriendly relationship with him right in the beginning over something as minor as this."

He put up a hand and cut her off as she started to speak. "I know, I know. You're still thinking about how he snatched Ben up and scared him, but there wasn't anything to that and if Ben was scared it was more his own fault than Burton's. It seems to me that he should have been much more afraid of the dog than the man. It was just plain stupid for him to get down on his hands and knees like that in front of such an animal." He shook his head disgustedly. "I don't know what we're going to do with that boy."

"Will, don't talk like that, please." She touched his arm gently. "Ben's just shy with people, you know that. He's spent his whole life so far right here on Hawk's Hill. He'll open up and get over it once he starts school next September. You'll see."

MacDonald smacked his fist angrily into the palm of his other hand. "No, all along that's what we've been telling ourselves, but it's more than just being shy and it's time we faced up to it. Esther, something's wrong with Ben, more than just his being so small and shy. Why won't he talk, except just now and then to you or maybe to John? Why is he always going off by himself somewhere, all quiet and acting sort of frightened of us all the time, instead of joining in with the family when we do things? Esther, he's six years old now! He's been like this since he could only crawl around, and ever since he was four we've been telling each other that he'll come out of it pretty soon, but he hasn't. And I don't think school's going to help him any. There's just no communicating with him. How can he change any if he won't listen and he won't talk to anyone and if he won't do anything except act like he's scared to death all the time?"

"But, Will, he's so small."

"Exactly the point! He's so small that how do you think he's going to respond when next fall comes and we send him off to school at North Corners and every child in his class—to say nothing of those in the upper classes—will practically tower over him? Esther, the boy only weighs a little over thirty pounds. He should weigh fifty or more! He only stands shoulder high to normal children his own age and—"

"William!"

The word had slipped out unconsciously and MacDonald was immediately contrite. "All right," he said hastily, "I didn't mean that. I meant that the normal . . . the *average* children his age are so much bigger and . . ."

He suddenly slapped his hand to the back of his neck in exasperation. "Oh, what's the use of trying to fool ourselves? He isn't normal, Esther, and we both know it, whether or not you're willing to admit it. He not only isn't normal physically, he's not normal mentally, either. Look how he acts toward animals. And for that matter, look how animals—*wild* animals as well as farm animals—act toward him. Even they can sense that he's different. Look at how that mean dog of Burton's acted. We've just got to face facts and admit to ourselves—"

"No!" Esther interrupted, her voice shrill, unnatural. "No, I won't listen to that, Will. I won't! He's small, yes, and he's shy and quiet, yes. But William MacDonald, you listen to me, our Benjamin is *not* abnormal. What he needs is our understanding and our love and help, not condemnation and despair."

She moved around to stand in front of him, hands on hips, and continued, "You complain that sometimes he looks at you with fear. I know he does, I've seen it, and it's a knife to my heart when it happens, but have you ever stopped to wonder why? Do you ever try to talk with him?"

Now it was she who cut him off as he began to object. "Wait. I said talk *with* him, not *to* him. Do you ever try to understand him?

Do you ever give him the opportunity—the opening he needs—to talk with you? When have you ever really listened to him?

"When you speak to him—and it's rarely that you do that," she went on, "you give him orders, commands! You stand there looming over him like some giant with your hands locked behind your back —you never try to touch him!—and demand that he do this or that or the other. Do you ever make *any* effort to get down on his level, even a little? When was the last time you squatted down or even bent over when you talked to him? When was the last time you held out your arms to him? I could count on one hand the times you've picked him up since he's been out of his crib. When was the last time you complimented him for *anything*, regardless of how trivial an achievement it might have been?"

Rarely had William MacDonald ever seen Esther angry at anyone and never before had she been truly angry at him, but she was now and it was a shock to him, holding him speechless in his surprise, and he wasn't even sure how it all began. Her eyes were still flashing and though she was fully a head shorter than he, she stood indignantly before him and he felt dwarfed by her onslaught.

• • • •

IN THE ENSUING CHAPTERS, Ben begins a wary relationship with the most fearless and ferocious animal on the plains—a badger. Their relationship will deepen when three events occur: (1) the badger is caught in one of Burton's traps long enough to cause her new pups to starve to death, (2) Ben wanders away from his farm and seeks shelter in the badger's burrow during a fierce storm, and (3) the badger adopts the disoriented young boy in place of her pups.

Eckert has written three books specifically for children or young adults: *The Dark Tunnel* and *The Wand* (both fantasy novels) and *Blue Jacket: War Chief of the Shawnees*. In addition, mature readers will also enjoy *Savage Journey*; *The Court-Martial of Daniel Boone*, and his *Winning of America* series: *The Frontiersman, Wilderness Empire, The Conquerors, The Wilderness War*, and *Gateway to Empire*. His latest book, *Sorrow of the Heart: The Life of Tecumseh*, was nominated for a Pulitzer Prize for history. There is also a forty-minute excerpt from *Incident at Hawk's Hill* available on audiocassette.

Allan Eckert fans will find similar pleasure in the writings of

Gary Paulsen (page 461), the historical novels of Avi (page 381) and Scott O'Dell (page 355), and *The Wolfling* by Sterling North.

For those interested in the idea of children being "adopted" by wild animals, author Jane Yolen has written a fascinating novel, *Children of the Wolf*, based upon the wolf-girls discovered by a missionary in India in 1920.

Fantastic Tales

Two stories that could
never be. Or could they?

from **W**HEN THE TRIPODS CAME

by John Christopher

A New Twist on an Old Story

The story, invented by a former school-teacher and onetime high school drop-out, was regarded as "the first of its kind" and became an immediate best-seller. And yet, the plot was as old as the Greek myths: puny mortals battling invaders with supernatural powers. Additionally, a prime ingredient in the plot was as old as the stars in the heavens. Today, almost a century later, despite experts reminding us how improbable or impossible the story is, we keep asking for more of it and hoping against hope that it is somehow true. What was the famous story?

These sentences from the first paragraph might give you a clue: "No one would have believed in the last years of the nineteenth century that this world was being watched keenly and closely by intelligence greater than man's and yet as mortal as his own. . . . Yet across the gulf of space, minds that are to our minds as ours are to those of the beasts that perish, intellects vast and cool and unsympathetic, regarded this earth with envious eyes, and slowly and surely drew plans against us."

With those words in 1898, H. G. Wells, who, along with Jules Verne, is regarded as the father of science fiction, began *The War of the Worlds*. What Wells did was to take the ancient writer's tool known as "What if . . ." and apply it to outer space. Today, hardly a year passes without some novelist or moviemaker attempting a spin-off of his story. How successful they are depends on whether or not they can come up with a clever twist on the "What if . . ." formula. The movies *E. T.—The Extra-Terrestrial* and *Close Encounters of the Third Kind* are both excellent examples of unique twists on the old story.

Admittedly, a lot has changed since Wells wrote his marauding

Martians story. Man has walked on the moon, landed vehicles on Mars, and poked cameras deeper into the universe than Wells's scientists ever dreamed of doing. Though we have not yet found even a hint of life, we can't seem to stop wondering if anyone is out there, much the way the conscience wonders if God is watching.

Of the thousands of "invader" tales that have appeared in print since that first one, most lacked the "twist" to make them memorable and classic, and none excited the lasting interest of adolescents—until John Christopher came along.

To begin with, John Christopher, one of the most successful and popular science-fiction writers for children and young adults, is also Hilary Ford, William Godfrey, Peter Graaf, Peter Nichols, and Anthony Rye. All of them are, in fact, a British writer named C. S. Youd (rhymes with "loud").

In the 1960s, Youd was a prolific but struggling adult novelist trying to support a family of five children. He had an imagination keen enough and energy high enough to be writing detective thrillers, comedies, science fiction, poetry, and "serious" fiction under different pen names. Writers use pseudonyms for two reasons: (1) They are prolific enough to write more than one book a year but their publishers prefer not to publish more than that for fear the public or critics will think the author is "cranking out" the material instead of giving it serious thought; and (2) some readers come to expect a certain kind of book from certain authors and are disappointed (to say nothing of being lighter in the purse) when their favorite science-fiction writer, says, suddenly produces a detective story.

Despite an abundance of pseudonyms and talent, Youd was thinking of abandoning his writing career in favor of one that promised a regular paycheck when one day a publisher suggested he try doing some science fiction for children. The idea didn't excite him. He had recently grown weary of sci-fi writing and was more interested in history now. He didn't reject the proposal outright, however, and soon thereafter he applied the "What if . . ." formula to the suggestion. He thought, "What if I combine what *they* want with what *I* want, blending the past and future into one novel, maybe a Middle Ages in the future?"

The result was *The White Mountains*, a novel in which aliens invade the earth, appearing as gigantic tripodal creatures, and take control of the human population by Capping: "People are fitted at puberty with a metal helmet which can't be detached from the scalp and which acts as a mental governor, preventing them from harboring any rebellious or, indeed, creative, thoughts." Having taken control of earth, the aliens look for a method by which to rule it and adopt the feudal society from the Middle Ages. But because the aliens do not do the Capping until adolescence, when the skull has finished most of its growth, children are the only humans capable of thinking independently and resisting the invaders. This gives the story a touch of David and Goliath—kids against the adults.

Youd was so intent upon the plot and its unique features that he "blinkered" himself to the fact that he had inadvertently swiped a premise from H. G. Wells. In *The War of the Worlds*, the invaders traverse the earth using three-legged or tripodal vehicles. Youd's aliens do the same and are called Tripods. He never saw the similarity until he had finished the novel, and by then he was too exhausted from the ordeal to change it. The book he thought he'd finish in six months proved to be more than he'd expected.

Up to this point in his career, he was a self-described "one-draft writer." The editors for his thirty adult novels had more or less taken what he gave them, with few or no revisions. Assuming this book would be more of the same, he was not surprised when his British editor accepted it without changes. His new American editor at Macmillan was not so impressed. Susan Hirschman (today the editor in chief of the Greenwillow Books division of Morrow) thought the first chapter was good but the rest of the book needed to be completely rewritten.

His first inclination was to fire off a nasty letter to Hirschman. "But, before writing to this effect, I gave myself time to reflect, and the reflection brought two conclusions. One was that Susan Hirschman had plainly read the manuscript with great care, and her criticism was pertinent and intelligent. The second, and more painful, was a realization about myself—that I had written the book with the (unconscious) disposition that it was 'only a children's book': that I had not, in fact, given it the attention and concentration essential to everything a writer attempts." At that point, he set to rewriting the rest of the book.

The result of all this was twofold: Children and teenagers had a new and extremely creative science-fiction author and Youd had a renewed career. The public response to *The White Mountains* was so positive that two sequels followed almost immediately (*The City of Gold and Lead* and *The Pool of Fire*), forming what became known as "the Tripods Trilogy."

For the next twenty years, Youd was besieged with requests by readers for sequels to the trilogy, but he resisted them in favor of doing other books for children. Finally, however, he relented—but with a twist. *The White Mountains* opened years after the aliens had arrived and taken control of the population. What Youd had never fully described was how the Tripods arrived and made their conquest. The trilogy would become a quartet when Youd added what is termed a "prequel"—the story *before The White Mountains*. Here, then, are the first chapter and part of the second chapter from that prequel, *When the Tripods Came*.

• • • •

CHAPTER 1

AN EXPLOSION OF NOISE woke me. It sounded as if a dozen express trains were about to hit the shed. I rolled over in my blanket, trying to get out of the way, and was aware of a blaze of orange, lighting up boxes and bits of old farm equipment and tackle. An ancient rusting tractor looked briefly like an overgrown insect.

"What was that, Laurie?" Andy asked. I could see him sitting up, between me and the window.

"I don't know."

Both light and sound faded and died. A dog started barking— deep-throated, a Labrador maybe. I got up and walked to the window, banging my shin on something in the dark. It was dark outside, too, moon and stars hidden by cloud. A light came on in the farmhouse, which was a couple of hundred meters away, just below the ridge.

I said, "It's not raining. What *was* it?"

"Didn't someone at the camp say something about an artillery range on the moor?"

"Nowhere near here, though."

"Whatever they were firing could have gone astray."

Rubbing my shin, I said, "It didn't sound like a shell. And a shell wouldn't produce fireworks like that."

"A rocket, maybe." He yawned loudly. "It's all quiet now, anyway. No sweat. Go to sleep. We've a long trek in the morning."

I stood by the window for a while. Eventually the light in the house went out: the farmer presumably took the same view as Andy. In the pitch black I felt my way to the pile of straw which served as a bed. This was less fun than it had seemed the previous evening;

there was little protection from the hardness of the earth floor, and once awake I knew all about the aches in my muscles.

Andy was already asleep. I blamed him for our being here—for volunteering us into the orienteering expedition in the first place, and then for insisting on a left fork which had taken us miles out of our way. It had looked as though we would have to spend the night on the moor, but we'd come across this isolated farm as dusk was thickening. The rules were not to ask for help, so we'd settled down in the shed.

I thought my aches, and resenting Andy, would keep me awake, but I was dead tired. We had set out early from summer camp, and it had been a long day's slog. Drifting into sleep again, I was half aware of another explosion, but it was a distant one, and I was too weary really to wake up—I couldn't even be sure I wasn't dreaming.

ANDY WOKE ME with the gray light of dawn filtering in. He said, "Listen."

"What?"

"*Listen!*"

I struggled into wakefulness. The noise was coming from the direction of the farmhouse, but further away, a succession of loud thumpings, heavy and mechanical.

"Farm machinery?" I suggested.

"I don't think so."

Listening more carefully, I didn't either. The thumps came at intervals of a second or less, and they were getting nearer. There was even a sensation of the ground shaking under me.

"Something heading this way," Andy said. "Something big, by the sound of it."

We crowded together at the small window of the shed. The sun hadn't risen, but to the east the farmhouse was outlined against a pearly sky. Smoke from a chimney rose almost straight: farmers were early risers. It looked like a good day for the trek back to camp. Then I saw what was coming into view on the other side of the house.

The top appeared first, an enormous gray-green hemispherical capsule, flat side down, which seemed to be floating ponderously in midair. But it wasn't floating: a weird stiltlike leg moved in a vast arc across the sky and planted itself just to the right of the farmhouse. As it crashed down a second leg appeared, passing over the house and landing between it and the shed. I could see a third leg, too, which if it followed suit would come to ground close to us, if not on top of us. But at that point, it stopped. The gigantic object, more than twenty meters high, stood straddling the house.

A band of bright green glassy panels ran horizontally along the side of the capsule. It produced an effect that was a cross between multiple staring eyes and a grinning mouth. It wasn't a pleasant grin.

"Someone's making a film." Andy's voice was unsteady. I turned to him and he looked as scared as I felt. "That must be it. A science-fiction movie."

"So where are the cameras?" I felt my voice was coming out wrong, too.

"They probably have to get it into position first."

I didn't know whether he believed it. I didn't.

Something was moving beneath the capsule, curling and twisting and stretching out. It was like an elephant's trunk, or a snake, except that it was silvery and metallic. It corkscrewed down towards the roof of the house and brushed lightly against it. Then it moved to the chimney stack and grasped it with a curling tip. Bricks sprayed like confetti, and we heard them crashing onto the slates.

I was shivering. Inside the house a woman screamed. A door at the back burst open, and a man in shirt and trousers came out. He stared up at the machine looming above him and started running. Immediately a second tentacle uncurled, this time fast and purposeful. The tip caught him before he'd gone ten meters, fastened round his waist, and plucked him from the ground. He was screaming, too, now.

The tentacle lifted him up in front of the row of panels, and his screams turned to muffled groaning. After a few moments the tentacle twisted back on itself. A lenslike opening appeared at the base of the capsule; it carried him towards it and thrust him through. I thought of someone holding a morsel of food on a fork before popping it into his mouth, and felt sick.

His groans ended as the tentacle withdrew, and the opening closed. The woman in the house had also become quiet; but the silence was even more frightening. Resting on its spindly legs, the machine had the look of an insect digesting its prey. I remembered my glimpse of the derelict tractor in the night; this insect was as tall as King Kong.

For what seemed a long time, nothing happened. The thing didn't stir, and there was no sound or movement from the house. All was still; not even a bird chirped. The tentacle hovered in midair, motionless and rigid.

When, after a minute or so, the tentacle did move, it raised itself higher, as though making a salute. For a second or two it hung in the air, before slamming down violently against the roof. Slates scattered, and rafters showed through a gaping hole. The woman started to shriek again.

Methodically the tentacle smashed the house, and as methodically picked over the ruins, like a scavenger going through a garbage can. The shrieking stopped, leaving just the din of demolition. A second tentacle set to work alongside the first, and a third joined them.

They probed deep into the rubble, lifting things up to the level of the panels. Most of what was picked up was dropped or tossed aside—chairs, a sideboard, a double bed, a bathtub dangling the metal pipes from which it had been ripped. A few were taken inside: I noticed an electric kettle and a television set.

At last it was over, and dust settled as the tentacles retracted under the capsule.

"I think we ought to get away from here," Andy said. His voice was so low I could hardly hear him.

"How far do you think it can see?"

"I don't know. But if we dodge out quickly, and get round the back . . ."

I gripped his arm. Something was moving at the base of the rubble that had been the farmhouse: a black dog wriggled free and started running across the farmyard. It covered about ten meters before a tentacle arrowed towards it. The dog was lifted, howling, in front of the panels, and held there. I thought it was going to be taken inside, as the man had been; instead the tentacle flicked it away. Briefly the dog was a black blur against the dawn light, then a crumpled silent heap.

The sick feeling was back, and one of my legs was trembling. I thought of my first sight of the Eiffel Tower, the summer my mother left and Ilse came to live with us—and my panicky feeling over the way it stretched so far up into the sky. This was as if the Eiffel Tower had moved—had smashed a house to bits and swallowed up a man . . . tossed a dog to its death the way you might throw away an apple core.

Time passed more draggingly than I ever remembered. I looked at my watch, and the display read 05:56. I looked again after what seemed like half an hour, and it said 05:58. The sky was getting lighter and there was first a point of gold, then a sliver, finally a disk of sun beyond the ruins of the house. I looked at my watch again. It was 06:07.

Andy said, "Look!"

The legs hadn't moved but the capsule was tilting upwards and beginning a slow rotation. The row of panels was moving to the left. Soon we might be out of the field of vision and have a chance of sneaking away. But as the rotation continued, a second row of panels came into view. It could see all round.

When it had traversed a hundred and eighty degrees, the rotation stopped. After that, nothing happened. The monster just stayed there, fixed, as leaden minutes crawled by.

The first plane came over soon after eight. A fighter made two runs, east to west and then west to east at a lower level. The thing didn't move. A quarter of an hour later a helicopter circled round, taking photographs, probably. It was nearly midday before the armored brigade arrived. Tanks and other tracked vehicles drew up on open farmland, and, in the bit of the farm lane in view, we could see an important-looking car and some trucks, including a TV van, all keeping a careful distance.

After that, nothing happened for another long time. We learned later this was the period in which our side was attempting to make radio contact, trying different frequencies without result. Andy got impatient, and again suggested making a run for it, towards the tanks.

I said, "The fact it hasn't moved doesn't mean it won't. Remember the dog."

"I do. It might also decide to smash this hut."

"And if we run, and it starts something and the army starts something back . . . we're likely to catch it from both sides."

He reluctantly accepted that. "Why *hasn't* the army done something?"

"What do you think they ought to do?"

"Well, not just sit there."

"I suppose they don't want to rush things. . . ."

I broke off as an engine started up, followed by a rumble of tracks. We ran to the window. A single tank was moving forward. It had a pole attached to its turret, and a white flag fluttering from the pole.

The tank lurched across the field and stopped almost directly beneath the capsule. The engine switched off, and I heard a sparrow chirruping outside the shed. Then, unexpectedly, there was a burst of classical music.

I asked, "Where's that coming from?"

"From the tank, I think."

"But why?"

"Maybe they want to demonstrate that we're civilized, not barbarians. It's that bit from a Beethoven symphony, isn't it—the one that's sung as a European anthem?"

"That's crazy," I said.

"I don't know." Andy pointed. "Look."

The machine was showing signs of movement. Beneath the capsule a tentacle uncurled. It extended down towards the tank and began waving gently.

"What's it *doing*?" I asked.

"Maybe it's keeping time."

The weird thing was, he was right; it was moving in rhythm with the music. A second tentacle emerged, dipped, and brushed against the turret. As though it were getting the hang of things, the first tentacle started moving faster, in a more positive beat. The second felt its way round the tank from front to rear, then made a second approach from the side, moving over it and probing underneath. The tip dug down, rocking the tank slightly, and reemerged to complete an embrace. The tank rocked more violently as it was lifted, at first just clear of the ground, then sharply upward.

Abruptly the music gave way to the stridence of machine-gun fire. Tracer bullets flamed against the sky. The tank rose in the tentacle's grip until it was level with the panels. It hung there, spitting out sparks.

But pointlessly; at that angle the tracers were scouring empty sky. And they stopped abruptly, as the tentacle tightened its grip; armorplate crumpled like tinfoil. For two or three seconds it squeezed the tank, before uncurling and letting it drop. The tank fell like a stone, landing on its nose and balancing for an instant before toppling over. There was a furrow along the side where it had been compressed to less than half its original width.

Andy said, "That was a Challenger." He sounded shaken, but not as shaken as I felt. I could still see that terrible careless squeeze, the tank dropped like a toffee paper.

When I looked out again, one of the tentacles had retracted, but the other was waving still, and still in the rhythm it had picked up from the music. I wanted to run—somewhere, anywhere, not caring what came next—but I couldn't move a muscle. I wondered if anyone in the tank had survived. I didn't see how they could have.

Then, unexpectedly and shatteringly, there was a roar of aircraft as the fighter-bombers, which had been on standby, whooshed in from the south, launching rockets as they came. Of the six they fired, two scored hits. I saw the long spindly legs shatter, the capsule tilt and sway and crash. It landed between the ruins of the farmhouse and the wrecked tank, with an impact that shook the shed.

I could hardly believe how quickly it was over—and how completely. But there was the capsule lying on its side, with broken bits of leg sticking out. As we stared, a second wave of fighter-bombers swooped in, pulverizing the remains.

• • • •

CHAPTER 2

THE SCHOOL TERM started three weeks later. By then the big excitement—with Andy and me being interviewed on television and local radio and all that—was over, but people at school were still interested. They fired questions at us—mostly me, because Andy was less willing to talk. I talked too much and then regretted it. When Wild Bill brought the subject up in physics class, I no longer wanted to discuss it, least of all with him.

He didn't look wild and his name wasn't Bill; he was a small, neat gray-haired man with a clipped voice and a sarcastic manner. His name was Hockey, and he had a habit of swinging round from the board and throwing whatever was in his hand—a piece of chalk usually—at someone he thought might be misbehaving behind his back. On one occasion it was the board eraser, which was wooden and quite heavy, and he hit a boy in the back row on the forehead. We called him Wild Bill Hockey after Wild Bill Hickock.

"Come on, Cordray," he said, "don't be shy. Now that you're famous you owe something to those of us who aren't." Some of the girls tittered. "The first person to see a Tripod, as I gather the media has decided we shall call them. . . . You'll be in the history books for that, even if not for the Nobel Prize in Physics."

There was more tittering. I'd been second from bottom the previous term.

"It throws an interesting light on national psychology," Wild Bill went on, "to consider the various reactions to man's first encounter with creatures from another part of the universe."

He had a tendency, which most of us encouraged, to launch into discourses on things that interested him, some of them quite remote from physics. I was happier still if it got him off my back.

He said, "As you know, there were three landings; one in the United States, in Montana, one in Kazakhstan in the Soviet Union, and Cordray's little show on the edge of Dartmoor. The landings were roughly simultaneous, ours in the middle of the night, the American late the previous evening and the Russian in time for breakfast.

"The Americans spotted theirs first, after tracking it in on radar, and just surrounded it and waited. The Russians located the one in their territory fairly quickly too, and promptly liquidated it with a rocket strike. We played Beethoven to ours, sent in a single tank, and then smashed it after it had destroyed the tank. Is that a testimony to British moderation? Cordray?"

I said unwillingly, "I don't know, sir. After it wrecked the farmhouse, I didn't care how soon they finished it off."

"No, I don't suppose you did. But presumably you had no more notion than the military of what a pushover it was going to be. And that, of course, is the fascinating part." He ran his fingers through his thinning hair.

"When I was your age there was a war on. We had a physics class similar to this interrupted one afternoon by a V-2 rocket that landed a quarter of a mile away and killed fifteen people. It was alarming, but I didn't really find it *interesting*. What interested me more than the war was what I read in the science-fiction magazines of those days. Rockets being hurled from Germany to England to kill people struck me as dull, compared with the possibilities of their being used to take us across interplanetary space to discover exotic life forms—or maybe bring them here to us.

"Science-fiction writers have portrayed that second possibility in a variety of ways. We have read of, or more recently watched on screen, alien invaders of every shape and size, color and texture, from overgrown bloodsucking spiders to cuddly little creatures with long snouts. Their arrival has been shown as bringing both disaster and revelation. What no one anticipated was a Close Encounter of the Absurd Kind, a cosmic farce. Why do I say farce, Cordray?"

"I don't know, sir."

"Well, you saw it, didn't you? Consider the Tripods themselves, for a start. What sort of goons would dream up something so clumsy and inefficient as a means of getting around?"

Hilda Goossens, a tall, bony redhead who was the class genius and his favorite, said, "But they must have had very advanced technology. We know they couldn't have come from within our solar system, so they must have traveled light-years to get here."

Wild Bill nodded. "Agreed. But consider further. Although the Americans didn't approach their Tripod, they did try the experiment of driving animals close in. Night had fallen by that time. And the Tripod switched on ordinary white light—searchlight beams, you could say—to find out what was happening beneath its feet. So it looks as though they don't even have infrared!

"And having gone to the considerable trouble of dropping these three machines at various points of the planet, think of what they used them for. Two out of three just sat around; the third demolished a farmhouse and *then* sat around. And a single sortie from a single air force squadron was sufficient to reduce it to mechanical garbage. The other two put up no better defense; the one in America actually self-destructed without being attacked. In fact, altogether the dreaded invasion from outer space proved to be the comic show of the century."

Some laughed. Although I'd done my bit of crawling to Wild Bill in the past, I didn't join in. I could still see it too clearly—the insectlike shape towering above the ruins of the farmhouse, the snaky tentacles plucking up pathetic bits and pieces and tossing them away. . . . It hadn't been funny then, and it wasn't now.

• • • •

Fans of the Tripod series will also enjoy the other John Christopher series, including *The Sword Trilogy* (*The Prince in Waiting, Beyond the Burning Lands*, and *The Sword of the Spirits*) and *The Fireball Trilogy* (*Fireball, New Found Land*, and *Dragon Dance*). He is also the author of *The Lotus Caves, The Guardians, Wild Jack*, and *Empty World*.

Science-fiction fans will also enjoy *The War of the Worlds* by H. G. Wells and these books by Robert A. Heinlein: *Farmer in the Sky, Have Space Suit—Will Travel*, and *The Star Beast*. The famous 1938 radio broadcast of *War of the Worlds* starring Orson Welles is available from most libraries and from The Mind's Eye as an audiocassette.

from THE WONDERFUL STORY OF HENRY SUGAR

by Roald Dahl

Launching a Career Over Lunch

This anecdote has been written and told elsewhere but I think it bears repeating here for those who might have missed it.

In 1942, an injured British pilot was sent to the United States to recuperate, as well as to serve as a kind of goodwill ambassador. America had only recently joined Britain in the war against Germany, and many Americans still didn't see the threat of Hitler and thus the point of the war. It was hoped that representatives such as this British airman would make a positive and inspiring impression on U.S. citizens. And to a small degree he did. But nowhere near the impression he would make twenty-five years later when he became one of the most popular authors among American schoolchildren.

But back in 1942, he wasn't a writer and had no ambitions to become one. He was a reader, however, and therefore pleased to learn shortly after his arrival that he was going to lunch with one of that generation's most famous novelists. C. S. Forester wrote the popular seafaring series about Horatio Hornblower, as well as *The African Queen*, from which the Academy Award–winning movie was made. Forester's idea, as well as that of the British War Office, was for the airman simply to recount some of his war adventures for the novelist over lunch, and Forester would convert them into an article for *The Saturday Evening Post*, then the most widely read weekly magazine in America.

It soon became apparent to the airman, however, that the note-taking was ruining Forester's lunch. "How about if I return to the hotel this evening, jot down my experiences, and post them to you in the morning?" suggested the airman. "That way you can relax and enjoy your lunch." Forester thought that would be splendid and put away his pen.

The airman dutifully wrote an accurate description of his war ordeal and sent it off the next day. Two weeks later came a response. Not only was Forester impressed with the story, he thought it good enough to use without changing a word, and sent it to the *Post* with the airman named as author—Roald Dahl.

The editors felt the same and sent Dahl a thousand-dollar check, along with a request for whatever else he could offer. Having never written professionally before, Dahl was stunned—and thrilled. He certainly wanted to continue writing, especially at those prices, but he had no more personal war stories.

So he began to make them up—all kinds of stories, not just war experiences. Over the next fifteen years he became one of the leading short-story writers for adults in the English-speaking world. Only when he ran out of ideas for adult stories, around 1959, did Dahl think about writing for children. That's when *James and the Giant Peach* and *Charlie and the Chocolate Factory* were born.

Several times during his nearly thirty years writing for children, Dahl took favorite old stories he had written originally for adults and expanded, modified, or completely rewrote them for a younger audience. *Danny, the Champion of the World* was one such story. And so was the title story from Dahl's collection for young adults, *The Wonderful Story of Henry Sugar and Six More*. In its first and slightly different life, the story appeared as "The Amazing Eyes of Kudda Box," in *Argosy* magazine.

"The Wonderful Story of Henry Sugar" is really a long short story, sometimes called a novella. It opens one rainy weekend in an English manor house where the gathered gentlemen are playing cards. This particular game can only be played by four, so the fifth man, Henry Sugar, has wandered elsewhere in the house. Sugar is one of those wealthy people who has never had to work a day in his life. Most of his time is spent gambling, which keeps him from getting bored and helps him grow even richer than he already is. He wouldn't be successful, though, if he wasn't also fairly accomplished at cheating.

That Sunday, Sugar's wandering ultimately takes him to the mansion's library. The shelves are filled with classical writers, none of whom interest him, and he is about to turn away when he notices a student notebook tucked away among the leather-bound volumes. On the first page he finds these words:

A REPORT OF AN INTERVIEW WITH IMHRAT KHAN
THE MAN WHO COULD SEE WITHOUT HIS EYES
By John F. Cartwright, M.D.
Bombay, India—December 1934

Sugar is immediately intrigued. Here, in Chapter 2 of the story, is the beginning of both Dr. Cartwright's journal and a grand adventure for Henry Sugar.

PRONUNCIATION GUIDE
Imhrat Khan (IM-rot Con)

• • • •

CHAPTER 2

THIS IS WHAT HENRY READ in the little blue exercise book:
I, John Cartwright, am a surgeon at Bombay General Hospital. On the morning of the second of December, 1934, I was in the doctors' rest room having a cup of tea. There were three other doctors there with me, all having a well-earned tea break. They were Dr. Marshall, Dr. Phillips and Dr. Macfarlane. There was a knock on the door. "Come in," I said.

The door opened and an Indian came in who smiled at us and said, "Excuse me, please. Could I ask you gentlemen a favor?"

The doctors' rest room was a most private place. Nobody other than a doctor was allowed to enter it except in an emergency.

"This is a private room," Dr. Macfarlane said sharply.

"Yes, yes," he answered. "I know that and I am very sorry to be bursting in like this, sirs, but I have a most interesting thing to show you."

All four of us were pretty annoyed and we didn't say anything.

"Gentlemen," he said. "I am a man who can see without using his eyes."

We still didn't invite him to go on. But we didn't kick him out either.

"You can cover my eyes in any way you wish," he said. "You can bandage my head with fifty bandages and I will still be able to read you a book."

He seemed perfectly serious. I felt my curiosity beginning to stir. "Come here," I said. He came over to me. "Turn around." He turned around. I placed my hands firmly over his eyes, holding the lids closed. "Now," I said, "one of the other doctors in the room is going to hold up some fingers. Tell me how many he's holding up."

Dr. Marshall held up seven fingers.

"Seven," the Indian said.

"Once more," I said.

Dr. Marshall clenched both fists and hid all his fingers.

"No fingers," the Indian said.

I removed my hands from his eyes. "Not bad," I said.

"Hold on," Dr. Marshall said. "Let's try this." There was a doctor's white coat hanging from a peg on the door. Dr. Marshall took it down and rolled in into a sort of long scarf. He then wound it around the Indian's head and held the ends tight at the back. "Try him now," Dr. Marshall said.

I took a key from my pocket. "What is this?" I asked.

"A key," he answered.

I put the key back and held up an empty hand. "What is this object?" I asked him.

"There isn't any object," the Indian said. "Your hand is empty."

Dr. Marshall removed the covering from the man's eyes. "How do you do it?" he asked. "What's the trick?"

"There is no trick," the Indian said. "It is a genuine thing that I have managed after years of training."

"What sort of training?" I asked.

"Forgive me, sir," he said, "but that is a private matter."

"Then why did you come here?" I asked.

"I came to request a favor of you," he said.

The Indian was a tall man of about thirty with light brown skin the color of a coconut. He had a small black mustache. Also, there was a curious matting of black hair growing all over the outsides of his ears. He wore a white cotton robe, and he had sandals on his bare feet.

"You see, gentlemen," he went on. "I am at present earning my living by working in a traveling theater, and we have just arrived here in Bombay. Tonight we give our opening performance."

"Where do you give it?" I asked.

"In the Royal Palace Hall," he answered. "In Acacia Street. I am the star performer. I am billed on the program as 'Imhrat Khan, the man who sees without his eyes.' And it is my duty to advertise the show in a big way. If we don't sell tickets, we don't eat."

"What does this have to do with us?" I asked him.

"Very interesting for you," he said. "Lots of fun. Let me explain. You see, whenever our theater arrives in a new town, I myself go straight to the largest hospital and I ask the doctors there to bandage my eyes. I ask them to do it in the most expert fashion. They must make sure my eyes are completely covered many times over. It is important that this job is done by doctors, otherwise people will think I am cheating. Then, when I am fully bandaged, I go out into the street and I do a dangerous thing."

"What do you mean by that?" I asked.

"What I mean is that I do something that is extremely dangerous for someone who cannot see."

"What do you do?" I asked.

"It is very interesting," he said. "And you will see me do it if you will be so kind as to bandage me up first. It would be a great favor to me if you will do this little thing, sirs."

I looked at the other three doctors. Dr. Phillips said he had to go back to his patients. Dr. Macfarlane said the same. Dr. Marshall said, "Well, why not? It might be amusing. It won't take a minute."

"I'm with you," I said. "But let's do the job properly. Let's make absolutely sure he can't peep."

"You are extremely kind," the Indian said. "Please do whatever you wish."

Dr. Phillips and Dr. Macfarlane left the room.

"Before we bandage him," I said to Dr. Marshall, "let's first of all seal down his eyelids. When we've done that, we'll fill his eye sockets with something soft and solid and sticky."

"Such as what?" Dr. Marshall asked.

"What about dough?"

"Dough would be perfect," Dr. Marshall said.

"Right," I said. "If you will nip down to the hospital bakery and get some dough, I'll take him into the surgery and seal his lids."

I led the Indian out of the rest room and down the long hospital corridor to the surgery. "Lie down there," I said, indicating the high bed. He lay down. I took a small bottle from the cupboard. It had an eyedropper in the top. "This is something called colodion," I told him. "It will harden over your closed eyelids so that it is impossible for you to open them."

"How do I get it off afterward?" he asked me.

"Alcohol will dissolve it away quite easily," I said. "It's perfectly harmless. Close your eyes now."

The Indian closed his eyes. I applied colodion to both lids. "Keep them closed," I said. "Wait for it to harden."

In a couple of minutes, the colodion had made a hard film over the eyelids, sticking them down tight. "Try to open them," I said.

He tried but couldn't.

Dr. Marshall came in with a basin of dough. It was the ordinary white dough used for baking bread. It was nice and soft. I took a lump of the dough and plastered it over one of the Indian's eyes. I filled the whole socket and let the dough overlap onto the surrounding skin. Then I pressed the edges down hard. I did the same with the other eye.

"That isn't too uncomfortable, is it?" I asked.

"No," the Indian said. "It's fine."

"You do the bandaging," I said to Dr. Marshall. "My fingers are too sticky."

"A pleasure," Dr. Marshall said. "Watch this." He took a thick wad of cotton wool and laid it on top of the Indian's dough-filled eyes. The cotton-wool stuck to the dough and stayed in place. "Sit down, please," Dr. Marshall said.

The Indian sat on the bed.

Dr. Marshall took a roll of three-inch bandage and proceeded to wrap it round and round the man's head. The bandage held the cotton wool and the dough firmly in place. Dr. Marshall pinned the bandage. After that, he took a second bandage and began to wrap that one not only around the man's eyes but around his entire face and head.

"Please to leave my nose free for breathing," the Indian said.

"Of course," Dr. Marshall answered. He finished the job and pinned down the end of the bandage. "How's that?" he asked.

"Splendid," I said. "There's no way he can possibly see through that."

The whole of the Indian's head was now swathed in thick white bandage, and the only thing you could see was the end of the nose sticking out. He looked like a man who had had some terrible brain operation.

"How does that feel?" Dr. Marshall asked him.

"It feels good," the Indian said. "I must compliment you gentlemen on doing such a fine job."

"Off you go, then," Dr. Marshall said, grinning at me. "Show us how clever you are at seeing things now."

The Indian got off the bed and walked straight to the door. He opened the door and went out.

"Great Scott!" I said. "Did you see that? He put his hand right on the doorknob!"

Dr. Marshall had stopped grinning. His face had suddenly gone white. "I'm going after him," he said, rushing for the door. I rushed for the door as well.

The Indian was walking quite normally along the hospital corridor. Dr. Marshall and I were about five yards behind him. And very spooky it was to watch this man with the enormous white and totally bandaged head strolling casually along the corridor just like anyone else. It was especially spooky when you knew for a certainty that his eyelids were sealed, that his eye sockets were filled with dough, and that there was a great wad of cotton wool and bandages on top of that.

I saw a native orderly coming along the corridor toward the Indian. He was pushing a food trolley. Suddenly the orderly caught sight of the man with the white head, and he froze. The bandaged Indian stepped casually to one side of the trolley and went on.

"He saw it!" I cried. "He must have seen that trolley! He walked right round it! This is absolutely unbelievable!"

Dr. Marshall didn't answer me. His cheeks were white, his whole face rigid with shocked disbelief.

The Indian came to the stairs and started to go down them. He went down with no trouble at all. He didn't even put a hand on the handrail. Several people were coming up the stairs. Each of them stopped, gasped, stared and quickly got out of the way.

At the bottom of the stairs, the Indian turned right and headed for the doors that led out into the street. Dr. Marshall and I kept close behind him.

The entrance to our hospital stands back a little from the street, and there is a rather grand series of steps leading down from the entrance into a small courtyard with acacia trees around it. Dr. Marshall and I came out into the blazing sunshine and stood at the top of the steps. Below us, in the courtyard, we saw a crowd of maybe a hundred people. At least half of them were barefoot children, and as our white-headed Indian walked down the steps, they all cheered and shouted and surged toward him. He greeted them by holding both hands above his head.

Suddenly I saw the bicycle. It was over to one side at the bottom of the steps, and a small boy was holding it. The bicycle itself was quite ordinary, but on the back of it, fixed somehow to the rear wheel frame, was a huge placard, about five feet square. On the placard were written the following words:

Imhrat Khan, The Man Who Sees Without His Eyes!
Today my eyes have been bandaged by hospital doctors!
Appearing Tonight and all this week at
The Royal Palace Hall, Acacia Street, at 7 P.M.
Don't miss it! You will see miracles performed!

Our Indian had reached the bottom of the steps and now he walked straight over to the bicycle. He said something to the boy, and the boy smiled. The Indian mounted the bicycle. The crowd made way for him. Then, lo and behold, this fellow with the blocked-up bandaged eyes now proceeded to ride across the courtyard and straight out into the bustling honking traffic of the street beyond! The crowd cheered louder than ever. The barefoot children ran after him, squealing and laughing. For a minute or so, we were able to keep him in sight. We saw him riding superbly down the busy street with cars whizzing past him and a bunch of children running in his wake. Then he turned a corner and was gone.

"I feel quite giddy," Dr. Marshall said. "I can't bring myself to believe it."

"We have to believe it," I said. "He couldn't possibly have removed the dough from under the bandages. We never let him out of our sight. And as for unsealing his eyelids, that job would take him five minutes with cotton wool and alcohol."

"Do you know what I think," Dr. Marshall said. "I think we have witnessed a miracle."

We turned and walked slowly back into the hospital.

. . . .

IN READING THE DOCTOR'S JOURNAL, Sugar discovers the personal eye exercises used by Khan that enabled him to see through solid objects. It doesn't take him long to make the fabulous connection between Khan's achievement and *playing cards*. Imagine the enormous advantage—and economic reward—if you could train yourself to see through the cards and thus determine which cards your opponent was holding.

In short order, Henry Sugar begins an arduous training regimen that leads him eventually to the top casinos of the world, but with unexpected results for both himself and the reader.

As improbable as Khan's story might seem, I recall reading somewhere that the U.S. Air Force was studying the meditation methods used by Indian gurus who are able to lower their body temperatures nearly twenty degrees through meditation. Air force interest was piqued by how such a technique might be used by airmen in cold-weather survival situations.

Fans of *Henry Sugar* will enjoy Ray Bradbury's short story collection *The Illustrated Man*.

Classics

Three old favorites,
one set in India, one in
the Middle Ages, and the
last in ancient Egypt.

RIKKI-TIKKI-TAVI

by Rudyard Kipling

The Jungle Books' Forgotten Origins

Few people are familiar enough with Kipling's life to know that Mowgli, the lost and naked baby who wandered into the wolves' jungle den, may have represented Kipling himself, who had been "abandoned" by his parents as a young child. So let us begin with that.

Kipling was born in India, where his English father was an artist and curator of a museum. He was also quickly spoiled by his doting parents. If you add to that a natural and quick intelligence, you have a child who, by three years of age, was often out of control and described by relatives as a child "with strange gifts for upsetting any household." About the only thing that calmed him was when his mother read aloud to him.

Because of India's climate, diseases, and culture, it was customary in those days for English families living there to board out their children in England during the school years. Thus it was that five-and-a-half-year-old "Ruddy," along with his three-year-old sister, Trix, were left with an English family whom the parents had located through a newspaper ad. It would prove to be a near disaster and might very well have been the inspiration for Mowgli's experience as a jungle orphan.

Since his English relatives lived not far away and were willing to take in the two children, experts can only guess at why the parents preferred the two strangers to family; their estimate is that they felt Rudyard's strong-willed behavior might have been too upsetting to relatives.

So without any real explanation and with the urging that he learn to read so they could write to him, the two parents left the children with Mr. and Mrs. Holloway and did not return *for six years.* During that period in the home that he and his sister came to call "the House of Desolation," the ill-mannered Ruddy more than met his match in Mrs. Holloway, a cruel religious fanatic who took great delight in punishing the children with either her hands or twenty-four-hour solitary confinement for crimes such as spilling food, forgetting chores, or weeping when their parents' letters were read to them.

As if that were not bad enough, there was yet another menace in the home. Kipling's biographer Lord Birkenhead described him this way: "The Holloways' son Harry—'the Devil Boy,' as Rudyard thought of him—was the children's most painful cause of suffering, deeply religious, mentally and physically cruel, and adored by his mother. Rudyard was condemned to share an attic with him, sleeping in a hard iron bed against the wall . . . and the nights were rendered hideous by Harry. . . ."

The terrors of the jungle for a lost child couldn't have been any worse than those met by the brother and sister. Birkenhead describes one experience: "There came a moment in March 1877 when he was shut away from Trix for two days on the grounds that he was a 'moral leper.' On a Monday morning with a bitter wind blowing, Trix, who had not seen Ruddy since Friday, was told to practice the piano and not to move from the stool for 45 minutes. . . . She asked to see her brother, but was scolded and told he was going to school and 'perhaps you'll never seen him again, and a good job too.'

"She waited till she heard the attic door unlocked, then she . . . drew the lace curtains well over the window. She heard 'Aunty' storming at Ruddy in the little hall, and drowned the noise by playing strident scales. Then, looking out of the window, she saw him going down the little garden, walking like an old man. A placard covered the whole of his back—it was strong cardboard—neatly printed by Harry: KIPLING THE LIAR."

It may also have been during this period of listening for the devilish Harry and "Aunty" that Kipling developed a kind of animal wariness and secretive nature that would mark (and haunt) his adult relationships with the public and press.

When he finally learned to read at the age of seven, which was considered late for those times, he took to it with urgent zeal, finding books the only means of escape from his daily prison. He read everything he could put his hands on despite a congenital eye problem of severe shortsightedness—a condition that dramatically worsened during his six-year confinement.

When his mother finally returned, the children were too intimidated to tell her of the horrors, but Ruddy's condition spoke louder than words: He was nearly blind, a nervous wreck, and threw up his hand to ward off punishment when she bent to kiss him goodnight. Not surprisingly, he was removed immediately from the House of Desolation, but strangely, Trix was allowed to stay several more years.

According to biographers, because of the children's reluctance to talk about the ordeal, the parents never knew the full extent of the ordeal until Kipling published the short story "Baa Baa Black Sheep" many years later. There was never, however, even a hint in Kipling's writings that he doubted his parents' love for him or his sister. Moreover, he maintained a long and devoted relationship with them all his life. As best we can determine, he felt they had merely been doing what was expected of English parents living in a foreign land—as painful as that might have been for the children.

After high school, and without any college training, Kipling took a job his father secured for him in India as a reporter. He represented one half of the paper's staff, however, and was forced to work in temperatures that often reached 128 degrees, in a community constantly shadowed by death from cholera, typhoid, and numerous incurable oriental diseases. During those seven years as a reporter he covered the full range of imperial British and Indian society, often immersing himself in the deepest and darkest corners of Indian life, filling journals with personal observations, which soon became the basis for a flood of poems and seventy short stories. Thus the reporter's trade would serve him as both polishing agent and story seedbed, just as it did for Charles Dickens earlier and Allan Eckert years later (page 114).

Kipling was an intrepid reporter, investigative, still ill-mannered, and often an embarrassment to English society in India. Strangely, the memory of those days as a prying journalist would be lost to him when he became famous. At that point he became extremely suspicious of the press, refused interviews, and went to great lengths to protect his privacy—eventually leaving his beloved India and England in 1892 to settle in a remote corner of the world called Brattleboro, Vermont.

His new wife's family owned property in the Brattleboro area, nestled in the shadow of magnificent Mount Monadnock, and surrounded by snow (which Kipling had never seen). Isolated here, he could write in peace and raise a family among the American people, whom his heart went out to "beyond all other peoples." The restless world traveler, who seemed homeless everywhere he went, had finally found a "snow castle" home—only to have it melt in the flames of anger and humiliation within four years.

In Vermont, Kipling's creative powers were renewed, and he produced one of the most world-famous stories of India—*The Jungle Book*. (The sequel, which soon followed, was called *The Second Jungle Book*, which still makes for a degree of confusion all these years later.)

While he was writing *The Jungle Books*, his wife, Carrie, established herself as his personal secretary, money manager, and guardian against intruders. This was no small task once the local and national press discovered the presence of the celebrated man in rural New England. Nonetheless, Kipling and his wife refused to grant interviews of any kind.

As any politician will attest, the more you challenge the press from a hiding place, the greater their determination to discover your whereabouts. Once a woman reporter came by sled to the Kipling estate in the dead of winter. She was unprepared for the intense cold and collapsed before being brought inside by the Kiplings, who warmed her with tea and blankets. When they discovered she was a reporter, however, she was promptly sent back out into the cold.

Kipling's passion for privacy, however, did not apply to children, who found him a ready listener and witty storyteller. He adored all children, often loaned his toboggans to neighboring schoolchildren, and wrote more than six hundred letters just to his own children during their lifetimes.

His undoing was his brother-in-law, Beatty Balestier. Ironically, Beatty had been Kipling's boon companion and host upon Kipling's arrival in Vermont. Kipling and his wife made him the construction foreman for their huge mansion home, and they spent their first Christmas in America with his family, and even gave him one of the earliest manuscripts of *The Jungle Book*. Beatty was also the alcoholic black sheep of the family, something the Kiplings thought they could work around. They were wrong.

No "local yokel," Beatty was an extremely complicated man. One of his neighbors, a writer, described him this way: "Men cursed him in one breath and laughed at him in the next. . . . Men have been mobbed for smaller offenses than Beatty committed. He went his way, scathing and unscathed. . . . He crammed enough excitement, enough swashbuckling, enough defiant, deliberate riot into his sixty-odd years to supply a half dozen ordinary lives. . . . [He] had a tongue like a skinning knife. . . . He was a pain to the pious, a thorn to the respectable, an affront to the abstemious. He had a brilliant mind that he refused to harness for profitable toil; a will that mocked all scruple or stricture. . . ."

By the time the Kiplings and Beatty had a falling-out over some family pastureland, Beatty was keenly aware of Rudyard's weaknesses. When he heard his sister and brother-in-law had been making disparaging remarks about his indebtedness, he gave Kipling a week to retract the lies or he would blow out his brains. Kipling, fearing Beatty really would kill him during one of his drunken rages, went to the sheriff and preferred charges. He hoped this stern measure would be enough to frighten Beatty and alert him to the seriousness of his behavior. In other words, he'd show Beatty who was boss.

Kipling had not taken into consideration what a criminal hearing would do to his privacy—but Beatty had. He even refused to accept the bail that Kipling offered to post for his release from jail. And just as Beatty expected, reporters and correspondents came from all over America and gleefully flashed word around the world that wealthy Rudyard Kipling had thrown his penny-poor brother-in-law into jail. A preliminary hearing supported much of Kipling's testimony, but the press couldn't refrain from teasing him about the affair, even parodying his poetry in columns and editorials.

When the trial itself was postponed until the fall term, the Kiplings saw nothing left of their future in America and fled the country in August 1896 before the trial could take place.

They left behind their "snow castle" (which was closer to being a monstrous wooden ark) with all its effects, even a bank box in a Brattleboro vault. The home has largely stood empty through the decades, with bats collecting in the barns, Kipling's golf clubs and red golf balls (for playing in the snow) forever unused, and much of the original Victorian furniture gathering the dust of ages. In 1992 it was finally bought by a private British charity, which hopes to restore it as a landmark.

And what of the two brothers-in-law? They never met or spoke again. The affair left Kipling with such bitter taste for Americans that he henceforth declared them to be among the world's "lesser breeds." Beatty, on his deathbed, expressed his regrets about the whole affair and said he'd turn out all the bands in Brattleboro to welcome Kipling back if he'd come. Though they died just months apart, they succumbed worlds apart. Kipling, the first English writer to win the

Nobel Prize for literature, died wealthy and world famous, buried in Westminster Abbey beside Charles Dickens and Thomas Hardy. Beatty died penniless in Brattleboro, forgotten except for a few lines buried in Kipling's biographies years later.

In the intervening years, much of Kipling's professional reputation has diminished because so much of his writing was a chauvinistic celebration of British imperialism. Strangely, he is still highly regarded in India, where his works provide students with a vivid picture of "the way it was" in their country during the nineteenth century. Only infrequently do you hear a line of Kipling poetry today, and when people hear the phrase "You're a better man than I am, Gunga Din" or "East is east and west is west," or listen to Frank Sinatra singing "The Road to Mandalay," few realize they are hearing Kipling poetry.

The Kipling works that have not suffered in reputation are his children's stories, especially *The Jungle Books*, in which his greatest strength—storytelling—still shines. Almost as soon as they were written, the two volumes became immediate favorites with children throughout the world, in large part because of the Mowgli tales, which actually constitute only seven of the fifteen stories in the two books.

Mowgli, the Indian boy raised by jungle wolves, is one of the most famous characters in children's literature and one of the many who celebrate the survival of the lost or abandoned child—from the mythic twins Romulus and Remus and Joseph sold into Egypt to Oliver Twist and Dorothy blown away to Oz. One could build a very strong case that Mowgli was the literary father of Tarzan. All of these figures owe much of their popularity to the fact that being a child without parents is also one of the recurring dreams *and* nightmares of childhood in all countries and all times. In this way, then, the *Jungle Book* stories are really fairy tales in the tradition of "Hänsel and Gretel" and "Cinderella."

Shortly after *The Jungle Books* began winning young readers, their survival theme was also very much on the mind of another Britisher who had just established an organization to train adolescent boys in leadership and citizenship. The movement had met with such enthusiasm that its founder, Robert Baden-Powell, was thinking of establishing a junior program for younger boys, and when he read of Mowgli's training among the wolf cubs, he had the perfect name for his group: Cub Scouts.

One of my favorite short stories in *The Jungle Book* is "Rikki-tikki-tavi." Independent of the Mowgli stories, it is both a murder story and a testimonial to the savagery and nobility of the jungle.

PRONUNCIATION GUIDE
Rikki-tikki-tavi (Ricky-ticky-TAH-vee)
Segowlee (Seh-GOW-lee)
Nagaina (Na-GAY-na)
Karait (Ka-RATE)

• • • •

THIS IS THE STORY of the great war that Rikki-tikki-tavi fought single-handed, through the bathrooms of the big bungalow in Segowlee cantonment. Darzee the tailorbird helped him, and Chuchundra the muskrat, who never comes out into the middle of the floor, but always creeps round by the wall, gave him advice; but Rikki-tikki did the real fighting.

He was a mongoose, rather like a little cat in his fur and his tail, but quite like a weasel in his head and his habits. His eyes and the end of his restless nose were pink; he could scratch himself anywhere he pleased with any leg, front or back, that he chose to use; he could fluff up his tail till it looked like a bottle brush, and his war cry as he scuttled through the long grass was: *Rikk-tikk-tikki-tikki-tchk!*

One day a high summer flood washed him out of the burrow where he lived with his father and mother, and carried him, kicking and clucking, down a roadside ditch. He found a little wisp of grass floating there and clung to it till he lost his senses. When he revived, he was lying in the hot sun on the middle of a garden path, very draggled indeed, and a small boy was saying: "Here's a dead mongoose. Let's have a funeral."

"No," said his mother, "let's take him in and dry him. Perhaps he isn't really dead."

They took him into the house, and a big man picked him up between his finger and thumb and said he was not dead but half choked, so they wrapped him in cotton wool, and warmed him over a little fire, and he opened his eyes and sneezed.

"Now," said the big man (he was an Englishman who had just moved into the bungalow), "don't frighten him, and we'll see what he'll do."

It is the hardest thing in the world to frighten a mongoose, because he is eaten up from nose to tail with curiosity. The motto of all the mongoose family is, "Run and find out," and Rikki-tikki was a true mongoose. He looked at the cotton wool, decided that it was not good to eat, ran all round the table, sat up and put his fur in order, scratched himself, and jumped on the small boy's shoulder.

"Don't be frightened, Teddy," said his father. "That's his way of making friends."

"Ouch! He's tickling under my chin," said Teddy.

Rikki-tikki looked down between the boy's collar and neck, snuffed at his ear, and climbed down to the floor, where he sat rubbing his nose.

"Good gracious," said Teddy's mother, "and that's a wild creature! I suppose he's so tame because we've been kind to him."

"All mongooses are like that," said her husband. "If Teddy doesn't pick him up by the tail, or try to put him in a cage, he'll run in and out of the house all day long. Let's give him something to eat."

They gave him a little piece of raw meat. Rikki-tikki liked it immensely, and when it was finished, he went out into the veranda and sat in the sunshine and fluffed up his fur to make it dry to the roots. Then he felt better.

"There are more things to find out about in this house," he said to himself, "than all my family could find out in all their lives. I shall certainly stay and find out."

He spent all that day roaming over the house. He nearly drowned himself in the bathtubs; put his nose into the ink on a writing table, and burnt it on the end of the big man's cigar, for he climbed up in the big man's lap to see how writing was done. At nightfall he ran into Teddy's nursery to watch how kerosene lamps were lighted, and when Teddy went to bed Rikki-tikki climbed up too; but he was a restless companion, because he had to get up and attend to every noise all through the night and find out what made it. Teddy's mother and father came in, the last thing, to look at their boy, and Rikki-tikki was awake on the pillow. "I don't like that," said Teddy's mother. "He may bite the child." "He'll do no such thing," said the father. "Teddy's safer with that little beast than if he had a bloodhound to watch him. If a snake came into the nursery now—"

But Teddy's mother wouldn't think of anything so awful.

Early in the morning Rikki-tikki came to early breakfast in the veranda riding on Teddy's shoulder, and they gave him banana and some boiled egg; and he sat on all their laps one after the other, because every well-brought-up mongoose always hopes to be a house mongoose someday and have rooms to run about in; and Rikki-tikki's mother (she used to live in the general's house at Segowlee) had carefully told Rikki what to do if ever he came across white men.

Then Rikki-tikki went out into the garden to see what was to be seen. It was a large garden, only half cultivated, with bushes, as big as summerhouses, of Marshal Niel roses; lime and orange trees, clumps of bamboos, and thickets of high grass. Rikki-tikki licked his lips. "This is a splendid hunting ground," he said, and his tail grew bottle-brushy at the thought of it, and he scuttled up and down the garden, snuffing here and there till he heard very sorrowful voices in a thornbush. It was Darzee the tailorbird and his wife. They had made a beautiful nest by pulling two big leaves together and stitching them up the edges with fibers, and had filled the hollow with cotton and downy fluff. The nest swayed to and fro, as they sat on the rim and cried.

"What is the matter?" asked Rikki-tikki.

"We are very miserable," said Darzee. "One of our babies fell out of the nest yesterday and Nag ate him."

"H'm!" said Rikki-tikki, "that is very sad—but I am a stranger here. Who is Nag?"

Darzee and his wife only cowered down in the nest without answering, for from the thick grass at the foot of the bush there came a low hiss—a horrid cold sound that made Rikki-tikki jump back two clear feet. Then inch by inch out of the grass rose up the head and spread hood of Nag, the big black cobra, and he was five feet long from tongue to tail. When he had lifted one-third of himself clear of the ground, he stayed balancing to and fro exactly as a dandelion tuft balances in the wind, and he looked at Rikki-tikki with the wicked snake's eyes that never change their expression, whatever the snake may be thinking of.

"Who is Nag?" said he. "*I* am Nag. The great god Brahm put his mark upon all our people, when the first cobra spread his hood to keep the sun off Brahm as he slept. Look, and be afraid!"

He spread out his hood more than ever, and Rikki-tikki saw the spectacle mark on the back of it that looks exactly like the eye part of a hook-and-eye fastening. He was afraid for the minute; but it is impossible for a mongoose to stay frightened for any length of time, and though Rikki-tikki had never met a live cobra before, his mother had fed him on dead ones, and he knew that all a grown mongoose's business in life was to fight and eat snakes: Nag knew that too and, at the bottom of his cold heart, he was afraid.

"Well," said Rikki-tikki, and his tail began to fluff up again, "marks or no marks, do you think it is right for you to eat fledglings out of a nest?"

Nag was thinking to himself and watching the least little movement in the grass behind Rikki-tikki. He knew that mongooses in the garden meant death sooner or later for him and his family; but he wanted to get Rikki-tikki off his guard. So he dropped his head a little and put it on one side.

"Let us talk," he said. "You eat eggs. Why should not I eat birds?"

"Behind you! Look behind you!" sang Darzee.

Rikki-tikki knew better than to waste time in staring. He jumped up in the air as high as he could go, and just under him whizzed by the head of Nagaina, Nag's wicked wife. She had crept up behind him as he was talking, to make an end of him; and he heard her savage hiss as the stroke missed. He came down almost across her back, and if he had been an old mongoose, he would have known that then was the time to break her back with one bite; but he was afraid of the terrible lashing return-stroke of the cobra. He bit, indeed, but did not bite long enough, and he jumped clear of the whisking tail, leaving Nagaina torn and angry.

"Wicked, wicked Darzee!" said Nag, lashing up as high as he could reach toward the nest in the thornbush; but Darzee had built it out of reach of snakes, and it only swayed to and fro.

Rikki-tikki felt his eyes growing red and hot (when a mongoose's eyes grow red, he is angry), and he sat back on his tail and hind legs like a little kangaroo, and looked all round him, and chattered with rage. But Nag and Nagaina had disappeared into the grass. When a snake misses its stroke, it never says anything or gives any sign of what it means to do next. Rikki-tikki did not care to follow them, for he did not feel sure that he could manage two snakes at once. So he trotted off to the gravel path near the house and sat down to think. It was a serious matter for him. If you read the old books of natural history, you will find they say that when the mongoose fights the snake and happens to get bitten, he runs off and eats some herb that cures him. That is not true. The victory is only a matter of quickness of eye and quickness of foot—snake's blow against mongoose's jump—and as no eye can follow the motion of a snake's head when it strikes, this makes things much more wonderful than any magic herb. Rikki-tikki knew he was a young mongoose, and it made him all the more pleased to think that he had managed to escape a blow from behind. It gave him confidence in himself, and when Teddy came running down the path, Rikki-tikki was ready to be petted. But just as Teddy was stooping, something wriggled a little in the dust, and a tiny voice said: "Be careful. I am Death." It was Karait, the dusty brown snakeling that lies for choice on the dusty earth; and his bite is as dangerous as the cobra's. But he is so small that nobody thinks of him, and so he does the more harm to people.

Rikki-tikki's eyes grew red again, and he danced up to Karait with the peculiar rocking, swaying motion that he had inherited from his family. It looks very funny, but it is so perfectly balanced a gait that you can fly off from it at any angle you please; and in dealing with snakes this is an advantage. If Rikki-tikki had only known—he was doing a much more dangerous thing than fighting Nag—for Karait is so small, and can turn so quickly, that unless Rikki bit him close to the back of the head, he would get the return-stroke in his eye or his lip. But Rikki did not know; his eyes were all red, and he rocked back and forth, looking for a good place to hold. Karait struck out; Rikki jumped sideways and tried to run in, but the wicked little dusty gray head lashed within a fraction of his shoulder, and he had to jump over the body, and the head followed his heels close.

Teddy shouted to the house: "Oh, look here! Our mongoose is killing a snake"; and Rikki-tikki heard a scream from Teddy's mother. His father ran out with a stick, but by the time he came up, Karait had lunged out once too far, and Rikki-tikki had sprung, jumped on the snake's back, dropped his head far between his forelegs, bitten as high up the back as he could get hold, and rolled away. That bite paralyzed Karait, and Rikki-tikki was just going to eat him up from the tail, after the custom of his family at dinner, when he remembered that a full meal makes a slow mongoose, and if he wanted all his strength and quickness ready, he must keep himself thin. He went away for a dust bath under the castor-oil bushes, while Teddy's father beat the dead Karait. "What is the use of that?" thought Rikki-tikki; "I have settled it all"; and then Teddy's mother picked him up from the dust and hugged him, crying that he had saved Teddy from death, and Teddy's father said that he was a providence, and Teddy looked on with big scared eyes. Rikki-tikki was rather amused at all the fuss, which, of course, he did not understand. Teddy's mother might just as well have petted Teddy for playing in the dust. Rikki was thoroughly enjoying himself.

That night at dinner, walking to and fro among the wineglasses on the table, he might have stuffed himself three times over with nice things; but he remembered Nag and Nagaina, and though it was very pleasant to be patted and petted by Teddy's mother and to sit on Teddy's shoulder, his eyes would get red from time to time, and he would go off into his long war cry of *"Rikk-tikk-tikki-tikki-tchk!"*

Teddy carried him off to bed and insisted on Rikki-tikki sleeping under his chin. Rikki-tikki was too well bred to bite or scratch, but as soon as Teddy was asleep he went off for his nightly walk round the house, and in the dark he ran up against Chuchundra the muskrat, creeping round by the wall. Chuchundra is a brokenhearted little beast. He whimpers and cheeps all the night, trying to make up his mind to run into the middle of the room; but he never gets there.

"Don't kill me," said Chuchundra, almost weeping. "Rikki-tikki, don't kill me!"

"Do you think a snake killer kills muskrats?" said Rikki-tikki scornfully.

"Those who kill snakes get killed by snakes," said Chuchundra, more sorrowfully than ever. "And how am I to be sure that Nag won't mistake me for you some dark night?"

"There's not the least danger," said Rikki-tikki. "But Nag is in the garden, and I know you don't go there."

"My cousin Chua the rat told me—" said Chuchundra, and then he stopped.

"Told you what?"

"H'sh! Nag is everywhere, Rikki-tikki. You should have talked to Chua in the garden."

"I didn't—so you must tell me. Quick, Chuchundra, or I'll bite you!"

Chuchundra sat down and cried till the tears rolled off his whiskers. "I am a very poor man," he sobbed. "I never had spirit enough to run out into the middle of the room. H'sh! I mustn't tell you anything. Can't you *hear*, Rikki-tikki?"

Rikki-tikki listened. The house was as still as still, but he thought he could just catch the faintest *scratch-scratch* in the world—a noise as faint as that of a wasp walking on a windowpane—the dry scratch of a snake's scales on brickwork.

"That's Nag or Nagaina," he said to himself, "and he is crawling into the bathroom sluice. You're right, Chuchundra; I should have talked to Chua."

He stole off to Teddy's bathroom, but there was nothing there, and then to Teddy's mother's bathroom. At the bottom of the smooth plaster wall there was a brick pulled out to make a sluice for the bathwater, and as Rikki-tikki stole in by the masonry curb where the bath is put, he heard Nag and Nagaina whispering together outside in the moonlight.

"When the house is emptied of people," said Nagaina to her husband, "*he* will have to go away, and then the garden will be our own again. Go in quietly, and remember that the big man who killed Karait is the first one to bite. Then come out and tell me, and we will hunt for Rikki-tikki together."

"But are you sure that there is anything to be gained by killing the people?" said Nag.

"Everything. When there were no people in the bungalow, did we have any mongoose in the garden? So long as the bungalow is empty, we are king and queen of the garden; and remember that as soon as our eggs in the melon bed hatch (as they may tomorrow), our children will need room and quiet."

"I had not thought of that," said Nag. "I will go, but there is no need that we should hunt for Rikki-tikki afterward. I will kill the big man and his wife, and the child if I can, and come away quietly. Then the bungalow will be empty, and Rikki-tikki will go."

Rikki-tikki tingled all over with rage and hatred at this, and then Nag's head came through the sluice, and his five feet of cold body followed it. Angry as he was, Rikki-tikki was very frightened as he saw the size of the big cobra. Nag coiled himself up, raised his head, and looked into the bathroom in the dark, and Rikki could see his eyes glitter.

"Now, if I kill him here, Nagaina will know; and if I fight him on the open floor, the odds are in his favor. What am I to do?" said Rikki-tikki-tavi.

Nag waved to and fro, and then Rikki-tikki heard him drinking from the biggest water jar that was used to fill the bath. "That is good," said the snake. "Now, when Karait was killed, the big man had a stick. He may have that stick still, but when he comes in to bathe in the morning he will not have a stick. I shall wait here till he comes. Nagaina—do you hear me?—I shall wait here in the cool till daytime."

There was no answer from outside, so Rikki-tikki knew Nagaina had gone away. Nag coiled himself down, coil by coil, round the bulge at the bottom of the water jar, and Rikki-tikki stayed still as death. After an hour he began to move, muscle by muscle, toward the jar. Nag was asleep, and Rikki-tikki looked at his big back, wondering which would be the best place for a good hold. "If I don't break his back at the first jump," said Rikki, "he can still fight; and if he fights—Oh, Rikki!" He looked at the thickness of the neck below the hood, but that was too much for him, and a bite near the tail would only make Nag savage.

"It must be the head," he said at last, "the head above the hood, and when I am once there, I must not let go."

Then he jumped. The head was lying a little clear of the water jar, under the curve of it; and, as his teeth met, Rikki braced his back against the bulge of the red earthenware to hold down the head. This gave him just one second's purchase, and he made the most of it. Then he was battered to and fro as a rat is shaken by a dog—to and fro on the floor, up and down, and round in great circles, but his eyes were red and he held on as the body cartwhipped over the floor, upsetting the tin dipper and the soap dish and the flesh brush, and banged against the tin side of the bath. As he held he closed his jaws tighter and tighter, for he made sure he would be banged to death, and, for the honor of his family, he preferred to be found with his teeth locked. He was dizzy, aching, and felt shaken to pieces when something went off like a thunderclap just behind him; a hot wind knocked him senseless and red fire singed his fur. The big man had been wakened by the noise, and had fired both barrels of a shotgun into Nag just behind the hood.

Rikki-tikki held on with his eyes shut, for now he was quite sure he was dead; but the head did not move, and the big man picked him up and said: "It's the mongoose again, Alice; the little chap has saved *our* lives now." Then Teddy's mother came in with a very white face and saw what was left of Nag, and Rikki-tikki dragged himself to Teddy's bedroom and spent half the rest of the night shaking himself tenderly to find out whether he really was broken into forty pieces, as he fancied.

When morning came, he was very stiff, but well pleased with his doings. "Now I have Nagaina to settle with, and she will be worse than five Nags, and there's no knowing when the eggs she spoke of will hatch. Goodness! I must go and see Darzee," he said.

Without waiting for breakfast, Rikki-tikki ran to the thornbush where Darzee was singing a song of triumph at the top of his voice.

The news of Nag's death was all over the garden, for the sweeper had thrown the body on the rubbish heap.

"Oh, you stupid tuft of feathers!" said Rikki-tikki angrily. "Is this the time to sing?"

"Nag is dead—is dead—is dead!" sang Darzee. "The valiant Rikki-tikki caught him by the head and held fast. The big man brought the bang stick, and Nag fell in two pieces! He will never eat my babies again."

"All that's true enough; but where's Nagaina?" said Rikki-tikki, looking carefully round him.

"Nagaina came to the bathroom sluice and called for Nag," Darzee went on, "and Nag came out on the end of a stick—the sweeper picked him up on the end of a stick and threw him upon the rubbish heap. Let us sing about the great, the red-eyed Rikki-tikki!" and Darzee filled his throat and sang.

"If I could get up to your nest, I'd roll your babies out!" said Rikki-tikki. "You don't know when to do the right thing at the right time. You're safe enough in your nest there, but it's war for me down here. Stop singing a minute, Darzee."

"For the great, the beautiful Rikki-tikki's sake I will stop," said Darzee. "What is it, O killer of the terrible Nag?"

"Where is Nagaina, for the third time?"

"On the rubbish heap by the stables, mourning for Nag. Great is Rikki-tikki with the white teeth."

"Bother my white teeth! Have you ever heard where she keeps her eggs?"

"In the melon bed, on the end nearest the wall, where the sun strikes nearly all day. She hid them there weeks ago."

"And you never thought it worthwhile to tell me? The end nearest the wall, you said?"

"Rikki-tikki, you are not going to eat her eggs?"

"Not eat exactly; no. Darzee, if you have a grain of sense, you will fly off to the stables and pretend that your wing is broken, and let Nagaina chase you away to this bush. I must get to the melon bed, and if I went there now, she'd see me."

Darzee was a featherbrained little fellow who could never hold more than one idea at a time in his head; and just because he knew that Nagaina's children were born in eggs like his own, he didn't think at first that it was fair to kill them. But his wife was a sensible bird, and she knew that cobra's eggs meant young cobras later on; so she flew off from the nest, and left Darzee to keep the babies warm, and continue his song about the death of Nag. Darzee was very like a man in some ways.

She fluttered in front of Nagaina by the rubbish heap, and cried out, "Oh, my wing is broken! The boy in the house threw a stone at me and broke it." Then she fluttered more desperately than ever.

Nagaina lifted up her head and hissed, "You warned Rikki-tikki when I would have killed him. Indeed and truly, you've chosen a bad place to be lame in." And she moved toward Darzee's wife, slipping along over the dust.

"The boy broke it with a stone!" shrieked Darzee's wife.

"Well! It may be some consolation to you when you're dead to know that I shall settle accounts with the boy. My husband lies on the rubbish heap this morning, but before night the boy in the house will lie very still. What is the use of running away? I am sure to catch you. Little fool, look at me!"

Darzee's wife knew better than to do *that*, for a bird who looks at a snake's eyes gets so frightened that she cannot move. Darzee's wife fluttered on, piping sorrowfully, and never leaving the ground, and Nagaina quickened her pace.

Rikki-tikki heard them going up the path from the stables, and he raced for the end of the melon patch near the wall. There, in the warm litter above the melons, very cunningly hidden, he found twenty-five eggs, about the size of a bantam's eggs, but with whitish skins instead of shells.

"I was not a day too soon," he said; for he could see the baby cobras curled up inside the skin, and he knew that the minute they were hatched they could each kill a man or a mongoose. He bit off the tops of the eggs as fast as he could, taking care to crush the young cobras, and turned over the litter from time to time to see whether he had missed any. At last there were only three eggs left, and Rikki-tikki began to chuckle to himself, when he heard Darzee's wife screaming:

"Rikki-tikki, I led Nagaina toward the house, and she has gone into the veranda, and—oh, come quickly—she means killing!"

Rikki-tikki smashed two eggs, and tumbled backward down the melon bed with the third egg in his mouth, and scuttled to the veranda as hard as he could put foot to the ground. Teddy and his mother and father were there at early breakfast; but Rikki-tikki saw that they were not eating anything. They sat stone-still, and their faces were white. Nagaina was coiled up on the matting by Teddy's chair, within easy striking distance of Teddy's bare leg, and she was swaying to and fro, singing a song of triumph.

"Son of the big man that killed Nag," she hissed, "stay still. I am not ready yet. Wait a little. Keep very still, all you three! If you move I strike, and if you do not move I strike. Oh, foolish people, who killed my Nag!"

Teddy's eyes were fixed on his father, and all his father could do was to whisper, "Sit still, Teddy. You mustn't move. Teddy, keep still."

Then Rikki-tikki came up and cried: "Turn round, Nagaina, turn and fight!"

"All in good time," said she, without moving her eyes. "I will settle my account with *you* presently. Look at your friends, Rikki-tikki. They are still and white. They are afraid. They dare not move, and if you come a step nearer I strike."

"Look at your eggs," said Rikki-tikki, "in the melon bed near the wall. Go and look, Nagaina!"

The big snake turned half round, and saw the egg on the veranda. "Ah-h! Give it to me," she said.

Rikki-tikki put his paws one on each side of the egg, and his eyes were bloodred. "What price for a snake's egg? For a young cobra? For a young king cobra? For the last—the very last of the brood? The ants are eating all the others down by the melon bed."

Nagaina spun clear round, forgetting everything for the sake of the one egg; and Rikki-tikki saw Teddy's father shoot out a big hand, catch Teddy by the shoulder and drag him across the little table with the teacups, safe and out of reach of Nagaina.

"Tricked! Tricked! Tricked! *Rikk-tck-tck!*" chuckled Rikki-tikki. "The boy is safe, and it was I—I—I that caught Nag by the hood last night in the bathroom." Then he began to jump up and down, all four feet together, his head close to the floor. "He threw me to and fro, but he could not shake me off. He was dead before the big man blew him in two. I did it! *Rikki-tikki-tck-tck!* Come then, Nagaina. Come and fight with me. You shall not be a widow long."

Nagaina saw that she had lost her chance of killing Teddy, and the egg lay between Rikki-tikki's paws. "Give me the egg, Rikki-tikki. Give me the last of my eggs, and I will go away and never come back," she said, lowering her hood.

"Yes, you will go away, and you will never come back; for you will go to the rubbish heap with Nag. Fight, widow! The big man has gone for his gun! Fight!"

Rikki-tikki was bounding all round Nagaina, keeping just out of reach of her stroke, his little eyes like hot coals. Nagaina gathered herself together, and flung out at him. Rikki-tikki jumped up and backward. Again and again and again she struck, and each time her head came with a whack on the matting of the veranda and she gathered herself together like a watch spring. Then Rikki-tikki danced in a circle to get behind her, and Nagaina spun round to keep her head to his head, so that the rustle of her tail on the matting sounded like dry leaves blown along by the wind.

He had forgotten the egg. It still lay on the veranda, and Nagaina came nearer and nearer to it, till at last, while Rikki-tikki was drawing breath, she caught it in her mouth, turned to the veranda steps, and flew like an arrow down the path, with Rikki-tikki behind her. When the cobra runs for her life, she goes like a whiplash flicked across a horse's neck. Rikki-tikki knew that he must catch her, or all the trouble would begin again. She headed straight for the long grass by the thornbush, and as he was running Rikki-tikki heard Darzee still singing his foolish little song of triumph. But Darzee's wife was wiser. She flew off her nest as Nagaina came along and flapped her wings about Nagaina's head. If Darzee had helped, they might have turned her; but Nagaina only lowered her hood and went on. Still, the instant's delay brought Rikki-tikki up to her, and as she plunged into the rathole where she and Nag used to live, his little white teeth were clenched on her tail, and he went down with her—and very few mongooses, however wise and old they may be, care to follow a cobra into its hole. It was dark in the hole, and Rikki-tikki never knew when it might open out and give Nagaina room to turn and strike at him. He held on savagely and stuck out his feet to act as brakes on the dark slope of the hot, moist earth. Then the grass by the mouth of the hole stopped waving, and Darzee said: "It is all over with Rikki-tikki! We must sing his death song. Valiant Rikki-tikki is dead! For Nagaina will surely kill him underground."

So he sang a very mournful song that he made up on the spur of the minute, and just as he got to the most touching part the grass quivered again, and Rikki-tikki, covered with dirt, dragged himself out of the hole leg by leg, licking his whiskers. Darzee stopped with a little shout. Rikki-tikki shook some of the dust out of his fur and sneezed. "It is all over," he said. "The widow will never come out again." And the red ants that live between the grass stems heard him, and began to troop down one after another to see if he had spoken the truth.

Rikki-tikki curled himself up in the grass and slept where he was—slept and slept till it was late in the afternoon, for he had done a hard day's work.

"Now," he said, when he awoke, "I will go back to the house. Tell the coppersmith, Darzee, and he will tell the garden that Nagaina is dead."

The coppersmith is a bird who makes a noise exactly like the beating of a little hammer on a copper pot; and the reason he is always making it is because he is the town crier to every Indian garden and tells all the news to everybody who cares to listen. As Rikki-tikki went up the path he heard his "attention" notes like a tiny dinner-gong; and then the steady "*Ding-dong-tock!* Nag is dead—*dong!* Nagaina is dead! *Ding-dong-tock!*" That set all the birds in the garden singing, and the frogs croaking; for Nag and Nagaina used to eat frogs as well as little birds.

When Rikki got to the house, Teddy and Teddy's mother (she looked very white still, for she had been fainting) and Teddy's father came out and almost cried over him; and that night he ate all that was given him till he could eat no more and went to bed on Teddy's shoulder, where Teddy's mother saw him when she came to look late at night.

"He saved our lives and Teddy's life," she said to her husband. "Just think, he saved all our lives."

Rikki-tikki woke up with a jump, for the mongooses are light sleepers.

"Oh, it's you," said he. "What are you bothering for? All the cobras are dead; and if they weren't, I'm here."

Rikki-tikki had a right to be proud of himself; but he did not grow too proud, and he kept that garden as a mongoose should keep it, with tooth and jump and spring and bite, till never a cobra dared show its head inside the walls.

• • • •

THIS TALE IS FOUND in the first *Jungle Book*, as well as on its own as *Rikki-tikki-tavi*, illustrated magnificently by Lambert Davis. Numerous publishers have combined *The Jungle Books* into single volumes.

For a related tale, see "Fear" by Rhys Davies on page 223.

It is strongly suspected that a certain amount of the Mowgli story sprang from actual cases of children being raised by wild animals. Author Jane Yolen wrote a fascinating novel, *Children of the Wolf*, based upon the wolf-girls discovered by a missionary in India in 1920. Yet another version of the feral child can be found in the novel *Incident at Hawk's Hill* by Allan Eckert, a chapter of which begins on page 117.

Far from the sticky-sweetness of the Disney version, the original movie version of *The Jungle Book*, starring Sabu, is now available in many video stores. Selections from *The Jungle Books* are available on a single audiocassette (JimCin), and the entire first *Jungle Book* (360 minutes) is also available from Books on Tape.

Remember when Teddy first found the apparently drowned mongoose? He immediately thought of a funeral, and he thought of it with considerable relish. For yet another angle on the same story, see page 408.

from **O**TTO OF THE SILVER HAND
by Howard Pyle

Lessons from Wounded Soldiers

At eight years of age, Howard Pyle stood by the railway in Wilmington, Delaware, and watched the young Union soldiers descend from their troop trains for food and water on their way south. When they departed, he raced home to pencil, watercolor, and paper to envision the glory that would soon be theirs. There would be barely enough room on his paper for all the blazing cannons, annihilation, muskets, and bayonets he would create as torture for the Confederates.

But in a world at war, little boys' dreams of pageantry and courage are like balloons in a rose garden. Henry Pitz, Pyle's eloquent biographer, describes the days when reality dawned for the child at the rail station: "Then came a different time when the trains came up from the South with the sick and wounded. Some were the enemy —they were the ragged ones, sometimes in gray. When they spoke, it was English but with a different inflection. Sometimes they were hard to understand, but they weren't terrifying. All the wounded were carried up the streets to the jerry-built hospitals and, on summer days, small boys were allowed to march beside the stretchers and fan the hot faces." And thus were planted the seeds of imagery that would blossom twenty years later in a daring antiwar novel for young American students.

Pyle was raised in a large and loving Quaker family, surrounded by books and magazines of every description, which his mother read aloud to him throughout his childhood. Along with the traditional Grimms' fairy tales, Washington Irving, and Hawthorne's *Wonder Book*, there were also Dickens and the tales that Dickens maintained were the biggest influence on his writing—the *Arabian Nights*.

Pyle's mother paid particular attention to the illustrations in their magazines and books, and soon cultivated within the child an insatiable appetite for both drawing and writing. Though he was extremely bright, Pyle never adapted to the routine of the classroom. Only in a small private art school at age sixteen did his intelligence and talent finally flourish. At the same time he read more widely, choosing more challenging books. At twenty years of age he attempted to open his own art school, but it never materialized. Twenty years later, however, he would be the mentor teacher for a class of professional artists that would dominate American commercial illustration unlike any group before or after. The class included N. C. Wyeth (father and teacher of Andrew Wyeth), Maxfield Parrish, Violet Oakley, and Frank Schoonover, and they would become known as the Brandywine school.

(Today, in Chadds Ford, Pennsylvania, forty-five minutes from Philadelphia and not far from where Pyle taught his famous students, the Brandywine River Museum houses a magnificent collection of these artists' works, as well as those of the entire Wyeth family. Nearby, in Wilmington, Delaware, the Delaware Art Museum offers the largest collection of Howard Pyle's work.)

Before his days as a teacher, though, Howard Pyle would have to ply his talents for the popular adult publishing houses in New York, gradually winning larger and more important commissions, until he was among the best on both sides of the Atlantic. One of his great strengths was the powerful sense of realism in the detail and costumes within his artwork. His devotion to detail prompted him to begin a collection of authentic period costumes that grew with his research until he was regarded as the leading figure in America on the subject.

Up to this point, he'd allowed his writing talents to rest in the shade of his artwork. At age thirty, he published his first book to rave reviews in the United States and abroad; it was *The Merry Adventures of Robin Hood of Great Renown, in Nottinghamshire*, a retelling of the popular legend. This was the beginning of a masterpiece collection of adventure books on knighthood, including *The Story of King Arthur and His Knights; Men of Iron*; and *Otto of the Silver Hand*.

Of all his novels, *Otto of the Silver Hand* remains the most accessible and powerful a century later. It is adventure and convincing historical fiction, but more important, it set a bold precedent in children's literature. Biographer Pitz explains: "It appeared at a time when, with only the fewest exceptions, children's authors timidly circled away from the bitterness of life or threw a veil over it. . . . Against a background of medieval Germany, it straightforwardly and touch-ingly told a story of family hatred, of the mutilation of a young boy, Otto, and the consequences of this brutality. . . . The Middle Ages enfolds the characters into its bitterness and beauty. Pyle produced a deeply moving story without a hint of preachiness."

It is unlikely he would ever have attempted such realism without first witnessing the emotional and physical devastation of war from the vantage point of an eight-year-old beside the troop trains in Amer-ica's own story of family hatred, the Civil War.

Here are two chapters from *Otto of the Silver Hand*, set in a time that Pyle describes as that "great black gulf in human history, a gulf of ignorance, of superstition, of cruelty, and of wickedness. That time we call the dark or middle ages." It was, however, his Christian belief that though the times were filled with evil, there were still a few virtuous men and women who guarded the candle of goodness through the night.

The book opens in what would be Germany today, inside the castle Drachenhausen, home of Baron Conrad, a robber baron who lives by robbing the caravans that come through the valley. His beau-tiful wife, Baroness Matilda, knows the dangers he faces each time he departs on one of his armed raiding parties, and in an unusual display of emotion she begs him to give up this dangerous life-style. Though he dearly loves her and would do anything else she asked, his pride and warring nature will not allow him to grant her wish.

As our selection begins, the Baroness is waiting for him to return from a raid, one that has run unusually long. She has important news to share with him and grows impatient as she and her ladies gather near the night fire in the castle. At last a bugle sounds the return of the Baron's party. When her husband's first guard, the one-eyed Hans, suddenly appears in the doorway, he wears a dark look upon his brow. Behind him come six men bearing a litter upon which rests Baron Conrad, white-faced, his eyes closed, and a dark red stain spilling across his armor.

And just as suddenly the horrified Baroness collapses to the floor. As her attendant looks up from her side, she cries fiercely to the one-eyed Hans, "Thou fool! Why didst thou bring him here? Thou has killed thy lady!"

(Keep in mind that Pyle uses some of the language of the Middle Ages in order to give his story a flavor of the times, and therefore some adjustment is necessary when you first hear or read his dialogue.)

• • • •

CHAPTER 3
How the Baron Came Home Shorn

BUT BARON CONRAD was not dead. For days he lay upon his hard bed, now muttering incoherent words beneath his red beard, now raving fiercely with the fever of his wound. But one day he woke again to the things about him.

He turned his head first to the one side and then to the other; there sat Schwartz Carl and the one-eyed Hans. Two or three other retainers stood by a great window that looked out into the courtyard beneath, jesting and laughing together in low tones, and one lay upon the heavy oaken bench that stood along by the wall, snoring in his sleep.

"Where is your lady?" said the Baron, presently; "and why is she not with me at this time?"

The man that lay upon the bench started up at the sound of his voice, and those at the window came hurrying to his bedside. But Schwartz Carl and the one-eyed Hans looked at one another, and neither of them spoke. The Baron saw the look and in it read a certain meaning that brought him to his elbow, though only to sink back upon his pillow again with a groan.

"Why do you not answer me?" said he at last, in a hollow voice; then to the one-eyed Hans, "Hast no tongue, fool, that thou standest gaping there like a fish? Answer me, where is thy mistress?"

"I—I do not know," stammered poor Hans.

For a while the Baron lay silently looking from one face to the other, then he spoke again. "How long have I been lying here?" said he.

"A sennight, my lord," said Master Rudolph, the steward, who had come into the room and who now stood among the others at the bedside.

"A sennight," repeated the Baron, in a low voice, and then to Master Rudolph, "And has the Baroness been often beside me in that time?" Master Rudolph hesitated. "Answer me," said the Baron, harshly.

"Not—not often," said Master Rudolph, hesitatingly.

The Baron lay silent for a long time. At last he passed his hands over his face and held them there for a minute, then of a sudden, before anyone knew what he was about to do, he rose upon his elbow and then sat upright upon the bed. The green wound broke out afresh and a dark red spot grew and spread upon the linen wrappings; his face was drawn and haggard with the pain of his moving, and his eyes wild and bloodshot. Great drops of sweat gathered and stood upon his forehead as he sat there swaying slightly from side to side.

"My shoes," said he, hoarsely.

Master Rudolph stepped forward. "But, my Lord Baron," he began and then stopped short, for the Baron shot him such a look that his tongue stood still in his head.

Hans saw that look out of his one eye. Down he dropped upon his knees and, fumbling under the bed, brought forth a pair of soft leathern shoes, which he slipped upon the Baron's feet and then laced the thongs above the instep.

"Your shoulder," said the Baron. He rose slowly to his feet, gripping Hans in the stress of his agony until the fellow winced again. For a moment he stood as though gathering strength, then doggedly started forth upon that quest which he had set upon himself.

At the door he stopped for a moment as though overcome by his weakness, and there Master Nicholas, his cousin, met him; for the steward had sent one of the retainers to tell the old man what the Baron was about to do.

"Thou must go back again, Conrad," said Master Nicholas; "thou art not fit to be abroad."

The Baron answered him never a word, but he glared at him from out of his bloodshot eyes and ground his teeth together. Then he started forth again upon his way.

Down the long hall he went, slowly and laboriously, the others following silently behind him, then up the steep winding stairs, step by step, now and then stopping to lean against the wall. So he reached a long and gloomy passage-way lit only by the light of a little window at the further end.

He stopped at the door of one of the rooms that opened into this passage-way, stood for a moment, then he pushed it open.

No one was within but old Ursela, who sat crooning over a fire with a bundle upon her knees. She did not see the Baron or know that he was there.

"Where is your lady?" said he, in a hollow voice.

Then the old nurse looked up with a start. "Jesu bless us," cried she, and crossed herself.

"Where is your lady?" said the Baron again, in the same hoarse voice; and then, not waiting for an answer, "Is she dead?"

The old woman looked at him for a minute blinking her watery eyes, and then suddenly broke into a shrill, long-drawn wail. The Baron needed to hear no more.

As though in answer to the old woman's cry, a thin piping complaint came from the bundle in her lap.

At the sound the red blood flashed up into the Baron's face. "What is that you have there?" said he, pointing to the bundle upon the old woman's knees.

She drew back the coverings and there lay a poor, weak, little baby, that once again raised its faint reedy pipe.

"It is your son," said Ursela, "that the dear Baroness left behind her when the holy angels took her to Paradise. She blessed him and called him Otto before she left us."

• • • •

CHAPTER 4
The White Cross on the Hill

WHERE THE GLASSY WATERS of the River Rhine, holding upon its bosom a mimic picture of the blue sky and white clouds floating above, runs smoothly around a jutting point of land, St. Michaelsburg, rising from the reedy banks of the stream, sweeps up with a smooth swell until it cuts sharp and clear against the sky. Stubby vineyards covered its earthy breast, and field and garden and orchard crowned its brow, where lay the Monastery of St. Michaelsburg—"*The White Cross on the Hill.*" There within the white walls, where the warm yellow sunlight slept, all was peaceful quietness, broken only now and then by the crowing of the cock or the clamorous cackle of a hen, the lowing of kine or the bleating of goats, a solitary voice in prayer, the faint accord of distant singing, or the resonant toll of the monastery bell from the high-peaked belfry that overlooked the hill and valley and the smooth, far-winding stream. No other sounds broke the stillness, for in this peaceful haven was never heard the clash of armor, the ring of iron-shod hoofs, or the hoarse call to arms.

All men were not wicked and cruel and fierce in that dark, far-away age; all were not robbers and terror-spreading tyrants, even in that time when men's hands were against their neighbors, and war and rapine dwelt in place of peace and justice.

Abbot Otto, of St. Michaelsburg, was a gentle, patient, pale-faced old man; his white hands were soft and smooth, and no one would have thought that they could have known the harsh touch of sword-hilt and lance. And yet, in the days of the Emperor Frederick—the grandson of the great Red-beard—no one stood higher in the prowess of arms than he. But all at once—for why, no man could tell—a change came over him, and in the flower of his youth and fame and growing power he gave up everything in life and entered the quiet sanctuary of that white monastery on the hill-side, so far away from the tumult and the conflict of the world in which he had lived.

Some said that it was because the lady he had loved had loved his brother, and that when they were married Otto of Wolbergen had left the church with a broken heart.

But such stories are old songs that have been sung before.

CLATTER! CLATTER! Jingle! jingle! It was a full-armed knight that came riding up the steep hill road that wound from left to right and right to left amid the vineyards on the slopes of St. Michaelsburg. Polished helm and corselet blazed in the noon sunlight, for no knight in those days dared to ride the roads except in full armor. In front of him the solitary knight carried a bundle wrapped in the folds of his coarse gray cloak.

It was a sorely sick man that rode up the heights of St. Michaelsburg. His head hung upon his breast through the faintness of weariness and pain; for it was the Baron Conrad.

He had left his bed of sickness that morning, had saddled his horse in the gray dawn with his own hands, and had ridden away into the misty twilight of the forest without the knowledge of anyone excepting the porter, who, winking and blinking in the bewilderment of his broken slumber, had opened the gates to the sick man, hardly knowing what he was doing, until he beheld his master far away, clattering down the steep bridle-path.

Eight leagues had he ridden that day with neither a stop nor a stay; but now at last the end of his journey had come, and he drew rein under the shade of the great wooden gateway of St. Michaelsburg.

He reached up to the knotted rope and gave it a pull, and from within sounded the answering ring of the porter's bell. By and by a little wicket opened in the great wooden portals, and the gentle, wrinkled face of old Brother Benedict, the porter, peeped out at the strange iron-clad visitor and the great black war-horse, streaked and wet with the sweat of the journey, flecked and dappled with flakes of foam. A few words passed between them, and then the little window was closed again; and within, the shuffling pat of the sandalled feet sounded fainter and fainter, as Brother Benedict bore the message from Baron Conrad to Abbot Otto, and the mail-clad figure was left alone, sitting there as silent as a statue.

By and by the footsteps sounded again; there came a noise of clattering chains and the rattle of the key in the lock, and the rasping of the bolts dragged back. Then the gate swung slowly open, and

Baron Conrad rode into the shelter of the White Cross, and as the hoofs of his war-horse clashed upon the stones of the courtyard within, the wooden gate swung slowly to behind him.

ABBOT OTTO STOOD by the table when Baron Conrad entered the high-vaulted room from the farther end. The light from the oriel window behind the old man shed broken rays of light upon him, and seemed to frame his thin gray hairs with a golden glory. His white, delicate hand rested upon the table beside him, and upon some sheets of parchment covered with rows of ancient Greek writing which he had been engaged in deciphering.

Clank! clank! clank! Baron Conrad strode across the stone floor, and then stopped short in front of the good old man.

"What dost thou seek here, my son?" said the Abbot.

"I seek sanctuary for my son and thy brother's grandson," said the Baron Conrad, and he flung back the folds of his cloak and showed the face of the sleeping babe.

For a while the Abbot said nothing, but stood gazing dreamily at the baby. After a while he looked up. "And the child's mother," said he—"what hath she to say at this?"

"She hath naught to say," said Baron Conrad, hoarsely, and then stopped short in his speech. "She is dead," said he, at last, in a husky voice, "and is with God's angels in paradise."

The Abbot looked intently in the Baron's face. "So!" said he, under his breath, and then for the first time noticed how white and drawn was the Baron's face. "Art sick thyself?" he asked.

"Ay," said the Baron, "I have come from death's door. But that is no matter. Wilt thou take this little babe into sanctuary? My house is a vile, rough place, and not fit for such as he, and his mother with the blessed saints in heaven." And once more Conrad of Drachenhausen's face began twitching with the pain of his thoughts.

"Yes," said the old man, gently, "he shall live here," and he stretched out his hands and took the babe. "Would," said he, "that all the little children in these dark times might be thus brought to the house of God, and there learn mercy and peace, instead of rapine and war."

For a while he stood looking down in silence at the baby in his arms, but with his mind far away upon other things. At last he roused himself with a start. "And thou," said he to the Baron Conrad—"hath not thy heart been chastened and softened by this? Surely thou wilt not go back to thy old life of rapine and extortion?"

"Nay," said Baron Conrad, gruffly, "I will rob the city swine no longer, for that was the last thing that my dear one asked of me."

The old Abbot's face lit up with a smile. "I am right glad that thy heart was softened, and that thou art willing at last to cease from war and violence."

"Nay," cried the Baron, roughly, "I said nothing of ceasing from war. By heaven, no! I will have revenge!" And he clashed his iron foot upon the floor and clinched his fists and ground his teeth together. "Listen," said he, "and I will tell thee how my troubles happened. A fortnight ago I rode out upon an expedition against a caravan of fat burghers in the valley of Gruenhoffen. They outnumbered us many to one, but city swine such as they are not of the stuff to stand against our kind for a long time. Nevertheless, while the men-at-arms who guarded the caravan were staying us with pike and cross-bow from behind a tree which they had felled in front of a high bridge the others had driven the pack-horses off, so that by the time we had forced the bridge they were a league or more away. We pushed after them as hard as we were able, but when we came up with them we found that they had been joined by Baron Frederick of Trutz-Drachen, to whom for three years and more the burghers of Gruenstadt have been paying a tribute for his protection against others. Then again they made a stand, and this time the Baron Frederick himself was with them. But though the dogs fought well, we were forcing them back, and might have got the better of them, had not my horse stumbled upon a sloping stone, and so fell and rolled over upon me. While I lay there with my horse upon me, Baron Frederick ran me down with his lance, and gave me that foul wound that came so near to slaying me—and did slay my dear wife. Nevertheless, my men were able to bring me out from that press and away, and we had bitten the Trutz-Drachen dogs so deep that they were too sore to follow us, and so let us go our way in peace. But when those fools of mine brought me to my castle they bore me lying upon a litter to my wife's chamber. There she beheld me, and, thinking me dead, swooned a death-swoon, so that she only lived long enough to bless her new-born babe and name it Otto, for you, her father's brother. But, by heavens! I will have revenge, root and branch, upon that vile tribe, the Roderburgs of Trutz-Drachen. Their great-grandsire built that castle in scorn of Baron Casper in the old days; their grandsire slew my father's grandsire; Baron Nicholas slew two of our kindred; and now this Baron

Frederick gives me that foul wound and kills my dear wife through my body." Here the Baron stopped short; then of a sudden, shaking his fist above his head, he cried out in his hoarse voice: "I swear by all the saints in heaven, either the red cock shall crow over the roof of Trutz-Drachen or else it shall crow over my house! The black dog shall sit on Baron Frederick's shoulders or else he shall sit on mine!" Again he stopped, and fixing his blazing eyes upon the old man, "Hearest thou that, priest?" said he, and broke into a great boisterous laugh.

Abbot Otto sighed heavily, but he tried no further to persuade the other into different thoughts.

"Thou art wounded," said he, at last, in a gentle voice; "at least stay here with us until thou art healed."

"Nay," said the Baron, roughly, "I will tarry no longer than to hear thee promise to care for my child."

"I promise," said the Abbot; "but lay aside thy armor, and rest."

"Nay," said the Baron, "I go back again to-day."

At this the Abbot cried out in amazement: "Sure thou, wounded man, would not take that long journey without a due stay for resting! Think! Night will be upon thee before thou canst reach home again, and the forests are beset with wolves."

The Baron laughed. "Those are not the wolves I fear," said he. "Urge me no further, I must return to-night; yet if thou hast a mind to do me a kindness thou canst give me some food to eat and a flask of your golden Michaelsburg; beyond these, I ask no further favor of any man, be he priest or layman."

"What comfort I can give thee thou shalt have," said the Abbot, in his patient voice, and so left the room to give the needful orders, bearing the babe with him.

• • • •

FOR THE NEXT TWELVE YEARS, young Otto lives among the simple, loving monks of the monastery, far from the bloody ways of his father. When the Baron finally returns, it is to claim him as his heir to glory and honor in warfare. So, against the wishes of the Abbot, the two depart for castle Drachenhausen, where a far from glorious fate awaits the boy.

Related books include: Roger L. Green's *The Adventures of Robin Hood* and *King Arthur and His Knights of the Round Table*; Julek Heller and Deirdre Headon's *Knights*; *Knights in Armor*, edited by John D. Clare; Bernard Miles's *Robin Hood: His Life and Legend*; and Robert Newman's *Merlin's Mistake* and *The Testing of Tertius*.

Also see *Castle*, a sixty-minute video tour of a thirteenth-century Welsh castle.

JOSEPH: HIS DREAM

by Walter de la Mare

From the World's Greatest Anthology

It would be the height of foolishness to compile an anthology of this kind without including something from the greatest anthology of all time. No anthology before or since has contained such beloved and widely read stories of romance, war, tragedy, travel, and history.

I mean, of course, the Bible—especially the Old Testament.

My favorite single paragraph to introduce the Old Testament is this one from biblical scholar Richard Elliott Friedman in his book *Who Wrote the Bible?*: "People have been reading the Bible for nearly two thousand years. They have taken it literally, figuratively, or symbolically. They have regarded it as divinely dictated, revealed, or inspired, or as a human creation. They have acquired more copies of it than any other book. It is quoted (or misquoted) more often than the others as well. It is called a great work of literature, the first work of history. It is at the heart of Christianity and Judaism. Ministers, priests, and rabbis preach it. Scholars spend their lives studying and teaching it in universities and seminaries. People read it, study it, admire it, disdain it, write about it, argue about it, and love it. People have lived by it and died for it. And we do not know who wrote it."

The consensus that evolved through the centuries of scholarly debate and bloody persecutions is this: The various books in the Old Testament were written by different people, as were the Five Books of Moses, but with no definite names. Through the ages the stories were gradually stitched together into one form. The word *Bible* comes from the Latin word *biblia*, plural for "books." The Holy Bible, as it is commonly accepted today, consists of the Old Testament and the New Testament, the former dealing with the Hebrew world before

Christ, the latter dealing with the life of Christ and his followers.

The Old Testament was originally written in Hebrew, mostly between 1100 B.C. and 100 B.C., and consists of laws, songs, stories or narratives, poems, maxims or proverbs, histories, and prayers. None of the *original* parchments or tablets have survived. All we have left is a text that has been transcribed by hand over and over through the centuries. In the process, it has been edited, compiled, translated, misread, misunderstood, misspelled, condensed, transposed, and annotated. For one American example of how changes have occurred through the ages, consider the translation of the Bible published in 1833 by Noah Webster, of dictionary fame. In it he removed socially offensive words such as *stink*.

The retelling or translation of the Bible into everyday language might seem as simple as translating a STOP sign from English into Spanish—unless you know the history of this special book and the people who established themselves as its special guardians. Until the early seventeenth century, the Bible was available only in Hebrew, Greek, and Latin. Since few commoners understood those languages, the religious hierarchy established themselves as the guardians and gatekeepers of God's Word.

In 1525, when an Englishman named William Tyndale dared to publish the New Testament in English so "every plough-boy" might be able to read it, the clergy saw him as a threat to their authority, pursued him through Europe, captured and tried him as a heretic, then strangled him and burned his body. Only through decades of persecution, courage, and rebellion was the Bible's freedom won for the plough-boy reader and his family. (See Scott O'Dell's novel about Tyndale, *The Hawk That Dare Not Hunt by Day*.)

The "anthology" called the Bible is considered the model for nearly all literature because it contains the most enduring and constant theme in all literature: quest. Someone loses a valuable possession, sets out to redeem it, faces difficult obstacles, and finally regains it. A quest is present in nearly all the myths, legends, folk and fairy tales, ballads, novels, and soap operas from yesterday and today. But the earliest record of quest is found in the Bible when Adam and Eve lose the eternal happiness of the Garden of Eden and must spend their earthly lives redeeming themselves in the eyes of God. It is not a big jump from their difficult quest to that of Oliver Twist, Hänsel and Gretel, Aladdin, Robin Hood, the Swiss Family Robinson, Peter Rabbit, Jim Hawkins, Huckleberry Finn, Dorothy in Oz, Mowgli, Runaway Ralph, and James in his Giant Peach. They're all on quests.

As for obstacles along the path of quest, not even Dickens could have filled his melodramas with the various obstacles a reader finds in the Bible: murder, famine, war, plague, flood, betrayal, kidnapping, poisoning, lynching, stoning, and enslavement. Little wonder that it is still regarded as the ultimate plot source, as well as the ultimate source of personal inspiration.

As uplifting and inspiring as the Bible might be, even its staunchest believers would not go as far as Menelik II, the emperor of Ethiopia who liberated his country from Italy and died' in 1913. As Clifton Fadiman explains in the *Little, Brown Book of Anecdotes*, Menelik was convinced that if he ate a few pages of the Bible whenever he was ill, it would cure his ailment. Whether his homemade remedy worked or not, it can be reported that it did no harm—until 1913, when he fell severely ill. At that point, he ordered the entire Book of Kings to be fed to him, page by page. He died before completing it. (I know this anecdote is hard to swallow, but it is true.)

It really doesn't matter whether you approach this next selection religiously or just as literature. In either case, it is still a powerful story. Two thousand years after it was written, its themes of jealousy, intrigue, punishment, and forgiveness are common commodities in the daily soap operas of the twentieth century—be they in the schoolyard, in the corporate boardroom, or on daytime television. It is the story of Joseph and his brothers from the Book of Genesis.

The schoolyard connection with this particular Bible story is not farfetched. In 1967, two college classmates in England wrote a musical version of "Joseph" at the urging of a schoolmaster, incorporating French café music, calypso, country, jazz, and rock music. When it was performed at St. Paul's Junior School in London, one of its audience enthusiasts was both a St. Paul's parent and the music critic for *The Sunday Times* of London. His subsequent review earned the play more public performances in London and off Broadway, and, with the years and various revisions, it became a kind of cult musical. Eventually, the two young collaborators, Andrew Lloyd Webber and Tim Rice, proceeded with other projects, such as *Jesus Christ Superstar* (1971) and *Evita* (1978). Finally, in 1982, their original musical arrived on Broadway, entitled *Joseph and the Amazing Technicolor Dreamcoat*, and it is still frequently revived and performed on the road today.

The retelling used here is by Walter de la Mare, a celebrated English poet, from his *Stories from the Bible*. I suppose it is appropriate that de la Mare should eventually take his turn as a religious storyteller, since he often claimed that the first coin he ever earned was from the archbishop of Canterbury, who paid him for holding his train during a processional at de la Mare's childhood school. De la Mare left school at age seventeen to become a bookkeeper, writing stories and verse in his spare time, until at age thirty-five he resigned to write full-time for both adults and children.

Keeping in mind the excitement they held for him as a child, the author hoped these retellings in contemporary language would render favorite Old Testament stories more accessible to young readers, without losing any of their flavor and drama. Here, then, is the beginning of the story of Joseph and his brothers, as retold by Walter de la Mare.

• • • •

AFTER THE DEATH of his father Isaac, Jacob, with his whole household, his sons, his servants, his flocks and herds and sheep-dogs, came to sojourn in the green and wooded vale of Hebron which is in Canaan. Here they pitched their tents, and led their flocks afield, for Hebron lies in a country rich in pastures and in clear well-springs of water.

Now of all his eleven sons Jacob loved Joseph the best. Until Benjamin was born, he was the youngest of them all, and he was too the only son of his beautiful mother Rachel, who was very dear to Jacob. Not only for this reason but for the child's own sake also, Joseph was Jacob's best-beloved; and, with no thought of any ill that might come of it, he favored him in all things, delighted to talk to him, and he gave him many presents.

He made him also a loose tunic coat of many colors, sewn together in delicate needlework in a bright pattern, and with sleeves to the wrists. And Joseph, being in age still little more than a child, delighted in his bright-colored coat. But when his brothers saw it, they envied and hated him. For in this his father had yet again shown his great love for Joseph and had favored him above themselves, and they could not speak a friendly or peaceable word to him.

As Joseph grew older, and in all that he was and did showed himself more and more unlike themselves, jealousy gnawed in their hearts like the fretting of a canker-worm. Above everything, they scorned, and even began to fear him, because of his dreams. They too, as they lay with their flocks, wrapped in their goat-skin cloaks beneath the dews and burning stars of the night, had their dreams; but these either vanished on waking or were broken and senseless.

But the dreams that came to Joseph in his sleep were not only of a strange reality, but seemed to carry with them a hidden meaning. They were like the crystal shimmering pictures of the air, called *mirage*, seen by wanderers in the desert, the reflections of things afar off—but far off in time not in space.

One late summer evening when he chanced to be with them in the fields, and sat a little apart from them, lost to all around him in the light of the moon—a moon so dazzling clear that even the colors of his coat were faintly distinguishable—they asked him sourly what ailed him.

"He sits out there," said one of them, "mumbling his thoughts like an old sheep too sick to graze." Joseph answered that he had been haunted all day by the memory of a dream. He was but a boy and he told his dream out to them, thinking no evil.

"I dreamed," he said, "it was the time of harvest, and we were reaping together in the fields. It was sunrise, and the corn being cut, we were tying it up into sheaves. Even now I seem to feel the roughness of the binder in my hand, though the place we were in was none I have ever seen in waking. I tied up my sheaf and laid it down, as you did your sheaves. And in my dream the sheaf that I had bound rose up as if of its own motion from the stubble and stood up there in the burning sunshine, and your own sheaves, that lay scattered around it, rose up also. And as I looked, they bowed themselves and made obeisance to my sheaf that was in the midst of them. Now what can be the meaning of such a dream, and why does it stay so continually in my mind?"

His brothers tried in vain to hide their anger.

"Meaning, forsooth!" they said. "Who art thou that we should bow ourselves down before thee, and that thou shouldst have dominion over us? The place for thee is with the women and sucklings in the tents." And they hated him the more.

Joseph was silent and made no answer, but the dream in its strangeness and beauty stayed on in his mind. He knew it must surely have a meaning, if only he could discover it; and when he dreamed again, he told his dream not only to his brothers, but to his father.

"I dreamed," he said, and his face was lit up at memory of it, "and, behold, in my dream it was the dead of night, yet the sun was in the heavens and the moon also. They shone there together, and I could see the stars. There was no wind, and all was still; and I counted the brightest stars, and they were eleven. And as I looked and wondered, it seemed that not only these eleven stars, but the sun and the moon stooped and bowed in their places in heaven before me and made obeisance. Then I awoke."

His brothers listened with louring faces, glancing covertly one at another, but Jacob his father rebuked him.

"Cast such crazy fancies out of thy mind," he said. "And God forbid that it should be even so much as in thy dreams that I and thy mother and thy brethren should come to bow ourselves down before thee and be humbled before thee!" None the less, the dream disquieted him, and there came a day when he remembered it again.

It chanced one evening after this, and when Joseph had passed his seventeenth birthday, that his father called him into his tent. He bade him set out on the morrow and go in search of his brothers, who had led their sheep to new pastures beyond the vale of Hebron, and not far distant from a town called Shechem.

"Go thy way early and seek them out," he said, "for they are among strangers and enemies. Ask them how they fare, and see thyself if it be well with them and with the flocks; and when you have rested, bring me word of them again. And may the Lord watch over you!"

Proud and happy in the trust his father put in him, Joseph rose up at daybreak next morning, kissed him, bade him good-bye, and set out at once. The day was calm and fair. It was springtime, the air was sweet with birds, and on the wayside and in the hollows of the hills hosts of wild flowers shone in their colors in the sun, crocus and anemone and narcissus. And as he went on his way, no omen chilled his heart of what was in store for him, and no foreboding that every step he took was towards a strange country from which in this life he would return home again no more.

He came at length to Shechem, an old walled and beautiful city of Samaria that with its gardens lay in a valley between two mountains, and rang with the music of more than a score of water-springs. But his brothers were no longer there, and loth to return to his father without news of them, he pressed on into country unknown to him, and lost his way.

A stranger met him as he was wandering at random in the wild. He saw how young he was, and that in spite of being anxious and footsore he still held on his way, so he hailed him and inquired whom he was seeking.

"It is my brothers," he said. "They are shepherds, but have gone on from Shechem where I looked to find them, and now I have lost my way. Tell me, I pray thee, what place is this and where it is likely they have gone?"

It chanced that this man had not only seen the shepherds but had overheard them in talk one with another, and he told Joseph they were now in all likelihood with their flocks near Dothan.

"It lies," he said, "on a hillside above its vineyards where there is a plentiful well of water." And he told him how he would find it. He repeated what he had said, "Follow on as I have told thee, and thou canst not miss the way."

He turned and watched until Joseph was out of sight. And Joseph hastened on eagerly, all weariness forgotten. Now on the northern side of Dothan there were hills, their slopes shagged with gray-green groves of olives, but on the side towards the south, it was flat country, so that his brothers, who were sitting there with their flocks and staring idly out across the grassy plain, spied out Joseph while he was still afar off. And they muttered morosely one to another: "Behold, the dreamer cometh!"

As they watched him making his way towards them in a coat of many colors, the hatred that had long smoldered in their hearts broke into flame, and some of them began devising together to murder him.

"He is alone and at our mercy," they said. "And here there is none to heed his cries or tell the tale. Let us kill him, then, and hide his body where it will never be found. Then we can go back with a tale that a wild beast must have attacked and devoured him. And who shall deny it?"

But Reuben, the eldest, overheard them muttering together. "No, no; shed no blood," he said. "If you must be rid of him, take him alive and fling him into that pit yonder. But use no violence, or let any harm come to him."

This he said because he himself intended, when the opportunity came, to set Joseph free, and to bring him back in safety again to his father. The rest of them argued and wrangled, some on this side and some on that, but at length they agreed together not to kill him. When Reuben was sure of it, and that no harm would come to Joseph until he could come back and take him into a place of safety, he left them and went away alone.

Joseph drew near, rejoiced to be at the end of his long journey and to see his brethren sitting in peace together with their flocks. But before he could so much as give them greeting or tell them why he had come, they seized him, stifled his cries, stripped off his coat of many colors, and bound him hand and foot. They carried him off to a deep dried-up pit or water-cistern. Into this pit they flung him down, and having dragged back the heavy stone again that had lain over the mouth of the pit, they left him there, returned to their camping-place, and sat down to eat.

While they were eating together, some jesting and others silent and uneasy, they heard in the distance shouts and voices borne on the windless air over the flat country. They lifted up their eyes and saw afar off a company of Ishmaelites, merchantmen, with their camels. These fierce swarthy tribesmen were journeying from Gilead which lay beyond the Jordan, a region famed for its balsam and groves of tree laurel, musical with the murmur of wood-doves and songs of birds. They were following the track of the great caravans that would bring them to the sand-dunes on the coast of the Great Sea, and then, on, and at length into Egypt. Their camels, neckleted with chains of metal, their links shaped like the crescent moon, were laden with sweet-smelling spiceries and fragrant gums which they had brought with them to barter or sell to the Egyptian embalmers and physicians.

When Judah, who had sat silent and aloof, saw these men with camels, he said to his brethren: "See now, here is a way out. If we leave the lad in the pit, he will perish of thirst and we shall be no less guilty of his death than if we had killed him with our own hands. Let us hail these accursed Ishmaelites, and sell him for what he will fetch. That way we shall see some profit in what we do, and we shall be for ever rid of him and his dreams. But not death, I say—for is he not our brother, the son of our father, and of our own flesh and blood?"

To this, though sullenly, they agreed. It was near sunset when, dragging away the heavy well-stone again, his brothers drew Joseph up out of the pit and freed him from the thongs with which they had bound him. He stood half-naked and trembling, faint with the heat of the pit. The sun smote blindingly on his eyes after the pitchy darkness in which he had lain—beaten and bruised and unable to stir hand or foot. He watched, while his brothers bargained with the crafty dark-browed Ishmaelites. They agreed at last to sell him to them for twenty pieces of silver, and divided the money between them. This done, the Ishmaelites knotted the cord that still shackled Joseph's wrists to the saddle of one of their camels, and continued on their way.

When Reuben came back at nightfall to the pit, called, and found it empty, he was smitten with remorse. He rent his clothes—as was the custom with these wandering tribesmen when to their anguish any great grief or disaster befell them—and he returned in despair to the camping-place. There he found his brethren and their flocks, hedged about with branches of thorn as a protection against wild animals.

"The lad is gone," he said, "and I, whither now shall *I* go?" But some of them pretended to be asleep, and none made answer.

Next day they killed a kid and dabbled Joseph's coat in its blood, then turned homewards with their flocks, and came at length to their own place and to their father's tent, and, with the pretence of grief on their faces, stood before him. His first thought was for Joseph, but he looked in vain for him.

Jacob questioned them anxiously. And when he told them how Joseph had been sent out to seek them in the valley of Shechem, they stared one at another, as though in horror and dismay. Then one of them named Simeon took out the torn and blood-bedabbled coat and spread it out before him.

"We knew nothing of what thou sayest until now," he said. "But on our way back from Dothan where we lay, we passed by a thicket of thorn trees in a wild and solitary place, and we found this. It is so bedraggled and drenched with blood that we cannot be sure if it be the coat you gave Joseph. See now, is this thy son's coat, or no?"

Jacob looked and trembled and turned away. "It is my son's coat," he said. "My son, Joseph! An evil beast hath devoured him; Joseph is without doubt rent in pieces. I shall never see his face again!"

He bowed himself in his grief and wept. He rent his clothes, and put on sackcloth like one who goes in mourning for the dead, and withdrew himself from them all, and remained in solitude for many days. His daughters and his sons, grown sick of their own treachery, came to him in hope to comfort him, but he refused to be comforted.

"Beyond the grave," he said, "but not until then, we two shall meet again. And my son Joseph will see how I have mourned for him." And he continued to grieve for Joseph, so great was the love he bore him. Only in Benjamin, who was his youngest son, did Jacob find solace as time went by. He loved and treasured him not only for his own sake but because, now that Joseph was gone, he was the only child left of his mother Rachel, for she had died when he was born.

• • • •

JOSEPH IS EVENTUALLY SOLD in the slave market, bought by an Egyptian who makes the boy his personal servant. Through the years he is given more and more responsibility, until he becomes overseer of everything the Egyptian owns. But when his master's lovesick wife shamelessly proposes that Joseph join her in betraying her husband's trust, Joseph spurns her advances. This so enrages her that she seeks revenge by lying to her husband about Joseph, and the young Hebrew is thrown into prison.

But the Lord continues to reward Joseph's trust, and eventually the young man wins such respect from the prison warden that he is put in charge of all other prisoners. Thus it is that he comes to meet the pharaoh's chief baker and butler, who have recently landed in prison. When each of them has a disquieting dream, Joseph is able to interpret the dreams correctly, each predicting moments in their future lives. This sets in motion the events by which Joseph will win not only his freedom, but also the opportunity to sit in judgment of his brothers.

There is an excellent audiocassette entitled *Walter de la Mare Speaking and Reading* (Harper-Caedmon).

Readers might also enjoy *Gods and Pharaohs from Egyptian Mythology* by Geraldine Harris.

Old Chestnuts

· · · · · · · · · · ·

Two famous poems and the
little-known stories behind them.

When Poetry
(and Oratory) Was King

In this section, we meet three members of an endangered species—famous poems. To truly understand why they are endangered, one needs to know the land and time from which they came.

These narrative verses began life almost a century ago, a time that was strikingly different from the one in which we live today. Contrary to what youth sometimes believes, in the "prehistoric" days before the automobile, radio, television, and videos, people did not live in a cultural vacuum, blowing out the candle every night at eight o'clock.

Local and traveling theater productions, recitations, and speeches were a regular part of community life at the opera house or the church hall. Having grown up tuned to the sounds of words instead of moving pictures, people in those times had extraordinary attention and listening spans. Lincoln's Gettysburg Address is an example of this phenomenon. Fifteen thousand visitors gathered in the tiny Pennsylvania village for the dedication of a new cemetery. What attracted them in such large numbers was not the appearance of the president of the United States. Indeed, the program printed for the occasion listed Lincoln for "Remarks," and that is just what he gave—272 memorable words in three minutes.

As the president knew fully well, the real attraction for the day was the man hired to give the "Oration," Edward Everett. The most famous orator in the country at that time, Everett was enough of a drawing card for the event's organizers to reschedule the day to fit his personal calendar. That day, speaking in the open air, with no microphone, no amphitheater, and no commercial interruption or coffee break, Everett riveted his audience for two solid hours—just what he was paid and expected to do.

Unlike the fifteen-second sound bites we meet on the nightly news, speeches of such length were commonplace in those days. The Lincoln-Douglas debates were three hours long. Just ten years after the death of Lincoln, an author traveled from one American city to another and stood on a stage beside a small table and a pitcher of water, reading at length from his books—no slides, overheads, or sound effects, just the spirited voice of Charles Dickens. His tour was hugely successful, drawing as many as six thousand people in an evening.

The public's interest in speech-making was fed directly by the classroom, where students were required to memorize famous historical speeches and long narrative poems from their textbooks and primers. Two of the most famous speakers of the last century—one free, the other enslaved, but both self-educated—were studying the same oratory textbook at almost the same time. Young Lincoln in Illinois and young Frederick Douglass in Maryland both memorized from *The Columbian Orator* (see page 295).

In keeping with the community's interest, schools and churches held oratory and debate competitions that were the equivalent of today's dance or music recitals—except the performers then were displaying their memories instead of their dance steps.

Though some graduates went on to apply their verbal gymnastics to the world of politics, most did not. They were content simply to move on to the community platform, where narrative poems and ballads had become increasingly popular as entertainment. In part, this was because the rhythm and rhyme as well as the narrative made them easier to memorize. Another factor was that the audience loved them. After all, the people usually were gathered to be entertained and narrative worked best for this purpose, especially if there was some humor in it.

With the advent of electrical amusements, such gatherings began to decline (some would argue the decline actually began four centuries earlier, when printing first distracted people from listening to reading). Though schools valiantly continued to emphasize formal recitations until the 1950s, by then many educators were convinced that such rote memorization stilted a child's imagination and initiative, like some kind of mental coloring book. By 1960, just about all that remained of academic memorization was the multiplication tables.

My generation (I was born in 1941) was perhaps the last to experience the classroom or home interest in speeches or narrative poems. I can recall vividly the sight and sound of my father shaving each morning while reciting a poem or speech he had learned as a child in the classroom. When I grew up and married I discovered an Irish father-in-law who needed no encouragement to launch into a long poem from his Boston childhood.

The community gatherings of a century ago whetted the public's appetite for poetry and simultaneously spread the fame of new poems. This general interest was reflected in the fact that most newspapers ran poetry—by both their own writers and their readers. Some papers turned over a whole page each week to verse. In fact, the initial popularity of "The Star-Spangled Banner" can be attributed to its appearance as a poem in newspapers throughout America long before anyone thought of it as an anthem. As late as the 1950s, one of New York's tabloid newspapers was still running the daily verse of a Broadway columnist named Nick Kenny, the last of his breed.

Recently a best-selling novelist declined the adjective *famous* in conjunction with his profession. His reasoning was this: In order for a novelist to be famous, his novels must be famous. And today, he said, that is impossible. The word *famous* can be defined as "widely talked about." People today, he argued, do not widely discuss books. They talk about videos, movie stars, talk-show hosts—but not writers.

Apply that argument to poetry. Compare today with a time when poems were commonly recited and applauded, and one could say, as I did earlier, that famous poets and famous poems are an endangered species. So before they disappear entirely, here are "Casey at the Bat" and "The Cremation of Sam Magee," two old chestnuts that brought audiences to their feet for decades. They are still familiar enough for some Americans to have at least heard about them. What few know, however, are the stories behind them and their authors.

CASEY AT THE BAT

by Ernest Lawrence Thayer

and

CASEY'S REVENGE

by Grantland Rice

Ernest Lawrence Thayer

A Legendary One-Hit Poet

Arguably the most famous and certainly one of the most beloved poems in American history has led a charmed life.

It is a poem not about war or the flag, not about flowers or sunsets, not about fences or roads less traveled. It is about a sport, a sport the author wasn't even interested in. He apparently wasn't all that interested in the poem either, because he never bothered to sign his name to it. Within a handful of years the poem became a national favorite, yet the poet, a straight-A Harvard graduate, earned only five dollars from it and never wrote anything significant again.

A history professor named Eugene C. Murdock once wrote an entire book on the history of the poem (*Mighty Casey: All-American*), which pointed to a string of lucky circumstances that needed to occur in order for the poem to have survived. As I explain the poem's history, consider what Murdock was referring to.

The poem's author, Ernest Lawrence Thayer, was the son of a wealthy New England mill owner. He graduated with high honors in philosophy from Harvard (note his class picture with this profile), and then took a year off to travel in Europe. Upon returning, he received a request from a college classmate who had dropped out of school. The classmate had left Harvard before he could be thrown out for having small porcelain toilet bowls delivered to all his professors with their names inscribed on them. Eventually he would become one of the most influential men in America, as well as the notorious real-life inspiration for the movie classic *Citizen Kane*, but when he contacted Thayer he was only William Randolph Hearst, the boy publisher of the *San Francisco Chronicle*, which was owned by his wealthy father. Hearst remembered Thayer's sense of humor and brightness from their days together on the college humor magazine and he wondered if Thayer would be interested in writing for the *Chronicle*.

Thayer had no ambitions to be a journalist, but he did want to see another part of the country, and so he took the job. Soon thereafter he read a collection of ballads and was inspired to try writing some himself. For the next few months, he wrote one for each Sunday edition—for which he was paid the sum of five dollars per poem. The byline under each was simply "Phin," short for his college nickname, "Phinny." This would subsequently cause him considerable headaches when a variety of people freely and falsely laid claim to being the poem's real author.

Be that as it may, on Sunday morning, June 3, 1888, the following title appeared above a poem on page 4 of the *Chronicle*:

CASEY AT THE BAT
A Ballad of the Republic, Sung in the Year 1888

Thayer never explained the reason for the subtitle, but poet Donald Hall, in his brilliant essay to commemorate the hundredth anniversary of the poem (*Casey at the Bat: A Centennial Edition*), explained that the nation was still healing its wounds from the Civil War twenty-five years earlier. Perhaps Thayer believed the game could aid in that healing process, since it was already the national pastime and had been played by Yankee and Confederate soldiers alike during rest periods and in prison camps.

There was no immediate public response to its printing, and no other newspapers republished it. To all outward appearances, "Casey at the Bat" came and went as quietly as the fog in the bay. And that's where it all would have ended were it not for the lucky circumstance that a celebrated novelist of the time, Archibald Clavering Gunter, was in San Francisco that weekend and was impressed enough by the poem to cut it out and stuff it into his wallet.

The clipping rested there in obscurity for the next year. And then, another chance circumstance: Gunter happened to see a notice in a New York newspaper announcing that the McCaull Light Opera

Company was scheduling a "baseball night." Two actors in the company, Digby Bell and De Wolf Hopper, were devoted baseball fans, and they had convinced the management that such a promotion would pack the house, especially if they invited the New York Giants and their day's opponents to be honored guests. Gunter immediately called on the manager of the theater company and offered the wrinkled newspaper clipping as the perfect piece for Hopper to recite for the event. McCaull and Hopper agreed.

Once more, however, fate wavered. Since the verse was brief, Hopper postponed memorizing it until the Thursday evening before the Friday-night performance. What he thought would be a routine task, however, suddenly became impossible. On that day he received a telegram from New England notifying him that his young son had contracted diphtheria, an often fatal disease. They would know by the next morning if the boy would survive.

Hopper slept little that night and gave no thought to the poem. The morning brought him no relief because a severe winter storm had severed the telegraph lines in southern New England and delayed the news. Hopper finally told the company's head, "I can't commit this piece. I can't call my name until I hear how the boy is."

When word arrived at 11:00 A.M. that the boy had survived, the rejoicing Hopper memorized the poem in an hour. That evening it met thunderous applause from the audience. Yet, as good as the reception was, Hopper did not have occasion to recite it again for two years. And then one evening, finding a musical comedy's performance lagging, he recalled the earlier impact of the piece and inserted it into the program. Once again the audience went wild. From that point on, it became the staple of Hopper's performances. In his lifetime, he recited or performed it more than ten thousand times.

Meanwhile, what had happened to "Casey's" author? The pressure of daily creativity, each day trying to outdo the previous day, jumping from writing advertisements to reporting to features to obituaries to editorials—all of it proved to be too much for Thayer. After eighteen months at the *Chronicle* his health began to break and he returned to the East. He did write a few ballads for the *New York Journal* a few years later, but they were as forgettable as everything else he wrote—except for "Casey."

For four years, Hopper tried unsuccessfully to locate the author named "Phin." Finally, by happy circumstance, he was performing in Worcester, Massachusetts, when he received a note inviting him to meet the poem's author at a local club. Thayer was by then managing his father's manufacturing properties in the area and had no idea of the poem's growing national fame until he met Hopper that night. During their meeting, Thayer was persuaded to recite the poem himself. Slightly built and slightly deaf, he spoke in a soft, Harvard-accented voice. In his memoirs years later, Hopper recalled the thousands of people he'd heard perform the poem. Thayer's performance, he admitted candidly, was "the worst of all."

As the poem's fame grew, not only did numerous people come forth professing to be the poem's author, even more claimed to be the famous Casey himself. Baseball historians debated at great length who it might have been, but few wanted to hear the truth, as often as Thayer told it in later years. It was too bland to be true. He declared that there was no basis in fact for Casey's performance. (As an aside, the famous Charles Dillon "Casey" Stengel had nothing to do with the poem. His nickname was derived from the initials of his hometown, Kansas City—"K.C.")

Casey himself, however, was based on a real person, and his depiction revealed a trace of the ethnic prejudice that saturated New England during Thayer's youth. As the social underclass of the time, the Irish were routinely scorned by the upper and middle classes, and "Irish Need Not Apply" signs hung in many store windows to ward off job inquiries from Irish immigrants. During this period, Thayer was attending high school. He was also self-publishing a small (two inches by three inches) sheet of humorous and mocking school notes, which he distributed among his peers. One of Thayer's teasing targets was a large Irish boy named Casey, and years later he recalled the boy's humorless response to the newsletter: "He didn't like it and he told me so, and, as he discoursed, his big, clenched, red hands were white at the knuckles." The diminutive Thayer was smart enough to drop Casey's name from his writings—until, that is, one Sunday a decade later and two thousand miles away, when he mockingly inserted the name twenty-two times into what he thought would be an obscure little poem. "I hope he never catches me," Thayer said, still looking over his shoulder years later.

Thanks in large part to De Wolf Hopper's traveling stage performances, which, in turn, inspired local amateurs to perform it as well, "Casey's" fame spread quickly to every corner of the continent. The absence of adequate copyright laws allowed easy replication, as well as numerous imitations, sequels, and parodies. The prevalence of newspaper poetry during the first half of this century also helped. Thus it was that through the years there were portrayals of Casey playing football, Casey as pitcher instead of hitter, Casey as a fan, gambler, cricketer, ghost, and African-American. There were also poems about Mrs. Casey, Casey's sister, his son, and his daughter. There were more than one hundred parodies through the years, including several in *Mad* magazine. In the 1950s, composer William Schuman, president of the Juilliard School of Music and later president of New York's Lincoln Center, wrote and staged a "Casey" opera (*The Mighty Casey*).

The human craving for sequels obviously did not begin with the movie *Rocky*. Human beings have always wanted to know, "What happened after that?" (I once heard someone describe the New Testament as a sequel.) The most successful of all the "Casey" sequels came from Grantland Rice, a classically trained scholar and poet from Tennessee who became the most widely known sportswriter of the 1930s and 1940s. It was Rice who nicknamed the 1924 Notre Dame backfield "the Four Horsemen," and many of his seven thousand poems graced the tens of thousands of columns and magazine pieces he wrote in praise of sport. Though not as widely known as the original, "Casey's Revenge" retains much of its predecessor's flavor and offers an added dimension to the legend. For those reasons I have included that 1906 sequel here, following "Casey at the Bat."

Whether "Casey's" longevity has anything to do with the quality of its poetry is open to debate. Some critics have labeled it nothing more than sentimental pop lit, but William Lyon Phelps of Yale called it a "masterpiece," pointing to its powerful understanding of human psychology and the tragedy of destiny. Some of its charm certainly can be attributed to the nature of the game it portrays. Domed stadiums and designated hitters notwithstanding, baseball is relatively unchanged from the days of Casey. And unlike football, basketball, and hockey, in which the action is incessant, sometimes blinding, and always controlled by the clock, baseball has a leisurely, timeless pace that invites the spectator to sit back and build a story around the game.

Baseball's roots are so deep they reach our everyday speech—in season or out. Consider just a few of the common expressions that originated on the diamond: *screwball, curveball, covering all bases, touching base, bench warmer, ground rules, plenty on the ball, cleanup man, rookie, here's the pitch, slip one past him,* and *go to bat for.*

The poem's long life might also be attributed to how emotional its fans become about the sport. The reason for that was best explained by its wisest commissioner, Bart Giamatti (a former Yale president), who once observed: "[Baseball] breaks your heart. It is designed to break your heart." Casey's strikeout epitomizes both the game itself and life itself. More than two dozen teams begin each spring with hope flowering in their hearts, and all but one will be defeated by the fall. Even the best hitters make two outs to every one hit. And in life, more often than not, we get neither the promotion nor the winning lottery ticket. That's life—and that's "Casey" too.

• • • •

CASEY AT THE BAT
A Ballad of the Republic, Sung in the Year 1888

The outlook wasn't brilliant for the Mudville nine that day,
The score stood four to two with but one inning more to play;
And then when Cooney died at first and Barrows did the same,
A sickly silence fell upon the patrons of the game.

A straggling few got up to go in deep despair. The rest
Clung to that hope which springs eternal in the human breast;
They thought if only Casey could but get a whack at that—
We'd put up even money now with Casey at the bat.

But Flynn preceded Casey, as did also Jimmy Blake,
And the former was a lulu and the latter was a cake;
So upon that stricken multitude grim melancholy sat,
For there seemed but little chance of Casey's getting to the bat.

But Flynn let drive a single, to the wonderment of all,
And Blake, the much despised, tore the cover off the ball;
And when the dust had lifted, and the men saw what had occurred,
There was Jimmy safe at second and Flynn a-hugging third.

Then from 5,000 throats and more there rose a lusty yell,
It rumbled through the valley, it rattled in the dell;
It knocked upon the mountain and recoiled upon the flat,
For Casey, mighty Casey, was advancing to the bat.

There was ease in Casey's manner as he stepped into his place,
There was pride in Casey's bearing and a smile on Casey's face;
And when responding to the cheers, he lightly doffed his hat,
No stranger in the crowd could doubt 'twas Casey at the bat.

Ten thousand eyes were on him as he rubbed his hands with dirt,
Five thousand tongues applauded when he wiped them on his shirt;
Then while the writhing pitcher ground the ball into his hip,
Defiance gleamed in Casey's eye, a sneer curled Casey's lip.

And now the leather-covered sphere came hurtling through the air;
And Casey stood a-watching it in haughty grandeur there;
Close by the sturdy batsman the ball unheeded sped—
"That ain't my style," said Casey. "Strike one," the umpire said.

From the benches, black with people, there went up a muffled roar,
Like the beating of the storm-waves on a stern and distant shore;
"Kill him! Kill the umpire!" shouted some one on the stand,
And it's likely they'd have killed him had not Casey raised his hand.

With a smile of Christian charity great Casey's visage shone,
He stilled the rising tumult; he bade the game go on;
He signaled to the pitcher, and once more the spheroid flew,
But Casey still ignored it, and the umpire said, "Strike two."

"Fraud!" cried the maddened thousands, and echo answered fraud,
But one scornful look from Casey and the audience was awed;
They saw his face grow stern and cold, they saw his muscles strain,
And they knew that Casey wouldn't let that ball go by again.

The sneer is gone from Casey's lip, his teeth are clenched in hate,
He pounds with cruel violence his bat upon the plate;
And now the pitcher holds the ball, and now he lets it go,
And now the air is shattered by the force of Casey's blow.

Oh, somewhere in this favored land the sun is shining bright,
The band is playing somewhere, and somewhere hearts are light;
And somewhere men are laughing, and somewhere children shout,
But there is no joy in Mudville—mighty Casey has struck out.

• • • •

CASEY'S REVENGE
By Grantland Rice

There were saddened hearts in Mudville for a week or even more,
There were muttered oaths and curses—every fan in town was sore;
"Just think," said one, "how soft it looked with Casey at the bat,
And then to think he'd go and spring a bush league trick like that!"

All his past fame was forgotten—he was now a hopeless "shine,"
They called him "Strike-Out Casey," from the mayor down the line;
And as he came to bat each day his bosom heaved a sigh,
While a look of hopeless fury shone in mighty Casey's eye.

He pondered in the days gone by that he had been their king,
That when he strolled up to the plate they made the welkin ring;
But now his nerve had vanished for when he heard them hoot,
He "fanned" or "popped out" daily, like some minor league recruit.

He soon began to sulk and loaf, his batting eye went lame,
No home runs on the score card now were chalked against his name;
The fans without exception gave the manager no peace,
For one and all kept clamoring for Casey's quick release.

The Mudville squad began to slump, the team was in the air,
Their playing went from bad to worse—nobody seemed to care;
"Back to the woods with Casey!" was the cry from Rooters' Row,
"Get some one who can hit the ball, and let that big dub go!"

The lane is long, some one has said, that never turns again,
And Fate, though fickle, often gives another chance to men;
And Casey smiled, his rugged face no longer wore a frown—
The pitcher who had started all the trouble came to town.

All Mudville had assembled—ten thousand fans had come,
To see the twirler who had put big Casey on the bum;
And when he stepped into the box, the multitude went wild,
He doffed his cap in proud disdain, but Casey only smiled.

"Play Ball!" the umpire's voice rang out, and then the game began,
But in that throng of thousands there was not a single fan
Who thought that Mudville had a chance, and with the setting sun,
Their hopes sank low—the rival team was leading "four to one."

The last half of the ninth came round, with no change in the score,
But when the first man up hit safe, the crowd began to roar;
The din increased, the echo of ten thousand shouts was heard,
When the pitcher hit the second and gave "four balls" to the third.

Three men on base—nobody out—three runs to tie the game!
A triple meant the highest niche in Mudville's hall of fame;
But here the rally ended and the gloom was deep as night,
When the fourth one "fouled to catcher" and the fifth "flew out to
right."

A dismal groan in chorus came, a scowl was on each face,
When Casey walked up, bat in hand, and slowly took his place;
His bloodshot eyes in fury gleamed, his teeth were clenched in hate,
He gave his cap a vicious hook and pounded on the plate.

But fame is fleeting as the wind and glory fades away,
There were no wild and woolly cheers, no glad acclaim this day;
They hissed and groaned and hooted as they clamored: "Strike him
out!"
But Casey gave no outward sign that he had heard this shout.

The pitcher smiled and cut one loose—across the plate it sped,
Another hiss, another groan, "Strike one!" the umpire said;
Zip! Like a shot the second curve broke just below the knee,
"Strike two!" the umpire roared aloud, but Casey made no plea.

No roasting for the umpire now—his was an easy lot,
But here the pitcher whirled again—was that a rifle shot?
A whack, a crack, and out through the space the leather pellet flew,
A blot against the distant sky, a speck against the blue.

Above the fence in center field in rapid whirling flight,
The sphere sailed on—the blot grew dim and then was lost to sight;
Ten thousand hats were thrown in air, ten thousand threw a fit,
But no one ever found the ball that mighty Casey hit.

O, somewhere in this favored land dark clouds may hide the sun,
And somewhere bands no longer play and children have no fun!
And somewhere over blighted lives there hangs a heavy pall,
But Mudville hearts are happy now, for Casey hit the ball.

• • • •

HERE ARE THE THREE BEST "Casey at the Bat" books: *The Annotated "Casey at the Bat": A Collection of Ballads about the Mighty Casey* by Martin Gardner, *Casey at the Bat: A Centennial Edition* by Ernest Lawrence Thayer, and *Mighty Casey: All-American* by Eugene C. Murdock.

Two more baseball stories can be found in the section "Out to the Ball Game," beginning on page 273, and a list of sports books can be found on pages 283 and 284.

THE CREMATION OF SAM McGEE

by Robert W. Service

"There's Gold in Them Thar Words"

When he was expelled from high school, few would have guessed he one day would write one of America's most famous poems. And you wouldn't have guessed it if you saw him a few years later as an unwashed vagrant slouched on a Los Angeles park bench. Not even four years later, when he was cleaned up and occasionally entertaining folks at the church hall with his recitations of Ernest Lawrence Thayer's "Casey at the Bat." Certainly the banker who shot at him one night would not have guessed it.

Would you have guessed it if you'd been at the breakfast table when he was six and invented his own rhyming grace before meals?

"God bless the cakes and bless the jam,
Bless the cheese and the cold boiled ham,
Bless the scones Aunt Jenny makes,
And save us all from belly-aches. Amen."

If environment is anything, Robert W. Service had that going for him, having been raised in Scotland, the homeland of Sir Walter Scott, Robert Louis Stevenson, and Robert Burns. In fact, Burns had been a friend of his great-grandfather.

Service was one of ten children and, as often happened in large families in those days, he was sent to live with his grandfather and three maiden aunts. The extended family can be a powerful stimulant for creative children if the relatives serve as encouraging audiences— as they did for Hans Christian Andersen, Langston Hughes, Moss Hart, Cynthia Rylant, Gary Paulsen, and Ray Bradbury. And that's what happened with Service's relatives. After his creative grace, he went on to alter the melodies and verses of church hymns to suit his comedic whims. One would think his old-fashioned aunts and grand-father would have frowned on such behavior, but they tolerated it—largely because of their Scottish fondness for poetry. If it rhymed, they reasoned, how wrong could it be?

By five years of age he had discovered his own powerful gift for storytelling. "I never believed in fairy tales," he said in his biography, "but I could make others do so."

Under the indulgence of his aunts, however, his behavior grad-ually worsened until his mother thought it best for him to rejoin the family. His exhibitionism continued, however, throughout his school years, until he was finally expelled from high school at fourteen for defying the drillmaster. (In those times, boys were often trained in marching by retired soldiers as part of their physical education program.)

Though he had barely passed his schoolwork, at the public library he read ravenously through adventure books and *Punch*, the English satire magazine. The adventure novels, combined with an adolescent summer living beside the sea, sowed the seeds of wanderlust.

At age fifteen he was apprenticed to a local bank. His days were spent working, reading as much as he could, and writing poetry that local weeklies found pleasant enough to publish. He tried college a few years later but lasted only three months.

His readings were now running from Poe to Rudyard Kipling and Jack London (the latter two being exciting new names in popular fiction), and he grew increasingly restless at home and on the job. At night he dreamed of "cowboys, gold-seekers, beach-combers."

Finally he took the leap and migrated to America. He ended up working a farm on Victoria Island in western Canada, haying, sawing wood, lifting stones, and milking cows—hardly the stuff of dreams or Jack London. Nonetheless, he felt he had to *live* experiences before he could *write* about them, and here was a beginning.

After two years of hard labor, he headed south for the United States, the land of opportunity and adventure. That, too, quickly wore thin. San Francisco, where his days were spent "among the misery of a great city, its derelicts, its down-and-outs," filling him with disgust instead of romantic excitement.

Service saw himself turning into a "human doormat" but couldn't get off the treadmill without compromising his idea that experience must come before creativity. In 1897, nearing twenty-four years of age, he was living with vagrants in a Los Angeles evangelical mission, and using the nearby public library daily to read poetry. (Thirty years later another young newcomer to L.A. would make that same daily trek to the Los Angeles library for sustenance—Ray Bradbury.) Service's dream at this point was to write "newspaper poetry, the kind that simple folks clip out and paste in scrap-books," but the bitter reality was that most of his days were spent wearing pasteboards to advertise some business, or picking oranges.

He reached rock bottom one night early in 1898 when he had to sleep in a pile of leaves to avoid a suspected killer who had invaded the hut of railroad ties Service was living in. The following day, he sat on a park bench and pondered his fate and future. It was then that his romantic "destiny" reached out and touched him. He noticed the newspaper that had been left on the bench. The headlines proclaimed that gold had been discovered in the Klondike.

If it had stopped with that, Service's interest would not have been stirred, but the article went on to state that "no doubt another Bret Harte will arise and sing of it in colorful verse." Harte, who became famous writing about the California gold rush years earlier, had been a favorite of Service's since childhood and one of the reasons for Service's attraction to the American West. With nothing more than this one line from a newspaper as a beacon, Service headed north, working a series of odd jobs for the next few years, until he reached Canada again. There he secured a job much like the one he'd left in Scotland seven years earlier—bank clerk.

Within two years he was transferred to Whitehorse in the heart of the Yukon, six years after he'd read that California newspaper article. He didn't know it, but the fortune that thousands of others had found in the Yukon was also waiting for him, buried not beneath its creeks but in streams of words.

Most of the excitement and "rush" was over by the time Service arrived in the Klondike, though thousands still worked the mines and streams. Service took to the good cheer and comradeship of the settlement, and his poetic voice returned stronger than ever. He worked his way up to teller at the bank, sent some verse to the local newspaper, and was playing the role of entertainer by reciting Kipling's "Gunga Din" and the newly popular "Casey at the Bat" before audiences in Whitehorse theatricals and church socials. But through it all he was more often observer than participant. He watched, listened, and took note of the colorful life around him. If he couldn't *live* it, perhaps he could *watch* it.

At last, one Saturday night in 1906, with the settlement's bars overflowing with noise and excitement, he hit upon an especially good idea for a poem. Looking for an isolated spot away from the din of the saloons, he headed for the peace and quiet of his teller's cage at the bank. It was quiet all right, until the ledger keeper sleeping in the guardroom thought he was a thief and shot at him. The shot missed Service, who immediately identified himself, then sat down to write his first important poem (with no pun intended), "The Shooting of Dan McGrew," finishing it at 5:00 A.M.

Unlike his other efforts, he didn't submit this poem to the local newspaper. Instead he began immediately to think of his next one. A month later it dawned on him in the middle of a local party where a miner from Dawson told a humorous story of the Yukon cold. Service knew immediately that here was the spark for the perfect ballad, *the* one he'd been in search of for nearly ten years. Walking the moonlit paths, Service worked out the entire poem in his head and put it on paper in the morning. With its hardy blend of whimsy and reality, it would become his most famous poem—"The Cremation of Sam McGee."

He knew he had created something special, but in his wildest dreams he probably couldn't have foreseen that "McGee" would quickly take the public stage beside "Casey at the Bat" as a favorite recitation piece throughout North America.

In the months that followed, Service wrote enough poems for a small book. Taking his Christmas bonus money from the bank, he sent it to Toronto to be printed by a Methodist church publisher who was a friend of his father's. The response was immediate, both in Canada and in the United States. Leaving the bank soon thereafter, he immersed himself in the land and its character to become the "poet of the North." With the exception of Jack London, no one has captured the lure and the lore of the wilderness North so convincingly.

• • • •

There are strange things done in the midnight sun
    By the men who moil for gold;
The Arctic trails have their secret tales
    That would make your blood run cold;
The Northern Lights have seen queer sights,
    But the queerest they ever did see

Was that night on the marge of Lake Lebarge
I cremated Sam McGee.

Now Sam McGee was from Tennessee,
    where the cotton blooms and blows.
Why he left his home in the South to roam
    'round the Pole, God only knows.
He was always cold, but the land of gold
    seemed to hold him like a spell;
Though he'd often say in his homely way
    that he'd "sooner live in Hell."

On a Christmas Day we were mushing our way
    over the Dawson trail.
Talk of your cold! through the parka's fold
    it stabbed like a driven nail.
If our eyes we'd close, then the lashes froze
    till sometimes we couldn't see,
It wasn't much fun, but the only one
    to whimper was Sam McGee.

And that very night, as we lay packed tight
    in our robes beneath the snow,
And the dogs were fed, and the stars o'erhead
    were dancing heel and toe,
He turned to me, and "Cap," says he,
    "I'll cash in this trip, I guess;
And if I do, I'm asking that you
    won't refuse my last request."

Well, he seemed so low that I couldn't say no;
    then he says with a sort of moan,
"It's the cursed cold, and it's got right hold
    till I'm chilled clean through to the bone.
Yet 'taint being dead—it's my awful dread
    of the icy grave that pains;
So I want you to swear that, foul or fair,
    you'll cremate my last remains."

A pal's last need is a thing to heed,
    so I swore I would not fail;
And we started on at the streak of dawn;
    but God! he looked ghastly pale.

He crouched on the sleigh, and he raved all day
    of his home in Tennessee;
  And before nightfall a corpse was all
    that was left of Sam McGee.

There wasn't a breath in that land of death,
    and I hurried, horror-driven,
  With a corpse half hid that I couldn't get rid,
    because of a promise given;
It was lashed to the sleigh, and it seemed to say:
    "You may tax your brawn and brains,
  But you promised true, and it's up to you
    to cremate these last remains."

Now a promise made is a debt unpaid,
    and the trail has its own stern code.
  In the days to come, though my lips were dumb,
    in my heart how I cursed that load!
In the long, long night, by the lone firelight,
    while the huskies, round in a ring,
  Howled out their woes to the homeless snows—
    Oh God, how I loathed the thing!

And every day that quiet clay
    seemed to heavy and heavier grow;
  And on I went, though the dogs were spent
    and the grub was getting low.
The trail was bad, and I felt half mad,
    but I swore I would not give in;
  And I'd often sing to the hateful thing,
    and it hearkened with a grin.

Till I came to the marge of Lake Lebarge,
    and a derelict there lay;
  It was jammed in the ice, but I saw in a trice
    it was called the *Alice May*.
And I looked at it, and I thought a bit,
    and I looked at my frozen chum;
  Then "Here," said I, with a sudden cry,
    "is my cre-ma-tor-eum!"

Some planks I tore from the cabin floor,
    and I lit the boiler fire;

Some coal I found that was lying around,
    and I heaped the fuel higher;
The flames just soared, and the furnace roared—
    such a blaze you seldom see,
And I burrowed a hole in the glowing coal,
    and I stuffed in Sam McGee.

Then I made a hike, for I didn't like
    to hear him sizzle so;
And the heavens scowled, and the huskies howled,
    and the wind began to blow.
It was icy cold, but the hot sweat rolled
    down my cheeks, and I don't know why;
And the greasy smoke in an inky cloak
    went streaking down the sky.

I do not know how long in the snow
    I wrestled with grisly fear;
But the stars came out and they danced about
    ere again I ventured near;
I was sick with dread, but I bravely said,
    "I'll just take a peep inside.
I guess he's cooked, and it's time I looked."
    Then the door I opened wide.

And there sat Sam, looking cool and calm,
    in the heart of the furnace roar;
And he wore a smile you could see a mile,
    and he said, "Please close that door.
It's fine in here, but I greatly fear
    you'll let in the cold and storm—
Since I left Plumtree, down in Tennessee,
    it's the first time I've been warm."

There are strange things done in the midnight sun
    By the men who moil for gold;
The Arctic trails have their secret tales
    That would make your blood run cold;
The Northern Lights have seen queer sights,
    But the queerest they ever did see
Was that night on the marge of Lake Lebarge
    I cremated Sam McGee.

. . . .

SERVICE EVENTUALLY LEFT the Klondike for Europe, where he worked with the Red Cross during the First World War. His collected poems from that war, *Rhymes of a Red Cross Man*, became the best-selling nonfiction book of the years 1917 and 1918—the first and last time a book of poetry held that distinction in the United States. He eventually settled in France, where he died in 1958.

Among his poetry collections still available: *The Best of Robert Service*, *The Collected Poems of Robert Service*, *The Cremation of Sam McGee*, *The Shooting of Dan McGrew*, and *The Spell of the Yukon*. His two autobiographies (available only through libraries) are *Ploughman of the Moon* and *Harper of Heaven*. See also *Robert Service*, a biography by Carl F. Klinck.

An audiocassette is also available of some of his poetry: *The Poetry of Robert W. Service* (read by Ed Begley, one hour).

For realistic fiction about the North, check out Jack London's *The Call of the Wild* and *White Fang*, and *Lost in the Barrens* by Farley Mowat. See also *The Iceberg Hermit* by Arthur Roth (page 371).

Chilling Tales

Five stories, shadowed by fear:
a game of hide-and-seek,
two night walks, and two rides—
one in an elevator
and another in a train.

FEAR

by Rhys Davies

The Roots of Our Fears

There was once a great teacher in New Zealand (Sylvia Ashton-Warner) who helped her kindergarten students learn to read by having them tell her their favorite or most important words. She would then write each on a card for the child to keep —*truck, car, mother, father, gun*, and so on. They never had trouble reading those "important" cards.

Keeping track of the cards, she found the most frequently mentioned words over the years were *kiss* and *ghost*. As newly formed as they might have been, these children instinctively knew the symbols of the two most dominant feelings of childhood and adulthood—love and fear.

For half a century, most writers for children and young adults steered only to the "love" and away from the "fear." Today, however, we know that ignoring or denying fears will not make them disappear. Confronting them, however, often serves to purge them—as any good psychologist or folklorist will attest. Amusement-park operators will second the motion. Their most popular rides with adolescents are often the scariest. Librarians and booksellers claim the most requested type of book is "scary stories."

In an interview with Leonard Marcus in the children's literature journal *The Lion and Unicorn*, folklorist Alvin Schwartz explained children's interest in scary stories: "Stories of this kind enable people to explore the outer edges of their experiences. Death, the unknown, strangeness, things that are not explainable and cannot be explained. You have to provide your own explanation. Traditionally, stories have served this function. . . . All these stories, and there are scads of them, are really saying: 'Watch out. The world's a dangerous place. You are going out on your own. Be careful.' . . . . It's just a story. People like that. There's no danger. It's what the English call 'having a gentle or a good fright.' It's like having a good cry.''

The next five stories contain a strong element of fear. Although adults were the primary audience for these stories when they were first printed, each is accessible to young adults. No one in this world knows fear the way a child does. As an adult, I can go months without once being truly afraid. On the other hand, most children can't go one day without knowing fear firsthand. To begin with, they live the first fifteen years of their lives in a land controlled by giants—sometimes moody and unreasonable giants.

So let us begin with children and fear. The first story comes from Rhys (REESE) Davies, born and raised in Wales, the son of a strict shopkeeper. Caught between rigid puritanism at home and the terror of the world outside—mining slums, unemployment, strikes, riots, and drunkenness—he began as a child to create fantasy worlds and stories. The Bible was his most important stimulant and storehouse of story ideas.

Davies, who died in 1978 and was a recipient of the Mystery Writers of America Edgar Allan Poe Award, possessed another mark of great writers: As you will see in this tale, he never forgot what it was like to be a child. Although nearly all of his writing was done with an adult audience in mind, this tale is one that younger audiences will appreciate as well.

To give the story its due, it might be helpful to note several things about its setting and characters. It takes place in England and involves an English boy and an Indian man—an Indian from India, not a Native American.

An Indian traveling on an English train is not unusual. At the same time England was colonizing America, it began full-scale commercial enterprises in India that would lead to its eventual control and rule of India. For most of their two-hundred-year relationship, the British and Indians had a more or less harmonious but one-sided relationship. English merchants and politicians controlled India, turning it into England's most powerful and richest colony, and Indians were allowed to visit, study, and work in England. Finally, in 1947, after a painful half century that saw the famous Mohandas Gandhi lead the simmering nation in nonviolent rebellion, England agreed to India's (and Pakistan's) independence.

Because of this long history together, the Indian population in

Great Britain is appreciably larger than that of any other ethnic group there. But because of this history, the English-Indian relationship is often a suspicious or tenuous one—similar to that of whites and African-Americans in the United States. Indeed, Rhys Davies could have set this short story in any country where two separate cultures —or two people divided by age—are suddenly forced to share the same confined space for a period of time.

• • • •

A S SOON AS THE BOY got into the compartment he felt there was something queer in it. The only other occupant was a slight, dusky man who sat in a corner with that air of propriety and unassertiveness which his race—he looked like an Indian—tend to display in England. There was also a faint sickly scent. For years afterwards, whenever he smelled that musk odor again, the terror of this afternoon came back to him.

He went to the other end of the compartment, sat in the opposite corner. There were no corridors in these local trains. The man looked at him and smiled friendlily. The boy returned the smile briefly, not quite knowing what he was thinking, only aware of a deep, vague unease. But it would look so silly to jump out of the compartment now. The train gave a jerk and began to move.

Then, immediately with the jerk, the man began to utter a low humming chant, slow but with a definite rhythm. His lips did not open or even move, yet the hum penetrated above the noise of the train's wheels. It was in a sort of dreamy rhythm, enticing, lonely and antique; it suggested monotonous deserts, an eternal patience, a soothing wisdom. It went on and on. It was the kind of archaic chant that brings to the mind images of slowly swaying bodies in some endless ceremony in a barbaric temple.

Startled, and very alive to this proof of there being something odd in the compartment, the boy turned from staring out of the window—already the train was deep in the country among lonely fields and dark wooded slopes—and forced himself to glance at the man.

The man was looking at him. They faced each other across the compartment's length. Something coiled up in the boy. It was as if his soul took primitive fear and crouched to hide. The man's brown lips became stretched in a mysterious smile, though that humming chant continued, wordlessly swaying out of his mouth. His eyes, dark and unfathomable, never moved from the boy. The musk scent was stronger.

Yet this was not all. The boy could not imagine what other fearful thing lurked in the compartment. But he seemed to sense a secret power of something evilly antipathetic. Did it come from the man's long pinky-brown hands, the sinewy but fleshless hands of a sun-scorched race? Long tribal hands like claws. Or only from the fact that the man was of a far country whose ways were utterly alien to ours? And he continued to smile. A faint and subtle smile, while his eyes surveyed the boy as if he contemplated action. Something had flickered in and out of those shadowy eyes, like a dancing malice.

The boy sat stiffly. Somehow he could not return to his staring out of the window. But he tried not to look at the man again. The humming did not stop. And suddenly it took a higher note, like an unhurried wail, yet keeping within its strict and narrow compass. A liquid exultance wavered in and out of the wail. The noise of the train, the flying fields and woods, even the walls of the compartment had vanished. There was only this chant, the man who was uttering it, and himself. He did not know that now he could not move his eyes from those of the man.

Abruptly the compartment was plunged into blackness. There was a shrieking rush of air. The train had entered a tunnel. With a sudden jerk the boy crouched down. He coiled into the seat's corner, shuddering, yet with every sense electrically alive now.

Then, above the roar of the air and the hurling grind of the train, that hum rose, dominantly established its insidious power. It called, it unhurriedly exhorted obedience, it soothed. Again it seemed to obliterate the louder, harsher noises. Spent and defeated, helplessly awaiting whatever menace lay in the darkness, the boy crouched. He knew the man's eyes were gazing towards him; he thought he saw their gleam triumphantly piercing the darkness. What was this strange presence of evil in the air, stronger now in the dark?

Suddenly crashing into the compartment, the hard blue and white daylight was like a blow. The train had gained speed in the tunnel, and now hurled on through the light with the same agonizing impetus, as if it would rush on for ever. Spent in the dread which had almost canceled out his senses, the boy stared dully at the man. Still he seemed to hear the humming, though actually it had ceased. He saw the man's lips part in a full enticing smile, he saw teeth dazzlingly white between the dusky lips.

"You not like dark tunnel?" The smile continued seductively; once more the flecks of light danced wickedly in his eyes. "Come!" He beckoned with a long wrinkled finger.

The boy did not move.

"You like pomegranates?" He rose and took from the luggage rack a brown wicker basket. It was the kind of basket in which a large cat would be sent on a journey. "Come!" he smiled friendlily and, as the boy still did not move, he crossed over and sat down beside him, but leaving a polite distance.

The staring boy did not flinch.

"Pomegranates from the East! English boy like, eh?" There seemed a collaboration in his intimate voice; he too was a boy going to share fruit with his friend. "Nice pomegranates," he smiled with good-humor. There was also something stupid in his manner, a fatuous mysteriousness.

The basket lay on his knees. He began to hum again. The boy watched, still without movement, cold and abstract in his nonapprehension of this friendliness. But he was aware of the sickly perfume beside him and, more pronounced than ever, of an insidious presence that was utterly alien. That evil power lay in his immediate vicinity. The man looked at him again and, still humming, drew a rod and lifted the basket's lid.

There was no glow of magically gleaming fruits, no yellow-and-rose-tinted rinds enclosing honeycombs of luscious seeds. But from the basket's depth rose the head of a snake. It rose slowly to the enchantment of the hum. It rose from its sleepy coil, rearing its long brownish-gold throat dreamily, the head swaying out in languor towards the man's lips. Its eyes seemed to look blindly at nothing. It was a cobra.

Something happened to the boy. An old warning of the muscles and the vulnerable flesh. He leapt and flung himself headlong across the compartment. He was not aware that he gave a sharp shriek. He curled against the opposite seat's back, his knees pressing into the cushion. But, half turning, his eyes could not tear themselves from that reared head.

And it was with other senses that he knew most deeply he had evoked rage. The cobra was writhing in disturbed anger, shooting its head in his direction. He saw wakened pin-point eyes of black malice. More fearful was the dilation of the throat, its skin swelling evilly into a hood in which shone two palpitating sparks. In some cell of his being he knew that the hood was swelling in destructive fury. He became very still.

The man did not stop humming. But now his narrowed eyes were focused in glittering concentration on the snake. And into that hum had crept a new note of tenacious decision. It was a pitting of subtle power against the snake's wishes and it was also an appeasement. A man was addressing a snake. He was offering a snake tribute and acknowledgment of its right to anger; he was honeyed and soothing. At the same time he did not relax an announcement of being master. There was courtesy towards one of the supreme powers of the animal kingdom, but also there was the ancient pride of man's supremacy.

And the snake was pacified. Its strange reared collar of skin sank back into its neck; its head ceased to lunge towards the boy. The humming slackened into a dreamy lullaby. Narrowly intent now, the man's eyes did not move. The length of tawny body slowly sank back. Its skin had a dull glisten, the glisten of an unhealthy torpidity. Now the snake looked effete, shorn of its venomous power. The drugged head sank. Unhurriedly the man closed the basket and slipped its rod secure.

He turned angrily to the boy; he made a contemptuous sound, like a hiss. "I show you cobra and you jump and shout, heh! Make him angry!" There was more rebuke than real rage in his exclamations. But also his brown face was puckered in a kind of childish stupidity; he might have been another boy of twelve. "I give you free performance with cobra, and you jump and scream like little girl." The indignation died out of his eyes; they became focused in a more adult perception. "I sing to keep cobra quiet in train," he explained. "Cobra not like train."

The boy had not stirred. "You not like cobra?" the man asked in injured surprise. "Nice snake now, no poison! But not liking you jump and shout."

There was no reply or movement; centuries and continents lay between him and the boy's still repudiation. The man gazed at him in silence and added worriedly: "You going to fair in Newport? You see me? Ali the Snake Charmer. You come in free and see me make cobra dance—".

But the train was drawing into the station. It was not the boy's station. He made a sudden blind leap away from the man, opened the door, saw it was not on the platform side, but jumped. There was a shout from someone. He ran up the track, he dived under some wire railings. He ran with amazingly quick short leaps up a field—like a hare that knows its life is precarious among the colossal dangers of the open world and has suddenly sensed one of them.

• • • •

WHO'S AFRAID?

by Philippa Pearce

A Scary Party Story

The daily headlines and nightly newscasts of the last twenty years cast a frightening image of our times. Tens of thousands of children and teenagers wandering America's urban streets each night, seeking money, violence, or simply shelter. Thousands of "missing children" pictured on milk cartons or fliers tacked to community bulletin boards. You would almost believe it is the worst of times—unless you know history.

History shows that homelessness and runaways did not begin in the 1980s or 1990s. Indeed, in the latter half of the last century, the streets of New York and London were filled with tens of thousands of homeless children and runaways. These children had either been discarded by parents and relatives who considered them to be unwanted baggage, or they had been abused by adults who saw them as helpless pack animals to be used for cheap labor in workhouses, factories, mills, and mines. Kidnapping or stealing a child for use as a slave or servant was so common for centuries that it wasn't even a crime until the early 1800s. These were the children and conditions Dickens described so vividly in his novels and writings at the end of the nineteenth century (*David Copperfield; Oliver Twist; Nicholas Nickleby*).

Through such writings the public became more aware of the problems, and laws were passed eventually to protect children both from their relatives and from other adults. The wave of child-abuse cases and new laws during the last two decades shows how slow and painful is the road to goodness.

One of the most important events along this road occurred in 1884 in England with the founding of the National Society for the Prevention of Cruelty to Children (NSPCC). It was founded, I might add, years *after* similar societies for the protection of animals were founded in England and America. In 1984, England's Society of Authors observed the hundredth anniversary of the NSPCC by publishing a collection of stories by its authors—all using "one hundred" as a theme. Some were humorous, some serious, some in pictures, others in verse or prose.

This story originated with that anthology. It is especially relevant to the subject of children and cruelty because it makes a bold suggestion: Cruelty does not begin in adulthood. It starts in backyards and playgrounds, along bicycle paths and inside gymnasiums. It even sprouts at birthday parties—as you will see.

The author, Philippa Pearce, is one of England's most esteemed writers for children and young adults. There are no wasted words in her stories, due in part to her many years as a radio scriptwriter and producer, when she often had to craft stories for tight-fitting time slots. Her writing career began when, as an adult, she was hospitalized with tuberculosis and was searching for something to fill in the empty hours. Pearce's tales often have a strong sense of suspense and an odor of fear, and they are set in an eerie twilight or darkness. Into such a setting steps the tormented child you are about to meet.

• • • •

"WILL MY COUSIN Dicky be there?"

"Everyone's been asked. Cousins, aunts, uncles, great-aunts, great-uncles—the lot. I've told you: it's your great-grandmother's hundredth birthday party."

"But will Dicky Hutt be there?"

"I'm sure he will be."

"Anyway, Joe, why do you want to know?"

Joe's mother and father were staring at Joe; and Joe said, "I hate Dicky."

"Now, Joe!" said his mother; and his father asked: "Why on earth do you hate Dicky?"

"I just do," said Joe. He turned away, to end the conversation; but inside his head he was saying: "I'd like to kill Dicky Hutt. Before he tries to kill me."

When the day of the birthday came, everyone—just as Joe's mother had said—was there. Relations of all ages swarmed over the little house where Great-grandmother lived, looked after by Great-aunt Madge. Fortunately, Great-grandmother had been born in the summer, and now—a hundred years later—the sun shone warmly on her celebrations. Great-aunt Madge shooed everyone into the garden for the photograph. The grown-ups sat on chairs, or stood in rows, and the children sat cross-legged in a row in the very front. (At one end, Joe; at the other, Dicky; and Dicky's stare at Joe said: "If I catch you, I'll kill you . . .") There was a gap in the center of this front row for a table with the tiered birthday cake and its hundred candles.

And behind the cake sat Great-grandmother in her wheelchair, with one shawl over her knees and another round her shoulders. Great-aunt Madge stood just behind her.

Great-grandmother faced the camera with a steady gaze from eyes that saw nothing by now—she had become blind in old age. Whether she heard much was doubtful. Certainly, she never spoke or turned her head even a fraction as if to listen.

After the photograph and the cutting of the cake, the grown-ups stood around drinking tea and talking. (Great-grandmother had been wheeled off somewhere indoors for a rest.) The children, if they were very young, clung to their parents; the older ones sidled about aimlessly—aimlessly, except that Joe could see Dicky always sidling towards him, staring his hatred. So Joe sidled away and sidled away . . .

"Children!" cried Great-aunt Madge. "What about a good old game? What about hide-and-seek? There's the garden to hide in, and most of the house."

Some of the children still clung to their parents; others said "yes" to hide-and-seek. Dicky Hutt said "yes." Joe said "no"; but his father said impatiently: "Don't be soft! Go off and play with the others."

Dicky Hutt shouted: "I'll be He!" So he was. Dicky Hutt shut his eyes and began to count at once. When he had counted a hundred, he would open his eyes and begin to search.

Joe knew whom he would search for with the bitterest thoroughness: himself.

Joe was afraid—too afraid to think well. He thought at first that he would hide in the garden, where there were at least grown-ups about—but then he didn't trust Dicky not to be secretly watching under his eyelashes, to see exactly where he went. Joe couldn't bear the thought of that.

So, after all, he went indoors to hide; but by then some of the best hiding-places had been taken. And out in the garden Dicky Hutt was counting fast, shouting aloud his total at every count of ten.

"Seventy!" he was shouting now; and Joe had just looked behind the sofa in the front room, and there was already someone crouching there. And there was also someone hiding under the pile of visitors' coats—"Eighty!" came Dicky Hutt's voice from the garden—and two children already in the stair-cupboard, when he thought of that hiding-place. So he must go on looking for somewhere—anywhere—to hide—and "Ninety!" from outside—*anywhere* to hide—and for the second time he came to the door with the notice pinned to it that said: "Keep out! Signed: Madge."

"A hundred! I'm coming!" shouted Dicky Hutt. And Joe turned the handle of the forbidden door and slipped inside and shut the door behind him.

The room was very dim, because the curtains had been drawn close; and its quietness seemed empty. But Joe's eyes began to be able to pick out the furnishings of the room, even in the half-light: table, chair, roll-top desk, and also—like just another piece of furniture, and just as immobile—Great-grandmother's wheelchair and Great-grandmother sitting in it.

He stood, she sat, both silent, still; and Dicky Hutt's thundering footsteps and voice were outside, passing the door, and then far away.

He thought she did not know that he had come into her room; but a low, slow voice reached him: "Who's there?"

He whispered: "It's only me—Joe."

Silence; and then the low, slow voice again: "Who's there?"

He was moving towards her, to speak in her very ear, when she spoke a third time: "Who's there?"

And this time he heard in her voice the little tremble of fear: he recognized it. He came to her chair, and laid his hand on hers. For a second he felt her weakly pull away, and then she let his hand rest, but turned her own, so that his hand fell into hers. She held his hand, fingered it slowly. He wanted her to know that he meant her no harm; he wanted her to say: "This is a small hand, a child's hand. You are only a child, after all."

But she did not speak again.

He stood there; she sat there; and the excited screams and laughter and running footsteps of hide-and-seek were very far away.

At last, Joe could tell from the sounds outside that the game of hide-and-seek was nearly over. He must be the last player not to be found and chased by Dicky Hutt. For now Dicky Hutt was wandering about, calling: "Come out, Joe! I know where you're hiding, Joe, so you might as well come out! I shall find you, Joe—I shall find you!"

The roving footsteps passed the forbidden doorway several times; but—no, this time they did not pass. Dicky Hutt had stopped outside.

The silence outside the door made Joe tremble: he tried to stop trembling, for the sake of the hand that held his, but he could not. He felt that old, old skin-and-bony hand close on his, as if questioning what was happening, what was wrong.

But he had no voice to explain to her. He had no voice at all.

His eyes were on the knob of the door. Even through the gloom he could see that it was turning. Then the door was creeping open— not fast, but steadily; not far, but far enough—

It opened far enough for Dicky Hutt to slip through. He stood there, inside the dim room. Joe could see his bulk there: Dicky Hutt had always been bigger than he was; now he loomed huge. And he was staring directly at Joe.

Joe's whole body was shaking. He felt as if he were shaking to pieces. He wished that he could.

His great-grandmother held his shaking hand in hers.

Dicky Hutt took a step forward into the room.

Joe had no hope. He felt his great-grandmother lean forward a little in her chair, tautening her grip on his hand as she did so. In her low, slow voice she was saying: "Who—" And Joe thought, He won't bother to answer her; he'll just come for me. He'll *come* for me . . .

But the low, slow voice went on: "Whoooooooooooooooooo—" She was hooting like some ghost-throated owl; and then the hooting raised itself into a thin, eerie wailing. Next, through the wailing, she began to gibber, with effect so startling—so horrifying—that Joe forgot Dicky Hutt for a moment, and turned to look at her. His great-grandmother's mouth was partly open, and she was making her false teeth do a kind of devil's dance inside it.

And when Joe looked towards Dicky Hutt again, he had gone. The door was closing, the knob turning. The door clicked shut, and Joe could hear Dicky Hutt's feet tiptoeing away.

When Joe looked at his great-grandmother again, she was sitting back in her chair. Her mouth was closed; the gibbering and the hooting and the wailing had ceased. She looked exhausted—or had she died? But no, she was just looking unbelievably old.

He did not disturb her. He stood by her chair some time longer. Then he heard his parents calling over the house for him: they wanted to go home.

He moved his hand out of hers—the grasp was slack now: perhaps she had fallen asleep. He thought he wanted to kiss her goodbye;

but then he did not want the feel of that century-old cheek against his lips.

So he simply slipped away from her and out of the room.

He never saw her again. Nearly a year later, at home, the news came of her death. Joe's mother said: "Poor old thing . . ."

Joe's father (whose grandmother Great-grandmother had been) said: "When I was a little boy, she was fun. I remember her. Joky, then; full of tricks . . ."

Joe's mother said: "Well, she'd outlived all that. Outlived everything. Too old to be any use to herself—or to anyone else. A burden, only."

Joe said nothing; but he wished now that he had kissed her cheek, to say goodbye, and to thank her.

• • • •

WITH THEIR DISTINCT and creative imaginations, no two authors or artists or musicians ever arrange the same elements in the same way. A perfect example of that can be found in comparing this Philippa Pearce tale with another story with some of the same events—threatened violence in the dark, an old woman, and a young boy—"Thank You, Ma'am" by Langston Hughes (page 82).

In 1959 Pearce won the Carnegie Medal (the British equivalent of America's Newbery Medal) for a supernatural time-travel story, *Tom's Midnight Garden*, set in the yard area behind an English apartment that turns into a Victorian home after midnight each evening. It is regarded as one of this century's classics of English children's literature. She is also the author of *Who's Afraid? and Other Strange Stories*, *The Shadow-Cage and Other Tales of the Supernatural*, *Minnow on the Say*, *The Way to Sattin Shore*, *What the Neighbors Did and Other Stories*, *A Dog So Small*, and *The Squirrel Wife*.

THE ELEVATOR

by William Sleator

The Profession with an Open-Door Policy

Writing, unlike the professions of medicine and engineering, is one of those wonderful career "bus stops" that allow for easy transfers. If you're a thirty-five-year-old accountant and you suddenly think you'd like to become a doctor, you'll soon realize you've missed the bus. But authorship seems to thrive on diversity and late bloomers.

Of just the authors in this book, consider the diversity of the backgrounds from which they came to writing:

Rudyard Kipling ("Rikki-tikki-tavi")—newspaper reporter

Avi (*The True Confessions of Charlotte Doyle*)—librarian

Christopher de Vinck ("Power of the Powerless")—high school English teacher

Allan Eckert (*Incident at Hawk's Hill*)—factory worker

Loren Eiseley (*All the Strange Hours*)—anthropologist

Harper Lee (*To Kill a Mockingbird*)—airline reservationist and law student

Gary Paulsen (*Woodsong*)—aerospace engineer

Robert W. Service ("The Cremation of Sam McGee")—bank teller

Maya Angelou (*I Know Why the Caged Bird Sings*)—dancer

Leon Garfield (*The December Rose*)—biochemical technician

Robert Newton Peck (*A Day No Pigs Would Die*)—advertising

Roald Dahl ("The Wonderful Story of Henry Sugar")—airman

Scott O'Dell (*Sarah Bishop*)—motion picture technician

Howard Pyle (*Otto of the Silver Hand*)—artist

It should therefore come as no surprise that William Sleator, the author of our next story as well as a dozen "psychological science-fantasy novels," pursued a music degree at Harvard University, switched to English, then went back to music and was working as a pianist when he wrote his first novel, *Blackbriar*.

Though he is the only one in his family not trained as a scientist, his home environment quickly led him to reading as a child and eventually to writing science-fiction tales. His stories are known for an escalating sense of menace that envelops both the characters and the reader, often suggesting there is someone out there, watching and waiting for you. Much of that flavoring can be credited to his parents.

His mother was an unassuming, free-spirit pediatrician and his father a laid-back university professor. How unassuming and laid back? They couldn't make up their minds what to name their last child, calling him Newby (new baby) for his first twenty-four months of life, until finally settling on Tycho Barney George Clement Newby Sleator. Honest.

Because Mrs. Sleator was "unconcerned about things like hygiene, foul language, and personal appearance," their home was the neighborhood hangout. It was such a breeding ground for far-out behavior that Sleator called his 1993 book of childhood reminiscences *Oddballs*.

The eerie tone of the story included here should come as no surprise to Sleator's childhood friends. During the time when Sleator was in the fifth and sixth grades, his mother would organize Halloween parties, allowing the kids to paint a gigantic gruesome mural on William's third-floor attic wall. The highlight, though, was her candle-lit reading of ghost stories that were scary enough to provoke some of the kids to call home.

Not to be outdone, Sleator's father had an equally offbeat taste for the unusual. He often took his children to his university medical school laboratory on weekends and would pretend to accidentally lock them in the laboratory freezer with the various dead animals.

The twists and turns of plot lines in fiction are hardly overwhelming to Sleator, considering the early training he received from his father's weekend "Hänsel and Gretel" games. Dad would blindfold the kids, drive them to an unknown part of the city, remove their blindfolds, and drive away—leaving them there to find their way home alone. And they loved it. (They did have a dime just in case they got lost and needed help.)

His adolescent characters are often found in bizarre psychological conflicts that require painful decisions. Typical is *The Duplicate*, in which a sixteen-year-old boy discovers a machine that will create another being who looks exactly like himself. The complication is that the duplicate does not *feel* or *act* the way he does. He is, in fact, truly evil—but is he human? If he's *not* human, then how wrong would it be to kill him? But if he *is* . . .

For all the complexities in his work, Sleator still has one primary goal with each story: "to entertain my audience and get them to read. I want them to know that reading is the best entertainment there is."

In this tale, Sleator takes a conventional source of anxiety—an elevator—and gives it an unsettling twist. It came as a result of a very realistic and frightening dream he had involving an elevator. The challenge was to come up with the right mix of menacing passenger and victim.

• • • •

IT WAS AN OLD BUILDING with an old elevator—a very small elevator, with a maximum capacity of three people. Martin, a thin twelve-year-old, felt nervous in it from the first day he and his father moved into the apartment. Of course he was always uncomfortable in elevators, afraid that they would fall, but there was something especially unpleasant about this one. Perhaps its baleful atmosphere was due to the light from the single fluorescent ceiling strip, bleak and dim on the dirty brown walls. Perhaps the problem was the door, which never stayed open quite long enough, and slammed shut with such ominous, clanging finality. Perhaps it was the way the mechanism shuddered in a kind of exhaustion each time it left a floor, as though it might never reach the next one. Maybe it was simply the dimensions of the contraption that bothered him, so small that it felt uncomfortably crowded even when there was only one other person in it.

Coming home from school the day after they moved in, Martin tried the stairs. But they were almost as bad, windowless, shadowy, with several dark landings where the light bulbs had burned out. His footsteps echoed behind him like slaps on the cement, as though there was another person climbing, getting closer. By the time he reached the seventeenth floor, which seemed to take forever, he was winded and gasping.

His father, who worked at home, wanted to know why he was so out of breath. "But why didn't you take the elevator?" he asked, frowning at Martin when he explained about the stairs. Not only are you skinny and weak and bad at sports, his expression seemed to say, but you're also a coward. After that, Martin forced himself to take the elevator. He would have to get used to it, he told himself, just the way he got used to being bullied at school, and always picked last when they chose teams. The elevator was an undeniable fact of life.

He didn't get used to it. He remained tense in the trembling little box, his eyes fixed on the numbers over the door that blinked on and off so haltingly, as if at any moment they might simply give up. Sometimes he forced himself to look away from them, to the Emergency Stop button, or the red Alarm button. What would happen if he pushed one of them? Would a bell ring? Would the elevator stop between floors? And if it did, how would they get him out?

That was what he hated about being alone on the thing—the fear of being trapped there for hours by himself. But it wasn't much better when there were other passengers. He felt too close to any other rider, too intimate. And he was always very conscious of the effort people made *not* to look at one another, staring fixedly at nothing. Being short, in this one situation, was an advantage, since his face was below the eye level of adults, and after a brief glance they ignored him.

Until the morning the elevator stopped at the fourteenth floor, and the fat lady got on. She wore a threadbare green coat that ballooned around her; her ankles bulged above dirty sneakers. As she waddled into the elevator, Martin was sure he felt it sink under her weight. She was so big that she filled the cubicle; her coat brushed against him, and he had to squeeze into the corner to make room for her— there certainly wouldn't have been room for another passenger. The door slammed quickly behind her. And then, unlike everyone else, she did not stand facing the door. She stood with her back to the door, wheezing, staring directly at Martin.

For a moment he met her gaze. Her features seemed very small, squashed together by the loose, fleshy mounds of her cheeks. She had no chin, only a great swollen mass of neck, barely contained by the collar of her coat. Her sparse red hair was pinned back by a plastic barrette. And her blue eyes, though tiny, were sharp and penetrating, boring into Martin's face.

Abruptly he looked away from her to the numbers over the door. She didn't turn around. Was she still looking at him? His eyes slipped back to hers, then quickly away. She *was* still watching him. He wanted to close his eyes; he wanted to turn around and stare into the corner, but how could he? The elevator creaked down to twelve, down to eleven. Martin looked at his watch; he looked at the numbers again. They weren't even down to nine yet. And then, against his will, his eyes slipped back to her face. She was still watching him. Her nose tilted up; there was a large space between her nostrils and her upper lip, giving her a piggish look. He looked away again, clenching his teeth, fighting the impulse to squeeze his eyes shut against her.

She had to be crazy. Why else would she stare at him this way? What was she going to do next?

She did nothing. She only watched him, breathing audibly, until the elevator reached the first floor at last. Martin would have rushed past her to get out, but there was no room. He could only wait as she turned—reluctantly, it seemed to him—and moved so slowly out into the lobby. And then he ran. He didn't care what she thought. He ran past her, outside into the fresh air, and he ran almost all the way to school. He had never felt such relief in his life.

He thought about her all day. Did she live in the building? He had never seen her before, and the building wasn't very big—only four apartments on each floor. It seemed likely that she didn't live there, and had only been visiting somebody.

But if she were only visiting somebody, why was she leaving the building at seven thirty in the morning? People didn't make visits at that time of day. Did that mean she *did* live in the building? If so, it was likely—it was a certainty—that sometime he would be riding with her on the elevator again.

He was apprehensive as he approached the building after school. In the lobby, he considered the stairs. But that was ridiculous. Why should he be afraid of an old lady? If he *was* afraid of her, if he let it control him, then he was worse than all the names they called him at school. He pressed the button; he stepped into the empty elevator. He stared at the lights, urging the elevator on. It stopped on three.

At least it's not fourteen, he told himself; the person she was visiting lives on fourteen. He watched the door slide open—revealing a green coat, a piggish face, blue eyes already fixed on him as though she knew he'd be there.

It wasn't possible. It was like a nightmare. But there she was, massively real. "Going up!" he said, his voice a humiliating squeak.

She nodded, her flesh quivering, and stepped on. The door slammed. He watched her pudgy hand move toward the buttons. She pressed, not fourteen, but eighteen, the top floor, one floor above his own. The elevator trembled and began its ascent. The fat lady watched him.

He knew she had gotten on at fourteen this morning. So why was she on three, going up to eighteen now? The only floors *he* ever went to were seventeen and one. What was she doing? Had she been waiting for him? Was she riding with him on purpose?

But that was crazy. Maybe she had a lot of friends in the building. Or else she was a cleaning lady who worked in different apartments. That had to be it. He felt her eyes on him as he stared at the numbers slowly blinking on and off—slower than usual, it seemed to him. Maybe the elevator was having trouble because of how heavy she was. It was supposed to carry three adults, but it was old. What if it got stuck between floors? What if it fell?

They were on five now. It occurred to him to press seven, get off there, and walk the rest of the way. And he would have done it, if he could have reached the buttons. But there was no room to get past her without squeezing against her, and he could not bear the thought of any physical contact with her. He concentrated on being in his room. He would be home soon, only another minute or so. He could stand anything for a minute, even this crazy lady watching him.

Unless the elevator got stuck between floors. Then what would he do? He tried to push the thought away, but it kept coming back. He looked at her. She was still staring at him, no expression at all on her squashed little features.

When the elevator stopped on his floor, she barely moved out of the way. He had to inch past her, rubbing against her horrible scratchy coat, terrified the door would close before he made it through. She quickly turned and watched him as the door slammed shut. And he thought, *Now she knows I live on seventeen.*

"Did you ever notice a strange fat lady on the elevator?" he asked his father that evening.

"Can't say as I have," he said, not looking away from the television.

He knew he was probably making a mistake, but he had to tell somebody. "Well, she was on the elevator with me twice today. And the funny thing was, she just kept staring at me, she never stopped looking at me for a minute. You think . . . you know of anybody who has a weird cleaning lady or anything?"

"What are you so worked up about now?" his father said, turning impatiently away from the television.

"I'm not worked up. It was just funny the way she kept staring at me. You know how people never look at each other in the elevator. Well, she just kept looking at me."

"What am I going to do with you, Martin?" his father said. He sighed and shook his head. "Honestly, now you're afraid of some poor old lady."

"I'm not afraid."

"You're afraid," said his father, with total assurance. "When are you going to grow up and act like a man? Are you going to be timid all your life?"

He managed not to cry until he got to his room—but his father probably knew he was crying anyway. He slept very little.

And in the morning, when the elevator door opened, the fat lady was waiting for him.

She was expecting him. She knew he lived on seventeen. He stood there, unable to move, and then backed away. And as he did so, her expression changed. She smiled as the door slammed.

He ran for the stairs. Luckily, the unlit flight on which he fell was between sixteen and fifteen. He only had to drag himself up one and a half flights with the terrible pain in his leg. His father was silent on the way to the hospital, disappointed and annoyed at him for being such a coward and a fool.

It was a simple fracture. He didn't need a wheelchair, only a cast and crutches. But he was condemned to the elevator now. Was that why the fat lady had smiled? Had she known it would happen this way?

At least his father was with him on the elevator on the way back from the hospital. There was no room for the fat lady to get on. And even if she did, his father would see her, he would realize how peculiar she was, and then maybe he would understand. And once they got home, he could stay in the apartment for a few days—the doctor had said he should use the leg as little as possible. A week, maybe—a whole week without going on the elevator. Riding up with his father, leaning on his crutches, he looked around the little cubicle and felt a kind of triumph. He had beaten the elevator, and the fat lady, for the time being. And the end of the week was very far away.

"Oh, I almost forgot," his father reached out his hand and pressed nine.

"What are you doing? You're not getting off, are you?" he asked him, trying not to sound panicky.

"I promised Terry Ullman I'd drop in on her," his father said, looking at his watch as he stepped off.

"Let me go with you. I want to visit her, too," Martin pleaded, struggling forward on his crutches.

But the door was already closing. "Afraid to be on the elevator alone?" his father said, with a look of total scorn. "Grow up, Martin." The door slammed shut.

Martin hobbled to the buttons and pressed nine, but it didn't do any good. The elevator stopped at ten, where the fat lady was waiting for him. She moved in quickly; he was too slow, too unsteady on his crutches to work his way past her in time. The door sealed them in; the elevator started up.

"Hello, Martin," she said, and laughed, and pushed the Stop button.

• • • •

I FOUND "THE ELEVATOR" in *Things That Go Bump in the Night: A Collection of Original Stories*, edited by Jane Yolen and Martin H. Greenberg.

Books by Sleator include: *Among the Dolls*, a psychological thriller for younger grades; *The Green Futures of Tycho*, a tale of time travel to the future; *Interstellar Pig*, a novel about menacing aliens posing as neighbors; *Oddballs*, semiautobiographical short stories; *Run*, a thriller in which a storm brings three teenagers together in an isolated house; and *Singularity*, a novel in which twin boys discover coexisting dimensions and universes.

Fans of William Sleator will also enjoy the work of Ray Bradbury (page 252) and John Christopher (page 131).

THE NIGHT WATCHMAN

by David Braly

A Story From the Shadows of Childhood

"The Night Watchman" by David Braly (BRAWL-ee) is an example of how the moon and the stars work in a writer's life, how certain events lying dormant in the subconscious—randomly stuffed in there over the years like old clothes and furniture in the attic—one day come together at a single moment to make a story.

To begin with, Braly has lived his entire life in the lumber community of Prineville, Oregon, once the ponderosa pine capital of the world. There are six thousand residents now, but when he was a boy there were only half as many. Among those few, he recalls, was a night watchman who would check the doors of the stores nightly. "I truthfully don't know if he was paid by the merchants or the police. The town was so small in those days, we didn't *need* much of a police force." Braly never met the watchman close up, though he saw him from a distance, and that was enough for him to file away in his memory bank.

Sometime in high school Braly also saw one of the movie clones of *The Exorcist*, a film called *The Possessed*. He remembers being chilled by the film's eerie setting—a girls' school housed in dark Gothic buildings, with a menacing tree on campus. And he filed it away.

Several years later he chanced to see the picture again at Reed College, where he was going to school. There was more than the usual student interest in the movie because it had been filmed on location at the Reed campus. "That film taught me one of the great lessons of my life. The eerie building in the film was actually Eliot Hall that I passed every day and the tree was the same one sitting outside the campus library. Suddenly I saw how you could take familiar things in your own environment and use them dramatically in a film or story."

While at Reed, Braly took a brief writing workshop in which he was required to hand in a short story or poem for the class to critique. An early version of "The Night Watchman" was written for that class. "I thought it was perfect," he recalls, "and wondered how they could find anything wrong with it. Well, they tore it to pieces."

By the time he graduated with a degree in history and social science a few years later, he'd decided to become a writer. So out came "The Night Watchman" to be rewritten and sent out to *Alfred Hitchcock's Mystery Magazine*, where it appeared in 1983.

• • • •

H E HAD WALKED THE SIDEWALKS of Sawyerville at night for as long as anyone could remember. He never hurried, never strolled, just proceeded in a slow but businesslike manner from one door to the next, turning each knob to make sure that every store in town was safely locked. To think of Sawyerville at night without thinking of its watchman was impossible.

And yet, while he was familiar to everyone, it was as an old building or weathered face is familiar, not as is a living, breathing person. People readily recognized his tall, lean figure, his slouching wide-brim hat, his low-strapped holster and gun, and his long, lead-handled flashlight. They knew his lumbering walk, his habit of staying close to the walls, within the shadows. They were familiar with all these things about him, but not with the man himself.

Somebody must have interviewed him for the job, must have shown him around the town when he first arrived, but no one could remember who. For in the whole town of Sawyerville, there was not one man or woman who claimed personal knowledge of the watchman. Where he lived and what his name was were as unknown as were his origins and past life. No one claimed him as their kin, friend, or acquaintance. No one could say what color his clothes or hat might be, although almost everyone assumed they were dark colors, just as they assumed that his skin, eyes, and hair were dark. His features were unknown, his face forever hidden by the night and by the slouching brim of his hat. In fact, there was even an argument about his features in the Golden Star Tavern one night in 1964. One man claimed that the watchman looked like Jimmy Stewart, another said that he resembled Anthony Quinn.

After that argument, when men saw the night watchman making his rounds they looked closely, trying to see the features of his face. But the night and the slouching hat and the distance prevented them. Perhaps if they'd walked up to the watchman they might have seen his face. And yet no man ever approached him. Nor, by some co-incidence, was any person ever approached by the watchman, although he never appeared to avoid anyone. Every night he followed his route down the dark sidewalks and back alleys and no person ever happened to be directly on that route either by accident or by design.

What annoyed people about the watchman was that he wasn't satisfied to walk that route. He could and did go anywhere he wanted, and no one knew from one night to the next where he might be. Old men staggering out of the taverns on Main Street would see a shadow moving against a building on the opposite side of the street and think that it was he. Young men whistling as they walked home on the edge of town would suddenly feel that they were being watched, and they would think that he was there, somewhere, in the night. Women hurrying down the dark sidewalks would feel his eyes following them. Teenagers sneaking down the deserted alleys after curfew would sud-denly notice that the watchman was standing in the distance, looking at them. Small children were afraid to venture out of their yards after dusk, fearing an encounter with him, and they would imagine that every movement in the darkness was he.

For all that, the watchman was never a subject of much specu-lation or conversation. He was there, he'd always been there, people wondered who he was and where he lived, and that was all.

However, there was one person in Sawyerville who wondered more than the others about the watchman. Even as a child Thomas Perkins had wondered. He continued to wonder as an adult. His curiosity increased, and occasionally he voiced it to his friends in the bank or at whatever tavern he happened to be patronizing.

Thomas Perkins was the last member of one of Sawyerville's pioneer families. Amos Perkins, his great-grandfather, had come there from Missouri in 1878. He had originally ranched on land nearby, but over a period of many years he had by hard work and cunning op-portunism built for himself and his family a great enterprise based upon land and livestock but also embracing several mercantile stores, two gold mines, and a freight line. The Perkins fief was shattered by the Great Depression, and by the time Thomas Perkins inherited its ruins, all that remained was five hundred acres of land along the creek, leased to a neighboring farmer, and a half interest in an abandoned cinnabar mine inhabited by bats.

There also remained the faded green three-story house on Walton Street, its steep gray roof and half-dozen chimneys towering above the nearby elms and the neighboring houses. A meter-high fence of slender green pickets enclosed its yard, that was planted with shrubs instead of grass. Thomas Perkins lived there alone. The only other person who ever went into the house was the old cleaning woman who busied herself there every day while Perkins was at the bank, where he had secured employment as a cashier. Early in the evening, after the sun had gone down but before the sky had blackened, Perkins would sit in his chair atop the high, covered porch of the big house, a tall, thin young man with black hair and piercing brown eyes who was overdressed in a blue three-piece suit, looking out at the front gate, at Walton Street, and out toward the center of town that was half a mile away and obscured by the nearby houses and trees.

When night came, Perkins would walk the several blocks to the taverns on Main, or drive his beat-up old Chevy to one of those at the edge of town. There he would drink whisky and talk with other men. Usually he talked about sports, politics, or local affairs, sometimes he talked gossip, and occasionally he talked about the watchman. Rarely his subject was the watchman, yet he talked more than any other man about him.

As time passed, Thomas Perkins warmed to his subject. Each year he talked more about him than the previous year, until men noticed that speculating about the watchman had become his favorite activity. His talk increased their own curiosity about the watchman, but mostly it caused them to wonder about Perkins himself, about why he was so absorbed in the subject.

Eventually the cashier became obsessed by the watchman. Never an evening passed that Perkins didn't mention him at some tavern. His attitude, the way he would spring mention of him into any conversation on the slightest pretext, revealed the depth of his obsession. It was clear to almost everyone who knew Thomas Perkins that the young man was thinking about the watchman during the whole of his days, and possibly dreaming about him at night. Old friends avoided him because they were tired of hearing his pointless speculation, and one or two men were heard to say that they feared Perkins was losing his mind.

Perkins probably noticed that he was driving away his friends.

But apparently he could not stop himself. And their indifference to the mystery annoyed him.

"What's the matter with you people?" he exploded one night. "Don't you understand? Don't you see how strange it is? As long as the oldest people in this town can remember, that night watchman has always been making his rounds. Don't you realize how old he has to be?"

"Now, Tom," said his friend Carl Lockwood. "We both know that the watchman those old folks remember and this man can't be the same fellow. There must have been another one before this man."

"When was the current watchman hired?"

"I don't know."

"And who does he work for?"

"Why, the merchants of course."

Thomas Perkins wasn't satisfied by these answers. During his spring break in 1981 he decided to conduct his own, private investigation. It involved going through the files of the *Sawyerville News* and the records of the municipal and county governments, as well as his questioning people of knowledge and authority in the sheriff's department, the Sawyerville police department, the Chamber of Commerce, and the Sawyerville Merchants Association. What he learned was that there was no record or recollection of *anyone's* having ever hired the watchman.

Perkins reported his findings to his friends and to others who were willing to listen. Almost everyone he talked to expressed interest, but no one appeared to be alarmed by what he had discovered. Carl Lockwood listened attentively while Perkins revealed his findings, then shrugged his shoulders and suggested that Perkins write a letter about it to the editor of the newspaper.

Herb Sudbury had a better suggestion. Sudbury was a short, heavyset, bald man in his early sixties who had once been a millworker but who now did all sorts of odd jobs around town in order to earn enough money to pay for his shabby second-floor room at one of the old boarding houses on Thompson Street and an inadequate supply (to his own way of thinking) of whisky. Sudbury was also the father of the girl Perkins had almost married and one of the few friends he had who for brief moments could halfway match his interest in the mystery of the watchman. And his suggestion to Perkins was simple: "Let's follow him and see where he goes."

The next night Perkins and Sudbury huddled together beneath the bridge that spanned the creek. From his investigation Perkins knew

that many nights the bridge was the last place where the watchman
had been seen. And so they waited there, listening for footfalls on the
pedestrian walk above, hearing for the most part only the creek water
splashing over rocks. Occasionally they did hear someone walking on
the bridge. When they did, Perkins would sneak out onto the south
bank where he would stare from behind a bush until he was certain
that the person he was looking at was not the watchman.

Finally, at eleven o'clock, Perkins recognized through the leaves
of the bush the tall, lean, hatted figure of the watchman. He turned
east after he left the bridge, walking down the narrow road that
bordered the north bank. Perkins slipped back under the bridge, where
he whispered to Sudbury that their quarry had arrived. Sudbury, sober
for once, only reluctantly followed Perkins up the north bank and
onto the road.

Just as they stepped onto the road, the watchman turned full
around and switched on his flashlight, pinning Perkins and Sudbury
in its beam.

"He sees us," gasped Sudbury.

"Stay calm."

"Calm, nothing. Man-oh-man!"

Perkins stared into the light. He didn't move.

Sudbury moved, but not much. He looked down at the bank,
calculating his chances if he tried to escape. He knew that he was old
and weak, that he could never outrun any man who had a reservoir
of strength, and still less could he outrun a bullet. He remained where
he was, anxious to flee but afraid to move.

Perkins started walking toward the watchman.

"What're you doing?" whispered Sudbury.

"I'm going up to him and look him right in the eye."

"Are you crazy? Come back . . . Tom . . . Tom!"

But Perkins continued to walk down the leafy road toward the
watchman, eighty feet distant from Sudbury. Soon Perkins was so
close that his body shielded Sudbury from the flashlight beam.

Sudbury stared, horrified, afraid to speak or to move. All that
he could see was the shrinking black form of Perkins's back, outlined
by the watchman's light. All that he could hear was the splashing
waters of the creek and a gentle breeze swaying the upper branches
of the elms and willows that lined its banks.

Suddenly the light disappeared.

Sudbury assumed that either Perkins was now so close to it that
his bulk completely blocked it out or else the watchman had switched

it off. Eventually he decided that the latter had happened. No matter how close Perkins was to the flashlight some of the light would be visible unless the watchman had switched it off.

Sudbury squinted in an effort to see what was happening. He could almost make out the form of Perkins standing on the road, but the watchman wasn't visible. The night was late, and dark, and its blackness was alleviated only by the quarter moon, the stars, and the light that came from the windows of a few houses on the other side of the creek through the elms and willows.

For ten minutes Sudbury waited for something to happen. Nothing did. And during the time of his wait his panic subsided, until finally it vanished altogether. He came to believe that Thomas Perkins and the watchman were standing on the road ahead talking to each other, maybe even having a good laugh about the way the cashier had thought the watchman so strange and mysterious. Yes, and he, Sudbury, was missing the conversation.

He began walking down the road, slowly at first but faster after he got his legs working good. He walked toward the black form of Perkins's back, listening for the conversation, for the laughs, but hearing only the splashing water and the swaying leaves.

Sudbury was less than ten feet from Perkins before he realized that the cashier was alone.

When he did reach him, he found Perkins staring straight ahead, wide-eyed, his mouth half-open and his face immobile.

"Where is he? Tom? Where's the watchman? . . . What happened? . . . Tom? . . . What's wrong? . . . Tom!"

Thomas Perkins never said a word to Herb Sudbury. And, although he did recover his ability to speak during the months that followed, he refused to talk about what had happened on the tree-shadowed road.

The watchman made his rounds as usual the following night, and all the nights that came after. Several police officers were heard to say that he would be questioned about what had happened the night Perkins suffered his breakdown, but they never did get around to doing it. Certainly no one else has tried to question or even approach the watchman, who still makes his nightly rounds down the sidewalks and back alleys of Sawyerville.

And most certain of all is the fact that Perkins has never again confronted him. He was released from the Portland hospital in October, 1982. He was rehired by the bank, but for shorter hours. Neither there, nor at the taverns, which he visits now only infrequently, will he discuss the night he met the watchman nor the watchman himself. Knowing that he went through a terrible year and a half after that meeting, no one ever talks about those things in his presence.

However, everyone believes that while Thomas Perkins, wearing his blue three-piece suit, sits on his chair on the porch of his huge, faded green house watching the arrival of dusk, he is thinking about one particular night in the spring of 1981—and about the watchman.

• • • •

Fans of Braly's story will also enjoy Ray Bradbury's writing (page 252) and William Sleator's (page 236), as well as the following books by anthologist Helen Hoke: *Horrifying and Hideous Hauntings*; *Spooks, Spirits, and Other Sinister Creatures*; *Tales of Fear and Frightening Phenomena*; and *Uncanny Tales and Unearthly and Unexpected Horrors*. See also *Things That Go Bump in the Night: A Collection of Original Stories*, edited by Jane Yolen and Martin H. Greenberg; and *Young Mutants* and *Young Monsters*, both edited by Isaac Asimov, Martin Greenberg, and Charles Waugh.

THE RAVINE

by Ray Bradbury

The Boy with His Head in the Stars

Raymond was different from the other fifth-graders. He couldn't catch a ball, or hit one either. He always had this far-away look about him, as though he could see things the others couldn't. And then there was his collection of "Buck Rogers" strips from the *Waukegan News-Sun* comics page, the one he was always talking about at school. His classmates finally began to taunt him about it, telling him how stupid that rocket stuff was and how stupid he must be too.

On the playground, Raymond listened to the jeers, crushed by his critics. When he couldn't take it anymore, he went home and tore the collection to shreds. But a week later the nine-year-old realized he'd torn himself apart too. They're wrong, he told himself, they don't understand. So he withdrew from the playground crowd and rebuilt his collection.

He never rejoined the crowd. He went to the library instead, reading all the Tom Swift and Tarzan books, then *John Carter of Mars, 20,000 Leagues Under the Sea*, and H. G. Wells's *War of the Worlds*. You could go to the library any Monday night and there would be Raymond, loading up for the week. Finally, when he was around twelve, his head bursting with everything he'd put into it, he started writing a thousand words a day. Not as a homework assignment, a term paper, or a secret diary—just stuff he dreamed about.

Today, more than sixty years later, Raymond is still Raymond. He still sees things others can't and he's still collecting that "rocket stuff," too, but nobody calls him stupid anymore. They call him rich, and brilliant, and cool. That's what they call Ray Bradbury, the most successful science-fiction writer in American publishing history.

Since 1942, he has sold more than five hundred short stories, poems, plays, operas, novels, screenplays, television scripts, and essays on such diverse subjects as horror, fantasy, science fiction, mystery, romance, fiction, nonfiction, and history, and they have been translated into more than thirty languages. Is there another writer on the face of the planet, dead or alive, who has sold work to *Weird Tales, The New Yorker, Cosmopolitan,* and *Nation's Business*?

It all began, as it often does with great writers, with the good fortune of having a mother and an aunt who read to him as a young child. His mother steeped him in Grimms' fairy tales and the Oz books. Like Hans Christian Andersen (whose father had built him a puppet theater) and Moss Hart (whose aunt took him to the theater each week—see page 303), Bradbury had a special relative—Aunt Neva, a costume designer, who helped him to make masks and puppets for acting out his stories. She also read Edgar Allan Poe to him and took him to his first stage plays.

While Bradbury's classmates didn't always understand him, there was a teacher who did. Her name was Jennet Johnson and she taught the tenth-grade short-story class he took at Los Angeles High School. His first story for her was science fiction—long before it was fashionable in America—and it was returned to him with this message: "I don't know what you're doing but you can *write!*" Her ten words of encouragement spurred him to write twice as much as the rest of the class, even to borrow the typing room during lunchtime. Looking back on their relationship, he recalled, "When I left high school, I took Miss Johnson along as a friend, and saw her frequently over the years. Every time she saw me, she asked, 'What have you been reading?' And I told her and she graded me on the spot." When his eventual fame brought him banquet honors, he would bring Miss Johnson along to be honored as well.

Miss Johnson's interest in his reading led to the next phase of his development. As has been pointed out elsewhere, Bradbury is the only one of science fiction's giant ABC (Isaac Asimov, Ray Bradbury, and Arthur C. Clarke) who was not trained as a scientist. That is correct only if you are talking about the conventional classroom laboratory. True, Bradbury couldn't afford to go to college—after he finished high school in 1938, he sold newspapers for three years. But consider how he was training his mind outside the classroom. The weekly visits to the library that began in elementary school grew into daily experiences for him when the family moved to Los Angeles for his high school years.

Then, with no college options, he put himself into the Los Angeles library and "graduated from there when I was twenty-eight," he explains. "I read everything that I could in every section. I gave myself an education in art history, philosophy, theology, the short story, the mystery story, essays, poetry, you name it. In some places, not very deep. In other places, complete. I just ran amok. I ramble libraries, I don't plan anything. I just climb the stacks like a chimpanzee."

Bradbury's love affair with the library should not be construed to mean he had no outside interests. Far from it. He was an inveterate moviegoer and radio listener. At one point in junior high school, he and a friend discovered where George Burns and Gracie Allen did their radio broadcasts. The two boys then waited outside the studio each week and badgered Burns until he allowed them inside—where they were an audience of two.

Not content with this, Bradbury began writing scripts for the show and pressing them on Burns each week. Though Burns accepted them with a smile, he never indicated whether he read them. He did, however, assure the boys that they were geniuses and should continue with their writing.

Eventually, Bradbury and his friend went on to other endeavors and George and Gracie went on to television and movies. Fifty-four years later, Burns and Bradbury had a tearful surprise reunion at a Hollywood banquet where Burns exclaimed, "Ray, was that really you back there in 1934? I *remember* you!"

While he was educating himself in the library, he divided his time between writing stories, sending them to pulp magazines, and opening the rejection letters. Finally, at age twenty-two, he sold his first one—for $20, to a magazine called *Weird Tales*. If he was going to earn a living at writing, he would have to mine every creative vein in his body. So for the next few years he averaged about forty stories a year—which brought him the glorious total of eight hundred dollars a year.

Those lean early years taught him that everything had a story lurking behind it. And oftentimes one story led to the next. For example, in the early 1950s, walking along the California beach one evening, Bradbury and his new wife came upon the ruins of the old Venice Beach Pier with its tracks and beams sticking eerily out of the sand and sea. "What's that dinosaur doing here on the beach?" he asked his wife. Into his subconscious it went until the next night, when he heard the Santa Monica foghorn. Story idea: an ancient dinosaur lured out of the sea by the mating call of the foghorn on the lighthouse. The short story, "The Fog Horn," appeared in *The Saturday Evening Post* (it would later be made into a popular sci-fi movie, *The Beast from 20,000 Fathoms*) and caught the eye of director John Huston, who wanted to make a movie of *Moby-Dick*. Would Bradbury consider doing the screenplay? Of course!

Bradbury then took some of the research he did on Herman Melville for *Moby-Dick* and used it as an introduction for a new translation of *20,000 Leagues Under the Sea*. That was seen by the organizers of the 1964 World's Fair in New York. Would he take charge of the creation of the top floor of the U.S. pavilion? Of course! And that's where the Disney folks first saw his genius. Would he like to design the dreams for Spaceship Earth at EPCOT Center? Do puppies like to chew on shoes? When you see the spaceship at EPCOT, remember how it began—in a creative genius's encounter with the ruins of an old ocean pier thirty years ago.

The story you are about to encounter here is from *Dandelion Wine*, a novel only Ray Bradbury would create. Most of its chapters had previous and separate lives as short stories in magazines. They were all related, nevertheless, by the fact that they sprang from the stashed-away memories of Bradbury's childhood—a toy, sneakers, lawn mowers, firecrackers, dandelions, and carnivals. In the mid-1950s, Bradbury hit upon the idea of a unique anthology. Suppose, he thought, I took some of my favorite stories and wove them together with a continuous plot that spread through one summer of a kid's life. Would it work? To date, *Dandelion Wine* has sold more than one million copies and is regarded as a modern classic in fantasy fiction.

Bradbury follows in the tradition of writers who often return to the well of their childhood homes (Kipling, Andersen, Frances Hodgson Burnett, Harper Lee, Gary Paulsen). *Dandelion Wine* is set in fictitious Green Town, which was really Waukegan, Illinois, where Bradbury grew up next door to his grandparents. The ravine included in this story is just like the one in Waukegan, and there really was an eccentric called "the Lonely One" who once haunted the dark corners of Waukegan.

For Bradbury, that ravine was the darkest nightmare of his childhood, "especially on those nights when walking home late across town, after seeing Lon Chaney's delicious fright *The Phantom of the Opera*, my brother Skip would run ahead and hide out under the ravine-creek bridge like the Lonely One and leap out and grab me, shrieking, so I ran, fell, and ran again, gibbering all the way home. That was great stuff." Bradbury once took his daughters back to

Waukegan to see if the ravine was as dark and deep as he remembered. It was worse.

. . . .

THE COURTHOUSE CLOCK chimed seven times. The echoes of the chimes faded.

Warm summer twilight here in upper Illinois country in this little town deep far away from everything, kept to itself by a river and a forest and a meadow and a lake. The sidewalks still scorched. The stores closing and the streets shadowed. And there were two moons; the clock moon with four faces in four night directions above the solemn black courthouse, and the real moon rising in vanilla whiteness from the dark east.

In the drugstore fans whispered in the high ceiling. In the rococo shade of porches, a few invisible people sat. Cigars glowed pink, on occasion. Screen doors whined their springs and slammed. On the purple bricks of the summer-night streets, Douglas Spaulding ran; dogs and boys followed after.

"Hi, Miss Lavinia!"

The boys loped away. Waving after them quietly, Lavinia Nebbs sat all alone with a tall cool lemonade in her white fingers, tapping it to her lips, sipping, waiting.

"Here I am, Lavinia."

She turned and there was Francine, all in snow white, at the bottom steps of the porch, in the smell of zinnias and hibiscus.

Lavinia Nebbs locked her front door and, leaving her lemonade glass half empty on the porch, said, "It's a fine night for the movie."

They walked down the street.

"Where you going, girls?" cried Miss Fern and Miss Roberta from their porch over the way.

Lavinia called back through the soft ocean of darkness: "To the Elite Theater to see CHARLIE CHAPLIN!"

"Won't catch us out on no night like this," wailed Miss Fern. "Not with the Lonely One strangling women. Lock ourselves up in our closet with a gun."

"Oh, bosh!" Lavinia heard the old women's door bang and lock, and she drifted on, feeling the warm breath of summer night shimmering off the oven-baked sidewalks. It was like walking on a hard crust of freshly warmed bread. The heat pulsed under your dress, along your legs, with a stealthy and not unpleasant sense of invasion.

"Lavinia, you don't believe all that about the Lonely One, do you?"

"Those women like to see their tongues dance."

"Just the same, Hattie McDollis was killed two months ago, Roberta Ferry the month before, and now Elizabeth Ramsell's disappeared. . . ."

"Hattie McDollis was a silly girl, walked off with a traveling man, I bet."

"But the others, all of them, strangled, their tongues sticking out their mouths, they say."

They stood upon the edge of the ravine that cut the town half in two. Behind them were the lit houses and music, ahead was deepness, moistness, fireflies and dark.

"Maybe we shouldn't go to the show tonight," said Francine. "The Lonely One might follow and kill us. I don't like that ravine. Look at it, will you!"

Lavinia looked and the ravine was a dynamo that never stopped running, night or day; there was a great moving hum, a bumbling and murmuring of creature, insect, or plant life. It smelled like a greenhouse, of secret vapors and ancient, washed shales and quicksands. And always the black dynamo humming, with sparkles like great electricity where fireflies moved on the air.

"It won't be *me* coming back through this old ravine tonight late, so darned late; it'll be you, Lavinia, you down the steps and over the bridge and maybe the Lonely One there."

"Bosh!" said Lavinia Nebbs.

"It'll be you alone on the path, listening to your shoes, not me. You all alone on the way back to your house. Lavinia, don't you get lonely living in that house?"

"Old maids love to live alone." Lavinia pointed at the hot shadowy path leading down into the dark. "Let's take the short cut."

"I'm afraid!"

"It's early. Lonely One won't be out till late." Lavinia took the other's arm and led her down and down the crooked path into the cricket warmth and frog sound and mosquito-delicate silence. They brushed through summer-scorched grass, burs prickling at their bare ankles.

"Let's run!" gasped Francine.

"No!"

They turned a curve in the path—and there it was.

In the singing deep night, in the shade of warm trees, as if she had laid herself out to enjoy the soft stars and the easy wind, her hands at either side of her like the oars of a delicate craft, lay Elizabeth Ramsell!

Francine screamed.

"Don't scream!" Lavinia put out her hands to hold onto Francine, who was whimpering and choking. "Don't! Don't!"

The woman lay as if she had floated there, her face moonlit, her eyes wide and like flint, her tongue sticking from her mouth.

"She's dead!" said Francine. "Oh, she's dead, dead! She's dead!"

Lavinia stood in the middle of a thousand warm shadows with the crickets screaming and the frogs loud.

"We'd better get the police," she said at last.

"Hold me, Lavinia, hold me, I'm cold, oh, I've never been so cold in all my life!"

Lavinia held Francine and the policemen were brushing through the crackling grass, flashlights ducked about, voices mingled, and the night grew toward eight-thirty.

"It's like December. I need a sweater," said Francine, eyes shut, against Lavinia.

The policeman said, "I guess you can go now, ladies. You might drop by the station tomorrow for a little more questioning."

Lavinia and Francine walked away from the police and the sheet over the delicate thing upon the ravine grass.

Lavinia felt her heart going loudly in her and she was cold, too, with a February cold; there were bits of sudden snow all over her flesh, and the moon washed her brittle fingers whiter, and she remembered doing all the talking while Francine just sobbed against her.

A voice called from far off, "You want an escort, ladies?"

"No, we'll make it," said Lavinia to nobody, and they walked on. They walked through the nuzzling, whispering ravine, the ravine of whispers and clicks, the little world of investigation growing small behind them with its lights and voices.

"I've never seen a dead person before," said Francine.

Lavinia examined her watch as if it was a thousand miles away on an arm and wrist grown impossibly distant. "It's only eight-thirty. We'll pick up Helen and get on to the show."

"The show!" Francine jerked.

"It's what we need. We've got to forget this. It's not good to remember. If we went home now we'd remember. We'll go to the show as if nothing happened."

"Lavinia, you don't *mean* it!"

"I never meant anything more in my life. We need to laugh now and forget."

"But Elizabeth's back there—your friend, my friend——"

"We can't help her; we can only help ourselves. Come on."

They started up the ravine side, on the stony path, in the dark. And suddenly there, barring their way, standing very still in one spot, not seeing them, but looking on down at the moving lights and the body and listening to the official voices, was Douglas Spaulding.

He stood there, white as a mushroom, with his hands at his sides, staring down into the ravine.

"Get home!" cried Francine.

He did not hear.

"You!" shrieked Francine. "Get home, get out of this place, you hear? Get home, get home, get *home*!"

Douglas jerked his head, stared at them as if they were not there. His mouth moved. He gave a bleating sound. Then, silently, he whirled about and ran. He ran silently up the distant hills into the warm darkness.

Francine sobbed and cried again and, doing this, walked on with Lavinia Nebbs.

"THERE YOU ARE! I thought you ladies'd never come!" Helen Greer stood tapping her foot atop her porch steps. "You're only an hour late, that's all. What happened?"

"We——" started Francine.

Lavinia clutched her arm tight. "There was a commotion. Somebody found Elizabeth Ramsell in the ravine."

"Dead? Was she—dead?"

Lavinia nodded. Helen gasped and put her hand to her throat. "Who found her?"

Lavinia held Francine's wrist firmly. "We don't know."

The three young women stood in the summer night looking at each other. "I've got a notion to go in the house and lock the doors," said Helen at last.

But finally she went to get a sweater, for though it was still warm, she, too, complained of the sudden winter night. While she was gone Francine whispered frantically, "Why didn't you *tell* her?"

"Why upset her?" said Lavinia. "Tomorrow. Tomorrow's plenty of time."

The three women moved along the street under the black trees, past suddenly locked houses. How soon the news had spread outward from the ravine, from house to house, porch to porch, telephone to telephone. Now, passing, the three women felt eyes looking out at them from curtained windows as locks rattled into place. How strange the popsicle, the vanilla night, the night of close-packed ice cream, of mosquito-lotioned wrists, the night of running children suddenly veered from their games and put away behind glass, behind wood, the popsicles in melting puddles of lime and strawberry where they fell when the children were scooped indoors. Strange the hot rooms with the sweating people pressed tightly back into them behind the bronze knobs and knockers. Baseball bats and balls lay upon the un-footprinted lawns. A half-drawn, white-chalk game of hopscotch lay on the broiled, steamed sidewalk. It was as if someone had predicted freezing weather a moment ago.

"We're crazy being out on a night like this," said Helen.

"Lonely One won't kill three ladies," said Lavinia. "There's safety in numbers. And besides, it's too soon. The killings always come a month separated."

A shadow fell across their terrified faces. A figure loomed behind a tree. As if someone had struck an organ a terrible blow with his fist, the three women gave off a scream, in three different shrill notes.

"Got you!" roared a voice. The man plunged at them. He came into the light, laughing. He leaned against a tree, pointing at the ladies weakly, laughing again.

"Hey! I'm the Lonely One!" said Frank Dillon.

"Frank Dillon!"

"Frank!"

"Frank," said Lavinia, "if you ever do a childish thing like that again, may someone riddle you with bullets!"

"What a thing to do!"

Francine began to cry hysterically.

Frank Dillon stopped smiling. "Say, I'm sorry."

"Go away!" said Lavinia. "Haven't you heard about Elizabeth Ramsell—found dead in the ravine? You running around scaring women! Don't speak to us again!"

"Aw, now——"

They moved. He moved to follow.

"Stay right there, Mr. Lonely One, and scare yourself. Go take

a look at Elizabeth Ramsell's face and see if it's funny. Good night!"
Lavinia took the other two on along the street of trees and stars,
Francine holding a kerchief to her face.

"Francine, it was only a joke." Helen turned to Lavinia. "Why's
she crying so hard?"

"We'll tell you when we get downtown. We're going to the
show no matter what! Enough's enough. Come on now, get your
money ready, we're almost there!"

THE DRUGSTORE was a small pool of sluggish air which the great
wooden fans stirred in tides of arnica and tonic and soda-smell out
onto the brick streets.

"I need a nickel's worth of green peppermint chews," said Lavinia
to the druggist. His face was set and pale, like all the faces they had
seen on the half-empty streets. "For eating in the show," said Lavinia
as the druggist weighed out a nickel's worth of the green candy with
a silver shovel.

"You sure look pretty tonight, ladies. You looked cool this afternoon, Miss Lavinia, when you was in for a chocolate soda. So cool
and nice that someone asked after you."

"Oh?"

"Man sitting at the counter—watched you walk out. Said to me,
'Say, who's that?' Why, that's Lavinia Nebbs, prettiest maiden lady
in town, I said. 'She's beautiful,' he said. 'Where does she live?'"
Here the druggist paused uncomfortably.

"You didn't!" said Francine. "You didn't give him her address,
I hope? You didn't!"

"I guess I didn't think. I said, 'Oh, over on Park Street, you
know, near the ravine.' A casual remark. But now, tonight, them
finding the body, I heard a minute ago, I thought, My God, what've
I done!" He handed over the package, much too full.

"You fool!" cried Francine, and tears were in her eyes.

"I'm sorry. Course, maybe it was nothing."

Lavinia stood with the three people looking at her, staring at her.
She felt nothing. Except, perhaps, the slightest prickle of excitement
in her throat. She held out her money automatically.

"There's no charge on those peppermints," said the druggist,
turning to shuffle some papers.

"Well, I know what I'm going to do right now!" Helen stalked
out of the drugshop. "I'm calling a taxi to take us all home. I'll be no
part of a hunting party for you, Lavinia. That man was up to no

good. Asking about you. You want to be dead in the ravine next?"

"It was just a man," said Lavinia, turning in a slow circle to look at the town.

"So is Frank Dillon a man, but maybe he's the Lonely One."

Francine hadn't come out with them, they noticed, and turning, they found her arriving. "I made him give me a description—the druggist. I made him tell what the man looked like. A stranger," she said, "in a dark suit. Sort of pale and thin."

"We're all overwrought," said Lavinia. "I simply won't take a taxi if you get one. If I'm the next victim, let me *be* the next. There's all too little excitement in life, especially for a maiden lady thirty-three years old, so don't you mind if I enjoy it. Anyway, it's silly; I'm not beautiful."

"Oh, but you are, Lavinia; you're the loveliest lady in town, now that Elizabeth is——" Francine stopped. "You keep men off at a distance. If you'd only relax, you'd been married years ago!"

"Stop sniveling, Francine! Here's the theater box office, I'm paying forty-one cents to see Charlie Chaplin. If you two want a taxi, go on. I'll sit alone and go home alone."

"Lavinia, you're crazy; we can't let you do that——"

They entered the theater.

The first showing was over, intermission was on, and the dim auditorium was sparsely populated. The three ladies sat halfway down front, in the smell of ancient brass polish, and watched the manager step through the worn red velvet curtains to make an announcement.

"The police have asked us to close early tonight so everyone can be out at a decent hour. Therefore we are cutting our short subjects and running our feature again immediately. The show will be over at eleven. Everyone is advised to go straight home. Don't linger on the streets."

"That means us, Lavinia!" whispered Francine.

The lights went out. The screen leaped to life.

"Lavinia," whispered Helen.

"What?"

"As we came in, a man in a dark suit, across the street, crossed over. He just walked down the aisle and is sitting in the row behind us."

"Oh, Helen!"

"Right behind us?"

One by one the three women turned to look.

They saw a white face there, flickering with unholy light from the silver screen. It seemed to be all men's faces hovering there in the dark.

"I'm going to get the manager!" Helen was gone up the aisle. "Stop the film! Lights!"

"Helen, come back!" cried Lavinia, rising.

THEY TAPPED their empty soda glasses down, each with a vanilla mustache on their upper lip, which they found with their tongues, laughing.

"You see how silly?" said Lavinia. "All that riot for nothing. How embarrassing."

"I'm sorry," said Helen faintly.

The clock said eleven-thirty now. They had come out of the dark theater, away from the fluttering rush of men and women hurrying everywhere, nowhere, on the street while laughing at Helen. Helen was trying to laugh at herself.

"Helen, when you ran up that aisle crying, 'Lights!' I thought I'd *die*! That *poor* man!"

"The theater manager's brother from Racine!"

"I apologized," said Helen, looking up at the great fan still whirling, whirling the warm late night air, stirring, restirring the smells of vanilla, raspberry, peppermint and Lysol.

"We shouldn't have stopped for these sodas. The police warned——"

"Oh, bosh the police," laughed Lavinia. "I'm not afraid of anything. The Lonely One is a million miles away now. He won't be back for weeks and the police'll get him then, just wait. Wasn't the film wonderful?"

"Closing up, ladies." The druggist switched off the lights in the cool white-tiled silence.

Outside, the streets were swept clean and empty of cars or trucks or people. Bright lights still burned in the small store windows where the warm wax dummies lifted pink wax hands fired with blue-white diamond rings, or flourished orange wax legs to reveal hosiery. The hot blue-glass eyes of the mannequins watched as the ladies drifted down the empty river bottom street, their images shimmering in windows like blossoms seen under darkly moving waters.

"Do you suppose if we screamed they'd do anything?"

"Who?"

"The dummies, the window people."

"Oh, Francine."

"Well . . ."

There were a thousand people in the windows, stiff and silent, and three people on the street, the echoes following like gunshots from store fronts across the way when they tapped their heels on the baked pavement.

A red neon sign flickered dimly, buzzed like a dying insect, as they passed.

Baked and white, the long avenues lay ahead. Blowing and tall in a wind that touched only their leafy summits, the trees stood on either side of the three small women. Seen from the courthouse peak, they appeared like three thistles far away.

"First, we'll walk you home, Francine."

"No, I'll walk *you* home."

"Don't be silly. You live way out at Electric Park. If you walked me home you'd have to come back across the ravine alone, yourself. And if so much as a leaf fell on you, you'd drop dead."

Francine said, "I can stay the night at your house. You're the *pretty* one!"

And so they walked, they drifted like three prim clothes forms over a moonlit sea of lawn and concrete, Lavinia watching the black trees flit by each side of her, listening to the voices of her friends murmuring, trying to laugh; and the night seemed to quicken, they seemed to run while walking slowly, everything seemed fast and the color of hot snow.

"Let's sing," said Lavinia.

They sang, "Shine On, Shine On, Harvest Moon . . ."

They sang sweetly and quietly, arm in arm, not looking back. They felt the hot sidewalk cooling underfoot, moving, moving.

"Listen!" said Lavinia.

They listened to the summer night. The summer-night crickets and the far-off tone of the courthouse clock making it eleven forty-five.

"Listen!"

Lavinia listened. A porch swing creaked in the dark and there was Mr. Terle, not saying anything to anybody, alone on his swing, having a last cigar. They saw the pink ash swinging gently to and fro.

Now the lights were going, going, gone. The little house lights and big house lights and yellow lights and green hurricane lights, the candles and oil lamps and porch lights, and everything felt locked up in brass and iron and steel, everything, thought Lavinia, is boxed and locked and wrapped and shaded. She imagined the people in their moonlit beds. And their breathing in the summer-night rooms, safe and together. And here we are, thought Lavinia, our footsteps on along the baked summer evening sidewalk. And above us the lonely street lights shining down, making a drunken shadow.

"Here's your house, Francine. Good night."

"Lavinia, Helen, stay here tonight. It's late, almost midnight now. You can sleep in the parlor. I'll make hot chocolate—it'll be such fun!" Francine was holding them both now, close to her.

"No, thanks," said Lavinia.

And Francine began to cry.

"Oh, not again, Francine," said Lavinia.

"I don't want you dead," sobbed Francine, the tears running straight down her cheeks. "You're so fine and nice, I want you alive. Please, oh, please!"

"Francine, I didn't know how much this has done to you. I promise I'll phone when I get home."

"Oh, will you?"

"And tell you I'm safe, yes. And tomorrow we'll have a picnic lunch at Electric Park. With ham sandwiches I'll make myself, how's that? You'll see, I'll live forever!"

"You'll phone, then?"

"I promised, didn't I?"

"Good night, good night!" Rushing upstairs, Francine whisked behind a door, which slammed to be snap-bolted tight on the instant.

"Now," said Lavinia to Helen, "I'll walk *you* home."

THE COURTHOUSE CLOCK struck the hour. The sounds blew across a town that was empty, emptier than it had ever been. Over empty streets and empty lots and empty lawns the sound faded.

"Nine, ten, eleven, twelve," counted Lavinia, with Helen on her arm.

"Don't you feel funny?" asked Helen.

"How do you mean?"

"When you think of us being out here on the sidewalks, under the trees, and all those people safe behind locked doors, lying in their beds. We're practically the only walking people out in the open in a thousand miles, I bet."

The sound of the deep warm dark ravine came near.

In a minute they stood before Helen's house, looking at each other for a long time. The wind blew the odor of cut grass between

them. The moon was sinking in a sky that was beginning to cloud.
"I don't suppose it's any use asking you to stay, Lavinia?"

"I'll be going on."

"Sometimes——"

"Sometimes what?"

"Sometimes I think people *want* to die. You've acted odd all evening."

"I'm just not afraid," said Lavinia. "And I'm curious, I suppose. And I'm using my head. Logically, the Lonely One can't be around. The police and all."

"The police are home with their covers up over their ears."

"Let's just say I'm enjoying myself, precariously, but safely. If there was any real chance of anything happening to me, I'd stay here with you, you can be sure of that."

"Maybe part of you doesn't want to live anymore."

"You and Francine. Honestly!"

"I feel so guilty. I'll be drinking some hot cocoa just as you reach the ravine bottom and walk on the bridge."

"Drink a cup for me. Good night."

Lavinia Nebbs walked alone down the midnight street, down the late summer-night silence. She saw houses with the dark windows and far away she heard a dog barking. In five minutes, she thought, I'll be safe at home. In five minutes I'll be phoning silly little Francine. I'll——

She heard the man's voice.

A man's voice singing far away among the trees.

"Oh, give me a June night, the moonlight and you . . ."

She walked a little faster.

The voice sang, "In my arms . . . with all your charms . . ."

Down the street in the dim moonlight a man walked slowly and casually along.

I can run knock on one of these doors, thought Lavinia, if I must.

"Oh, give me a June night," sang the man, and he carried a long club in his hand. "The moonlight and you. Well, look who's *here*! What a time of night for you to be out, Miss Nebbs!"

"Officer Kennedy!"

And that's who it was, of course.

"I'd better see you home!"

"Thanks, I'll make it."

"But you live across the ravine. . . ."

Yes, she thought, but I won't walk through the ravine with any man, not even an officer. How do I know who the Lonely One is? "No," she said, "I'll hurry."

"I'll wait right here," he said. "If you need any help, give a yell. Voices carry good here. I'll come running."

"Thank you."

She went on, leaving him under a light, humming to himself, alone.

Here I am, she thought.

The ravine.

She stood on the edge of the one hundred and thirteen steps that went down the steep hill and then across the bridge seventy yards and up the hills leading to Park Street. And only one lantern to see by. Three minutes from now, she thought, I'll be putting my key in my house door. Nothing can happen in just one hundred eighty seconds.

She started down the long dark-green steps into the deep ravine.

"One, two, three, four, five, six, seven, eight, nine, ten steps," she counted in a whisper.

She felt she was running, but she was not running.

"Fifteen, sixteen, seventeen, eighteen, nineteen, twenty steps," she breathed.

"One fifth of the way!" she announced to herself.

The ravine was deep, black and black, black! And the world was gone behind, the world of safe people in bed, the locked doors, the town, the drugstore, the theater, the lights, everything was gone. Only the ravine existed and lived, black and huge, about her.

"Nothing's happened, has it? No one around, is there? Twenty-four, twenty-five steps. Remember that old ghost story you told each other when you were children?"

She listened to her shoes on the steps.

"The story about the dark man coming in your house and you upstairs in bed. And now he's at the first step coming up to your room. And now he's at the second step. And now he's at the third step and the fourth step and the fifth! Oh, how you used to laugh and scream at that story! And now the horrid dark man's at the twelfth step and now he's opening the door of your room and now he's standing by your bed. 'I GOT YOU!' "

She screamed. It was like nothing she'd ever heard, that scream. She had never screamed that loud in her life. She stopped, she froze, she clung to the wooden banister. Her heart exploded in her. The sound of the terrified beating filled the universe.

"There, *there*!" she screamed to herself. "At the bottom of the steps. A man, under the light! No, now he's gone! He was *waiting* there!"

She listened.

Silence.

The bridge was empty.

Nothing, she thought, holding her heart. Nothing. Fool! That story I told myself. How silly. What shall I do?

Her heartbeats faded.

Shall I call the officer—did he hear me scream?

She listened. Nothing. Nothing.

I'll go the rest of the way. That silly story.

She began again, counting the steps.

"Thirty-five, thirty-six, careful, don't fall. Oh, I am a fool. Thirty-seven steps, thirty-eight, nine and forty, and two makes forty-two—almost halfway."

She froze again.

Wait, she told herself.

She took a step. There was an echo.

She took another step.

Another echo. Another step, just a fraction of a moment later.

"Someone's following me," she whispered to the ravine, to the black crickets and dark-green hidden frogs and the black stream. "Someone's on the steps behind me. I don't dare turn around."

Another step, another echo.

"Every time I take a step, they take one."

A step and an echo.

Weakly she asked of the ravine, "Officer Kennedy, is that *you*?"

The crickets were still.

The crickets were *listening*. The night was listening to *her*. For a change, all of the far summer-night meadows and close summer-night trees were suspending motion; leaf, shrub, star, and meadow grass ceased their particular tremors and were listening to Lavinia Nebbs's heart. And perhaps a thousand miles away, across locomotive-lonely country, in an empty way station, a single traveler reading a dim newspaper under a solitary naked bulb, might raise up his head, listen, and think, What's that? and decide, Only a woodchuck, surely, beating on a hollow log. But it was Lavinia Nebbs, it was most surely the heart of Lavinia Nebbs.

Silence. A summer-night silence which lay for a thousand miles, which covered the earth like a white and shadowy sea.

Faster, faster! She went down the steps.

Run!

She heard music. In a mad way, in a silly way, she heard the great surge of music that pounded at her, and she realized as she ran, as she ran in panic and terror, that some part of her mind was dramatizing, borrowing from the turbulent musical score of some private drama, and the music was rushing and pushing her now, higher and higher, faster, faster, plummeting and scurrying, down, and down into the pit of the ravine.

Only a little way, she prayed. One hundred eight, nine, one hundred ten steps! The bottom! Now, run! Across the bridge!

She told her legs what to do, her arms, her body, her terror; she advised all parts of herself in this white and terrible moment, over the roaring creek waters, on the hollow, thudding, swaying, almost alive, resilient bridge planks she ran, followed by the wild footsteps behind, behind, with the music following, too, the music shrieking and babbling.

He's following, don't turn, don't look, if you see him, you'll not be able to move, you'll be so frightened. Just run, run!

She ran across the bridge.

Oh, God, God, please, please let me get up the hill! Now up, the path, now between the hills, oh God, it's dark, and everything so far away. If I screamed now it wouldn't help; I can't scream anyway. Here's the top of the path, here's the street, oh, God, please let me be safe, if I get home safe I'll never go out alone; I was a fool, let me admit it, I was a fool, I didn't know what terror was, but if you let me get home from this I'll never go without Helen or Francine again! Here's the street. Across the street!

She crossed the street and rushed up the sidewalk.

Oh God, the porch! My house! Oh God, please give me time to get inside and lock the door and I'll be safe!

And there—silly thing to notice—why did she notice, instantly, no time, no time—but there it was anyway, flashing by—there on the porch rail, the half-filled glass of lemonade she had abandoned a long time, a year, half an evening ago! The lemonade glass sitting calmly, imperturbably there on the rail . . . and . . .

She heard her clumsy feet on the porch and listened and felt her hands scrabbling and ripping at the lock with the key. She heard her heart. She heard her inner voice screaming.

The key fit.

Unlock the door, quick, quick!

The door opened.

Now, inside. Slam it!

She slammed the door.

"Now lock it, bar it, lock it!" she gasped wretchedly.

"Lock it, tight, *tight*!"

The door was locked and bolted tight.

The music stopped. She listened to her heart again and the sound of it diminishing into silence.

Home! Oh God, safe at home! Safe, safe and safe at home! She slumped against the door. Safe, safe. Listen. Not a sound. Safe, safe, oh thank God, safe at home. I'll never go out at night again. I'll stay home. I won't go over that ravine again ever. Safe, oh safe, safe home, so good, so good, safe! Safe inside, the door locked. Wait.

Look out the window.

She looked.

Why, there's no one there at all! Nobody. There was nobody following me at all. Nobody running after me. She got her breath and almost laughed at herself. It stands to *reason*. If a man *had* been following me, he'd have *caught* me! I'm not a fast runner. . . . There's no one on the porch or in the yard. How silly of me. I wasn't running from anything. That ravine's as safe as anyplace. Just the same, it's nice to be home. Home's the really good warm place, the only place to be.

She put her hand out to the light switch and stopped.

"What?" she asked. "What? *What?*"

Behind her in the living room, someone cleared his throat.

•   •   •   •

A LONG WITH *Dandelion Wine*, Bradbury's fantasy books include *The Illustrated Man, The Halloween Tree*, and *Something Wicked This Way Comes*. Among his best science-fiction books are *The Martian Chronicles, R Is for Rocket*, and *The Golden Apples of the Sun*. The best retrospective collection of his stories is *The Stories of Ray Bradbury*. Others include *Classic Stories 1* and *Classic Stories 2*.

Much of Ray Bradbury's work is available on audiocassette, including: *Bradbury Thirteen* (dramatizations, seven hours, Mind's Eye); *Dandelion Wine* (read by Michael Prichard, eight hours, Books on Tape); *Fantastic Tales of Ray Bradbury* (read by Bradbury, fourteen stories, abridged, four hours, forty-eight minutes, Listening Library); *The Golden Apples of the Sun* (read by Michael Prichard, seven hours,

Books on Tape); *The Illustrated Man* (read by Michael Prichard, eight hours); and *The Martian Chronicles* (read by Bradbury, six and one-half hours, Listening Library).

Fans of Ray Bradbury will also enjoy the works of William Sleator (page 236) and John Christopher (page 131), as well as *Tales from Isaac Asimov's Science Fiction Magazine*, selected by Sheila Williams and Cynthia Manson; *Young Mutants*, edited by Isaac Asimov, Martin Greenberg, and Charles Waugh; and *Young Monsters*, edited by Isaac Asimov, Martin Greenberg, and Charles Waugh.

Out to the Ball Game

What may be the greatest
"fan" story of all time, and
a near-tragic one.

THE ANDY STRASBERG STORY

as told to Mike Bryan

The Ultimate Fan Story

Andy Strasberg and Roger Maris

A *good* writer can sit down with anyone and dig up at least one good story. A crowded beach, a park, a bus station—each represents a mother lode of gold to a writer who knows two things: how to ask questions and how to listen. A perfect example of that is the story of Mike Bryan and Andy Strasberg. In my estimation, it is the ultimate "fan" story, and a *thousand* writers walked by it for more than a decade before one of them discovered it.

It begins in 1987 with a Texas-born writer named Mike Bryan who was looking around for his next writing project. He and his editor had been impressed by the oral histories Studs Terkel had done over the years (*Working, Hard Times, The Good War*) and wondered about the possibility of something similar being done with baseball. Bryan had done a season-long book with all-star first baseman Keith Hernandez a few years earlier (*If at First*) and knew there were as many colorful characters *off* the field as on it. Without the fans, scorekeepers, groundskeepers, scouts, minor-league managers, stadium announcers, agents, tavern keepers, baseball-card collectors, and so on, we would call it a business instead of a game.

Bryan then approached the public-relations directors of each major-league team and told them about his project. The PR people are usually former sportswriters themselves and retain a fine eye for what makes a good story. They gave Bryan numerous leads, which in turn led to others: "But ya know who would be terrific for this? I know this guy who used to scout the Appalachian League. I'm tellin' ya, the guy is incredible!" Thus it was that when he approached the PR director for the San Diego Padres, he was immediately told, "You've *got* to talk to Andy Strasberg."

Strasberg was the marketing director for the Padres. Without the slightest premonition that he was about to begin the greatest interview of his career, Bryan turned on his tape recorder and asked Strasberg to tell him what it's like to sell baseball. A look of disappointment passed over Strasberg's face. "Can I tell you about *before* I got into this job? Can I tell you about Roger Maris?" he asked.

What followed needed only to be transcribed from the tape recorder and edited slightly. The interview was a dream come true for Bryan, but for every fan who ever dreamed of meeting his or her hero, who ever cut pictures from a magazine and tacked them on a bedroom door, who ever waited hopefully outside a stadium or a theater for an autograph, it was living proof that sometimes dreams come true.

• • • •

I GREW UP IN THE SHADOWS of Yankee Stadium—if it was a long, long shadow! We were really about five miles from the ballpark. One of my fondest memories is when my dad first took me to the Polo Grounds. In the middle of Harlem was this immense cathedral and inside was all this green, green grass. Incredible.

On that particular day the Giants were playing the Phillies and the Phillies were wearing the old-style uniforms, with the oversized red numbers on the back. My dad had purchased tickets to sit in the upper deck, general admission, and then in about the fourth inning he said, "I'll be back in just a minute," and went downstairs. I was sitting there all alone. After about fifteen minutes he came back and motioned for me to come with him and we sat down about four rows from the field. He slipped the usher some money and the guy wiped off the seat. And I just fell in love with baseball. That was 1957 when I was eight years old and throughout my life, every time I started to drift away from the game, something brought me back, something incredible, something very special.

In 1960, when Roger Maris came to the Yankees from Kansas City, I was burned in a fire in August and so I was laid up for a while. I followed baseball even closer because of that. I remember a headline in *Sports Illustrated* saying that Roger Maris "rejuvenates" the New York Yankees. I had never heard the word "rejuvenate," but it triggered in my mind that this person Roger Maris was someone special.

That's just like yesterday to me. That was the year, you may recall, that Roger won the Most Valuable Player Award.

For me, there was just something about the way he swung the bat, the way he played right field, the way he looked. Now I had an idol. In 1961, the entire country was wrapped up in the home-run race between Roger Maris and Mickey Mantle and Babe Ruth's ghost. I cut out every single article on Roger Maris and said to myself when I get older and can afford it, I'm going to have these professionally bound. When I was in college I actually went back to microfilms of 1957, '58, and '59 newspapers and magazines and made copies of box scores and stories on Roger Maris. About eight years ago I had all of it bound into eleven albums.

I always sat in section 31, box 163-A, seat 1 in Yankee Stadium. Right field. I would buy a general admission ticket, but I knew the policeman so I would always sit there. You have to understand, I'd get to the ballpark about two hours before they'd open up and I'd remain two hours after. I would see Roger park his car and I would say hello and tell him what a big fan I was. After a while he started to notice me. He threw me a baseball in batting practice and I am embarrassed to tell you what happened. I was so stunned I couldn't lift my arms. The ball fell off and somebody else got it and I yelled to Rog that I didn't get the ball. So he stopped on the way in and spoke to Phil Linz, a utility infielder. Linz came over, took a ball out of his back pocket and said "Put out your hand." I put out my hand and he said, "This is from Roger Maris."

He put the ball in my hand. But you know how cruel kids can be. All my friends said, "That ball's from Phil Linz, not Roger Maris." So later on I asked Roger for a ball and he did give me a baseball. My friends kept pushing me, challenging me. "Why don't you ask him for one of his home-run bats?"

Well, one day he was standing by the fence during batting practice. He would not sign autographs when the players were on the field, and I don't recall anyone even asking him for an autograph, but I made the request for the bat and he said, "Sure, next time I break the bat."

The Yankees had a West Coast trip and they were playing against the Angels and I was listening on the radio late at night, in bed, with the lights out. You know how kids did it. I'm sure they probably still do. And Roger cracked a bat. He had to go back to the bat rack. The next morning my old friend from high school called me: "Did you hear Roger crack his bat? That's *your* bat."

I said, "We'll see."

When the club came back my friend and I went to the stadium and during batting practice Rog walks straight over to me and before I even open up my mouth he says, "I've got that bat for you."

I said, "Oh, my God, I can't thank you enough."

Before the game starts I go to the dugout and there's a police officer there and I mean it is just impossible to get close unless you've got tickets. I went up to this great policeman and just poured my heart out as quick as I could: "You have to understand, please understand, Roger Maris told me to come here, I was supposed to pick up a bat, it's the most important thing. I wouldn't fool you, I'm not trying to pull the wool over your eyes, you gotta let me—"

"No problem. Stand over here."

I thought, geez, this is too easy, because I was expecting the worst. Just before the game starts Rog comes up out of the runway and hands me the bat. One of the most incredible moments in my life. Here is the bat from my idol and he thought enough of me to bring it back and give it to me. I went to the right-field seats and I was the only kid, obviously, in right field with a bat.

I brought the bat home and told all my friends and they said, "Now that you have the bat, why don't you ask him for one of his home-run baseballs?"

So I ask Roger for one of his home-run baseballs and he says, "You're gonna have to catch one 'cause I don't have any."

This is when the story starts to get unbelievable. In 1967 I go off to college at the University of Akron, in Ohio. My roommate has a picture of Raquel Welch on his wall and I've got a picture of Roger Maris. Everyone throughout the school knows that I'm a big Roger Maris fan. Maris had been traded to St. Louis for Charley Smith on December 6, and it was a real dark day as far as I was concerned, because Roger Maris was no longer a New York Yankee.

One day in speech class, I had to give a convincing speech and the subject I decided on was going to a baseball game. The conclusion of my speech was that I think so much of going to a baseball game that I am leaving after this class, driving with five of my friends two and a half hours to Pittsburgh to see the St. Louis Cardinals play the Pittsburgh Pirates.

My five friends had said, "You told us that you know Roger Maris. Let's just go see."

It's May 9, 1967. We get to Forbes Field approximately two hours before the game and there is the red number 9. It's the first time in my life I had ever seen Roger Maris outside of Yankee Stadium, and I figured he doesn't know who I am because the setting is different and I'm very, very nervous. *Extremely* nervous, because I now have five guys with me. I go down to the edge of the fence and my voice is quivering and I just say, "Ah, Rog. Rog . . ."

He turns around and says, "Andy Strasberg, what the hell are you doing here in Pittsburgh?"

That was the first time I knew he knew my name. I look at him and I look at my friends and I say, "Well, Rog, I'm with some guys from college. They wanted to meet you and I just wanted to come out and say hello." The five of them paraded by and shook hands and they couldn't believe it. I wished Rog the traditional good luck and he said, "Wait a minute. I want to give you an autograph on a National League ball." And he went into the dugout and got a ball and signed it. I put it in my pocket and I felt like a million dollars.

I'm very superstitious when it comes to baseball. Out in right field I sat in row 9, seat 9. In the third inning Roger Maris hit his first National League home run off Woody Fryman.

I caught the ball.

It's the most amazing thing that will ever happen to me in my life. My friends were jumping all over me. Five friends. Tears were rolling down my face. I couldn't believe it. He came running out at the conclusion of the inning—you've got to remember that Rog knew where I was and it wasn't crowded that particular game—and said, "I can't believe it."

I said, "You can't? I can't!"

I asked Roger if he would sign it and he said, "Why don't I sign it back in New York?"

My friends and I got back to the dorm about one, one-thirty in the morning and it was like wildfire. The whole school found out what had happened and I just had people coming in all night long, asking to see the baseball, asking me to tell them my story. I stayed up the entire night. I was also afraid that someone was going to steal or hide the ball, so the next morning I did not go to class. I went to the Akron Dime National Bank, explained the situation to the president and asked if he would put the ball in a safe-deposit box until I left Akron. And he did. No charge.

I came home for the summer and Roger signed the ball when the Cardinals came to Shea Stadium. My family had moved from the Bronx to White Plains and the local paper there had the story and a picture of me with the bat and the ball—the first time I had ever been interviewed. I might as well tell you that the bat and the ball are part of the family now. The bat's name is Woodrow, we call him Woody, and we just celebrated his twenty-third birthday. The ball's name is Homer.

You would think that the story of Roger Maris is over with now. I had caught the baseball. But it just snowballs. I graduate from college and I'm still in touch with him. He has now retired. In fact in 1968 I flew out to St. Louis to see Roger Maris's last game. For me it was a real tough time because I knew my childhood was coming to an end. I got real emotional at the end of the game. He ran out to right field and then they sent in a substitute and he came running in. I was sitting somewhat behind the dugout watching the proceedings and he didn't acknowledge me and by now I felt that we had a pretty good rapport and I felt a little bit bad. But he must have seen me because then he popped his head out and winked and went back in. This really touched my heart. I was interviewed by *The Sporting News,* who found out that I had made that trip from New York expressly to see Roger retire. The reporter asked Roger Maris about me specifically and Roger said, "Andy Strasberg was my most loyal fan."

On the front page of *The Sporting News.* There it was in print for the first time. I was his most loyal, his number-one fan.

I CONTINUED WITH MY LIFE and he continued with his. We started exchanging Christmas cards and the relationship kind of grew. I graduated from college in 1971 with a degree in English Literature and was getting to be somewhat of an adult and traveled around the United States in a yellow Chevy off and on for two or three years, looking for a job in baseball, visiting every major and minor league club I could find. I was a dishwasher in Arizona, a gardener in Maine, an editor for a football publication in New York. I delivered flowers, pressed clothes, drove a cab.

One time I was on the road in Spokane, Washington, with a friend from college nicknamed "Maps" because that was all he ever read. Maps sat in the car while I made my pitch to the general manager. Usually I would wind up such a conversation by asking whether it would be possible to get a couple of tickets for tonight's game. "Sure," they usually said, but in Spokane the man said, "Young man, if I were to give free tickets to everyone trying to get a job in baseball, I wouldn't have any to sell."

Maps asked, "Did you get the job?"

"No."

"Well, at least we're going to the ball game."

"The hell we are."

Finally in 1973 I settled in a camera store in Long Beach, California. The traveling was getting to be too much. In the beginning I had said if I didn't find the job by the time I was twenty-one I wouldn't frustrate the family any further. I pushed that up to twenty-two . . . twenty-three . . . twenty-four . . . twenty-five.

In 1975 I finally got a job with the San Diego Padres, from Elten Schiller, the man who had turned me down in Spokane. He denies that story about the tickets, but it's true.

When I drove down from Long Beach to talk about the opening with the Padres, Elten asked me, "How much money are we talking about? What would it take for you to come and work for the San Diego Padres?"

I figured that many people had probably said they would work for free, or at minimum wage, so I looked at Elten and said, "The most I could pay the Padres would be $100 a month."

Again, he denies this story, but it's true.

I contacted Roger, telling him that I had gotten the job. He wrote me a nice note of congratulations.

I got married in 1976, at home plate at Jack Murphy Stadium here in San Diego. A nice, small ballpark wedding. I wouldn't allow the media in because I didn't do it for the publicity. I did it because I had promised myself I was going to get married, if I ever did, at home plate. But I didn't think it would be a *major*-league ballpark. On our first date I had suggested a ball game. "No, too boring," Patti said, so we went to the movies. But she appreciates baseball. She understands it. She's just not obsessed with it. *Obsessed*, that's the word for me. I have half a million baseball cards—nowhere near the record—categorized by years, bound in books; seventy-one different recordings of "Take Me Out to the Ball Game," most of them in a jukebox, including the first one ever produced, back in the early 1900's; a collection of seats from the old parks.

Rog and his wife Pat sent me a wedding gift, which to this day is one of only two gifts that we still have in our house. I started to call Roger about once or twice a year and we would visit on the phone and it was great because, although he was still my idol and still my hero, I was a little more down-to-earth and able to talk to him about normal things instead of "How'd you feel when you hit your 61st?"

In 1980, Roger and Pat were in Los Angeles for the All-Star game and my dad, who had never met Rog, flew in from New York. He ran into Roger Maris in the lobby of the Biltmore Hotel. It was a great meeting and they started kidding about me. That night we went out for dinner, my wife and my dad, Roger and his wife, and someone else in this organization. I sat next to Roger throughout the dinner; I hadn't seen him for several years.

Roger started talking about his first National League home run and how I caught it. I had never heard his version of the story. I had told it a number of times and usually the response was, "It's not true. You're lying." It was great to hear his version about how he had an injury to his right hand, how it was tough to get around on the ball. When he was through, the fellow from our office, Jim Weigel, said to me, "I've got to tell you, Andy. Up until now, I never believed that story."

I GUESS THE NEXT SCENE is when Roger passed away, in December of 1985. He lived in Gainesville, Florida, but he grew up in Fargo, and I made arrangements to go to Fargo for the funeral. It was brutally cold. I went there not knowing anyone but his wife. After the ceremony I sat and waited because I didn't want to go up to Pat when everyone else was there. Then I went to her and expressed how sorry I felt and she hugged me and kissed me. She couldn't thank me enough for coming. Then she said, "I want you to meet the rest of my family." I had never met the kids. Six children. She turned to them and said, "I want to introduce someone really special. Kids, this is Andy Strasberg—" and Roger Maris, Jr., said, "You're Dad's number-one fan."

I couldn't keep my composure. The family reached out to me and I reached out to them and I thought it was just a nice ending to a great story, but it wasn't the end. It was just the beginning. I have gone back to Fargo every year for a charity golf tournament and auction to benefit the Hospice of the Red River Valley. I have gotten to know the family well enough that Randy Maris and his wife have spent a week with my family. I've spent a couple of days at their house. I wouldn't say I'm part of the family because I'm not, but I'm part of the many, many close friends that they have. If you open up the first page of last year's souvenir program you'll see what they did for me, which I thought was so super. My wife was embarrassed because my picture made the front page, and the Maris family made the second page.

One year I went out to the cemetery to pay my respects, at no scheduled time. I just did it on my own and without my knowledge there was a photographer present. In the Jewish religion, you place a stone on the grave. The picture of me placing the stone was on the front page of the little newspaper.

Another year I asked for the opportunity to address the banquet. There were about 700 people there. I said, "You've heard from Roger's family, Roger's friends, his teammates, but there is another side, and that is Roger's *fans*, and this video tells it all."

The lights went down and I played this three-and-a-half minute video I had put together with a friend—pictures of Maris, of Maris and me together, with Lou Rawls singing, "Did you ever know that you are my hero? I can fly higher than an eagle, you are the wind beneath my wings." It gave me an opportunity to tell everyone how he was no longer just the player Roger Maris. He was the *man*. He was a very frank person and some people took that as being surly, but he was just an honest, straightforward person.

One year in Fargo this gal came up in her wheelchair and told me how Roger used to visit her in the hospital before he even made the majors. Then Roger sent her an invitation to his wedding. She told him she couldn't go because she had no way of getting there. Roger said, "I'll pick you up an hour before the ceremony."

• • • •

TOWARD THE END OF THIS STORY, Andy Strasberg noted his closeness to the Maris family but conceded he wasn't *part* of the family. Since the book was published, that has changed. On August 3, 1991, a son was born to Randy and Fran Maris (Roger's son and daughter-in-law). Guess what they named the child and whom they chose for a godfather. Andy Strasberg, thirty-one years after he began his relationship with Roger Maris, officially became a part of the family.

Andy Strasberg (who is now the Padres' vice-president for public relations) is but one of the fifty-four people contained in Mike Bryan's book *Baseball Lives: Men and Women of the Game Talk About Their Jobs, Their Lives, and the National Pastime.*

There are two more baseball selections in this anthology: one of the most famous baseball tales ever written (page 202), and the true story of a near-tragic incident at the ballpark and how it affected a father and son (page 285).

Here is a list of outstanding sports books: *The Twentieth Century Treasury of Sports*, edited by Al Silverman and Brian Silverman; *The*

Fireside Book of Baseball/Volume IV, edited by Charles Einstein; Tom Boswell's two books, *How Life Imitates the World Series* and *Why Time Begins on Opening Day*; Roger Kahn's *The Boys of Summer*; *Once More Around the Park: A Baseball Reader* by Roger Angell; and *A Year in the Sun: The Games, the Players, and the Pleasure of Sports* by George Vecsey. A unique venture in recent years was the publication of an excellent literature textbook entitled *Sports in Literature: Experiencing Literature Through Poems, Stories, and Non-fiction About Sports*, edited by Bruce Emra.

From the late 1930s through the 1950s, the best American writer of adolescent sports novels was John R. Tunis. Many of his books are still relevant today and are back in print, including: *All-American; Champion's Choice; City for Lincoln; The Duke Decides; Go, Team, Go!; Highpockets; The Iron Duke; Keystone Kids; The Kid Comes Back; The Kid from Tomkinsville; Rookie of the Year; Schoolboy Johnson; World Series; Yea! Wildcats*; and *Young Razzle*.

The most highly praised teenage sports novel in the last twenty-five years is Bob Lipsyte's boxing book *The Contender*. Today's most prolific writer in the sports novel genre is Thomas J. Dygard, whose books include *Forward Pass, Halfback Tough, Outside Shooter, Point Spread, Quarterback Walk-On, Rebound Caper, The Rookie Arrives, Soccer Duel, Tournament Upstart, Wilderness Peril*, and *Winning Kicker*.

TRIP TO FENWAY DRIVES HOME TRUTH— RIGHT OFF THE BAT

by Jim Trelease

Close Call at the Ballpark

There is an old cliché that calls baseball "a game of inches." Playing it as a child, covering it as a sportswriter, and watching it as a fan, I had given the phrase only cursory attention and then only as it applied to what happened on the field. I knew the stories about the perfect symmetry of the game, how much it would have changed the game if the distance between the bases had not been ninety feet, that the sixty feet, six inches to the pitcher's mound could not be changed by even an inch without dramatically changing the relationship between pitcher and hitter.

Then one day I took my son to Fenway Park in Boston for his first major-league game. That day, I *lived* the cliché. I can tell you firsthand: It *is* a game of inches. In fact, that day I was willing to expand the expression to "*Life* is a game of inches." But I also learned that day, if I had not known it before, that baseball is just a game. Yes, there are more important things on a sunny day.

When we returned home after the game, I went immediately to a typewriter and wrote this story. I had started in the newspaper business almost twenty years earlier as a sportswriter but had left that department after few years to become the paper's staff artist. I continued, however, to write feature stories as I came across them. In 1980, this was the only story I wrote. It won the New England Associated Press features award that year.

• • • •

H E WAITED UNTIL THE BOY was fully awake. He sat on his bed in the morning and savored the look on the child's face when he told him they were going to Fenway Park.

The father had waited until his son was 10, waited until he was sure he would understand the game, appreciate the beauty of Fenway in the spring. He waited for the right day, a sunny day game in the middle of a vacation week, a game minus the weekend drunks. He wanted the boy's first game to be perfect.

He wanted it to be better than his own first game—a hot afternoon at Yankee Stadium in 1950 with the sun in his eyes and the players too far away.

The boy had his mother's eyes and good looks, his father's sensitivities; he was a laugher and a worrier—sometimes in the same hour. He liked sports. He didn't love them; just liked them. And that was fine with his father because that's the way he felt, too.

But *this* day! This would be a special one. This would be a day the two of them could treasure all of their lives. The boy's first day at Fenway—the day they'd both waited so long for.

They drove down the Pike, the father detailing the history of Fenway and its uniqueness in sports, the boy testing their borrowed binoculars on road signs and a solitary cloud over Framingham.

They parked in the Grove St. MBTA lot and rode the trolley into town.

"A lot quieter than a subway, huh, Dad?" the boy commented. And the man silently recalled how he and his father had ridden the noisy and frightening New York subway up to the Bronx for that first game together and that of all the memories from that day, the only pleasurable one was the security he felt with the closeness of his father in the subway.

This year, father and son arrived by the second inning, took a chance at the reserved seat ticket window and were rewarded with a pair of lower box seats next to the Red Sox on-deck circle. The father could not believe his good fortune.

The boy sat in the second row and stared in disbelief at the great green wall in left and the white doubleknit uniforms just a few feet away from him.

And the father watched him and felt his heart bursting with joy.

If there were a way, he thought, to capture even a part of this day and put it in a bottle, it would glow forever.

They did all the things the man had planned: Fenway franks, ice cream sandwiches, how to read the scoreboard, crowd watching, foul ball chasing, cheering for Yaz.

This is what life's all about, the father thought. A boy and his dad and baseball. Nothing beats it!

With the Sox ahead 9-2 in the ninth, the stands began to empty. But these two didn't leave. Here was a day and game to be savored until the very end.

"How 'bout another frank?"

"Sure, Dad."

"Wait here," the father said. "Even if the game ends—just stay in your seat. I'll be right back."

The concession was closed and in minutes the father was struggling against the exiting crowd to return to his seat. And then suddenly the crowd wasn't pushing any more. It was standing still. Then leaning. The aisle was clogged. The father couldn't see the box seat section. He stood on his toes and peered over the shoulders. There—there were the two women from the adjacent box. But the boy was missing.

Something seemed wrong down on the field. Play had stopped. There were ushers congesting the aisle.

The father felt his legs go weak and his hands tremble. He remembered the woman advising him and his son that "you've really got to watch yourself with the foul tips when you're sitting in these box seats." Somehow he fought his way down the aisle. There was no sign of the boy. Everyone was bent toward the steps where ushers were ministering to a boy.

"Got the split end of the bat in the face," the father heard someone say over his shoulder.

"Is . . . is that my son?" he asked aloud to the strangers. "Is it my son?"

No one answered.

He knelt on the blood-smeared cement steps and peered through at the body that was face down in the spot where he'd left his son minutes before. The jacket was the same color as his son's.

But the collar—it was different. It's not him! he told himself. It can't be. This couldn't happen. It happens to other people, not to us, he thought.

He was shaken with doubts. What if they'd placed someone's jacket around the boy. Still on his knees, he reached through the ushers' legs and gently touched the boy's hair. Was it the hair he'd tousled and caressed so many thousands of times? He couldn't be sure or wouldn't allow himself to be sure.

His hands were shaking as he turned back the coat's sheepskin collar and saw the red shirt beneath. His son had been wearing blue!

He stood up quickly, his face hot, his voice trembling, "Where's my son?" he asked the woman who had warned them. Together they scanned the crowd and finally came to the tiny figure in the front row —alone in the seats that had been vacated by the helpers and voyeurs.

He was standing stiffly, facing centerfield, both hands covering his eyes.

Suddenly it was all different. A father and son held each other in the lengthening shadows of a Fenway afternoon. It was a moment they would remember for a long time.

The father will remember the long ride home and what they talked about. How the splintered bat had spun into the stands, glanced off the spectator across the aisle and bounced off the shoulder of his son.

Yes, they talked about the game, Yaz's hits and how much Fred Lynn looked like Willie Wonka on TV. But always they came back to what was important: not a game or runs or hot dogs but that they were together, alive and well and that they loved each other. *That* is what life is all about, thought the father. And he prayed silently that they both always would remember their first game together and the lesson it carried.

• • • •

A FEW DAYS AFTER THE ARTICLE APPEARED, an old college friend, Dick Bresciani, who was then the public-relations director for the Boston Red Sox, sent word to me that the youngster who had been struck by the bat had recovered and was OK.

Off-the-field mishaps at the ballpark can be as common as on-the-field errors, and ministering to the medical needs of sports fans is often as nerve-racking as a pennant race, according to *The Wall Street Journal*'s July 15, 1992, front-page story "It's a Bloody Business Being a Baseball Fan; Ask Mr. Giampietro" by Timothy Smith. (Back issues of the *Journal* can found in your local library's reference room.)

A list of excellent sports books can be found on pages 283 and 284.

Escape Reading

Reading

• • • • • • • • • •

Five memoirs of being rescued
by books—rescued from slavery,
poverty, traumas, and prison.

Mapping Escape Routes

The average American spends almost fifteen hundred hours a year watching television, and a family uses the telephone almost four thousand times in the same year. All of these programs and calls are accomplished without much knowledge or appreciation of how those pictures or voices are able to materialize out of little black wires.

Where once Americans were dumbstruck by the miracle of such inventions, today's citizen cannot recall a day without them. What's so miraculous about the ordinary? On the other hand, computers still startle many of us. But of all the discoveries experienced by humans, none has been as revolutionary, world-changing, mind-boggling, enchanting, inspirational, and powerful as the skill called literacy.

For the majority of us who have been reading since first grade, it often becomes as routine as a telephone. Consider, however, the description offered by Arthur Gordon: "Isn't it amazing how we take them for granted, those little black marks on paper! Twenty-six different shapes known as letters, arranged in endless combinations known as words. Lifeless, until someone's eyes fall upon them. But then a miracle happens. Along the optic nerve, almost at the speed of light, these tiny symbols are flashed to the brain, where they are instantly decoded into ideas, images, concepts, meanings. The eye's owner is changed too. The little black marks can make him love or hate, laugh or cry, fight or run away. And what do we call this incredible chain of events? Reading."

Romance novels and adventure stories are often labeled *escapist literature*. The obvious and somewhat shallow meaning in the phrase refers to people who read such stories in order to escape the moment or the life they are leading—the weary housewife and bus driver who hoard their free minutes to read something that will take them "out of the house" or "off the route." There is, however, a deeper, truer meaning to *escapist literature*, and the following five selections explore that meaning from the vantage points of different centuries, continents, times, and locales.

The novelist Avi recalls how the aboriginal people of Australia had no written literature, just an oral one. Their spoken stories, however, were crucial to their nomadic way of life because of references to specific people and places in the stories. In a very real sense, they used these tales like maps to get from place to place. The selections you are about to read offer dramatic examples of how remarkably successful people used books or stories as maps in achieving their destinies. Each of them found a map in their reading, a map by which they could escape their personal dungeons. All five selections are from their autobiographies, and thus they are history as well—slices of the way things once were, pieces of crystallized time and experience to chew on and compare with our own.

from NARRATIVE OF THE LIFE OF FREDERICK DOUGLASS

by Frederick Douglass

A Slave's Secret Education

Escapist literature is the perfect term to describe the early reading done by the young boy born into slavery as Frederick Bailey in Tuckahoe, Maryland, across Chesapeake Bay on Maryland's Eastern Shore in 1818. Before he was finished reading, he would command the attention of eight presidents and be the most famous black man in the world.

He had no real memory of his mother for the first six years of his life, though she worked in nearby fields. She may have only visited him a half-dozen times in his entire childhood, and therefore he had no emotional attachment to her. Slavery had robbed him of not only a father, but for all intents and purposes a mother as well.

Knowing the intellectual heights to which he eventually rose, one cannot help but wonder who or what filled the void when he was deprived of both parents and forced to live for twenty years in the environment of slavery. To begin with, there was the extraordinary gift of natural intelligence. From the very beginning, people (white and black) recognized him as a remarkable child. But the biggest asset came in the person whose cabin he would live in for the first six years of his life, who would be the role model for his strength and determination—his grandmother Betsy Bailey.

Douglass's biographer William McFeely describes her this way: "Intelligent and physically powerful, she had made herself an expert in fishing and farming. The nets she wove were in 'great demand' in the nearby towns . . . and she also put them to good use herself. Douglass remembered her being 'in the water half the day' gathering in the abundant shad and herring. When spring came, she not only planted her own sweet potatoes but was called on to help others in the neighborhood get theirs into the ground properly. At harvest time, her fork went into the ground so deftly that none of the crop was pierced or lost, and she had foresight to put aside sound seed potatoes for planting the next season."

It was his grandmother who would play the role of first teacher, answering his questions, asking her own, nurturing his curiosity, inviting him to join her in some task, praising his efforts, and challenging him to do more. It was also his good fortune that his grandmother was required to do no fieldwork for the plantation. Her task was to raise the grandchildren, "freeing" the parents to spend their energies and lives laboring in the fields. "Raising" the children meant not just the care and feeding, but training them for the jobs that would soon await them.

Thus it was that Frederick, at the age of six, walked the twelve miles with his grandmother to the master's house. Here, much to his angry and tearful dismay, his life with Betsy Bailey ended. Their days together in the fields and streams were over. He would join the 180 other slaves in the home-place.

But fortune blessed him again. Daniel, the eleven-year-old son of the master, took a liking to Frederick and they became fast friends and playmates. Though they spent less than two years with each other, those years were of monumental importance to Frederick. Not only did they play together, they were also tutored together. Daniel's parents hired a tutor from Massachusetts to educate the boy and, though Frederick was allowed to be only a passive spectator, his keen ears and eyes were open to everything before him. The talent for mimicry that his grandmother had nurtured ("Do it this way. Here—watch me!") would be applied to the speech of these white people whose lives he was touching. He learned the nuances of their speech patterns, vocabulary, and body language that someday would win him not only freedom but standing ovations throughout the world. And he pestered Daniel with incessant questions about everything.

After two years, he was shipped with livestock to be the eight-year-old houseboy for his master's brother in Baltimore. For the next five and a half years, he would be the only slave in the shipbuilder's home, servant for the parents, and protector for their two-year-old son. And it would be here that he would discover—openly and secretly—the mysteries of reading that changed his life forever.

It should be noted that it was against the law in many states and against accepted tradition everywhere in the South to teach slaves to read. The goal of slave traders, merchants, and owners was to keep the slave anonymous, so disoriented and without hope or heritage that he would be nothing more than trade goods in the eyes of both himself and whites. Any portrayal of slaves as more than "things"— especially, God forbid, as human—threatened the balance of owner-slave relationships and could not be tolerated. Once slaves became literate, the chains would start to fall from their minds. They would have access to the same information as whites and soon would begin to dream of freeing their bodies as well.

Just how Douglass managed to become literate—against his master's wishes—is the subject of the chapter included in this selection. Before going to that, let us jump ahead to what he accomplished once he became literate.

Through his readings, Douglass discovered that a powerful anti-slavery movement was growing in certain corners of the country. Various church groups (usually made up of women) saw slavery as "unchristian" and worked to keep new states slave-free. The campaign became known as the abolitionist movement, and from it sprang the "Underground Railroad" that clandestinely shuttled fleeing slaves from the South to the North and freedom.

By twelve years of age, Douglass had managed to hoard the grand total of fifty cents, which he used to buy a copy of *The Columbian Orator*, an anthology of historically famous speeches. The reigning theory for many years before and afterward was that such speeches, when memorized, gave young boys the essential ingredients for oral leadership. If they learned the noble thoughts and words of emperors, generals, poets, politicians, and ministers, they had a powerful lever to move their world.

So with his new purchase in hand, Douglass retreated behind a shipyard wall and began to read the book aloud, practicing the white man's diction, mimicking many of the nuances he'd learned at Daniel's side years earlier, dissecting the meanings of words, and finally memorizing the speeches. Those secret hours of labor with mind and tongue would eventually bear fruit in ways the young slave boy could never have imagined. Ironically, a young man whose fate was inextricably entwined with Douglass's was also educating himself using *The Columbian Orator* as a textbook—Abraham Lincoln.

Nine years later, at age twenty-one, having escaped from Baltimore and his life as a slave, he was living and working in New Bedford, Massachusetts, attending a church meeting. There, for the first time, he spontaneously rose to condemn the evil of slavery publicly, and he shared a portion of his firsthand knowledge. Soon thereafter, one of the antislavery movement's leaders who heard him that day spotted him in another audience and asked him to share his life's story with the crowd. It was the awakening of a sleeping giant in the abolitionist movement.

Here was the man they were looking for: six feet tall, ruggedly handsome and dignified, with a deep baritone voice, someone who could detail with chilling effect the horrors of slavery. Within months, and after some small coaching from professional speakers, he was accomplishing his task with what one editor called "wit, argument, sarcasm and pathos."

In the ensuing years, as he crisscrossed the free states on the lecture circuit, he was almost too good to be true. He was so refined and educated in his speeches, audiences began to wonder how a former slave could speak so eloquently. To document both his case and his capabilities, he wrote his autobiography—seven years before the publication of Uncle Tom's Cabin. His influence was such that when the Civil War was ravaging the nation, President Lincoln sought both Douglass's advice and support in the White House. The president's respect for him moved Mrs. Lincoln to send Lincoln's walking stick to Douglass after the assassination.

It is a common mistake for people to confuse the two brilliant self-made men named Douglas(s) in Lincoln's life. One was a black man who spelled his last name with a double s at the end (he had changed his name at the age of twenty upon arriving in Massachusetts, via the Underground Railroad, to confuse possible slave catchers; he chose "Douglass" from Sir Walter Scott's "Lady of the Lake"). The other was Stephen A. Douglas (one s), who debated and defeated Lincoln for a U.S. Senate seat from Illinois and helped precipitate the Civil War with his notorious Kansas-Nebraska slavery law. Both men, however, were loyal supporters of Lincoln during the war.

After the war, Douglass remained outspoken on reform, racism, and equality, and won three presidential appointments: marshal of the District of Columbia; its first black recorder of deeds; and, at seventy-one years of age, United States consul general to Haiti. His lifetime was so rich in experience and challenges that he wrote three autobiographies, though the first was regarded as the best. In short, he was the single most important and influential black leader of his time and for generations to come.

It is said that great men exist that there might be greater men. If that be true, then Frederick Douglass existed that there might be a W. E. B. Du Bois, a Martin Luther King, Jr., and a Jesse Jackson.

Here then is a chapter from his first autobiography, *Narrative of the Life of Frederick Douglass: An American Slave*, in which he describes how he achieved the literacy that would set him free.

• • • •

CHAPTER 7

I LIVED in Master Hugh's family about seven years. During this time, I succeeded in learning to read and write. In accomplishing this, I was compelled to resort to various stratagems. I had no regular teacher. My mistress, who had kindly commenced to instruct me, had, in compliance with the advice and direction of her husband, not only ceased to instruct, but had set her face against my being instructed by any one else. It is due, however, to my mistress to say of her, that she did not adopt this course of treatment immediately. She at first lacked the depravity indispensable to shutting me up in mental darkness. It was at least necessary for her to have some training in the exercise of irresponsible power, to make her equal to the task of treating me as though I were a brute.

My mistress was, as I have said, a kind and tender-hearted woman; and in the simplicity of her soul she commenced, when I first went to live with her, to treat me as she supposed one human being ought to treat another. In entering upon the duties of a slaveholder, she did not seem to perceive that I sustained to her the relation of a mere chattel, and that for her to treat me as a human being was not only wrong, but dangerously so. Slavery proved as injurious to her as it did to me. When I went there, she was a pious, warm, and tender-hearted woman. There was no sorrow or suffering for which she had not a tear. She had bread for the hungry, clothes for the naked, and comfort for every mourner that came within her reach. Slavery soon proved its ability to divest her of these heavenly qualities. Under its influence, the tender heart became stone, and the lamblike disposition gave way to one of tiger-like fierceness. The first step in her downward course was in her ceasing to instruct me. She now commenced to practise her husband's precepts. She finally became even more violent in her opposition than her husband himself. She was not satisfied with simply doing as well as he had commanded; she seemed anxious to do better. Nothing seemed to make her more angry than to see me with a newspaper. She seemed to think that here lay the danger. I have had her rush at me with a face made all up of fury, and snatch from me a newspaper, in a manner that fully revealed her apprehension. She was an apt woman; and a little experience soon demonstrated, to her satisfaction, that education and slavery were incompatible with each other.

From this time I was most narrowly watched. If I was in a separate room any considerable length of time, I was sure to be suspected of having a book, and was at once called to give an account of myself. All this, however, was too late. The first step had been taken. Mistress, in teaching me the alphabet, had given me the *inch*, and no precaution could prevent me from taking the *ell*.

The plan which I adopted, and the one by which I was most successful, was that of making friends of all the little white boys whom I met in the street. As many of these as I could, I converted into teachers. With their kindly aid, obtained at different times and in different places, I finally succeeded in learning to read. When I was sent on errands, I always took my book with me, and by doing one part of my errand quickly, I found time to get a lesson before my return. I used also to carry bread with me, enough of which was always in the house, and to which I was always welcome; for I was much better off in this regard than many of the poor white children in our neighborhood. This bread I used to bestow upon the hungry little urchins, who, in return, would give me that more valuable bread of knowledge. I am strongly tempted to give the names of two or three of those little boys, as a testimonial of the gratitude and affection I bear them; but prudence forbids;—not that it would injure me, but it might embarrass them; for it is almost an unpardonable offence to teach slaves to read in this Christian country. It is enough to say of the dear little fellows, that they lived on Philpot Street, very near Durgin and Bailey's ship-yard. I used to talk this matter of slavery over with them. I would sometimes say to them, I wished I could be as free as they would be when they got to be men. "You will be free as soon as you are twenty-one, *but I am a slave for life!* Have not I as good a right to be free as you have?" These words used to trouble them; they would express for me the liveliest sympathy, and console me with the hope that something would occur by which I might be free.

I was now about twelve years old, and the thought of being *a slave for life* began to bear heavily upon my heart. Just about this time, I got hold of a book entitled "The Columbian Orator." Every opportunity I got, I used to read this book. Among much of other interesting matter, I found in it a dialogue between a master and his slave. The slave was represented as having run away from his master three times. The dialogue represented the conversation which took place between them, when the slave was retaken the third time. In this dialogue, the whole argument in behalf of slavery was brought forward by the master, all of which was disposed of by the slave. The slave was made to say some very smart as well as impressive things in reply to his master—things which had the desired though unexpected effect; for the conversation resulted in the voluntary emancipation of the slave on the part of the master.

In the same book, I met with one of Sheridan's mighty speeches on and in behalf of Catholic emancipation. These were choice documents to me. I read them over and over again with unabated interest. They gave tongue to interesting thoughts of my own soul, which had frequently flashed through my mind, and died away for want of utterance. The moral which I gained from the dialogue was the power of truth over the conscience of even a slaveholder. What I got from Sheridan was a bold denunciation of slavery, and a powerful vindication of human rights. The reading of these documents enabled me to utter my thoughts, and to meet the arguments brought forward to sustain slavery; but while they relieved me of one difficulty, they brought on another even more painful than the one of which I was relieved. The more I read, the more I was led to abhor and detest my enslavers. I could regard them in no other light than a band of successful robbers, who had left their homes, and gone to Africa, and stolen us from our homes, and in a strange land reduced us to slavery. I loathed them as being the meanest as well as the most wicked of men. As I read and contemplated the subject, behold! that very discontentment which Master Hugh had predicted would follow my learning to read had already come, to torment and sting my soul to unutterable anguish. As I writhed under it, I would at times feel that learning to read had been a curse rather than a blessing. It had given me a view of my wretched condition, without the remedy. It opened my eyes to the horrible pit, but to no ladder upon which to get out. In moments of agony, I envied my fellow-slaves for their stupidity. I have often wished myself a beast. I preferred the condition of the meanest reptile to my own. Any thing, no matter what, to get rid of thinking! It was this everlasting thinking of my condition that tormented me. There was no getting rid of it. It was pressed upon me by every object within sight or hearing, animate or inanimate. The silver trump of freedom had roused my soul to eternal wakefulness. Freedom now appeared, to disappear no more forever. It was heard in every sound, and seen in every thing. It was ever present to torment me with a sense of my wretched condition. I saw nothing without seeing it, I heard nothing without hearing it, and felt nothing without feeling it. It looked from every star, it smiled in every calm, breathed in every wind, and moved in every storm.

I often found myself regretting my own existence, and wishing myself dead; and but for the hope of being free, I have no doubt but that I should have killed myself, or done something for which I should have been killed. While in this state of mind, I was eager to hear any one speak of slavery. I was a ready listener. Every little while, I could hear something about the abolitionists. It was some time before I found what the word meant. It was always used in such connections as to make it an interesting word to me. If a slave ran away and succeeded in getting clear, or if a slave killed his master, set fire to a barn, or did any thing very wrong in the mind of a slaveholder, it was spoken of as the fruit of *abolition*. Hearing the word in this connection very often, I set about learning what it meant. The dictionary afforded me little or no help. I found it was "the act of abolishing;" but then I did not know what was to be abolished. Here I was perplexed. I did not dare to ask any one about its meaning, for I was satisfied that it was something they wanted me to know very little about. After a patient waiting, I got one of our city papers, containing an account of the number of petitions from the north, praying for the abolition of slavery in the District of Columbia, and of the slave trade between the States. From this time I understood the words *abolition* and *abolitionist*, and always drew near when that word was spoken, expecting to hear something of importance to myself and fellow-slaves. The light broke in upon me by degrees. I went one day down on the wharf of Mr. Waters; and seeing two Irishmen unloading a scow of stone, I went, unasked, and helped them. When we had finished, one of them came to me and asked me if I were a slave. I told him I was. He asked, "Are ye a slave for life?" I told him that I was. The good Irishman seemed to be deeply affected by the statement. He said to the other that it was a pity so fine a little fellow as myself should be a slave for life. He said it was a shame to hold me. They both advised me to run away to the north; that I should find friends there, and that I should be free. I pretended not to be interested in what they said, and treated them as if I did not understand them; for I feared they might be treacherous. White men have been known to encourage slaves to escape, and then, to get the reward, catch them and return them to their masters. I was afraid that these seemingly good men might use me so; but I nevertheless remembered their advice, and from that time I resolved to run away. I looked forward to a time at which it would be safe for me to escape. I was too young to think of doing so immediately; besides, I wished to learn how to write, as I might have occasion to write my own pass. I consoled myself with the hope that I should one day find a good chance. Meanwhile, I would learn to write.

The idea as to how I might learn to write was suggested to me by being in Durgin and Bailey's ship-yard, and frequently seeing the ship carpenters, after hewing, and getting a piece of timber ready for use, write on the timber the name of that part of the ship for which it was intended. When a piece of timber was intended for the larboard side, it would be marked thus—"L." When a piece was for the starboard side, it would be marked thus—"S." A piece for the larboard side forward would be marked thus—"L. F." When a piece was for starboard side forward, it would be marked thus—"S. F." For larboard aft, it would be marked thus—"L. A." For starboard aft, it would be marked thus—"S. A." I soon learned the names of these letters, and for what they were intended when placed upon a piece of timber in the ship-yard. I immediately commenced copying them, and in a short time was able to make the four letters named. After that, when I met with any boy who I knew could write, I would tell him I could write as well as he. The next word would be, "I don't believe you. Let me see you try it." I would then make the letters which I had been so fortunate as to learn, and ask him to beat that. In this way I got a good many lessons in writing, which it is quite possible I should never have gotten in any other way. During this time, my copy-book was the board fence, brick wall, and pavement; my pen and ink was a lump of chalk. With these, I learned mainly how to write. I then commenced and continued copying the Italics in Webster's Spelling Book, until I could make them all without looking on the book. By this time, my little Master Thomas had gone to school, and learned how to write, and had written over a number of copy-books. These had been brought home, and shown to some of our near neighbors, and then laid aside. My mistress used to go to class meeting at the Wilk Street meetinghouse every Monday afternoon, and leave me to take care of the house. When left thus, I used to spend the time in writing in the spaces left in Master Thomas's copy-book, copying what he had written. I continued to do this until I could write a hand very similar to that of Master Thomas. Thus, after a long, tedious effort for years, I finally succeeded in learning how to write.

• • • •

IN ADDITION to Douglass's autobiography, details of his life can be found in: *Escape to Freedom: A Play about Young Frederick Douglass* by Ossie Davis; *Frederick Douglass: The Black Lion* by Patricia and Frederick McKissack; and *The Story of Frederick Douglass: Voice of Freedom* by Eric Weiner. The definitive adult biography on him is William S. McFeely's *Frederick Douglass*.

The following (Harper-Caedmon) audiocassettes also offer readings from Douglass's works: *Black Pioneers in American History, Vol. I* (readings by Moses Gunn from Douglass's autobiography) and *Great Black Speeches* (Norman Matlock reads Douglass's condemnation of slavery to the British people).

Douglass's speaker's manual, *The Columbian Orator*, is no longer in print, but there are even greater resources now available: *The World's Great Speeches*, edited by Lewis Copeland and Lawrence W. Lamm, containing 278 of the great speeches from ancient times to the 1960s, and *Lend Me Your Ears: Great Speeches in History*, selected and introduced by William Safire.

Related books on black history include: *All Times, All People: A World History of Slavery* by Milton Meltzer; *Anthony Burns: The Defeat and Triumph of a Fugitive Slave* and *Many Thousand Gone: African Americans from Slavery to Freedom*, both by Virginia Hamilton; *Letters from a Slave Girl: The Story of Harriet Jacobs* by Mary E. Lyons; *Now Is Your Time! The African-American Struggle for Freedom* by Walter Dean Myers; *One More River to Cross: The Stories of Twelve Black Americans* by Jim Haskins; *Rosa Parks: My Story* by Rosa Parks; and *To Be a Slave* by Julius Lester.

Roots of Resistance: A Story of the Underground Railroad is an excellent sixty-minute video (PBS).

These novels are also related to the issue of slavery: *The Borning Room* by Paul Fleischman, *Something Upstairs* by Avi, and *Underground Man* by Milton Meltzer.

Mature readers will find many similarities between Douglass's struggle and that of two boys growing up in Chicago's worst public housing in the 1980s, as profiled by Alex Kotlowitz in his powerful nonfiction book, *There Are No Children Here: The Story of Two Boys Growing Up in the Other America*.

from ACT ONE
by Moss Hart

From Streetlights to Footlights

Eventually he became one of the power figures in the entertainment industry— from Broadway to Hollywood, from comedy to drama to musicals, what he touched as a writer or director turned to gold. But his thirty-year run of adult success was built on a foundation of childhood anguish and poverty. It has been said that theater people often turn to the stage when they are children in order to escape unhappy childhoods, and Moss Hart always agreed with that—with good reason.

Hart's first theatrical success was not in front of the footlights but under the streetlights as a young teenager trying to live down his lack of athletic prowess. That experience before a live audience is the subject of this selection, and it would weigh heavily in his success in show business. Hart's maternal grandfather had come to America from England as the disinherited black sheep in a wealthy Jewish family. A richly cultured man, he married an illiterate woman, worked as a cigar maker (hand-wrapping cigars), and lived on the edge of poverty most of his life.

With no money available for entertainment, the family had to make do with his nightly readings aloud from the novels of Charles Dickens, who was then at the pinnacle of his fame. The day Moss Hart was born, his seventy-nine-year-old grandfather immediately adopted him as his personal project, something that was made easier by the fact that Hart's parents lived with the grandfather. For all intents and purposes, though, his mother was an indentured servant to his grandfather. The grandfather's domineering nature made him a genuine monster to the adults in the family, but he was a gentle giant to his grandchild. In a sense, he became the boy's father.

It was the grandfather who took the boy for his first haircut and caught butterflies in the park with him. He also brought him into the dining room for meetings of the Friday Night Literary Society and applauded when the child succeeded in reciting lines from Dickens's "A Christmas Carol." And it was the grandfather who brought him to his first theater production.

When the grandfather died, the boy turned not to his parents but to an extroverted, eccentric aunt who also lived with them and was begrudgingly supported by Hart's father (also a cigar maker). She had managed to blackmail a small allowance from her English relatives and used this to create a fantasy world for herself in the audience of the New York theater world. Each week, in a house that was too often filled with sullen silences or tearful outbursts, the boy would eagerly await her breathless report on the play she had just seen. In a world where there was no radio or television, these reports were as good as a front-row seat—until he was old enough to go with her. Knowing his father would never approve (there was an undeclared war between the aunt and his father), Hart was secretly kept out of school every Thursday afternoon and smuggled off to the theater with her. Eventually Saturday matinees were added.

These journeys had an incalculable impact on the boy. As he recalled, "At school I was a lonely and alien figure. My given name, to begin with, was a strange one, and children are quick to hold suspect and to damn anything different from themselves, even a name. Added to this was the fact that I spoke with a faint English accent; my manner of speaking, I'm afraid, was a trifle too literate, if not downright theatrical. . . . It is easy to understand how my aunt became for me a refuge against the world of reality and how the fantasy world of the theater quickly became an escape and a solace."

And then, at the age of ten, that world collapsed. His father and aunt had a cataclysmic confrontation which saw her depart their home forever. Add to that the arrival of the cigar-making machines that put his father out of work. The result was that, upon completing eighth grade, Hart was forced to drop out of school to find a job that would help support the family—a task he would carry for the rest of his life.

Almost immediately he set his sights on two targets: poverty and the Broadway theater. The dark specter of poverty and all of its attendant miseries had stalked him since infancy. Somehow he would find a way to kill it. And the theater would be the gun he would use. He began by working two and a half years in a furrier's vault; he then secured a job as an office boy for a theatrical agency, wrote a play that lost his boss forty-five thousand dollars and received one of the worst reviews imaginable, served six years as the activities and social director for adult summer camps, directed local theater groups, and finally wrote more plays—mostly bad ones—until his big break came when he and George S. Kaufman became a theatrical comedy writing team.

By the time he died at the young age of fifty-eight, he had shared a Pulitzer Prize for writing *You Can't Take It with You* (1937) and had won a Tony Award (1956) for directing *My Fair Lady*, one of the most successful plays in the history of the Broadway theater. He had also written the screenplay for *Gentleman's Agreement*, which won the 1947 Academy Award for best picture.

The selection here is from his autobiography, *Act One*, one of the best-selling and perhaps the finest theater book of its kind. It describes the summer between his seventh- and eighth-grade years, when he discovered that he owned the powerful tool that would someday lift him out of poverty.

• • • •

I WANTED, OF COURSE, to be an actor. It never occurred to me that these godlike creatures did not themselves make up the words that flowed so effortlessly and magnificently from their lips. I think I believed they created a play as they went along—a belief, I am convinced, that some portions of a matinée audience still cling to. More than once, sitting in the audience at a play of mine, I have heard the lady behind me exclaim, "The clever things actors say! Aren't they wonderful!" And I have been tempted to say, "Not *that* wonderful, madame!" But I have understood her bewitchment. Not even in my wildest dreams of glory did I ever imagine that I would one day write the words for actors to speak on the stage, and not until long afterward did I come to know that there were more important figures in the theatre than the gods of my idolatry.

Had I had the wit to perceive it, there was already a hint that I was a dramatist; even then I could dramatize a story and hold an audience, and when I inadvertently stumbled on this gift, I used it the way other boys use a good pitching arm or a long reach in basketball. It gave me the only standing I was ever to have in the tough and ruthless world of boys of my own age, and I wielded the tiny sense of power it gave me hungrily and shrewdly. Even in the long-ago days when I was growing up, the cult of "toughness" in American life was beginning to blossom and flower. The non-athletic boy, the youngster who liked to read or listen to music, who could not fight or was afraid to, or the boy who had some special interest that was strange or alien to the rest, like the theatre in my case, was banished from the companionship of the others by rules of the "tough" world that was already beginning to prevail.

It is a mistake to believe that this cult of "toughness" was limited to the poor neighborhood in which we lived. It had begun to pervade other levels of American life, and I suspect that today's bland dismissal of the intellectual and the overwhelming emphasis placed on the necessity of competing and of success are due in part to the strange taboo we have set against that softness in ourselves which brings men closest to the angels. A nation of poets would be no more desirable than a nation of athletes, but I wonder if that toughness and competitiveness, which have become an ingrained part of our character as a people and a symbol of our way of life as a nation, are not a sign of weakness as well as of strength. Is our cultural life not robbed of a necessary dimension and our emotional life of an element of grace? And I wonder if the fear of a lack of toughness in our children does not sometimes rob them of an awakening awareness and sensitivity in the realm of the spirit that are each child's birthright and his weapon of rebellion against the accepted norm of his time. This lack of toughness and the inability to compete were a constant agony of my own childhood, and I lived it through as best I could.

A city child's summer is spent in the street in front of his home, and all through the long summer vacations I sat on the curb and watched the other boys on the block play baseball or prisoner's base or gutter hockey. I was never asked to take part even when one team had a member missing—not out of any special cruelty, but because they took it for granted I would be no good at it. They were right, of course. Yet much of the bitterness and envy and loneliness I suffered in those years could have been borne better if a single wise teacher or a knowledgeable parent had made me understand that there were compensations for the untough and the nonathletic; that the world would not always be bounded by the curbstone in front of the house.

One of those compensations I blundered into myself, and its effect was electric on both me and the tough world of the boys on the block. I have never forgotten the joy of that wonderful evening when it happened. There was no daylight-saving in those days, and the baseball and other games ended about eight or eight thirty, when it grew dark. Then it was the custom of the boys to retire to a little stoop that jutted out from the candy store on the corner and that somehow had become theirs through tribal right. No grownup ever sat there or attempted to. There the boys would sit, talking aimlessly for hours on end. There were the usual probings of sex and dirty jokes, not too well defined or clearly understood; but mostly the talk was of the games played during the day and of the game to be played tomorrow. Ultimately, long silences would fall and then the boys would wander off one by one. It was just after one of those long silences that my life as an outsider changed, and for one glorious summer I was accepted on my own terms as one of the tribe. I can no longer remember which boy it was that summer evening who broke the silence with a question; but whoever he was, I nod to him in gratitude now. "What's in those books you're always reading?" he asked idly. "Stories," I answered. "What kind?" asked somebody else without much interest.

Nor do I know what impelled me to behave as I did, for usually I just sat there in silence, glad enough to be allowed to remain among them; but instead of answering his question, I launched full tilt into the book I was immersed in at the moment. The book was *Sister Carrie* and I told them the story of Sister Carrie for two full hours. They listened bug-eyed and breathless. I must have told it well, but I think there was another and deeper reason that made them so flattering an audience. Listening to a tale being told in the dark is one of the most ancient of man's entertainments, but I was offering them as well, without being aware of doing it, a new and exciting experience.

The books they themselves read were the *Rover Boys* or *Tom Swift* or G. A. Henty. I had read them too, but at thirteen I had long since left them behind. Since I was much alone I had become an omnivorous reader and I had gone through the books-for-boys-series in one vast gulp. In those days there was no intermediate reading material between children's and grownups' books, or I could find none, and since there was no one to say me nay, I had gone right from *Tom Swift and His Flying Machine* to Theodore Dreiser and *Sister Carrie*. Dreiser had hit my young mind and senses with the impact of a thunderbolt, and they listened to me tell the story with some of the wonder that I had had in reading it.

It was, in part, the excitement of discovery—the discovery that there could be another kind of story that gave them a deeper kind of pleasure than the *Rover Boys*—blunderingly, I was giving them a glimpse of the riches contained outside the world of *Tom Swift*. Not one of them left the stoop until I had finished, and I went upstairs that wonderful evening not only a member of the tribe but a figure in my own right among them.

The next night and many nights thereafter, a kind of unspoken ritual took place. As it grew dark, I would take my place in the center of the stoop and, like Scheherazade, begin the evening's tale. Some nights, in order to savor my triumph more completely, I cheated. I would stop at the most exciting part of a story by Jack London or Frank Norris or Bret Harte, and without warning tell them that that was as far as I had gone in the book and it would have to be continued the following evening. It was not true, of course; but I had to make certain of my new-found power and position, and with a sense of drama that I did not know I possessed, I spun out the long summer evenings until school began again in the fall. Other words of mine have been listened to by larger and more fashionable audiences, but for that tough and grimy one that huddled on the stoop outside the candy store, I have an unreasoning affection that will last forever. It was a memorable summer, and it was the last I was to spend with the boys on the block.

• • • •

NEARLY TEN YEARS LATER, Moss Hart returned to that stoop beside the candy store, this time with a crisis far deeper than adolescence. He and his family had since moved from the old neighborhood, and fallen to their deepest level of poverty yet. Their furniture was in storage, the rent was due, they had no money, and everyone in the family was unemployed. On the edge of panic, Hart wandered back to his old neighborhood and recalled wistfully those summer nights on the stoop with the boys and thought about how far away they seemed at the moment. In the candy store nearby, he stood before the pay telephone and racked his brain to think of someone—anyone—who would loan him two hundred dollars to save his family, someone who would invest two hundred dollars in a playwright who had never done anything more than direct silly summer camp productions. His everlasting fortune was that he found someone to do just that.

When he finally met success, he embraced it, then shared it with everyone he knew. Moss Hart was described this way by Brooks Atkinson, the drama critic for *The New York Times*: ". . . since 1930, when *Once in a Lifetime* began to pour money into all his pockets, he has taken a frank delight in living expensively surrounded by friends. There is nothing mean or prudent about him in character or purse. He leaves a trail of expensive gifts wherever he goes. He spends money with the eager lavishness of a man who once had none. . . . [He] wants everyone to enjoy his good fortune. . . ."

Related book: Jackie French Koller has written an excellent young-adult novel about the time period and neighborhoods in which Moss Hart grew up, *Nothing to Fear*.

from **A**LL THE STRANGE HOURS
by Loren Eiseley

The Immense Journey from Pond to Professor

When Professor Loren Eiseley died, he was celebrated as one of America's most distinguished writers and scientists. Today, more than fifteen years later, many of his books are still in print, and *The Immense Journey* remains one of the best-selling "popular-science" books of all time. His own personal journey to fame was an arduous and painful one.

In order to understand how long that journey was, one must first understand what Eiseley became—an anthropologist. In the simplest terms, an anthropologist is a scientist who examines the history of mankind from the viewpoints of biology (body and bones) and sociology (the things one says and builds with that body). The examination often is done by digging into the earth (geology) in hopes of discovering fossils (paleontology) from ancient times. In other words, the anthropologist must know a little bit about a lot of different things.

Now, let us examine the "artifacts" in Loren Eiseley's life. Neither his mother nor his father had gone beyond eighth grade. Both, however, were avid readers. His father had read most of Shakespeare by the time he was twenty, memorizing long passages, and years later often recited them for his son. His mother, Daisy, had contracted an unknown disease during childhood that gradually withered her hearing until she became deaf early in adulthood, a factor that would greatly affect her son's life.

When Eiseley was four, the family moved to Lincoln, Nebraska, to the home that would be the most important in his life. Gale Christianson, Eiseley's biographer, describes it this way: "Loren sensed that something was seriously wrong shortly after the family moved into Lincoln. It was a time of hushed and troubled voices: 'The whispering, always the whispering of [Aunt] Grace, grandmother and the rest. [Ours] was a house of whispers.' It was also a house unto itself. Visitors rarely came, and those few who crossed the threshold were not encouraged to stay long. The shuttered and curtained windows not only kept the sun at bay but discouraged curious neighbors from establishing contact with those who dwelled within. The Eiseleys were dismissed as peculiar, though harmless and unimportant, social outcasts of their own making."

The strangeness was a result of his mother, who had grown increasingly abnormal in her behavior, often verbally assaulting her husband for his lowly pay as a hardware salesman. Young Eiseley frequently had to act as a referee between his parents. The common rites of family life—as simple as a family picnic—were unknown to the child. (He had one picnic—with his first-grade class.)

As he grew older, his mother became paranoid about losing him. She insisted on knowing his whereabouts at all times and limited his play space to within a block of their home. When he was old enough to wander farther afield, his mother "often pursued [him] and his friends through the streets and into the farmland, shouting at Loren in her eerie voice and embarrassing him in front of his playmates."

Increasingly isolated, the young boy began to look for friendship in the plants, insects, and small animals in the fields and ponds around him. It was the birth of both the scientist and the melancholy "loner." Fortunately, the public library was one of the few places his mother always allowed him to visit unattended.

By his sophomore year in high school the emotional deterioration of his family forced him to live with his uncle and aunt. Soon thereafter he dropped out of high school when social pressures from the affluent student body became more than he could bear. Fortunately, his uncle knew the head of a local experimental high school that gave individual attention to its students, and he convinced the boy to give it a try. The change worked wonders and Eiseley graduated two years later, captain of the football team and class president (though there were only forty members in his class). More important, he and his teachers had discovered the creative writer within him. It was the first public recognition of his talent and worth.

He attended the University of Nebraska in Lincoln, but poverty, along with personal insecurity, tuberculosis, and family concerns, turned college into what he called a "prison term." Instead of graduating in four years, he required eight. He flunked out once, and dropped out other times.

During his absences from school, he often joined the waves of hoboes and vagrants hopping freight trains headed west. These personal expeditions along the rails allowed him to expand the habit of quiet contemplation he'd begun as a child. Now, instead of examining the species in his aquariums, he was examining the human species that sat beside him in the light of the hobo campfires. The restlessness, however, would stay with him all his life—as evidenced by the paths he wore in the living-room carpets as he paced through the night, pondering or worrying through a problem. Like Hans Christian Andersen, another product of an unhappy and poverty-stricken childhood, he would spend his entire adult life living in apartments—he never owned a home, even though he had the wealth to do so.

In the study of anthropology he found his first "home," and after a succession of college and university professorships he became head of the anthropology department at the University of Pennsylvania. Along the way he developed a writing style that would elevate him above the other scientists of his time. They would have brains and insight greater than his, but they didn't have the gift with language to translate what they knew into what could be understood by nonscientists.

With his poetic vision, Eiseley was able to write successfully for scientific journals such as the *American Scholar* and *American Anthropologist* as well as for popular periodicals such as *Reader's Digest, Harper's*, and *The Saturday Evening Post*. Many of his essays were sculpted like small short stories. Indeed, another struggling young writer—who knew nothing of Eiseley's background—read his articles, recognized immediately a kindred spirit, and wrote him fan letters. The correspondent would soon be famous for his own science —science *fiction*: Ray Bradbury (page 252). Eventually Eiseley's literary style came to be known as "the concealed essay"—writings that were so easy and pleasurable to read, the reader didn't know he was learning something at the same time.

The excerpt here is from Eiseley's book *All the Strange Hours*. Though autobiographical in nature, it is really a collection of interesting essays about his own life.

In setting the scene for this selection, it should be noted that Eiseley had a brother from his father's previous marriage, Leo, who was fourteen years older. By the time Loren was five, Leo was living and working outside the home, leaving the younger child to live as a kind of castaway on a deserted island. Leo, however, did give his brother the tools and materials to escape the island—and Eiseley describes them in this selection.

He also reports a conversation he had with his father about three escaped convicts. The compassion his father requested for the men would linger with Eiseley for his entire life, but most vividly during the times he traveled with the hoboes and drifters, a few of whom were criminals, but most of whom were simply ill-starred victims in a strange play called life.

At the beginning of Chapter 16, Eiseley is thrust back to his childhood when he stumbles across an unanswered fan letter he had received after writing several articles for *Harper's* magazine. Still unanswered after twenty-five years, it had come from Jimmy Dawes, his closest companion in childhood, the boy who had dropped him as a friend when his well-to-do father decided it was socially unacceptable for Jimmy to be palling around with the Eiseley boy now that they were in high school. Dawes was the last classmate or friend ever to enter Eiseley's childhood home.

• • • •

from CHAPTER 16
The Letter

ON THE SHELF where I had started to fumble when Jimmy Dawes' letter arrived was an old book, bound in green cloth with a stylized fish in gold stamped on the cover, a book bearing the unimpressive title *The Home Aquarium: How to Care for It*. A man equally obscure had published that book in 1902, five years before I was born. His name was Eugene Smith and whatever else he did in life I do not know. The introduction was written in Hoboken, New Jersey.

The copy I possess is not the one I borrowed and read from the Lincoln City Library while I was still in grade school. So profound had been its influence upon me, however, that in adulthood, after coming East, I had sought for it unsuccessfully in old book stores. One day, in my first year in graduate school, I had been turning over books on a sales table largely strewn with trivia in Leary's famous old store in Philadelphia, a store now vanished. To my utter surprise there lay three copies with the stamp of the golden fish upon their covers. It was all I could do to restrain myself from purchasing all three. It was the first and last time I ever saw the work in a book store. The name B. W. Griffiths and the date 1903 was inscribed on the fly leaf. To this I added my own scrawled signature and the date 1933. Now, in the year 1975, I still possess it. I have spoken in the past of hidden teachers. This book was one such to me.

It is true there had been my early delvings in sandpiles, and so strong is childhood memory, that I can still recollect the precise circumstances under which I first discovered a trapdoor spider's nest. My amazing, unpredictable mother was the person who explained it to me. How, then, did this pedestrian work on the home aquarium happen to light up my whole inner existence?

There were, I think, two very precise reasons having nothing to do with literature as such that intrigued me about this old volume. Most of the aquarium books of today start with the assumption that you go to a pet store and buy tanks, thermometers, specialized aeration equipment, and even your assemblage of flora and fauna "ready made." Smith's book contained no such assumption. You got the glass, you cut it yourself, you made bottoms and sides of wood. Then, somewhere, you obtained tar to waterproof the wood and the joints. Moreover, Smith had given a simple running account, not alone of easily accessible fresh-water fish, but of local invertebrates with which aquariums could be stocked.

I genuinely believe that it was from the pages of his book that I first learned about the green fresh-water polyp *Hydra viridis*, so that later I identified it in one of my own aquariums, not from the wild. In other words, there had been placed within my hands the possibility of being the director, the overseer of living worlds of my own. If one has the temperament and takes this seriously one will feel forever afterward responsible for the life that cannot survive without one's constant attention. One learns unconsciously about ecological balance, what things may the most readily survive together, and, if one spends long hours observing, as I later came to do, one makes one's own discoveries and is not confined to textbooks.

This leads me to the other value gained from Smith's plain little volume. I spent no time, as a midlander, yearning after tropical marine fish or other exotic specimens. I would have to make my own aquariums and stock them as well. Furthermore, for a lad inclined as I was, one need not confine oneself to fish. One could also make smaller aquariums devoted to invertebrate pond life.

By chance I encountered Smith's book in midwinter and it would be a normal parental expectation that all of this interest in "slippery things" would have worn itself out while the natural world was asleep under pond ice. In the flaming heat of enthusiasm, however, I grew determined not to wait upon nature. I first secured some wood and glass scraps from a nearby building project and tar from a broken tar barrel. Though I had no great gifts as a carpenter I did the job by persistence from materials then strewn casually about every house under construction. I boiled and applied the warm tar myself. In one triumph, I even made a small aquarium from a cigar box.

In a few days I had enough worlds to start any number of creations. To do so I had to reverse the course of nature. Elders may quail but this is nothing for children. So it was winter? Snow lying thick over the countryside? Ponds under ice? Never mind. I knew where the streams and ponds were. I had also learned that many forms of life hibernate in the mud of ponds. All that was necessary was to improvise a net, again homemade, take a small lard bucket or two, and trudge off to the most accessible Walden.

The countryside was open in those days. On one visit to Lincoln several years ago I thought it might be good to tramp out to that old pond where so many generations of boys had swum, waded, or collected. Forbidding fences warned me away. It was now part of a country club of the sort doubtless frequented by the successors of the parents of Jimmy Dawes. I speak no ill. If a country club had not acquired the ponds and landscaped the greens, all would have been filled in by suburban developments in any case. But this was all wild once, and the feeling that is left is somehow lost and bittersweet. The pond is there. It is not the same pond. It is "reserved." It has been tamed for rich men to play beside. Either that or the developers come. One takes one's choice. No. Not really. One has no choice.

On that winter day so long ago I almost lost my life. I arrived at the pond and chopped an experimental hole near the shore where I worked my clumsy mud-dredging apparatus back and forth. My plan was successful. I was drawing up a few sleeping water boatmen, whirligig beetles, and dragonfly larvae, along with other more microscopic animalcules. These I placed in my lard buckets and prepared to go home and begin the stocking of my little aquariums. A forced spring had come early to my captives.

There were skates on a strap hanging around my neck, and before leaving I thought I would take one quick run over the pond. It was a very cold day, the ice firm. I had no reason to anticipate disaster. I made two swift passages out over what I knew to be deeper water. On the second pass, as I stepped up speed, there was a sudden, instantaneous splintering of ice. The leg to which I had just applied skating pressure went hip deep into the water. I came down upon my face. I lay there a moment half stunned. No one was with me. What if the rest of the ice broke? Even if one held on to the edge one would freeze very quickly.

I waited anxiously, trying not to extend the ice-fracture by struggling. I was scared enough to yell, but it was useless. No one but a boy infused with the momentary idea of becoming a creator would be out on a day like this. Slowly I slid forward, arms spread, and withdrew my soaking leg from the hole. I must have struck an ice bubble with that one foot. The freezing weather fortunately permitted no general collapse of the ice. In one sweating moment I was safe, but I had to jog all the way home with my closed buckets.

After such an event there was no one's arms in which to fall at home. If one did, there would be only hysterical admonitions, and I would be lucky to be allowed out. Slowly my inner life was continuing to adjust to this fact. I had to rely on silence. It was like creeping away from death out of an ice hole an inch at a time. You did it alone.

Critics, good friends in academia, sometimes ask, as is so frequently the custom, what impelled me to become a writer, what I read, who influenced me. Again, if pressed, I feel as though I were still inching out of that smashed ice bubble. Any educated man is bound to live in the cultural stream of his time. If I say, however, that I have read Thoreau, then it has been Thoreau who has been my mentor; this in spite of the fact that I did not read Thoreau until well into my middle years. Or it is Melville, Poe, anyone but me. If I mention a living writer whom I know, he is my inspiration, my fount of knowledge.

Or it is the editor of my first book who must have taught me this arcane art, because if one writes one must indeed publish a first book and that requires an editor. Or if one remains perplexed and has no answer, then one is stupid and one's work is written by a ghost who is paid well for his silence. In one institution where I taught long ago, it was generally assumed that all of us young science instructors were too manly to engage in this dubious art. Our wives produced our papers.

I myself believe implicitly in what G. K. Chesterton wrote many years ago: "The man who makes a vow makes an appointment with himself at some distant time or place." I think this vow of which Chesterton speaks was made unconsciously by me three separate times in my childhood. These unconscious vows may not have determined the precise mode of whatever achievement may be accorded mine, or what crossroads I may have encountered on the way. I mean to imply simply that when a vow is made one will someday meet what it has made of oneself and, most likely, curse one's failure. In any event, one will meet one's self. Let me tell about the first of those vows. It was a vow to read, and surely the first step to writing is a vow to read, not to encounter an editor.

It so happened that when I was five years old my parents, in a rare moment of doting agreement, looked upon their solitary child and decided not to pack him off to kindergarten in that year. One can call them feckless, kind, or wise, according to one's notions of the result. Surprisingly, I can remember the gist of their conversation because I caught in its implications the feel of that looming weather which, in after years, we know as life.

"Let him be free another year," they said. I remember my astonishment at their agreement. "There'll be all his life to learn about the rest. Let him be free to play just one more time." They both smiled in sudden affection. The words come back from very far away. I rather think they are my mother's, though there is a soft inflection in them. For once, just once, there was total unanimity between my parents. A rare thing. And I pretended not to have heard that phrase "about the rest." Nevertheless when I went out to play in the sunshine I felt chilled.

I did not have to go to kindergarten to learn to read. I had already mastered the alphabet at some earlier point. I had little primers of my own, the see-John-run sort of thing or its equivalent in that year of 1912. Yes, in that fashion I could read. Sometime in the months that followed, my elder brother paid a brief visit home. He brought with him a full adult version of *Robinson Crusoe*. He proceeded to read it to me in spare moments. I lived for that story. I hung upon my brother's words. Then abruptly, as was always happening in the world above me in the lamplight, my brother had departed. We had reached only as far as the discovery of the footprint on the shore.

He left me the book, to be exact, but no reader. I never asked mother to read because her voice distressed me. Her inability to hear had made it harsh and jangling. My father read with great grace and beauty but he worked the long and dreadful hours of those years. There was only one thing evident to me. I had to get on with it, do it myself, otherwise I would never learn what happened to Crusoe.

I took Defoe's book and some little inadequate dictionary I found about the house, and proceeded to worry and chew my way like a puppy through the remaining pages. No doubt I lost the sense of a word here and there, but I mastered it. I had read it on my own. Papa bought me *Twenty Thousand Leagues Under the Sea* as a reward. I read that, too. I began to read everything I could lay my hands on.

Well, that was a kind of vow made to myself, was it not? Not just to handle ABC's, not to do the minimum for a school teacher, but to read books, read them for the joy of reading. When critics come to me again I shall say, "Put Daniel Defoe on the list, and myself, as well," because I kept the vow to read *Robinson Crusoe* and then to try to read all the books in the local library, or at least to examine them. I even learned to scan the papers for what a boy might hopefully understand.

That was 1912 and in the arctic winter of that year three prisoners blasted their way through the gates of the state penitentiary in our town. They left the warden and his deputy dead behind them. A blizzard howled across the landscape. This was long before the time of the fast getaway by car. The convicts were out somewhere shivering in the driving snow with the inevitable ruthless hunters drawing a narrowing circle for the kill.

That night papa tossed the paper on the table with a sigh. "They won't make it," he said and I could see by his eyes he was out there in the snow.

"But papa," I said, "the papers say they are bad men. They killed the warden."

"Yes, son," he said heavily. Then he paused, censoring his words carefully. "There are also bad prisons and bad wardens. You read your books now. Sit here by the lamp. Stay warm. Someday you will know more about people out in the cold. Try to think kindly, until then. These papers," he tapped the one he had brought in, "will not tell you everything. Someday when you are grown up you may remember this."

"Yes, papa," I said, and that was the second vow, though again I did not know it. The memory of that night stayed on, as did the darkness and the howling wind. Long after those fleeing men were dead I would re-enter that year to seek them out. I would dream once more about them. I would be— Never mind, I would be myself a fugitive. When once, just once, through sympathy, one enters the cold, one is always there. One eternally keeps an appointment with one's self, but I was much too young to know.

By the time of the aquarium episode I was several years older. That, too, was a vow, the sudden furious vow that induced me to create spring in midwinter. Record the homely writing of Eugene Smith, placing in my hand a tool and giving me command of tiny kingdoms. When I finally went away to graduate school I left them to the care of my grandmother Corey. I told her just how to manage them. She did so faithfully until her death. I think they brightened her final years—the little worlds we cared for. After the breakup of the house I searched for them. No one could tell me where they were. I would have greatly treasured them in the years remaining. I have never had an aquarium since, though expensive ones are now to be had.

I suppose, if I wrote till midnight and beyond, I could conjure up one last unstable vow—when at nineteen I watched, outwardly unmoved, the letter of my father crumble in the flames. I started, did I not, to explain why a man writes and how there is always supposed to be someone he had derived his inspiration from, following which the good scholar may seek out the predecessor of one's predecessor, until nothing original is left. I have said we all live in a moving stream, as surely as a catfish groping with its whiskers in the muddy dark. I have seized this opportunity nevertheless to ensure that my unhappy parents' part in this dubious creation of a writer is not forgotten, nor the role of my half-brother, who accidentally stimulated me into a gigantic reading effort. As for Eugene Smith, he gave me the gift of wanting to understand other lives, even if he almost stole my own upon that winter pond.

I would like to tell this dead man that I fondled his little handbook as I wrote this chapter. We are not important names, I would like to tell him. His is a very common one and all we are quickly vanishes. But still not quite. That is the wonder of words. They drift on and on beyond imagining. Did Eugene Smith of Hoboken think his book would have a lifelong impact on a boy in a small Nebraska town? I do not think so.

Ironically, one of the senior officers of the firm that published Smith's work asked me not long ago if he could interest me in a project and would I come to lunch. The letter was pleasantly flattering. I wrote the man that I would be glad to lunch with him, though in all honesty I was heavily committed elsewhere. After his original invitation, I was never accorded the dignity of a reply.

Sometimes this is called the world of publishing. It is a pity. I would have liked to tell this important man, over a cocktail, about a man named Smith whose book was published by his very own house before he, this generation's president, had been born. I would have been delighted to inform him that there was a stylized gold fish on the cover, and to what place the book had traveled, and how it had almost drowned, as well as uplifted, a small boy. Alas, this is a foolish dream. The presidents of great companies do not go to luncheons for such purposes. As for me, these strange chances in life intrigue me. I delight or shudder to hear of them.

• • • •

THE DEFINITIVE ADULT BIOGRAPHY of Loren Eiseley is *Fox at the Wood's Edge* by Gale Christianson.

Related books: For those wishing an overview of exactly what anthropologists do, I recommend *Buried in Ice: The Mystery of the Lost Arctic Expedition* by Owen Beattie and John Geiger, a sixty-four-page description of how a team of scientists discovered the remains of the mysterious 1845 Franklin Expedition in the Arctic that precipitated the greatest rescue mission in history—an effort that failed. In 1984, anthropologist Owen Beattie succeeded in finding out what *really* happened to the phantom ships and their crews.

The field of paleontology has not always had an honorable reputation. *My Daniel* by Pam Conrad is a powerful novel about the unsavory early years when museums were building their dinosaur collections.

And for those looking for an insight into the troubled times in which Loren Eiseley hopped his freights, I recommend two novels: *Nothing to Fear* by Jackie French Koller and *No Promises in the Wind* by Irene Hunt. Edwin Way Teale, the only nature writer to ever win the Pulitzer Prize, was a friend of Loren Eiseley's and the autobiography of his childhood, *Dune Boy: The Early Years of a Naturalist*, is very accessible for young adults. It can be found in many libraries.

from **A**LEXANDER DOLGUN'S STORY

by Alexander Dolgun with Patrick Watson

Using Stories as a Survival Tool

Like most twenty-two-year-old Americans, Alex Dolgun (DOLL-gun) knew the words to lots of songs. Because he loved books and movies, he also knew more than his share of plots and stories. What he did *not* know was how they would help to save his sanity and perhaps his life.

At that point in time, it was not known how important stories can be in keeping the balance between sanity and insanity. We wouldn't begin to study that for another twenty-five years, until the prisoners of war came home from Vietnam and the Middle East. Alex, of course, knew none of that when he left the American embassy in Moscow and went out for lunch on a chilly December day in 1948.

He never made it to lunch. Instead, he was stopped by a stranger claiming to be an old friend. Alex patiently explained there must be a mistake: "I have never seen you before in my life!" At that point, the stranger pulled a card from his pocket that identified him as a member of the Soviet secret police. At the same time, two more strangers appeared at Alex's side and shoved him into a car that stopped abruptly at the curb. It was the beginning of an eight-year nightmare that would literally and figuratively stretch Alex Dolgun's heart, mind, and body to the limits of human endurance.

The problem began in 1933 when Alex's Polish-born father, like a number of other engineers, was lured into leaving the United States to work for a year as an adviser to the Moscow Automotive Works. The pay was three times more than he would earn in the United States. At the time, America was in the throes of the Great Depression, so when the year's contract was up and the Soviets offered an extension, the elder Dolgun agreed—on the condition that he be allowed to bring his family to Moscow. That one-year extension stretched into another and another, until suddenly it was 1939 and the world was on the brink of war. At that point, Dolgun was told by the Soviets that not only could he and his family not return to the United States, but because he had stayed as long as he had he was now a Soviet citizen and was being drafted into the Red Army. Dolgun was not politically connected—all his contracts had been handled by the Soviet government—and therefore he didn't know of a possible recourse such as the American embassy.

By the time the war was over, the Dolgun family had adjusted to their difficult situation. Their son Alex, however, was rediscovering the America he left as an eight-year-old. Through his teen years he had taken to borrowing and memorizing every book or record the American embassy would loan to him. By the time he won a clerk's position at the embassy he was eyeing a return to the United States. At the same time, however, the Cold War between the U.S.S.R. and the free world had escalated, and each side was intensifying its search for spies. The secret police saw Alex Dolgun, a Soviet citizen working daily in the U.S. embassy, as an ideal prospect for espionage interrogation.

Once captured, he was brought to Lubyanka, the huge secret police stronghold just minutes from the U.S. embassy—though he might as well have been two thousand miles away for all anyone would know. Despite his protestations of innocence, he was accused of espionage and political terrorism and was ordered to confess everything. Toward that goal, a KGB colonel began to interrogate him—eighteen hours a day, a routine that would proceed for eighteen months. The interrogations would be laced with the foulest of verbal abuse and physical torture. When he was not being questioned, his sleep would be interrupted constantly in a cell where the temperature was kept below freezing. On average he slept fewer than three hours a night.

His hair began to fall out in large clumps and his weight dropped more than fifty pounds. When sleep would overtake him during interrogation, he often fell off his chair. If the fall didn't wake him, a bucket of ice water was dumped on him.

No one had lasted as long as six months under the strain before breaking and signing whatever the police wanted. Dolgun's iron determination lasted eighteen months. Much of his endurance can be attributed to his personal efforts to maintain his mental balance. To sustain it, Dolgun fell back on memory. Years later he recalled, "Memory keeps you alive. I firmly believe this. It's obvious you need food and water and air and shelter, of course. But lonely men have gone mad or killed themselves even when they were warm enough and had enough to eat. A man in my position—left in a dark room, not really enough food to keep his endurance going, cold, insulted and abused by the few people he does encounter, so that he doesn't see them as people anymore—needs a good memory to keep in touch with human beings who are somewhere else.

"If I had not been able to remember faces, names, plots of movies, words people had spoken to me, books I had read, restaurants I had eaten in, maps, the face of Europe, rooftops in Manhattan, I could never have survived the Moscow prisons," he explained.

When the police resigned themselves to Dolgun being a lost cause, they summarily sentenced him to one of the 165 slave-labor camps that arched across the Soviet Union. This network, eventually labeled the Gulag Archipelago (Empire of the Camps) by writer Aleksandr Solzhenitsyn (Sol-shen-EET-sen), was the largest penal system in the history of the world, housing 12 to 15 million prisoners. For purposes of comparison, all American prisons combined housed 1.2 million prisoners in 1991. Furthermore, while American prisons are intended only for criminal punishment, the Soviet camps were multipurpose: They housed the common, professional criminals (called *urki*) as well as political prisoners, while at the same time providing a gigantic slave-labor force to work mines and industries in areas where normal citizens would not freely think of working. Political prisoners were all those who were incarcerated for publicly or privately disagreeing with the policies of the Soviet government.

The frightening specter of the camps loomed so large in the minds of average Soviet citizens that most would do or say anything to avoid being sentenced to one. "Anything" included spying and reporting on their parents, children, friends, employers, and neighbors. All of this increased both the prison population and the paranoia among the population that someone was always listening and no one could be trusted. Only when he eventually was released from the camps did Dolgun learn that his parents had also been imprisoned and that his mother had been driven insane by the experience.

The selection you are about to encounter is from the book *Alexander Dolgun's Story: An American in the Gulag*, written by Dolgun in conjunction with journalist Patrick Watson and published in 1975, four years after Dolgun's sister and a handful of American politicians were able to win his return to freedom. The story fulfilled a promise he made to fellow prisoners who asked him to tell their story to the world. When he returned to the United States, he worked as a program analyst for U.S. and Soviet medicine in the U.S. Department of Education, developing health programs that could be shared between the two nations. Before he died in 1986, he predicted the fall of the Soviet system as well as years of transition hardships that would follow for citizens of the Soviet Union.

As you will discover, Dolgun's story is a testimonial to courage and ingenuity, but it also is brutally frank and hideous. To have portrayed the events in anything *but* that way would have been like pouring salt on the wound. This particular incident also adds a powerful dimension to the term *escapist literature*.

In this incident, Dolgun arrives at the cell of his first camp, where he and the other new prisoners "repeated our prayers" at the door. In this usage, *prayer* refers to each prisoner's compulsory oral recitation of his crime and punishment. And for purposes of comparison, when he describes the size of the cell, think in these terms: The average American car is sixteen feet long, and the distance from home plate to the pitcher's mound in baseball is sixty feet, six inches.

PRONUNCIATION GUIDE
urki (OORR-key)—professional or habitual criminals
dukharik (doo-HAR-eek)—a man with *soul* or *guts*
pakhan (pah-KHAN)—"chief" of professional criminals
Dzhezkazgan (Jiz-kaz-GHAN)—Siberian prison camp

• • • •

from CHAPTER 13

THE CELL that I and about fifteen others were taken to opened directly on the yard. It was cell number 12. At the door we formed a line and one by one repeated our prayers and then were roughly pushed inside. I stumbled going across the threshold and fell against a jumble of people just inside the door. I rolled on the floor and ended up against a wooden pole. I pulled myself up by grabbing this pole, found it was a support for some sort of long bunk, or shelf, and grabbed a space to sit down.

My first impression was of bedlam. The cell reverberated with chatter. Later I counted and found that we were 129 people in a cell sixteen feet wide and about forty feet long. Two layers of bunks, which were nothing more than hard plank platforms, ran down each of the long sides and across the end. At the far end was a large window, open in the warm air, with bars on the outside. In the glare from the window it was hard to see the far end of the cell clearly, but I know that it was already packed with people standing on the floor and sitting or lying on or under the sleeping platforms. By the door, at the opposite end from the window, was a large wooden barrel that served as a urinal. The floor around it was damp, as the barrel was too high to use without difficulty unless you were very tall. The smell of urine would have been suffocating if the window had not been open at the other end of the room.

I remember that several people came up to me almost immediately to hear news from outside. The first question was always, "Are you from freedom?" And then, even when I explained that I had been in prison for a year and a half, many still wanted to know what it was like outside; they had been in prison for five years, ten years, some for twenty years.

For some reason I was standing up. Perhaps I had been squeezed off the crowded bunk. I was weak, but sitting on hard wood with my buttocks gone was not comfortable and I know that I often stood up to relieve the pain on my hip bones. The talk around me went silent suddenly and the heads of the people who had gathered to hear my meager news swung around toward the central part of the room. Then they moved away from me anxiously. I saw three dirty, ragged young men advancing toward me, grinning wickedly. They stepped up to within a couple of feet of where I stood, hanging on to a bunk support, and looked me over with insolent eyes. I still had my navy surplus gray gabardine trousers, and even after a year and a half of prison they were in much better shape than most prisoners' clothes. These toughs were *shobla yobla*, the lowest of the *urki*, or criminal class. They were very nasty-looking guys. They looked at my pants with obvious interest. The one in the middle said to the others, "Look, brothers, he has my trousers on!" He started to feel the cloth.

I said, "What the hell are you talking about? These are mine. Hands off!"

The leader kept pushing at me roughly. "Now, look at this, brothers! A common thief wearing my pants! And claims they are his own! Well, well!"

Then he grabbed a bundle from one of the other young jackals and held it out to me, a bundle of rags. "*These* are your trousers," he said between his teeth, holding them under my nose and pushing his face very close. "Now give me mine and give them to me quick," and thrust out two fingers as if to jab them in my eyes.

I had been up against tougher guys than he for a year and a half, and I was certainly not going to take this lying down. I was too weak for a good swing, but I held tight to the post with my left hand and brought my right up from below in the hardest and fastest uppercut I could manage. It hurt my hand like hell because it connected beautifully, right on the button, and the kid went down on his back. He looked astonished and he looked ready to kill. The other two began to close in and they were still grinning, but the grin had hardened a lot and their hands were held out like wrestlers'.

The room had gone absolutely silent. All the friendly people who had been so eager to hear my news had melted away. I felt totally alone in this weird crowd. The guy on the floor got up, rubbing his chin. There was blood on his lip. He spread his hands and held the other two back. His eyes looked murder. "I'll take him," he said curtly. He took a step toward me. I tightened my grip on the post. I was trembling but I figured I could at least duck and butt him in the stomach with my head, and then go for the crotch of one of the others before he got me. I was pretty scared, but I was pretty mad, too, and quite ready to throw myself at them, as feeble as I was.

But it never happened. A loud call from the back of the room, where the glare from the window hid the speaker from me, stopped the *shobla yobla* cold.

"*Off!*" this voice said, very clear, with great authority. "Lay off, now. That man is a *dukharik!*" *Dukh* is the word for "soul," but it means pretty much the same, in this context, as the English word "guts."

"Bring him to me," the voice said, more quietly. I was squinting into the shadow under the glaring window to try to see who this was. All heads in the room were looking either at me or toward the invisible speaker at the end of the room.

The *shobla yobla* were cowed. One of them said, almost deferentially, "The *pakhan* calls you. You better go see him," and then he led me to the other end of the room.

Pakhan is underworld slang for "the chief." In rank and authority, this guy has the status of a robber king. In the Mafia he would be like the godfather, but I do not want to use that word, because there is a godfather in the labor camps and that is an entirely different thing. Besides, a *pakhan* can arise anywhere and does not have to be linked to a particular family. He is a man widely recognized in the underworld for his skill and experience and authority. To meet such a distinguished, high-class *urka* is a very rare event.

The man I saw on the lower shelf at the end of the cell when I got close enough not to be dazzled by the light from the window was impressive in every way. He was well over six feet tall. He had wide shoulders and strong brown hands. He sat cross-legged on the bunk in boots of fine black soft leather, very high boots, with blue trousers tucked into the tops. His whole suit was a rich blue and made of good cloth. He had a pink shirt and a flashy striped tie and a handkerchief in his jacket pocket. Perhaps the most astonishing thing of all, since I had just come through the most rigorous search and knew that anything as innocent as a teaspoon would be confiscated in case you had an idea of making a weapon from it, was that this man had in his hand a large polished hunting knife with a handle made of laminated discs of different-colored plastic. With the absolutely classical manner of a movie tough guy, he sat there on the bunk slicing pieces of smoked meat from a big chunk and popping them in his mouth. Not only that, but he had *white* bread, which I had not seen since December 13, 1948, almost eighteen months earlier. He looked me over with an amused smile, but a very friendly kind of amusement.

The *pakhan* said, "Here, sit." Immediately people made room beside him. I took my jacket out of my bundle and made a cushion out of it and sat. The *pakhan* looked me over and I looked over all the people around him. There was a short, fair-haired guy sitting at his right hand, and from time to time someone would come up and whisper to this short guy and the short guy would whisper back, or just nod or shake his head, and the supplicant would go away. He looked like the *pakhan*'s grand vizier, and that is almost exactly what he turned out to be.

The *pakhan* cut off a slice of smoked sausage and put it on a slice of white bread and handed it to me. I gobbled it down. I had not eaten such good food since my last breakfast at the American Embassy.

My benefactor opened his eyes at the speed with which his gift disappeared. He cut off another slice of meat and made a sandwich and offered it, and while I gobbled it down he waved his hand and a mug of water appeared, which he passed to me as soon as I had licked the last grease and crumbs from my fingers. He waited until I had drunk, then he said simply, "Well?"

I said, "I'm an American citizen. I was kidnapped by the Organs. I've just come from Sukhanovka. I've got twenty-five years and I think I'm going to Dzhezkazgan. My name is Alexander Dolgun."

"Then I call you Sasha the American, okay? This"—indicating the grand vizier—"is Sashka Kozyr." *Kozyr* is Russian for "trump." "He is my deputy. My name is Valentin Intellighent. You can call me Valka."

I said, "Thanks for the food. I really don't understand how you get all this stuff . . . and the knife? What's going on here?" I was totally mystified. Valentine the Intelligent just laughed.

"I will explain it to you sometime," he said in a very good-natured way, but also in a way that made clear that *he* was the chief and *he* would decide the order in which things were supposed to be done.

"Listen," he said, "if you're an American, you must have seen lots of movies, yes?"

I nodded.

"And you talk like an educated man, like myself, yes? Read a lot of books? Read novels a lot?"

I nodded again.

"Good. I think we may be able to have a good business relationship."

The *pakhan* grinned widely at my bewilderment. Then his mood shifted and he became very serious and intense, peering at me directly with only a hint of a mocking smile around his dark eyes. He was very handsome, his black hair was neatly combed, and he was clean shaven. With that knife, I thought. It looked sharp enough.

"Now listen," he said seriously. "Can you squeeze a novel?"

I said, "What do you mean, 'squeeze'?"

He said, "You know, 'squeeze' is our slang for 'tell.' Can you tell us novels, narrate the stories, same with movies? We have no storyteller here, and we need stories. Life is empty without a good story to keep you going every day. Can you do that?"

I said eagerly, "Sure I can. I've spent the last year and a half telling myself all the movies and novels I could remember. I'm getting very good at it."

"That's excellent!" Valentin said. "I'll call the brothers around and we can get started."

• • • •

Dolgun's story was a sensation with the prisoners. They sat spellbound, attending his every word. In the weeks that followed, he regaled them with mystery stories from Ellery Queen (page 53), detective stories, and movies. He even spent several nights serializing the Victor Hugo classic *Les Misérables*.

What Dolgun had discovered alone in his Moscow cell would be reinforced here in the filthy, insect-ridden prison camp: Human beings need stories, both for entertainment and to maintain their balance. When American POWs were released after the Vietnam War, and, later, when America's Middle East hostages were released, psychologists reported that certain ones survived the experience better than others. According to their studies, the ones who had the healthiest *imaginations*, who were able to mentally flee the captivity for a period of time each day, to come home and kiss their wives and hug their children, were the ones who suffered the least long-term damage from their captivity.

Additionally, we use stories to understand what happens to us, comparing one experience with another one stored in our memories. By such comparison we are able to predict what might happen next. This sense of control and balance keeps people sane. (Roger C. Schank has written the definitive book on this subject, *Tell Me a Story: A New Look at Real and Artificial Memory*.)

If Dolgun's portrait of his fellow prisoners is occasionally less than complimentary to the human species, one should not misread it as peculiar to the Soviet Union or a foreign country. Dolgun is reminded elsewhere in the book by a kindly physician-prisoner that "man deprived of liberty tends to degenerate morally." The greatest struggle among prisoners anywhere, next to staying alive, is to avoid the clutches of moral decay.

Evidence of the universality of such decay can be found in the daily diary of a quartermaster for Union forces in the Civil War. Originally published in 1881 and now available as *John Ransom's Andersonville Diary*, the book describes his year as a Confederate prisoner. As historian Bruce Catton points out in the book's introduction, the war's prison camps—North or South—killed *ten times* as many people as did the battlefields. Catton praises Ransom's account for showing that "much of the suffering undergone by Union men in Confederate camps was of their own making."

Consider these brief excerpts from Ransom's diary and how much they resemble Dolgun's:

Dec. 1, 1863: Have just seen a big fight among the prisoners; just like so many snarly dogs, cross and peevish. A great deal of fighting going on. Rebels collect around on the outside in crowds to see the Yankees bruise themselves and it is quite sport for them.

Dec. 6: A great deal of stealing is going on among the men. There are organized bands of raiders who do pretty much as they please. A ration of bread is often of more consequence than a man's life.

Jan. 5, 1864: Jimmy Devers spends the evenings with us and we have funny times talking over better days—and are nearly talked out. I have said all I can think, and am just beginning to talk it all over again. All our stories have been told from two, to three or four times, and are getting stale. We offer a reward for a new story.

Jan. 17: A good deal of raiding is going on among the men. One Captain Moseby (Union officer) commands a band of cut-throats who do nearly as they please, cheating, robbing and knocking down—operating principally upon new prisoners. . . .

May 10: New prisoners coming in every day with good clothes, blankets, etc., and occasionally money. These are victims for the raiders who pitch into them for plunder.

June 8: There are now over 23,000 confined here, and the death rate 100 to 130 per day. . . .

July 3: The greatest possible excitement. Hundreds (of prisoners) that have been neutral and non-committal are now joining a police force. Captains are appointed to take charge of the squads that have been furnished with clubs by (Capt.) Wirtz (Confederate prison commandant). As I write, this middle of the afternoon, the battle rages. The police go right to raider headquarters knock right and left and make arrests. Sometimes the police are whipped and have to retreat, but they rally their forces and again make a charge in which they are successful.

Like Dolgun's account a century later, Ransom's diary (which filled three volumes during his imprisonment) is both indictment and testimonial: indictment of man's inhumanity in times of stress; testimonial to the ultimate goodness that transcends the worst of times and conditions. Both books, I should caution you, are for mature readers and certainly not for the timid or fainthearted.

Related books include: *The Long Walk: A Gamble for Life* by Slavomir Rawicz as told to Ronald Downing (out of print but available in many libraries), the story of eight Soviet prisoners and their four-thousand-mile escape route from a Siberian prison; *North to Freedom* by Anne Holm (page 363); *One Day in the Life of Ivan Denisovich* by Aleksandr Solzhenitsyn, the most famous story on Soviet forced-labor camps, written by a man who survived their horrors and won the Nobel Prize for literature; *Three Came Home* by Agnes Newton Keith (out of print but available in many libraries and used-book stores), the inspiring true story of the author's wartime experiences with her husband and son in a Japanese prison camp; *The Wooden Horse* by Eric Williams (out of print but found in libraries and used-book stores), which is set in a German prisoner-of-war camp during World War II, and is one of the most famous escape stories ever printed.

You might also be interested in *Monuments to Failure: America's Prison Crisis* and *Memory of the Camps* (actual film footage of the Nazi concentration camps), both sixty-minute (PBS) videos.

from **I** KNOW WHY THE CAGED BIRD SINGS

by Maya Angelou

A Southern Writer Finds Her Voice

There is a maxim that says, "Prosperity is a great teacher, but adversity is greater." If that is true, then Marguerite Johnson had quite an education by the time she was twenty.

Her father was a doorman and her mother was a card dealer, beautician, registered nurse, and merchant sailor. At the age of three, she and her four-year-old brother, Bailey, were given up by their parents and sent fifteen hundred miles by train, alone, to live with their grandmother. At eight, she was raped by her mother's boyfriend. As a teenager, she was awkwardly skinny with broad feet, her eyes so small and squinty they provoked classmates to say her father must have been a "Chinaman." At the age of sixteen, she was pregnant and unmarried.

By the time she was in her sixties, each June found her besieged by twenty colleges and universities that wanted her to be their commencement speaker. Her name is now Maya Angelou (pronounced MY-a ON-jeh-low), and to date she has a remarkable list of accomplishments: She has

- authored seven books (including two volumes of poems), numerous plays, and documentaries, and composed songs for stage, screen, and television
- served as associate editor of an English-language newsweekly in Egypt and as feature editor of *African Review* in Ghana
- performed as a singer and dancer in more than thirty countries, learned six languages, and won an Emmy nomination for her performance as Kunta Kinte's grandmother in the television production of "Roots"

- taught modern dance in Italy and Israel
- worked as the Southern Christian Leadership Conference's northern coordinator for Dr. Martin Luther King, Jr.
- served as one of President Ford's appointees to the American Bicentennial Committee and was selected by another president to be his "inaugural poet"
- watched her son become the first black executive with Western Airlines
- received more than fifty honorary degrees from colleges and universities

Along the way she was also a cook, streetcar conductor, and cocktail waitress, among other jobs.

Perhaps her parents sensed the gift they were giving her and her brother when, after their marriage fell apart in California, they tagged the two children at the wrist with identification and put them on a train to fiercely segregated Stamps, Arkansas.

In Stamps their grandmother, Mrs. Annie Henderson, forever thence to be called "Momma" by her grandchildren, owned the general store—the *only* black-owned store in town—and the grandchildren joined her and their crippled uncle in their home behind the store. Mrs. Henderson's establishment was a rallying point and anchor for the black community. They brought and bought there: They brought their good news and troubles, sharing as the need might be, and they bought their food and household staples. They could even have their hair cut on Saturdays.

It was behind the store's counter and at her grandmother's knee that Maya Angelou learned the social graces of life—the way to begin and end sentences, how to answer and behave with elders, the hymns and graces of church and home, the need and power of education, the strength of both home and a grandmother's and uncle's hand. But more than anything else, she learned she was loved and a person of worth.

There were other lessons to be learned there, too—ones that would inspire her tenacity in the difficult years to come. At dawn each day during cotton season, Marguerite would listen at her grandmother's side to the happy banter of the field hands in the store as they waited to board the wagons for a day's labor. And she listened again, never to forget, the pickers' grim, "dirt-disappointed" murmuring as they returned at the end of the day, broken by the sun and the knowledge that their lowly wages would never be enough of a ladder to escape their dark hole. This, she vowed to herself, is not right and it will never happen to me.

Angelou recalls the days and heartbeats of her childhood with intensity and affection—but with full knowledge of their bitter edges. No amount of nostalgia could dull the memory of the Ku Klux Klan and their dreaded visits. She would watch as her grandmother emptied the store's vegetable bin so the crippled uncle could be helped into it, where he would lie buried beneath the potatoes and onions through the night, waiting in dread for the devilish hoofbeats.

Fifty years later, her life's path would epitomize the courage and tenacity that marked the American civil rights struggle since the days when the Klan ruled communities such as Stamps. By 1993, Angelou was a professor of American studies at Wake Forest University in Winston-Salem, North Carolina—a college that excluded blacks when she was a child. She was also the poet of choice for Bill Clinton, who asked her to create and recite to the nation a poem on the occasion of his inauguration as president. Clinton came to the presidency from the governorship of Arkansas—a state that just thirty-six years earlier had had a governor (Orval Faubus) who defied the Supreme Court and called up the state's national guard to block the integration of its schools, a confrontation that many called the most serious constitutional crisis since the Civil War.

The fullness and diversity of Angelou's life caught the attention of the celebrated writer James Baldwin, who convinced her to share it with others. There have been five volumes of autobiography to date, from childhood through her professional careers here and abroad. The writing, however, is not for the timid or sheltered—unless they welcome the harsh truth of other lives. She writes candidly, joyfully, and sometimes painfully of her mistakes and triumphs from childhood to parenthood and adulthood. A *New York Times* critic once described her writing style as "the product of a born writer's senses, nourished on black church singing and preaching, soft mother talk and salty street talk, and on literature."

In the autobiographies, she spreads her life's cards on the table, as if saying, "This is the hand I was dealt and here is how I played it. It might not have been the best way or the only way, but give it a look. You might learn something from it. I certainly did."

The selection included here follows a period when, as an eight-year-old, she and her brother rejoined their mother for a year in St. Louis. While there, she was molested and then raped by her mother's boyfriend. During the subsequent trial, her confusion and fear led her to lie inadvertently in response to a lawyer's question. As it turned out, the truth would not have mattered in the verdict—guilty—but the lie haunted her. When she learned that the man was murdered a few days later after his lawyer won his release, she associated her lie with his death. At that point—and for the next year—she stopped talking with everyone except her beloved brother. She was convinced her loose tongue could kill any adult she spoke to.

At the end of a year, she and Bailey were returned to "Momma" and to Stamps, where she drifted silently and aimlessly through the months. Finally, a neighbor woman would loosen her tongue, open her mind, and touch her soul. Here, from Chapter 15 of her autobiography *I Know Why the Caged Bird Sings*, Maya Angelou describes the poignant summer afternoon when the sun came back into her life.

• • • •

from CHAPTER 15

FOR NEARLY A YEAR, I sopped around the house, the Store, the school and the church, like an old biscuit, dirty and inedible. Then I met, or rather got to know, the lady who threw me my first life line.

Mrs. Bertha Flowers was the aristocrat of Black Stamps. She had the grace of control to appear warm in the coldest weather, and on the Arkansas summer days it seemed she had a private breeze which swirled around, cooling her. She was thin without the taut look of wiry people, and her printed voile dresses and flowered hats were as right for her as denim overalls for a farmer. She was our side's answer to the richest white woman in town.

Her skin was a rich black that would have peeled like a plum if snagged, but then no one would have thought of getting close enough to Mrs. Flowers to ruffle her dress, let alone snag her skin. She didn't encourage familiarity. She wore gloves too.

I don't think I ever saw Mrs. Flowers laugh, but she smiled often. A slow widening of her thin black lips to show even, small white teeth, then the slow effortless closing. When she chose to smile on me, I always wanted to thank her. The action was so graceful and inclusively benign.

She was one of the few gentlewomen I have ever known, and

has remained throughout my life the measure of what a human being can be.

Momma had a strange relationship with her. Most often when she passed on the road in front of the Store, she spoke to Momma in that soft yet carrying voice, "Good day, Mrs. Henderson." Momma responded with "How you, Sister Flowers?"

Mrs. Flowers didn't belong to our church, nor was she Momma's familiar. Why on earth did she insist on calling her Sister Flowers? Shame made me want to hide my face. Mrs. Flowers deserved better than to be called Sister. Then, Momma left out the verb. Why not ask, "How *are* you, *Mrs*. Flowers?" With the unbalanced passion of the young, I hated her for showing her ignorance to Mrs. Flowers. It didn't occur to me for many years that they were as alike as sisters, separated only by formal education.

Although I was upset, neither of the women was in the least shaken by what I thought an unceremonious greeting. Mrs. Flowers would continue her easy gait up the hill to her little bungalow, and Momma kept on shelling peas or doing whatever had brought her to the front porch.

Occasionally, though, Mrs. Flowers would drift off the road and down to the Store and Momma would say to me, "Sister, you go on and play." As I left I would hear the beginning of an intimate conversation. Momma persistently using the wrong verb, or none at all.

"Brother and Sister Wilcox is sho'ly the meanest—" "Is," Momma? "Is"? Oh, please, not "is," Momma, for two or more. But they talked, and from the side of the building where I waited for the ground to open up and swallow me, I heard the soft-voiced Mrs. Flowers and the textured voice of my grandmother merging and melting. They were interrupted from time to time by giggles that must have come from Mrs. Flowers (Momma never giggled in her life). Then she was gone.

She appealed to me because she was like people I had never met personally. Like women in English novels who walked the moors (whatever they were) with their loyal dogs racing at a respectful distance. Like the women who sat in front of roaring fireplaces, drinking tea incessantly from silver trays full of scones and crumpets. Women who walked over the "heath" and read morocco-bound books and had two last names divided by a hyphen. It would be safe to say that she made me proud to be Negro, just by being herself.

She acted just as refined as whitefolks in the movies and books and she was more beautiful, for none of them could have come near that warm color without looking gray by comparison.

It was fortunate that I never saw her in the company of powhitefolks. For since they tend to think of their whiteness as an evenizer, I'm certain that I would have had to hear her spoken to commonly as Bertha, and my image of her would have been shattered like the unmendable Humpty-Dumpty.

One summer afternoon, sweet-milk fresh in my memory, she stopped at the Store to buy provisions. Another Negro woman of her health and age would have been expected to carry the paper sacks home in one hand, but Momma said, "Sister Flowers, I'll send Bailey up to your house with these things."

She smiled that slow dragging smile, "Thank you, Mrs. Henderson. I'd prefer Marguerite, though." My name was beautiful when she said it. "I've been meaning to talk to her, anyway." They gave each other age-group looks.

Momma said, "Well, that's all right then. Sister, go and change your dress. You going to Sister Flowers's."

The chifforobe was a maze. What on earth did one put on to go to Mrs. Flowers' house? I knew I shouldn't put on a Sunday dress. It might be sacrilegious. Certainly not a house dress, since I was already wearing a fresh one. I chose a school dress, naturally. It was formal without suggesting that going to Mrs. Flowers' house was equivalent to attending church.

I trusted myself back into the Store.

"Now, don't you look nice." I had chosen the right thing, for once.

"Mrs. Henderson, you make most of the children's clothes, don't you?"

"Yes, ma'am. Sure do. Store-bought clothes ain't hardly worth the thread it take to stitch them."

"I'll say you do a lovely job, though, so neat. That dress looks professional."

Momma was enjoying the seldom-received compliments. Since everyone we knew (except Mrs. Flowers, of course) could sew competently, praise was rarely handed out for the commonly practiced craft.

"I try, with the help of the Lord, Sister Flowers, to finish the inside just like I does the outside. Come here, Sister."

I had buttoned up the collar and tied the belt, apronlike, in back.

Momma told me to turn around. With one hand she pulled the strings and the belt fell free at both sides of my waist. Then her large hands were at my neck, opening the button loops. I was terrified. What was happening?

"Take it off, Sister." She had her hands on the hem of the dress.

"I don't need to see the inside, Mrs. Henderson, I can tell . . ." But the dress was over my head and my arms were stuck in the sleeves. Momma said, "That'll do. See here, Sister Flowers, I French-seams around the armholes." Through the cloth film, I saw the shadow approach. "That makes it last longer. Children these days would bust out of sheet-metal clothes. They so rough."

"That is a very good job, Mrs. Henderson. You should be proud. You can put your dress back on, Marguerite."

"No ma'am. Pride is a sin. And 'cording to the Good Book, it goeth before a fall."

"That's right. So the Bible says. It's a good thing to keep in mind."

I wouldn't look at either of them. Momma hadn't thought that taking off my dress in front of Mrs. Flowers would kill me stone dead. If I had refused, she would have thought I was trying to be "womanish" and might have remembered St. Louis. Mrs. Flowers had known that I would be embarrassed and that was even worse. I picked up the groceries and went out to wait in the hot sunshine. It would be fitting if I got a sunstroke and died before they came outside. Just dropped dead on the slanting porch.

There was a little path beside the rocky road, and Mrs. Flowers walked in front swinging her arms and picking her way over the stones.

She said, without turning her head, to me, "I hear you're doing very good school work, Marguerite, but that it's all written. The teachers report that they have trouble getting you to talk in class." We passed the triangular farm on our left and the path widened to allow us to walk together. I hung back in the separate unasked and unanswerable questions.

"Come and walk along with me, Marguerite." I couldn't have refused even if I wanted to. She pronounced my name so nicely. Or more correctly, she spoke each word with such clarity that I was certain a foreigner who didn't understand English could have understood her.

"Now no one is going to make you talk—possibly no one can. But bear in mind, language is man's way of communicating with his fellow man and it is language alone which separates him from the lower animals." That was a totally new idea to me, and I would need time to think about it.

"Your grandmother says you read a lot. Every chance you get. That's good, but not good enough. Words mean more than what is set down on paper. It takes the human voice to infuse them with the shades of deeper meaning."

I memorized the part about the human voice infusing words. It seemed so valid and poetic.

She said she was going to give me some books and that I not only must read them, I must read them aloud. She suggested that I try to make a sentence sound in as many different ways as possible.

"I'll accept no excuse if you return a book to me that has been badly handled." My imagination boggled at the punishment I would deserve if in fact I did abuse a book of Mrs. Flowers'. Death would be too kind and brief.

The odors in the house surprised me. Somehow I had never connected Mrs. Flowers with food or eating or any other common experience of common people. There must have been an outhouse, too, but my mind never recorded it.

The sweet scent of vanilla had met us as she opened the door.

"I made tea cookies this morning. You see, I had planned to invite you for cookies and lemonade so we could have this little chat. The lemonade is in the icebox."

It followed that Mrs. Flowers would have ice on an ordinary day, when most families in our town bought ice late on Saturdays only a few times during the summer to be used in the wooden ice-cream freezers.

She took the bags from me and disappeared through the kitchen door. I looked around the room that I had never in my wildest fantasies imagined I would see. Browned photographs leered or threatened from the walls and the white, freshly done curtains pushed against themselves and against the wind. I wanted to gobble up the room entire and take it to Bailey, who would help me analyze and enjoy it.

"Have a seat, Marguerite. Over there by the table." She carried a platter covered with a tea towel. Although she warned that she hadn't tried her hand at baking sweets for some time, I was certain that like everything else about her the cookies would be perfect.

They were flat round wafers, slightly browned on the edges and butter-yellow in the center. With the cold lemonade they were sufficient for childhood's lifelong diet. Remembering my manners, I took nice little lady-like bites off the edges. She said she had made them expressly for me and that she had a few in the kitchen that I could take home to my brother. So I jammed one whole cake in my mouth and the rough crumbs scratched the insides of my jaws, and if I hadn't had to swallow, it would have been a dream come true.

As I ate she began the first of what we later called "my lessons in living." She said that I must always be intolerant of ignorance but understanding of illiteracy. That some people, unable to go to school, were more educated and even more intelligent than college professors. She encouraged me to listen carefully to what country people called mother wit. That in those homely sayings was couched the collective wisdom of generations.

When I finished the cookies she brushed off the table and brought a thick, small book from the bookcase. I had read *A Tale of Two Cities* and found it up to my standards as a romantic novel. She opened the first page and I heard poetry for the first time in my life.

"It was the best of times and the worst of times . . ." Her voice slid in and curved down through and over the words. She was nearly singing. I wanted to look at the pages. Were they the same that I had read? Or were there notes, music, lined on the pages, as in a hymn book? Her sounds began cascading gently. I knew from listening to a thousand preachers that she was nearing the end of her reading, and I hadn't really heard, heard to understand, a single word.

"How do you like that?"

It occurred to me that she expected a response. The sweet vanilla flavor was still on my tongue and her reading was a wonder in my ears. I had to speak.

I said, "Yes, ma'am." It was the least I could do, but it was the most also.

"There's one more thing. Take this book of poems and memorize one for me. Next time you pay me a visit, I want you to recite."

I have tried often to search behind the sophistication of years for the enchantment I so easily found in those gifts. The essence escapes but its aura remains. To be allowed, no, invited, into the private lives of strangers, and to share their joys and fears, was a chance to exchange the Southern bitter wormwood for a cup of mead with Beowulf or a hot cup of tea and milk with Oliver Twist. When I said aloud, "It is a far, far better thing that I do, than I have ever done . . ." tears of love filled my eyes at my selflessness.

On that first day, I ran down the hill and into the road (few cars ever came along it) and had the good sense to stop running before I reached the Store.

I was liked, and what a difference it made. I was respected not as Mrs. Henderson's grandchild or Bailey's sister but for just being Marguerite Johnson.

Childhood's logic never asks to be proved (all conclusions are absolute). I didn't question why Mrs. Flowers had singled me out for attention, nor did it occur to me that Momma might have asked her to give me a little talking to. All I cared about was that she had made tea cookies for *me* and read to *me* from her favorite book. It was enough to prove that she liked me.

• • • •

THE FIVE VOLUMES (in chronological order) of Maya Angelou's autobiographical series are *I Know Why the Caged Bird Sings*, *Gather Together in My Name*, *Singin' and Swingin' and Gettin' Merry Like Christmas*, *The Heart of a Woman*, and *All God's Children Need Traveling Shoes*.

I Know Why the Caged Bird Sings is available on audiocassette, abridged to three hours (Random Audio), and there is a powerful sixty-minute PBS video of Angelou's return to Stamps, Arkansas, accompanied by Bill Moyers. Also recommended: *The Autobiography of Miss Jane Pittman*, a 110-minute video (Prism); and *Eyes on the Prize*, a six-cassette PBS documentary, the most comprehensive portrayal of the American civil rights movement.

Two other stories about the southern experience can be found in this volume: a chapter from *Good Old Boy: A Delta Boyhood* by Mississippi's Willie Morris (page 105) and a chapter from *To Kill a Mockingbird* by Alabama's Harper Lee (page 67). Stories about the black experience include the chapter from *Narrative of the Life of Frederick Douglass* (page 293) and "Thank You, Ma'am" by Langston Hughes (page 82).

Books pertaining to African-American history and experiences include: *Now Is Your Time! The African-American Struggle for Freedom* by Walter Dean Myers; *One More River to Cross: The Stories of Twelve Black Americans* and *The Life and Death of Martin Luther King, Jr.*, both by Jim Haskins; *Roll of Thunder, Hear My Cry* by Mildred Taylor; and *Words by Heart* by Ouida Sebestyn.

Mature readers will find many similarities between Angelou's struggle and that of two boys growing up in Chicago's worst public housing in the 1980s, as profiled by Alex Kotlowitz in his powerful nonfiction book, *There Are No Children Here: The Story of Two Boys Growing Up in the Other America*. Also for mature readers: *The Water Is Wide* (sometimes *Conrack* in paperback), novelist Pat Conroy's sobering nonfiction book about his days teaching school on an all-black island off the coast of South Carolina in the 1960s.

Historical Fiction

• • • • • • • • • •

Five selections from novels that
show that the human condition
has changed little through the
centuries, on land or at sea.

from THE DECEMBER ROSE

by Leon Garfield

A Writer Who Gives His Characters the Dickens

There are few if any originals—in anything. All actors and actresses, all artists, and all athletes have stars in their eyes when they are starting out, and their idols or role models are always on their minds. A gesture here, an inflection there—just the way Brando or De Niro or Streep would do it. Young art students are required to repaint a masterpiece to learn its subtleties and shadings. Aspiring athletes mimic the moves of their heroes.

It is the same with writers. A hundred years ago a young Robert W. Service wanted to be like Bret Harte and Jack London and eventually succeeded with "The Cremation of Sam McGee" (page 212). Fifty years ago a teenaged Ray Bradbury wanted to create magical kingdoms like H. G. Wells and L. Frank Baum, and *The Martian Chronicles* serves as a testimonial to them. Very few authors, however, have come as close to playing the role of their heroes as novelist Leon Garfield has.

Though he was born in 1921 in Brighton, England, one could say Garfield was born into the nineteenth century as well. Brighton still retains much of the flavor from its nineteenth-century seaside heritage—a setting ready-made for Charles Dickens, that century's most famous chronicler. Now add to that the fact that Garfield's parents behaved as though they'd just stepped out of a Dickens novel: His flamboyant but irresponsible father and neurotic mother engaged in constant warfare while young Garfield often found himself helpless in the cross fire.

It therefore seemed only natural for Garfield to adopt—on purpose or by accident—the setting and style of Dickens. Indeed, his work was so often compared to the great nineteenth-century novelist that he attempted what few writers would even dream of doing. When Dickens died in 1870, he left behind one half of an unfinished psychological murder mystery called *The Mystery of Edwin Drood*. Who would possess the complicated mind needed for the task of finishing the book, never mind the audacity to walk in the shoes of a master writer? Garfield was the natural candidate, and the completed novel met excellent American reviews from skeptical critics when it was published here in 1981.

He didn't begin to write his first book until he was forty years old, and then it took him five years. He'd been working for almost twenty years as a biochemical technician when the seedling of a story set in the nineteenth century began to take root in him. What he had to learn was that good stories aren't born full grown. He was painfully dismayed at how much he didn't know about the nineteenth century: How long would it take to get from one place to another in those times? What was the money worth? How much would it buy?

His research led him even further back to the eighteenth-century writers Defoe (*Robinson Crusoe*) and Swift (*Gulliver's Travels*) for nautical information: "They were both very strong in it, and they appeared to get their effects from vivid personal experience. I was very depressed . . . until I discovered that both had got their information straight out of an old sailing manual. . . . They both knew no more about the sea than I did." He called it the most encouraging discovery he ever made.

Five years' worth of reading in decaying manuals, diaries, and map books netted him a treasure trove of detailed information, which he crafted into that first novel, *Jack Holburn*. Today, thoroughly steeped in the nineteenth century, he requires less time for research, but if he places a post office at Charing Cross in one of his stories, you can be sure there really was one there.

In the last thirty years Garfield has won a Carnegie Medal (the English equivalent of the Newbery Medal) and has been runner-up three times. His action-filled plots lend themselves naturally to screenplays, and at least seven have been adapted for British film and television. Conversely, one story originated as a BBC TV production and afterward was made into a novel called *The December Rose*, two chapters of which appear here.

There are no car chases in Garfield novels, but there are more than enough kidnappings, murders, mobbings, stolen documents, narrow escapes, pickpockets, menacing villains, and devilish apprentices, as well as bighearted heroes and heroines. And, as the second chapter demonstrates, Garfield knows the comic relief that Dickens used as counterbalance to a tale's grimness and terror.

Like Dickens, Garfield begins most stories with his hero as a child—the most frequent and most unprotected victim of the nineteenth century. Law and order were still very much beyond arm's reach in those times, which allows Garfield and Dickens the liberty to douse their characters in every imaginable catastrophe. In other words, each creates a melodrama—a sensational drama with a happy ending, or, as Garfield describes it, "that old-fashioned thing called a family novel, accessible to the twelve-year-old and readable by his elders."

All of this allows Garfield to avoid what he feels is the worst of traps—boring his readers. "They must never be bored," he states, "not for an instant. Words must live for them; so must people. That is what really matters. . . ." Therefore, Garfield wastes no time or space before launching his story. And unlike Dickens, who was paid by the word and sometimes used more adjectives and adverbs than were absolutely necessary to the story, Garfield has fine-tuned his writing over the years for the eye and ear of the twentieth century.

Here, then, are the first two chapters from *The December Rose*, a piece of the nineteenth century in living, colorful prose.

· · · ·

CHAPTER 1

AT ABOUT A QUARTER PAST FIVE on a Thursday afternoon early in September, a woman entered the Post Office at Charing Cross and inquired of one of the clerks if a letter was awaiting her. It was her third visit in as many days. On this occasion the clerk was able to oblige her. He handed her a letter which she opened immediately, without even stepping back from the counter. She glanced rapidly to see the name of the sender, as if to reassure herself, and then, clutching the letter in her hand, hastened outside with an air of strong nervous excitement.

Although the day was warm and summery, she was dressed entirely in black . . . which served to set off the extreme pallor of her complexion and the brilliancy of her eyes. Her name was Donia Vassilova. She was known as an enemy of the country and a grave risk to the security of the State.

Once outside, she hesitated briefly, glanced about her, and then set off in the direction of Charing Cross Road. She walked quickly, sometimes stepping out into the road rather than be restricted to the slower pace of those ahead of her.

From time to time she paused, looked behind her, and then hastened on. It was plain that she suspected she was being followed, but could not be sure who, among the shifting multitude behind her, was her pursuer.

She turned into Moor Street and then into Greek Street, where she stopped abruptly and gazed up searchingly at one of the houses on the right-hand side. Possibly she did this with the intention of deceiving her pursuer, or perhaps she hoped she would be seen by a confederate and her predicament understood.

After a few moments, during which she showed signs of agitation, she hurried northward into Oxford Street where she attempted to lose herself by mingling with the dense crowds. However, her striking appearance always rendered her an easy object for observation. Becoming aware of this, she sought out the less frequented streets to the north, doubtless hoping to isolate her pursuer and force him to show himself. On one occasion she stood for a full five minutes on a corner, intently staring back along the way she had come. Although she saw nothing to confirm her suspicion, she was by no means satisfied and continued with her evasive antics of hurrying from street to street, now north, now east, now south . . .

At half past eight, the evening, which had been increasing in heaviness, turned very dark and came on to rain. The woman, after sheltering briefly in a doorway, went into the Adam and Eve public house in the Tottenham Court Road, where she occupied a seat by the window from which she could observe the street outside. Then, for the first time since she had collected it from the Post Office, she read the letter. As she did so, it could be seen that her hand went continually to a trinket that she wore on a chain round her neck. It was a gold locket bearing an unusual design in black enamel: an eagle . . .

The rain persisted for just over an hour, during which time the woman remained in her place by the window, dividing her attention between her letter and the street, and speaking to no one apart from the waiter who served her. She left the public house at a quarter to ten, crossed the Tottenham Court Road, and walked in the direction of the City.

She seemed to have abandoned her earlier attempts at evasion. She no longer hesitated, but walked rapidly and with a definite sense of purpose. Perhaps she thought she had thrown off her pursuer— either that, or the need to meet with her confederates and inform them of the letter had become too urgent to admit of further delay. The only time she paused was in Fetter Lane, and then only briefly.

She looked behind her. She saw no one. The rain had emptied all the streets, and the lamps, shining on the wet, made watchers only of shadows. The pallor of her face was extraordinary; her eyes were enormous. It was possible that among the multitude of shadows that inhabited the doorways, one had suddenly seemed darker and more threatening than was natural. She drew in her breath and, with a violent shake of her head, hurried away towards Blackfriars.

She reached Bridge Street and then, after a moment's indecision, decided that, rather than crossing the bridge, her best course lay among the narrow lanes and alleys off Union Street. For a little while she negotiated them with the skill and cunning of an animal until, suddenly, in Stonecutter Alley, a deep puddle obstructed her way. Instinctively she shrank back, as if more careful for her skirts than for her life. Such folly!

She turned aside into Pilgrim Court. Even as she did so, she realized her mistake. Pilgrim Court was a dead end. There was no way out. Just before she vanished into the darkness, she turned, and her face was caught in the dim yellow of a street lamp. The expression on it was one that would have been better unseen. It was a look of terror, hatred and despair; and the hatred was the strongest and the worst.

She made no great struggle and uttered only the faintest of cries. All her strength and determination were directed towards clutching the locket. Indeed, her grip upon it remained so strong that it required considerable force to prize it from her hand before her body was tipped into the river off Blackfriars Stairs. She floated briefly, with her face upwards, before the stone that was attached to her waist by a rope dragged her down.

The chain on the locket had been broken, but otherwise it was quite undamaged: ". . . as you can see for yourself, m'lord."

• • • •

CHAPTER 2

THERE WAS A BOY up the chimney, but only God and Mister Roberts knew exactly where. How God came by His knowledge was, of course, a holy mystery; and how Mister Roberts came by his was almost as wonderful an affair. He'd only to lay his ear against a wall, medically so to speak, as if it was a wheezy chest, and it was enough! Leaving a black ear behind, he'd rush to the nearest fireplace, insert his head, and bellow upwards: "I knows yer, Barnacle! I knows ye're just squattin' up there, a-pickin' of yer nose! Git on with yer sweepin', lad, or I'll light a fire and scorch yer to a black little twig! So help me," he would add, for he was a devout man, "God!"

Up and up the dreadful threat would fly, booming and echoing through all the narrow, dark and twisty flues, until it found out Barnacle, exactly as Mister Roberts had divined, squatting in some sooty nook and, if there was room enough to move his arms, a-picking of his nose.

"I knows yer—yer—yer—yer . . . Git on—on—on—on . . . scorch yer—yer—yer—yer . . ."

Barnacle, neatly wedged in an elbow of broken brick, went on with picking his nose and waiting for "God!"

His proper name was Absalom Brown, but his owner, Mister Roberts, called him Barnacle on account of his amazing powers of holding on. He could attach himself to the inside of a flue by finger- and toe-holds at which even a fly might have blinked. It was a real gift, and the only one he had. Otherwise he was a child of darkness, no better, as Mister Roberts often had cause to shout, than a animal.

"So help me, God—God—God—God!" came Mister Roberts's voice, and Barnacle began brushing away at the soot, and dislodged a piece of brickwork for good measure. He heard it go bumping and rattling down until at last it clanged to a stop against the iron bars of a distant grate.

"Watch it, lad—lad—lad—lad!"

"Watch it, 'e says," marveled Barnacle, who was as tight in blackness as a stone in a plum. "An' wot wiv, might I arst?"

Eyes weren't any help, as it was as dark outside his head as it was within; and anyway he was too bone-idle to open them. It was fingers, elbows and knees that told him where he was, and it was his nose that told him where he was going, and, most important of all, it was his ears that warned him of what was to come: either the wrath of Mister Roberts or a sudden fall of stinking, choking soot that was always heralded by a tiny whispering click.

Cautiously he eased himself up the flue, clearing the soot as he went, partly with his brush and partly with the spiky stubble that grew out of his head. Once he'd had a cap, but he'd lost it in his infancy, trying to swipe at a pigeon as he'd come out of the top of a chimney-pot. He'd cried bitterly over the loss, not of the cap but of the handsome brass badge on the front of it that had proclaimed him to be a boy of importance, a climbing boy belonging to a master sweep.

Presently he found he could move more easily. Either he was shrinking or the flue was getting wider. He paused and sniffed. There was a new smell. Mingled in with the sulphurous stink of soot was a faint aroma of toast. He divined he was approaching a coming together of God knew how many flues rising up from God knew how many fireplaces, for the house he was crawling about in, like an earwig, was a real monster, big as Parliament, almost.

He went on a little further and tried the darkness again. To his great pleasure he found he could move his arms enough to pick his nose. He sighed and reclined luxuriously against a thick cushion of soot. For a few brief moments he was happy, being no more than a sensation in the dark.

He could hear voices. They were very faint, scarcely more than murmurs, drifting up from somewhere far below. He listened. He liked listening. In fact, it was his only schooling, and his lessons were made up out of whispers, quarrels, sly kisses, laughter and tears.

There were several voices and, little by little, he began to make them out. There was one that was smooth and thin, like a bone, and another that was a real wobbling fat-guts of a voice. There was a lady who laughed whenever she said anything, and there was a fourth voice that was hard to put a shape to. It was a voice with a kind of whistling edge to it, which seemed to cut through the quiet without even making it bleed.

". . . as you can see for yourself, m'lord," said Whistling Edge.

"Why, it's charming, charming," twittered Laughing Lady. "And so unusual, don't you think?"

"Well done," wobbled Fat-Guts. "Well done indeed!"

"A sorry business, but villains must pay the price," murmured Smooth-and-Bony. "We owe you much!"

"The *December Rose*," said Whistling Edge. "We will be waiting."

"The *December Rose!*" repeated Fat-Guts, and Smooth-and-Bony echoed him, "The *December Rose!*" while Laughing Lady chuckled, like pebbles in the rain.

Eagerly Barnacle poked a finger in his ear and reamed out the soot. He wanted to hear more. He leaned forward, perilously. Suddenly he felt something thin and cold creep up the side of his leg. A moment later he felt a sharp, stabbing pain, as if he'd been stung by a chimney snake!

It was Mister Roberts. Suspecting that his boy was idling, he'd shoved his sweeping rods up the chimney with a spike on the end of them instead of his brush. It was his own invention. "Nothin' like it," he'd declare, "for unstopperin' even the tightest lad!"

He was right. Barnacle howled—and jerked. He crashed his head, scraped his back and skinned his elbows and knees. Frantically he clutched at the blackness, kicked at the air, and howled again. He was falling. Despairingly he clawed at the rushing brickwork, but his amazing powers had deserted him, and he left only fingertips behind.

His rush down to hell—for that's where he was going and no mistake: everybody had always told him so—was tremendous, and accompanied by a furious storm of soot and rubble.

"Gawd 'elp us!" he shrieked, and awaited the iron fist of Grandmother Death.

A moment later, it came. His bones seemed to shoot out of their sockets and his teeth snapped together over the top of his head as, with immense force, he struck the bars of a grate. Then, with a contemptuous shrug of iron and brass, he was tossed out into a carpeted darkness that smelled of cigars and toast.

"What is it? What is it?"

"It's a nest—"

"It's an animal—"

"No, it's a boy," said Whistling Edge.

He was not in hell. Mister Roberts's spike had jerked him and tipped him down another flue. He was in the room of voices.

"Yes . . . a climbing boy . . . a sweep's boy . . . only a boy—"

He opened his eyes. Instantly light blazed and half-blinded him. The room was huge and gleaming, with a crusty ceiling, like a cake . . .

"Come to me, boy," said Whistling Edge, a dark and terrible figure, shaped like a coffin, with enormous square-toed boots.

"That's right, go to Inspector Creaker, boy," urged Smooth-and-Bony. "He won't hurt you."

Whistling Edge smiled a smile of a thousand teeth. Barnacle, dazed and terrified, dragged himself upright, clutching at the fire-irons for support.

"Put that down, boy!"

He'd got hold of a poker. Whistling Edge took a pace back, Laughing Lady screamed, and the room was full of glaring, frightened eyes.

"Oh my Gawd—oh my Gawd!" came a familiar voice, as the door opened and round it came the sooty head of Mister Roberts, with his hair bolt upright and shame and horror all over his face. "What the 'ell are you doin' in 'ere, lad? Beggin' yer honors' pardons! Come 'ere, you little turd! Drop that bleedin' poker or I'll kill yer, so 'elp me God, I will!"

He meant it; he always did. Barnacle screeched defiance and threw the poker at him. Something smashed, but it couldn't have been Mister Roberts, as he was able to shout, "Like a animal! Just like a animal, 'e is!"

Whistling Edge—Inspector Creaker—began to advance. Barnacle's terror increased until it filled him from frowsy top to stinking toe. He had a natural horror of policemen, and this one was the worst he'd ever seen. He threw the tongs at him; and then, without any thought of the consequences, and feeling only a desperate longing to be elsewhere, to escape, to dart into some dark hole, he began to throw everything he could lay his hands on.

Vases, dishes, ornaments, cups and plates, jugs, a silver teapot and a china bust of the queen flew through the air as if of their own accord, and crashed and banged against walls and furnishings while the little black figure of Barnacle hopped and darted hither and thither, frantically seeking a way out.

"Stop him! Stop him!" shouted Fat-Guts. "Stop him!" screamed Laughing Lady, shaking in a corner and blazing with beads. "I'll kill yer!" panted Mister Roberts. But Whistling Edge was the worst. He seemed to know Barnacle's every twist and turn. There was no escaping him. His eyes bulged like cobble-stones, and his great square hands came nearer and nearer . . .

"Come to me, boy, come to me . . ."

"I'm a goner!" thought Barnacle, desperately clawing across a table for something more to throw. "I'd 'ave been better orf in 'ell!"

He clutched a fistful of spoons and something glittering on a chain. He raised his fist, but even as he did so he knew that what he held was pitiful against a man like Whistling Edge.

"Come—" began the policeman, and then he stopped. He was staring at Barnacle's fist or, rather, at what was held in it. A strange look had come into his face, a look of infinite distress. He grew pale, as if his blood had turned to water and his flesh to stone.

For maybe two seconds—no more—he seemed unable to move. But two seconds were enough! With a scream of joy Barnacle darted under his outstretched arm, rushed across the room and hurled himself at the drawn curtains. Wood snapped, glass exploded and Barnacle, speckled with splinters, billowed through yellow velvet and out into the late afternoon!

He landed on grass, but only for an instant. No sooner had he touched it than he was off, like a black cinder whirled away by the wind. He ran and ran through streets and alleys and courts and squares, up hills, down steps, through markets and across wide thoroughfares thick with traffic. He ran until he could run no more. Gasping and panting, he leaned inside a doorway, trying to get back his breath. It was only then that he realized that there was still something clutched in his fist.

Cautiously he examined his prize. He frowned, and then he beamed. He was now the possessor of six silver teaspoons and a locket on a broken chain. It was a gold locket with a curiously enameled design: a bird, an eagle, black as the hand that held it.

• • • •

BARNACLE IS HOLDING A CHAIN but he is also *part* of a chain—a chain of terrifying events that will pit him against the sinister Inspector Creaker and drop him into the large, protective lap of Tom Gosling and the flamboyant Mrs. McDipper.

Garfield is also the author of *Devil in the Fog, Footsteps, Jack Holburn, The Night of the Comet,* and *The Strange Affair of Adelaide Harris.* One Garfield book is available unabridged on audiocassette: *The Ghost Downstairs,* two hours (G. K. Hall).

Columbia Pictures' Oscar-winning film *Oliver* (available in video) provides an excellent background setting for all of Garfield's work.

Fans of *The December Rose* will also enjoy Joan Aiken's *Midnight Is a Place* and Robert Newman's books (*The Case of the Baker Street Irregular, The Case of the Murdered Players, The Case of the Vanishing Corpse,* and *The Case of the Watching Boy*).

from SARAH BISHOP
by Scott O'Dell

Using Yesterday to Understand Today

Scott O'Dell's life was one of remarkable and diverse achievements—few of which will ever be matched.

To begin with, though he lived well into the modern age, he was definitely a product of another time and century. He was born in 1898 on an island off the coast of Southern California at a time when Los Angeles was a frontier town. His father's railroad job constantly took the family into pioneer villages throughout the West, and his earliest memories include the sound of a wildcat scratching the roof above his bedroom and the sound of waves washing under their house, which was built on stilts on Rattlesnake Island. If the characters in his historical novels tend toward dangerous adventures, they aren't much beyond what O'Dell did as a child when he and playmates would swim out to twelve-foot logs waiting to be sent to the sawmills, free one for each boy, and hand-paddle the splintered giants out to the sea for a day of salty adventure.

As a young cameraman in Hollywood filming the original *Ben-Hur* movie (1926), he carried the first Technicolor motion picture camera, made by hand at M.I.T. Before he turned to writing, his jobs in the motion picture industry ranged from cameraman to technical director to teaching a correspondence course in screenwriting.

O'Dell didn't write his first children's novel until he was sixty-two years old, after a successful career as an adult writer and book critic for Los Angeles newspapers. That first book, *Island of the Blue Dolphins*, won the grand prize for children's novels, the 1961 Newbery Medal. O'Dell went on to win three "second-place" Newbery Honor medals for *The King's Fifth*, *The Black Pearl*, and *Sing Down the Moon*—making him the most honored Newbery winner in the first seventy years of the award. (All his novels have remained in print for an unusually long time.)

O'Dell also may have set a longevity record for novelists. His literary powers, unlike those of most writers, did not greatly diminish with age. He wrote one novel a year through most of his eighties, including one of his strongest and most critically acclaimed books, *Streams to the River, River to the Sea: A Novel of Sacagawea*, at the age of eighty-six. He died in 1989 at age ninety-one while working on another novel.

Critics have cast O'Dell in the tradition of the great writers of historical fiction for young people—C. S. Forester, Nordhoff and Hall, Kenneth Roberts, Jack London, and Robert Louis Stevenson. Like many of these predecessors, he had a deep independent streak. For example, he attended four different colleges but graduated from none because he insisted upon taking only courses that interested him—regardless of whether they resulted in a diploma.

He saw himself as a "writer of books that children read" rather than a "writer of children's books," though he did concede that there were certain writing styles that naturally attracted young readers. Children, he felt, are more adept than adults at placing themselves into the characters of a story. With that in mind, he usually made the central character a young person and used first-person narrative. Before his death, O'Dell received an average of two thousand letters a year from his readers.

As a male novelist and historian, he was well ahead of his time. Long before the modern feminist movement ignited interest in strong female protagonists in young-adult novels, O'Dell was a firm believer that women could accomplish every noble thing men could. He routinely cast his novels with courageous women—Karana, the Robinson Crusoe–like girl in *Island of the Blue Dolphins*; Bright Morning, the Navajo girl in *Sing Down the Moon*; Serena Lynn, the heroine in *The Serpent Never Sleeps: A Novel of Jamestown and Pocahontas*; and Alexandra, the sponge diver, and Sarah Bishop, the colonial recluse, both from novels of the same names. In the same vein, twenty-five years before cultural diversity became a rallying point in American education, O'Dell blazed the trail with novels about Spanish, Indian, West Indian, and Mexican characters.

O'Dell was not a purist who believed in writing for the sake of writing. He did not believe the purpose of a book was just to be a book from which the reader could create his or her own meaning. He had a definite point of view about history and the human condition, believing strongly in Santayana's philosophy: "Those who cannot remember the past are condemned to repeat it." Knowing the truth about a society's past sins is a giant step toward curtailing them in the future.

Another factor in his writing was his concern about the absence of meaningful role models in modern society. Conversely, history offers a huge array of heroes and heroines—William Tyndale, for example. The hero of his historical novel *The Hawk That Dare Not Hunt by Day*, Tyndale was the martyred Englishman who violated church law by translating the Bible into English, and his story can serve as a powerful antidote to contemporary religious intolerance. O'Dell explained, "Today children don't feel there are important things to do. They take it out on sports—the football and baseball players are heroes, so that at any given time we've got five thousand heroes. But this is a very empty thing; it's heroism delegated. Nobody enjoys sports more than I do, but I don't enjoy them for that reason. I don't think they should be used as a substitute for the meaningful things in life."

The selection here is from *Sarah Bishop*, a story that began when O'Dell discovered a legendary cave near Waccabuc, New York, where he lived the last ten years of his life. O'Dell told *Language Arts* magazine that the cave was "a small place where a young woman named Sarah Bishop lived during the Revolutionary War. I became interested in this girl. I began my research, but the only information was one short paragraph about her in a newspaper of the time she died. I took that sparse information and created Sarah Bishop. I put fiction and fact together to create her."

One of the historical facts he applies to Sarah's story is this: Hard times bring out both the goodness and the hardness in human beings. In time of war or economic depression, human beings' tolerance for others' political and religious views grows dangerously narrow.

The novel opens on Long Island, New York, on the eve of the Revolutionary War. The Bishops—Sarah, her brother, Chad, and their widower father—are immigrant farmers from England, and the father is still stubbornly loyal to King George. This has made him an easy target for a band of local night riders who call themselves patriots but are closer to vigilantes. Lately some of them have taken to randomly firing shots at the Bishop farmhouse. The community is sinking deeper beneath a wave of fear, worrying whether various unfortunate events are caused by accident or by witches, Tories or patriots. When Sarah applies for credit at Purdy's mill, she is informed that there will be no more credit because of her father's views. Chad, on the other hand, is gripped by the rebel fever. In an emotional confrontation between father and son over the writings of Thomas Paine, he rejects his father's old-world views and departs to join the patriot militia. Soon thereafter, Sarah and her father depart Sunday church service to find their horses have been stolen—along with those of five other loyalist families.

• • • •

CHAPTER 6

FOR TWO WHOLE WEEKS nothing was heard about the stolen horses. Then Mr. Kinkade carted a load of early apples over to Newtown. While he was there he heard that a drover had been seen hurrying east just the day before, driving twelve horses. That was all we ever heard.

Father did not have the money for another team, but he sold some tools and managed to buy one horse, a mare. She wasn't much of a horse; she was spavined and at least as old as I. However, she could pull a wagon if it was not loaded full. No one knew her name, so I called her Samantha, because I liked the sound.

We started harvesting the corn three days after our team was stolen. It was beautiful corn, mostly four ears to the stalk, plump and the color of fresh butter. I took three half-loads to Purdy's mill and had them ground into meal. I paid Mr. Purdy what we owed and had some left for winter.

I caught only a glimpse of Quarme's bony head sticking up above a stack of barrels and his small, mean little eyes peering down at me. Mr. Purdy told me about the cat he had shot, how it had left a trail of blood behind, how afterward the mill hadn't stopped at midnight. I didn't tell him about Old Lady Ryder and her hand.

The next week we picked a few early Roxbury Russets, which always go to a good market. They are not a pretty apple, having sort of a brownish blush; but underneath the blush is a green-gold and the flesh is sweet and crisp. We also had a fine crop of Golden Russets coming on. It is a smaller apple than the Roxbury but richer to the taste.

I put up ten gallons of cider, thirty-three jugs of apple butter, and saved three small barrels to dry for winter eating. Some I sold in

Mott's Corner, going from house to house because you get more money that way than if you sell them to the store.

When I was no longer tired at night, Father brought out the Bible after supper and we sat at the table and he read to me. I'd had a lot of religious instruction from the Bible since the time I was old enough to listen, so this was more to help me to speak and write properly, now that I was not going to school anymore. I had given up the idea because Father was set against it.

Father was an admirer of William Tyndale. He never got tired of talking about him. Every night he told me something new about Tyndale.

"Imagine," he said one night. It was the night Birdsall's mob came to our place. "Imagine a young man, just out of the university, who wished to translate the Bible from the Greek language, in which it was first written, into English. But he couldn't because it was against the wishes of Henry the Eighth—he is the King who had many wives and cut the heads off two of them. Because his life was in danger, Tyndale had to leave England and flee to Germany. There he translated the Bible, printed it, and smuggled it down the Rhine River into England, though the King's spies were on his trail."

My father leaned across the table. He clasped his hands. His eyes shone steady in the candlelight. I could imagine him living long ago, having the courage to do the things William Tyndale did.

"Afterward, because the King's spies were searching everywhere for him, he hid out in cellars and garrets and cocklofts. He hid for many years in fear of his life, but all the while writing words in praise of Christ. Until he was finally captured, strangled, and burned at the stake. Today, Sarah, most of the words I read to you are of Tyndale's making. Listen to Matthew:

" 'Ye have heard that it hath been said, An eye for an eye, and a tooth for a tooth: But I say unto you, That ye resist not evil: but whosoever shall smite thee on thy right cheek, turn to him the other also.'

"And this: 'Ye have heard that it hath been said, Thou shalt love thy neighbour, and hate thine enemy. But I say unto you, Love your enemies, bless them that curse you, do good to them that hate you, and pray for them which despitefully use you, and persecute you.' "

Father closed the Bible and folded his hands on the table. "It is good in stressful times to hear the music of these words. To let it echo in the heart. But the meanings are something else besides. It is terribly hard for me to remember them when I think of Quarme or Purdy or Ben Birdsall. Could it be that I am not a Christian?"

"You are a Christian," I said.

"Are you, Sarah? Can you find it in your heart to forgive Birdsall and his mob?"

"I find it hard."

Father opened the Bible again and began to read from Kings, when from far off, in the direction of Purdy's mill, we heard the sound of hoofs striking stone. Father put the Bible away. He went to the door and listened and came back and blew out the candle. The sound of hoofs came closer. From the window I saw a line of horsemen against the sky. They were riding at a trot down the winding road toward our house. I heard the horses splash through the stream.

Father took up the old musket that he used for hunting waterfowl, the one Chad had asked for. He opened the door a crack and stood listening for a moment. Then he closed the door and bolted it.

I was standing back from the window, watching. There were ten horsemen. They rode up near the barn and sat there waiting while one of them slid from the saddle and came to the door. He held a torch in his hand. By its light I recognized Ben Birdsall, his head and fat little neck thrust out.

"Open up," he said and rapped twice.

"What do you want?" Father asked.

"I want to talk," came the reply, "and I can't do it through the door."

It was dark in the room except for a thread of light where Birdsall's torch shone through. Father shouldered his musket, slid the bolt, and opened the door. I stood back of him.

Birdsall held the torch up to see better. He was not carrying a gun, but he had a nose that was turned up in such a way that you peered right into his nostrils. In the torchlight they looked like the barrels of two pistols.

"Light the candle, Sarah," my father said.

"We don't need light," Birdsall answered. He held the torch higher and waved it. "I understand that you have a picture of King George hanging on your wall."

"I did have. It is there no longer."

"That's good to hear," said Birdsall.

The cows were restless, moving around in the barn, and one of them bawled.

"You know David Whitlock, do you not?" Birdsall said.

Father nodded. "He's a friend of my son. Why do you ask?"

"Young Whitlock reported to his father, who reported to me, that you took a book belonging to said father—a book by Thomas Paine called *Common Sense*—did willfully tear this book up, and did, without proper cause, scatter the pieces about in an angry manner. Why, may I ask?" He sounded as if he were reading from a paper, like David himself.

"It was not a book," Father said in an even voice. "It was a pamphlet, and I destroyed . . ."

"One or the other, it's no matter," Birdsall broke in. "What was the reason for such highhandedness?"

"Do you ask me honestly?"

"I do."

"Well, Colonel Birdsall, my answer is that the pamphlet is a pack of lies."

I was shocked by my father's blunt words, for he gained nothing by saying them. "My brother, Chad, joined the militia," I said. "He's a patriot soldier." Father was too proud and unbending ever to say this. "Chad is off somewhere fighting now."

Birdsall said nothing. He acted as if Chad's being a soldier with the patriot militia made no difference to him. His torch began to smoke and he held it out at arm's length, but its light still glinted on his upturned nose. It still looked like two black pistol barrels pointed straight at us.

The horsemen seemed to catch a signal from Ben Birdsall for something. They began to ride around in a circle. One of them lit a torch. The man held it while it sputtered and burst into flame. Then he flung it into a haymow beside the barn. Flames leaped high and caught the barn roof and licked their way swiftly upward to the ridgepole.

I was unable to move or think. I stood there staring at the flames and screaming at Birdsall. I have no idea what I said. Then I ran past him, thinking to lead the cows out of the milking shed. I had taken no more than a dozen steps when the old mare staggered out of the barn. Her throat had been cut and she fell sprawling at my feet.

Someone seized me from behind. Others bound my arms and legs. They pulled me off, away from the barn and the house, which was now also burning. They tied me to the trunk of a tree and left. One of them was Quarme.

The house and barn and the cow shed and the pigsty were now one mass of sparks and leaping flames. I heard strange sounds, men yelling at each other and laughter. When the moon came up I worked myself free from the tree.

I heard a wagon drive away. I heard horsemen galloping off up the hill. I kept moving through the grass toward our house, which was now only smoldering. I called out with all the strength I had left.

A figure came toward me out of the leaping shadows, through the trees, across the meadow. It was like a figure you set up in the field to scare away crows. But it was not such a figure. It was my father, with his arms stretched out toward me. He was covered with tar and feathers. They looked like the same feathers that I had used to make our sleeping pillows.

• • • •

TARRED AND FEATHERED, Sarah's father lives only a few hours. With the family homestead burned to the ground, she departs to find her brother and tell him of the tragic events. En route she is mistakenly accused of arson by the British. When she subsequently learns that Chad has died of battle wounds aboard a prison ship, she escapes and makes her way into the wilderness to escape forever the ravages of war.

Here is a complete listing of Scott O'Dell historical novels still in print: *Alexandra; The Amethyst Ring; The Black Pearl; The Captive; Carlota; The Cruise of the Arctic Star; The Dark Canoe; The Feathered Serpent; The Hawk That Dare Not Hunt by Day; Island of the Blue Dolphins; The King's Fifth; My Name Is Not Angelica; The Road to Damietta; Sarah Bishop; The Serpent Never Sleeps: A Novel of Jamestown and Pocahontas; Sing Down the Moon; Streams to the River, River to the Sea: A Novel of Sacagawea; Thunder Rolling in the Mountains* (written with Elizabeth Hall); and *Zia*.

Scott O'Dell fans will also enjoy the historical novels of Avi (page 381) and Allan Eckert (page 114). Christopher and James Lincoln Collier have written four excellent young adult novels about the Revolutionary period: *My Brother Sam Is Dead* (a Newberry Honor book) and the trilogy comprising *Jump Ship to Freedom, War Comes to Willy Freeman*, and *Who Is Carrie?*

from **N**ORTH TO FREEDOM
by Anne Holm

An Unknown Book
Too Good to Miss

North to Freedom by Anne Holm (translated from the Danish by L. W. Kingsland) is a novel I like to describe as a "sleeper"—which doesn't mean it's boring. Far from it. Published in the United States in 1965, *North to Freedom* usually can be found sleeping soundly and slightly dust-covered on library shelves, but seldom on bookstore shelves (though it is, thankfully, still in print). Despite this, I have yet to encounter a student or class that did not respond immediately and with great enthusiasm to its powerful story once it is brought to their attention. Afterward, teachers and parents ask me, "How is it I've never heard of this book before? Where has it been?"

One of the book's problems has always been its confusing title: *North to Freedom* suggests to most American readers a story about the Underground Railroad. As you will see from the selection that follows, it is not even set in America. In England and Canada, the same book is entitled *I Am David.*

Another unfortunate strike against the book is the fact the author is not American. As I have noted elsewhere, books originally published in foreign countries and translated into English don't usually become big sellers here (the exceptions being such classics as Andersen's and the Grimms' fairy tales, *Heidi,* and *Bambi.* Additionally, foreign authors are usually not available for book promotion tours and reading or library conferences here, and thus suffer from lack of exposure to the "movers and shakers" in children's literature.

Author Anne Holm was born and raised in Denmark and lived through the German occupation of her homeland during World War II. That experience, coupled with Denmark's proximity to the U.S.S.R. and its monstrous slave labor camp network, gave Holm a unique vantage point for this story of a twelve-year-old's flight from the concentration camp in which he has lived for as long as he can remember.

Knowing that it is only in childhood that we truly throw ourselves unreservedly into the books we read, Holm reasoned to herself, "Why waste such an opportunity by filling it with harmless entertainment instead of real, valuable literature?" The end product of that resolution was the award-winning *North to Freedom*. It has been the subject of a British television series as well as a Universal motion picture. Here, then, is a selection from its first chapter.

• • • •

from CHAPTER 1

D AVID LAY QUITE STILL in the darkness, listening to the men's low muttering. But this evening he was aware of their voices only as a vague, meaningless noise in the distance, and he paid no attention to what they were saying.

"You must get away tonight," the man had told him. "Stay awake so that you're ready just before the guard's changed. When you see me strike a match, the current will be cut off and you can climb over—you'll have half a minute for it, no more."

In his mind's eye David saw once again the gray, bare room he knew so well. He saw the man and was conscious, somewhere in the pit of his stomach, of the hard knot of hate he always felt whenever he saw him. The man's eyes were small, repulsive, light in color, their expression never changing; his face was gross and fat, yet at the same time square and angular. David had known him all his life, but he never spoke to him more than was necessary to answer his questions; and though he had known his name for as long as he could remember, he never said anything but "the man" when he spoke about him or thought of him. Giving him a name would be like admitting that he knew him; it would place him on an equal footing with the others.

But that evening he had spoken to him. He had said, "And if I don't escape?"

The man had shrugged his shoulders. "That'll be none of my business. I have to leave here tomorrow, and whatever my successor may decide to do about you, I shan't be able to interfere. But you'll soon be a big lad, and there's need in a good many places for those strong enough to work. Of course he may think that you aren't yet big enough but that it's still worthwhile feeding you here."

David knew only too well that those other places would not be any better than the camp where he now was. "And if I get away without being caught, what then?" he had asked.

"Just by the big tree in the thicket that lies on the road out to the mines, you'll find a bottle of water and a compass. Follow the compass southward till you get to Salonika, and then when no one's looking, go on board a ship and hide. You'll have to stay hidden while the ship's at sea, and you'll need the water then. Find a ship that's bound for Italy, and when you get there, go north till you come to a country called Denmark—you'll be safe there."

David had very nearly shown his astonishment, but he had controlled himself and, hiding his feelings, had merely said, "I don't know what a compass is."

The man had shown him one, telling him that the four letters indicated the four main points and that the needle, which was free to move, always pointed in the same direction. Then he had added, "The half minute the current's cut off is intended for you. If you try to take anyone with you, you can be sure that neither of you will get away. And now clear off before you're missed."

David did not know what had possessed him to say it. He had never asked the man for anything, partly because he knew it would be of no use, but chiefly because he would not—when you hated someone, you did not ask him for anything. But tonight he had done it: when he had reached the door, he had turned around and, looking straight into that coarse, heavy face, had said, "I'd like a piece of soap."

For a moment there had been complete silence in that bare, gray room. The man looked as if he were going to say something, but he did not, all the same. Instead, he picked up a cake of soap that lay by the side of the washbasin in the corner and threw it on the table. All he said was, "Now go."

So David had gone, as quickly as it was possible to go without appearing to be in a hurry.

The men's muttering was fainter now—some of them must have fallen asleep. The camp's latest arrival was still talking—David recognized his voice because it was less flat and grating than the others'. Whenever the newcomer dozed off to sleep, he was seized with a nightmare, and then they would all wake up again. The night before, this had happened just before the guard was changed, but if he took longer to fall asleep this evening, then it might be possible for David to slip out before the others were awakened again.

David was not yet sure whether he would make the attempt. He tried to figure out why the man had told him to do it. It was certainly a trap: just as he was climbing over, the searchlight would suddenly swing around and catch him in its beam, and then they would shoot. Perhaps something pleasant was going to happen tomorrow, and the man wanted him shot first. David had always known that the man hated him, just as much as David hated *him* in return. On the other hand, nothing pleasant had ever yet happened in the camp that David could remember, and he was now twelve years old—it said so on his identity card.

And then quite suddenly David decided he would do it. He had turned it over in his mind until his head was in a whirl, and he still could not understand why the man had told him to escape. David had no wish to make the attempt: it would only be a question of time before he was caught. But suppose it were a trap and they shot him —it would all be over quickly anyway. If you were fired at while trying to escape, you would be dead within a minute. Yes, David decided to try.

THERE COULD NOT BE many minutes left now. Over in the guardroom he could hear the men moving about and getting dressed, and he could hear the guard yawning as his pace grew slower. Then came the sound of new steps, and David pressed himself even more closely against the wall. It was the man: the faint, sleepy yellow light from the guardroom shone for a moment on his face as he passed the window. He went up to the guard, and David suddenly felt quite empty inside. He was sure that he would be unable to move when the time came. Then he saw before him the endless succession of days, months, and years that would pass if he did not. The waiting would kill him in the end, but it might take a long time: unless you were old, it might take years, as he had seen with all of them. And it would grow worse and worse, all the time; David clenched his teeth so hard that he felt the muscles of his throat grow taut. Then the man struck a match.

Nineteen, twenty . . . the half minute would be up when he had counted slowly to thirty . . . David set his foot in a gap higher up the barbed wire . . . When would the searchlight come? They could not be certain of hitting him in the dark . . . and if they did not hurry, he would be over.

A moment later he had touched the ground on the other side,

and as he ran, he said angrily to himself, "What a fool you are! There's plenty of ground to cover yet—all this great flat stretch without so much as the stump of a tree for shelter. They'll wait till you've nearly reached the thicket . . . they'll think it more amusing if you believe you've almost gotten to safety."

Why didn't they hurry up? The thought pounded through his head as every moment he expected to see the ground lit up in front of him. Then he stopped. He would run no more. When the beam of light caught him, they should see him walking away quite calmly. Then they would not enjoy it so much; they would feel cheated. The thought filled David with triumph.

When he was little, it had been his most burning desire to get the better of them, especially of the man. And now he would! They would be forced to shoot him at the very moment when he was walking quietly away and taking no notice of them!

David was so taken up with his victory over them that he had gone a dozen yards past the spot where the thicket hid him from the camp before he realized that no one had fired. He stopped short. What could have happened? He turned, found a place where the thicket was thin enough to peer through, and looked across at the low buildings outlined against the dark sky, like an even darker smudge of blackness. He could faintly hear the tread of the guard, but it came no nearer and sounded no different from usual, only farther off. Nothing at all appeared different: there was no sign of anything afoot.

David frowned in the darkness and stood for a moment undecided; it couldn't possibly . . . ? He trotted on, following the edge of the thicket toward the big tree, running faster the nearer he got, and when he reached the tree, he threw himself down on the ground, searching frantically around the trunk with his hands.

There was the bundle. David leaned up against the tree shivering with cold, although it was not cold at all. The bundle was a piece of cloth wrapped around something and tied in a knot. He fumbled with the knot, but his fingers were clumsy and would not respond—and then he suddenly realized that he dared not undo it. There would be something dangerous inside the bundle . . . He tried to gather his thoughts together sufficiently to think what it might be, but his imagination did not get beyond a bomb.

It would make little difference, he thought desperately—a bullet or a bomb—it would soon be over, either way. Frantically, his fingers awkward, he struggled with the cloth.

But there was no bomb in the cloth. It was a square handkerchief tied crosswise over a bottle of water and a compass, just as the man had said.

The thought now occurred to David for the first time that he might simply have walked past the bundle. He was quite alone: nobody was there to make him pick it up . . . He barely managed to turn aside before he was sick.

Afterward he felt carefully all around the square-shaped bundle. A bottle, a compass—there was something else. David's eyes had grown accustomed to the darkness; in the bundle there were also a box of matches, a large loaf of bread, and a pocketknife.

So the man had intended him to escape after all! He would send out a search party in the morning, but not before . . . The night was his, and it was up to him to make the most of it.

All this had taken only a few minutes, but to David it felt like hours. His hand closed tightly around the soap—he had not let go of it for a moment since he first got it. He recalled the hours he had spent that evening lying on his plank bed listening to the muttered conversation of the men and thinking over what the man had said. He remembered, too, that it would be only a matter of time before he was caught again; but that, like everything else, no longer seemed important. All that mattered now were his bundle and the freedom of the night that lay ahead. Slowly he tucked the piece of soap into a corner of the handkerchief, laid the bottle, bread, and knife on top, tied the ends together, took a firm grip on the knot, and looked at the compass in his hand.

Then he ran.

WHEN HE LOOKED BACK AFTERWARD, all he could recall of the five days that followed was running and looking all the time at the compass to make sure he was traveling in the right direction. Every night he ran, and he ran all night long. Once he slipped into a water hole, and the mud caked on him as it dried. Once he was so torn by branches that blood oozed from the scratches on his face, hands, and legs. He would never forget that night. He had come to a close thicket of thornbushes, and the needle indicated that he should go straight through it. He had hesitated a moment and then tried running a few yards along the edge of it, but the compass needle immediately swung around. Perhaps he could have recovered his direction a bit farther on, but he knew so little about compasses that he dared not risk it. And so he plunged into the thicket, elbows up to protect his face. The first branch that struck him hurt painfully, and so did the first gash along his arm, but after that he noticed nothing and just crashed his way through. The nights were usually completely quiet, but that night he could hear a whimpering moan the whole time. Not until afterward did he realize that the sound had come from himself.

He ran all the time, sometimes fairly slowly so that it took him hours to go a short way, sometimes so quickly that he felt his blood pounding. Every morning with the first glimmer of daylight he lay down to sleep. It was not very difficult to find somewhere to sleep in that sparsely inhabited district. David had no idea what the countryside looked like; for him it was only a place where he must run through the night and hide by day.

Two other incidents remained in his memory: they were moments when fear grew to a sharp-pointed terror that seemed to pierce him right through. The first one happened just as it was growing dark one evening. David was awakened by something warm and hairy touching his hand. He lay still, tense with fear . . . It was some minutes before he could bring himself to turn his head, and then he saw—a sheep.

But it spelled danger, nevertheless, for where there are sheep, there must also be people not far away, and that evening David did not stop to recover his breath for some hours afterward.

Yet he was glad enough to come across more sheep later that night. David was used to hard work and satisfied with very little food, and he had been as sparing as he could with the bread and water, but after two whole days the bottle was empty and the bread eaten. He could manage without bread, but it was dreadful to be so thirsty. In the end he could think of hardly anything but water, but where was he to get it?

At that point he almost stumbled over two shepherds who lay asleep on the ground wrapped in their cloaks. His heart, which had been thumping so loudly all through the night, missed a beat, so terror-stricken was he. But he stopped himself just in time; bare feet make no noise and the two men had heard nothing.

David was about to step back, slowly and cautiously, when he caught sight, in the moonlight, of a bucket with a lid and the embers of a burned-down fire. Food! And where there was food, there was probably water, too!

That night David went no farther. He kept watch till daybreak, far enough off to give him a chance to escape should that prove necessary, and yet near enough to be back in a moment as soon as the two shepherds were out of sight in the morning. There was little doubt that this was their regular camping place for the night, for they left their bundles and the bucket behind. Perhaps they would soon be back, but that was a risk David decided he must take. Without food, or at least without water, he would not be able to last many more hours. He was familiar enough, from his experiences in the camp, with what happened when a man was left without food and water.

What had nearly proved a catastrophe ended as a stroke of good fortune. There was some soup left in the bucket, and in one of the bundles he found a chunk of bread. He broke the bread unevenly, leaving a small piece behind. Then he filled his bottle with soup. He replaced the lid and knocked it off again with his elbow. He did not know whether sheep ate bread and soup, but if they did, he wanted to make it look as if they had been there.

After that night he took care to run at a more even pace and to stop more often, but for shorter periods, to recover his breath. He must not again risk being so tired that he saw nothing and stumbled on blindly.

• • • •

In the ensuing chapters, David continues his terrifying journey, traveling across Italy, Switzerland, and France and finally turning instinctively north toward what he eventually learns is his home. Along the way he must deal with the normal human experiences that were denied to him in prison. He lives wonderful but confusing moments when he encounters for the first time a crying baby, flowers, fruit, church bells, children playing, even a toothbrush.

The refugee experience is also described in these books for young adults: *The Endless Steppe: Growing Up in Siberia* by Esther Hautzig, *Goodnight Mr. Tom* by Michelle Magorian, and *So Far from the Bamboo Grove* by Yoko Watkins.

Mature readers and listeners will find a powerful picture of prison-camp life in the excerpt from *Alexander Dolgun's Story: An American in the Gulag* (page 321). There is also a list of related book titles at the end of that selection.

For middle-grade readers, here are two popular books on the Danish resistance and Nazi occupation: Newbery winner *Number the Stars* by Lois Lowry and *Snow Treasure* by Marie McSwigan.

from THE ICEBERG HERMIT
by Arthur Roth

"He'll Never Be Worth a Damn with Books"

Teachers, I have discovered, are best at teaching. They can tell you who the great writers are or were. But when it comes to who the great writers *will* be, they make poor fortune-tellers. For every one who spots a future Rudyard Kipling or Ray Bradbury, there are thousands who miss the chance to say of a Cynthia Rylant, a Gary Paulsen, or an Arthur Roth: "Someday you will be a great writer."

Roth is a perfect example. It wasn't until many years later that his Irish aunt told him what the schoolmaster had said when she debated her nephew's dropping out of school after eighth grade: "Put Arthur to work right away. He'll never be worth a damn with books." Of course, not even the best of fortune-tellers could have foreseen the thirty novels and Columbia University master's degree waiting at the end of all those orphanages and attempts to run away.

As Roth explained in *Something About the Author Autobiography Series*, his mother had been an Irish immigrant who worked as a maid while putting herself through a New York high school and then nurse's training. As a nurse, she met Roth's father when he was treated at her hospital for an injury. They married and had two children before she died suddenly of pneumonia at age thirty. The Great Depression had already taken the husband's job, and now, without his young wife, he didn't know how he could possibly raise two children. Eventually the madness of despair overtook his sanity and he was committed for life to a mental institution. His son and daughter, in turn, were shipped to a series of orphanages.

Six-year-old Arthur ran away from the first institution, as well as the second. The third stop was a reformatory run by the Christian

Brothers in New York City. Not only did he run away from there numerous times, he once escaped and, just for fun, broke into another orphanage where a friend's brother was living.

Institutional living for children in those days was far from enlightened. Roth habitually wet his bed and received daily whippings for it. Since there was little in the way of recreation (outside of fighting and escaping), he took to reading. "I became an avid reader and can thank the Christian Brothers for the lifelong habit."

When he was thirteen, a new crisis arose. The reformatory property was sold and the boys had to be dispersed, so young Roth found himself aboard an ocean liner bound for England and eventually his relatives in Belfast, Northern Ireland. Still plagued by itchy feet and a mischievous mind, Roth proved to be a poor student in everything but reading and quit school after eighth grade—with the enthusiastic support of the schoolmaster.

When he grew tired of his job as an apprentice auto mechanic, Roth "reverted to old habits and ran away." Located through lost-youth radio reports, he was returned, only to run away again. Eventually he was old enough to join the regular Irish army across the border from Northern Ireland, and he spent three years there as a soldier. After his discharge, his aunt persuaded him to return to America, where an uncle promised him a job as a bartender.

Roth and the uncle, however, proved incompatible, and he was ready to go back to Ireland when the uncle convinced him his future was here—if he would just give America a closer look. That look began a few months later when he arrived in San Francisco and began selling magazine subscriptions door-to-door, working his way into the Rocky Mountains. There he quit in order to work in a copper mine; he then joined the U.S. Forest Service as a fire watcher. Months later, a toss of the coin sent him to Arizona, where he successively picked cotton, sorted mail, lived on saltines and sardines, and joined the air national guard. That part-time job turned full-time when his unit was activated for the Korean War—an event that would finally halt his rolling-stone life-style.

While on active duty, Roth wrote a humorous letter to the base newspaper about the flies in the mess hall. When he was summoned to the captain's office, he figured a reprimand was on its way. Instead, he was offered a chance to write a weekly humor column for the paper. (How often have flies in the mess hall launched a writing career?) Now working beside Princeton and Yale graduates at the paper, Roth began to consider his future. Granted, he didn't have a high school diploma—he didn't have a *day* in high school. But I'm as smart as some of these guys, he thought, and if *they* could make it through college, why couldn't I? So upon discharge he enrolled at Arizona State; he invented a fictitious Irish high school he said was destroyed during the war, and claimed that as a result he couldn't produce his secondary school records. By the time university authorities uncovered his ruse, Roth's college grades were high enough to warrant his staying. Despite having to work nights in a factory, he graduated with distinction in just two years—the first in his family with a college degree.

His days at the base newspaper had convinced him there was a future for him in writing. A succession of adult novels eventually followed, as well as a master's degree from Columbia University, and then a chance meeting with an editor at Scholastic led him to try a young-adult novel about surfers, *Wipeout*. Bingo! He had hit the perfect genre for a former vagabond, and nineteen adolescent novels followed, the most successful of which is *The Iceberg Hermit*, with more than a half-million copies in print in six languages.

While reading Edward Rowe Snow's book *Great Sea Rescues and Tales of Survival*, Roth found a legendary tale, called "The Polar Robinson Crusoe," about a seventeen-year-old Scot marooned in the deadly clutches of an iceberg in 1757. One can only wonder what was going through Roth's mind when he read those pages. As an author, perhaps he saw only the outline for another survival novel. But it is also possible he saw himself forty years earlier, as a six-year-old, abandoned by fate to stone-cold orphanages.

When he was in England a few years later, he pursued the story, located the lad's hometown of Aberdeen, and discovered that the local public library contained extensive material on the tale—including the debate over its truthfulness. Indeed, the very first recording of the survival story had been done by "Bunty" Duff, the schoolmaster mentioned obliquely in the first chapter, the same one the reader meets in a later chapter in which the young seaman recalls the master telling his mother when he was twelve years old: "Another two years would be wasted on him. He's a good size now and ready for work. He's picked up a bit of reading but he's hopeless at writing. It's all he can do to write his name. Put him to work—he hasn't the brains for school."

Here, then, is the first chapter from *The Iceberg Hermit*.

• • • •

CHAPTER 1

"**M**ASTHEAD THERE! Look sharp, blast yeer eyes!" the captain roared. High on the lookout point on the main mast, seventeen-year-old Allan Gordon steadied himself and looked down. The captain and the first mate, two black dots far below on deck, were looking up at him. Allan watched the captain turn to the first mate and say something. Then angry voices rose again on the still cold air.

All around him Allan could hear ice scraping against the wooden sides of the *Anne Forbes*. He blew into his mittens, trying to warm his hands. The fog seemed to get inside his clothes, making him shiver. He put his hand into the pocket of his jacket and felt the small Bible his mother had given him when he left home. She had made him promise to read a page every day. So far he had only missed once, the day they had caught their first whale. In all the excitement he had forgotten his promise, but he had read two pages the next day to make up for it.

Allan had long ago decided that Captain Hughes was a liar and a bully. He shouted at everyone on the ship. Only Big Tom, the first mate, would stand up to him. But the other men, and Allan too, kept quiet when the captain began to rant and rave. Captain Hughes was the sort of man who was looking for any excuse to place a sailor in irons for mutiny. That way the captain and the shipowners would have one less share to pay out when the ship reached Aberdeen, its home port in Scotland. This was the year 1757, when sailors led a very hard life on their ships at sea.

Allan peered ahead into the whitish mist. These were iceberg seas, and he had to keep a sharp lookout. Now and again he would catch an angry word from far below as the captain and mate continued their argument.

The captain's bullying voice made Allan think of "Crab" McAfee, an old retired sailor who used to spend hours talking to Allan about life in the British Royal Navy. Crab had gone in the Royal Navy when he was only twelve. Once Crab told Allan about the bullying midshipman on one of the men-of-war who used to stand on the yardarm and stamp on the fingers of young boys as they climbed to his level. One day the midshipman fell, and his fall was seen by a dozen boys aloft in the rigging. They swung their hats and cheered the body all the way down to the deck. The doomed midshipman hit with such force that his leg bones were driven up into his body. For a moment Allan imagined the short squat body of Captain Hughes falling from the main mast, turning over and over in the air before it hit the deck. It was one way to get rid of a hated sea captain, but unfortunately Captain Hughes never climbed up into the rigging.

Through the still and windless air Allan heard the two men arguing below him.

"I don't like this fog rolling in," the captain shouted.

"Aye, we're paying now for your stubbornness," Big Tom answered.

"Oh we'll come out of it," the captain said. "I've sailed through worse than this."

"It's late in the season and we're still far to the north. We should have come about a week ago."

The captain said nothing. For the past week the first mate had been insisting that they begin the long voyage home to Scotland. Their whaling ship, the *Anne Forbes*, had spent the summer between the north of Greenland and Spitsbergen, along the edge of the polar ice-cap, chasing whales. Early in the season the ship had fallen in with a large school of whales that the captain had followed to the north, sailing ever deeper into the Arctic seas. Big Tom, an experienced whaler, kept urging the captain to turn about. He had never seen the sea that clear of ice so far to the north before, and he knew how suddenly treacherous the polar seas could become. Many a whaling ship had been caught in the ice and never heard of again.

But Captain Hughes was a stubborn man, and a greedy man, and he kept sailing north until the holds were almost full. Then one day, just after the whaleboat crew had lashed yet another whale to the ship's side, the captain suddenly grew alarmed. He ordered the fires under the try-pots put out and the huge iron kettles lashed down. It was time to run for home. The last whale was hauled up on deck, and for the next day or two, as the *Anne Forbes* was underway, the men cut the whale up into chunks of blubber that were packed away into barrels. The blubber from that last whale could always be melted down when the ship reached port.

But several days after hoisting sail, the *Anne Forbes* caught a northward current and made very little headway. Even worse, the polar seas were beginning to freeze over. Soon the vessel was surrounded by bobbing ice floes that every day grew more thick and numerous.

To add to their troubles, a heavy fog lay over the water. The mate guessed that the fog meant the nearby presence of an iceberg or large ice field. He had seen those Arctic fogs before. He knew too that whaling ships were sometimes trapped in the ice all winter, and when that happened the crews of such ships usually died from the cold, or from hunger, or from the dread sickness known as scurvy. And those were slow and painful ways to die, with none of the swift mercy of drowning.

Now the ice floes were closing in on all sides of the *Anne Forbes*. Even Allan Gordon, high up on his lookout platform on the main mast, could hear the scrape of ice against the wooden sides of the vessel. Allan peered into the fog. On all sides he could spot cakes of ice bobbing past. As far as he could see the water was dotted with ice floes of all shapes and sizes. Several times he spotted a large ice island, where dozens of floes had frozen to each other. But Allan was not worried. This was his first whaling trip into the northern seas and he did not realize the danger. High up on the mast he thought only of his return home. With fair sailing weather they could make it back to Scotland in a couple of weeks. It had been a good voyage, their holds were full, and Allan would make more money from this one trip than he had in three years of fishing. His mother would be pleased. Allan's father was dead, and they needed the money at home. He would also be able to buy a nice present for his girlfriend, Nancy.

Despite the cold and fog and ice, Allan was happy to be a whaler. He was in excellent health, making good money at an adventurous job, and he had already traveled more and seen more sights than most people did in a lifetime. What seventeen-year-old lad could ask for more?

Allan had signed on the *Anne Forbes* four months before, entitled to a full seaman's share of the profits from the voyage. In those days a seaman could make more money from whaling than any other kind of sea duty. The work was hard and dangerous, but it paid very well. Whale oil was in great demand. Before the discovery of crude oil, people burned whale oil in their lamps. Whalebone was used in ladies' garments, while perfume and cosmetics were made from other parts of the whale. Although Allan was only seventeen, he had already worked three years on fishing ships in his home port of Aberdeen. In those days it was common for twelve-, thirteen-, and fourteen-year-old boys to go to sea.

Allan had worked twelve hours a day, six days a week, for a tailor in Scotland, before he went to sea. So he was well used to hard work. He was a strong, well-built youth who stood five feet nine inches tall, and weighed 160 pounds. He had blue eyes and straw-colored hair and a tiny cleft in the point of his chin.

Around Allan the canvas sails flapped lazily in the odd breeze the ship caught. As usual with fog, there was little wind and the ship was making slow headway. Suddenly Allan came alert. For a moment he thought he spotted land ahead. He knew the *Anne Forbes* was not far from the north Greenland coast and it was possible that an uncharted island lay in the vessel's path. He lowered his head and narrowed his eyes as he tried to peer through the fog. But he could make out nothing. The afternoon light was failing and it was hard to see ahead for any distance.

But there! Now it loomed in front of him, a solid greenish-white wall of ice. He turned and shouted down with all his might.

"Berg! Dead ahead! Berg! Dead ahead!"

Down below Captain Hughes yelled a command to the helmsman. "Hard a port, blast yeer clumsy claws! Hard a port! Port! PORT!" The *Anne Forbes* slowly began a turn to port.

But it was too late. The ship hit the ice almost head on, a heavy smashing blow. Both mate and captain were thrown to the deck. The crash whipped the top of the mast forward like the tip of a fishing rod and Allan flew from his lookout post. He hit a sail below and clutched at it desperately, but his mittened fingers could not get a grip. He half slid, half fell, down the sail until he hit a spar. The blow knocked the breath from him but he had sense enough to hook one arm under a rope and hang on.

After several moments of just hanging there, he managed to pull himself up and onto the yardarm. Then he looked down. Spars were snapping off with such fury that they sounded like gunshots. Sails hung sideways, all fouled in the rigging. Already one mast had crashed on to the deck. Allan picked his way to the very end of the yardarm. There, some twenty feet below, was the flat surface of a ledge on the iceberg. Between the wreckage of the crippled ship and the smooth hard surface of the ice, Allan chose the ice and dropped from the end of the yardarm. This time the force of the fall knocked him out.

On board the *Anne Forbes* all was confusion. The ice wall against which the ship was pinned gave no foothold to anyone. The ship had started to sink, and an attempt was being made to lower one of the whaleboats on the sea side of the vessel. The whaleboat no sooner reached the water when a large ice floe smashed it to pieces against the side of the *Anne Forbes*. Bodies spilled into the sea. Other ice floes began to build against the seaward side of the ship. As the *Anne Forbes* settled lower in the water, large blocks of ice rode in over the side, forcing the vessel to list even more until the seawater came pouring in over her gunwales.

All the sailors were now up on deck, desperately trying to save themselves. Some threw hatchcovers into the sea and jumped in after them, hoping to use them as rafts. Quite a few had climbed the rigging, but with the tilt of the ship to seaward, they had no hope of reaching the top of the ice wall and were now simply hanging on to ropes and spars.

Captain Hughes had gone down to his cabin to snatch up the ship's log and other valuable papers. Big Tom, bracing himself against the slope of the deck, looked around at all the others. There was a slight smile on his face. The desperate efforts, the panic, the scurrying to and fro, the captain trying to save the log, all of this seemed senseless to the mate. For he knew too much, knew they were all doomed, knew that the men who had jumped overboard would only last minutes in the freezing water, knew it was only a matter of time before the Arctic claimed another fifty victims. He looked up in the rigging, wondering what had happened to Allan Gordon. He felt a wave of pity for the seventeen-year-old-youth out on his first voyage. Allan was nowhere to be seen and the mate decided that he must have been thrown into the water and was no doubt drowned by now.

"Get it over with," Big Tom muttered to himself, then ran down the sloping deck and dived cleanly over the rail to his death in the icy waters.

Above on the ice field Allan Gordon groaned, then forced himself to sit up. He was just in time to see the top of the ship's mast disappear from sight. The *Anne Forbes* had gone down in minutes, with all hands, and Allan was alone on a field of ice, somewhere off the coast of Greenland, with no food, no water and no hope of rescue.

Allan looked around. Nearby there were some dim white shapes that he knew to be ice boulders but they were the only things to be seen. Everywhere he looked there was fog and ice and piercing cold. He felt a desperate loneliness, as though he were the only person in the whole world. Without food, without water, with no way of keeping warm, he was doomed. Death would come in a matter of days, perhaps even hours.

It was so unfair, he thought. In one moment he was a happy young man on his way home to his family and girlfriend with plenty of money honestly earned, and in the next minute he was sitting all alone on a piece of ice in the middle of the Arctic seas, waiting for death to come.

He got to his feet, staggered over to one of the ice boulders and sank down behind it, trying to find some shelter from the cold. He wrapped his arms around his sides, hugging himself, and began to sway back and forth. "I'm going to die," he said aloud. "I'm going to die right here, all alone, and no one will ever know about it."

He thought then of his mother and of his three younger sisters: Jean, Flora, and Gladys. They would wait for word of the *Anne Forbes* and as the months and then the years passed, they would learn to accept the fact that Allan was dead. And wee "Bunty" Duff would finally be right about Allan. However, if the schoolmaster were right, then the old fortuneteller had to be wrong.

Thinking of his mother, Allan reached a hand into his pocket and took out the Bible. There was just enough light to read his daily page.

When he was finished reading, he carefully marked his place in the Bible with a thin, flat piece of whalebone that he used as a bookmark, then put the book away in his pocket and thought that in his present situation saying a prayer was about the only possible way he could help himself.

But he had little faith that prayer would save him either. Squinching down into his clothes as much as possible to keep warm, he sat there and waited for the end.

• • • •

THE END, HOWEVER, is a long way from coming. When Allan awakens he discovers he is surrounded by frozen seawater, which is filled with salt and unfit for drinking. He also has nothing to eat until he notices the carcass of a dead whale that had broken loose from the *Anne Forbes*. The whale, however, is actually the upturned bottom of the ship itself. In the ensuing days, the young seaman hacks his way through the ice and the ship's oaken ribs until he is able to crawl inside. Safe at last, he is then attacked by foraging polar bears. He is one thousand miles from help, and locked into an ice field; his future looks as bleak as a grave.

When Allan eventually returned to Scotland and recounted his tale, few believed it and most called it a hoax. By the time Roth read the material in the Aberdeen library two centuries later, scientific discoveries had lent new evidence in support of its claims. Roth made it his task to flesh out the original tale, leaving it up the reader to decide on its probability.

A related book, *Buried in Ice: The Mystery of the Lost Arctic Expedition* by Owen Beattie and John Geiger, is a sixty-four-page book on how a team of scientists discovered the remains of the mysterious 1845 Franklin Expedition in the Arctic that precipitated the greatest rescue mission in history—an effort that failed. In 1984, anthropologist Owen Beattie succeeded in finding out what *really* happened to the phantom ships and their crews.

If you enjoy *The Iceberg Hermit*, you will also enjoy these survival stories: three from Jean C. George—*Julie of the Wolves, My Side of the Mountain*, and its sequel, *On the Far Side of the Mountain*; Farley Mowat's *Lost in the Barrens*; Gary Paulsen's novels *Hatchet, The River*, and *The Voyage of the Frog*; Theodore Taylor's *The Cay*; and Elizabeth George Speare's *The Sign of the Beaver*.

from **T**HE TRUE CONFESSIONS
OF CHARLOTTE DOYLE

by Avi

The Award-Winning Novelist with a Writing Disability

Avi's books are like him—*inimitable.* You just can't put them or him into any other category. Consider these traits, quirks, and gifts:

- He has dysgraphia, a writing disability that causes him to transpose letters and words, much the way dyslexia confuses readers
- The only name he uses is Avi, a childhood nickname (there are lots of one-name singers, but how many authors?)
- He revises everything he writes at least twenty times
- To date he has written twenty-six books, including one novel (*Nothing but the Truth*) that is made up mostly of memos, letters, and newspaper stories, but no descriptions; another novel ("*Who Was That Masked Man, Anyway?*") that is all dialogue and contains not even one "he said" or "she said"; and a 190-page comic book, *City of Light/City of Dark*
- He has won two Newbery Honor Medals (for *The True Confessions of Charlotte Doyle* and *Nothing but the Truth*), yet once flunked out of high school and came within a whisker of flunking English at the next school he attended

Though he was unaware he had a specific writing disability until he was well into his forties, he and his family knew there was a problem. "It's a perceptual dysfunction," he explains. "I often transpose letters or words while I'm writing—putting down *true* instead of *blue*. The teacher reading my paper would immediately write it off as carelessness or sloppiness. What made it even more difficult was that it is an erratic problem. Sometimes I'd spell a word correctly, other times incorrectly. My aunt once said I was the only person she knew who could spell a five-letter word five different ways."

Complicating the matter was the fact that Avi came from a family of writers that extended as far back as his two great-grandfathers. Finally, a high school English teacher told his family that he would pass Avi *only* if he spent the entire summer being tutored in the basics of writing and spelling. In his one-to-one sessions with a family friend that summer, both Avi and the teacher came to the conclusion there was a writer working his way to the surface. Like columnist Bob Greene (page 411), Avi kept a secret daily journal during his senior year, nurturing a writer's dreams. His parents, one a psychiatrist and the other a psychiatric social worker, could only see the disability and, trying to protect him from failure, worked at dissuading him from becoming a writer. And the harder they pushed in one direction, the more stubbornly he pushed in the opposite. He would become a writer to spite them!

(His writing ambitions can be attributed less to genetics than to growing up in a home where books abounded. Like so many authors, Avi and his twin sister were read to daily, and he devoured comic books, as well as *The Wind in the Willows*, the Hardy Boys mysteries, and Robert Louis Stevenson.)

While dysgraphia cannot be cured, it can be overcome by doing what Avi does—he double-checks *everything* (phone numbers, driving instructions, grocery lists, and manuscripts). "I've also acknowledged to myself," he explains, "that I have a problem. I've learned to live with it and I'm not embarrassed."

In college he decided he would write plays and adult novels, and after graduating he worked unsuccessfully at those ambitions. The theater experience, however, would inspire and shape his future writings, just as Dickens's lifelong obsession with theater aided him in pacing his novels. (Dickens would even act out the various parts as he wrote, reciting lines aloud, racing to the mirror to check the curl of a lip or a scowl.)

Avi's writing didn't come into focus until he began working as a librarian and inventing nightly stories for his sons—and that's when he began to think of writing children's books. Best-selling children's author Roald Dahl had a similar experience. (See page 143.)

Avi is best known for his historical novels, which are rich in both action and accuracy. Typical is *The Fighting Ground*, a grim, minute-by-minute description of a twenty-four-hour period in the life of a thirteen-year-old boy during the Revolutionary War. It is also an example of how his playwriting background helps him to balance dramatic action and dialogue. Just as there are no long descriptive passages in plays, there are few in Avi's novels either. He wastes neither time nor words in launching his stories. *Wolf Rider* is a young-adult novel subtitled *A Tale of Terror*, and it is that and more: daring, controversial, riveting—beginning with the first page, on which a fifteen-year-old boy answers the phone and a stranger says, "I just killed someone."

As an author, Avi shies away from no subject. In writing of today or yesterday, he allows his characters to confront the issues that have always encumbered the human journey—prejudice, intolerance, and violence. He avoids the trite, happy-ever-after ending, and instead often goes for a troubling or thought-provoking finale that leaves the reader thinking deeply about the book afterward. The ending for *The True Confessions of Charlotte Doyle* was so original, so unexpected, that the producer who wanted to buy the rights for a TV-movie version insisted the ending be changed. Avi told her, "Thanks, but no thanks," and turned down the movie.

The selection here is the second chapter from that novel, set in 1832. The protagonist is Charlotte Doyle, a lovely thirteen-year-old American girl who has spent the last seven years with her family in England, where her father was employed. When her father is transferred back to America, he decrees that it would be best if the family departed for home immediately, but that Charlotte should finish her term at the Barrington School for Better Girls and then make the journey herself. The ship will be a merchant vessel owned by her father's employer, and there will be two families aboard who are friends of her parents. What can possibly go wrong? Charlotte's father also gives her a journal in which he expects her to keep a careful and accurately spelled record of her journey.

Chapter 1 opens with Charlotte being escorted along the docks by Mr. Grummage, a business associate of her father's. Her trunk has been dropped by two different porters, who, when they heard that its destination was Captain Jaggery's ship, the *Seahawk*, turned and fled. Mr. Grummage further learns that the two families have been delayed and, since the captain will not delay departure, Charlotte will have to travel alone. Startled, she balks at the idea of spending two months alone with a crew of men, exclaiming, "I am a girl. It would be wrong!"

Mr. Grummage draws himself up and replies, "Miss Doyle, in *my* world, judgments as to rights and wrongs are left to my Creator, *not* to children. Now, be so good as to board the *Seahawk*. At once!"

• • • •

CHAPTER 2

WITH MR. GRUMMAGE LEADING THE WAY I stepped finally, hesitantly, upon the deck of the *Seahawk*. A man was waiting for us.

He was a small man—most seafaring men are small—barely taller than I and dressed in a frayed green jacket over a white shirt that was none too clean. His complexion was weathered dark, his chin illshaven. His mouth was unsmiling. His fingers fidgeted and his feet shuffled. His darting, unfocused eyes, set deep in a narrow ferretlike face, gave the impression of one who is constantly on watch for threats that might appear from any quarter at any moment.

"Miss Doyle," Mr. Grummage intoned by way of introduction, "both Captain Jaggery and the first mate are ashore. May I present the second mate, Mr. Keetch."

"Miss Doyle," this Mr. Keetch said to me, speaking in an unnecessarily loud voice, "since Captain Jaggery isn't aboard I've no choice but to stand in his place. But it's my strong opinion, miss, that you should take another ship for your passage to America."

"And I," Mr. Grummage cut in before I could respond, "can allow of no such thing!"

This was hardly the welcome I had expected.

"But Mr. Grummage," I said, "I'm sure my father would not want me to be traveling without—"

Mr. Grummage silenced my objections with an upraised hand. "Miss Doyle," he said, "my orders were clear and allow for no other construction. I met you. I brought you here. I had you placed under the protection of this man, who, in the momentary absence of Captain Jaggery and the first mate, fulfilled his obligation by signing a receipt for you."

To prove his point Mr. Grummage waved a piece of paper at me. I might have been a bale of cotton.

"Therefore, Miss Doyle," he rushed on, "nothing remains save to wish you a most pleasant voyage to America."

Putting action to words he tipped his hat, and before I could utter a syllable he strode down the gangplank toward the shore.

"But Mr. Grummage!" I called desperately.

Whether Mr. Grummage heard me, or chose not to hear me, he continued to stride along the dock without so much as a backward glance. I was never to see him again.

A slight shuffling sound made me turn about. Beneath a lantern on the forecastle deck I saw a few wretched sailors hunched in apelike postures pounding oakum between the decking planks. Without doubt they had heard everything. Now they threw hostile glances over their shoulders in my direction.

I felt a touch at my elbow. Starting, I turned again and saw Mr. Keetch. He seemed more nervous than ever.

"Begging your pardon, Miss Doyle," he said in his awkward way, "there's nothing to be done now, is there? I'd best show you your cabin."

At that point I remembered my trunk of clothing, as if that collection of outward fashion—still ashore—had more claim to me than the ship. And since *it* was there, so should I be. "My trunk . . ." I murmured, making a half turn toward the dock.

"Not to worry, miss. We'll fetch it for you," Mr. Keetch said, cutting off my last excuse for retreat. Indeed, he held out a lantern, indicating an entryway in the wall of the quarterdeck that appeared to lead below.

What could I do? All my life I had been trained to obey, educated to accept. I could hardly change in a moment. "Please lead me," I mumbled, as near to fainting as one could be without actually succumbing.

"Very good, miss," he said, leading me across the deck and down a short flight of steps.

I found myself in a narrow, dark passageway with a low ceiling. The steerage, as this area is called, was hardly more than six feet wide and perhaps thirty feet in length. In the dimness I could make out a door on each side, one door at the far end. Like a massive tree rising right out of the floor and up through the ceiling was the mainmast. There was also a small table attached to the center of the flooring. No chairs.

The whole area was frightfully confining, offering no sense of comfort that I could see. And a stench of rot permeated the air.

"This way," I heard Mr. Keetch say again. He had opened a door on my left. "Your cabin, miss. The one contracted for." A gesture invited me to enter.

I gasped. The cabin was but six feet in length. Four feet wide. Four and a half feet high. I, none too tall, could only stoop to see in.

"Regular passengers pay a whole six pounds for this, miss," Mr. Keetch advised me, his voice much softer.

I forced myself to take a step into the cabin. Against the opposite wall I could make out a narrow shelf, partly framed by boarding. When I noticed something that looked like a pillow and a blanket, I realized it was meant to be a bed. Then, when Mr. Keetch held up the light, I saw something *crawl* over it.

"What's that?" I cried.

"Roach, miss. Every ship has 'em."

As for the rest of the furnishings, there were none save a small built-in chest in the bulkhead wall, the door of which dropped down and served as a desktop. There was nothing else. No porthole. No chair. Not so much as a single piece of polite ornamentation. It was ugly, unnatural, and, as I stooped there, impossible.

In a panic I turned toward Mr. Keetch, wanting to utter some new protest. Alas, he had gone—and had shut the door behind him as though to close the spring on a trap.

How long I remained hunched in that tiny, dark hole, I am not sure. What aroused me was a knock on the door. Startled, I gasped, "Come in."

The door opened. Standing there was a shockingly decrepit old sailor, a tattered tar-covered hat all but crushed in his gnarled and trembling hands. His clothing was poor, his manner cringing.

"Yes?" I managed to say.

"Miss, your trunk is here."

I looked beyond the door to the trunk's bulky outline. I saw at once how absurd it would be to even attempt bringing it into my space.

The sailor understood. "She's too big, isn't she?" he said.

"I think so," I stammered.

"Best put it in top cargo," he offered. "Right below. You can always fetch things there, miss."

"Yes, top cargo," I echoed without knowing what I was saying.

"Very good, miss," the man said, and then pulled his forelock as a signal of obedience and compliance to a suggestion that he himself had made. But instead of going he just stood there.

"Yes?" I asked miserably.

"Begging your pardon, miss," the man murmured, his look more hangdog than ever. "Barlow's the name and though it's not my business or place to tell you, miss, some of the others here, Jack Tars like myself, have deputized me to say that you shouldn't be on this ship. Not alone as you are. Not this ship. Not this voyage, miss."

"What do you mean?" I said, frightened anew. "Why would they say that?"

"You're being here will lead to no good, miss. No good at all. You'd be better off far from the *Seahawk*."

Though all my being agreed with him, my training—that it was wrong for a man of his low station to presume to advise me of *anything*—rose to the surface. I drew myself up. "Mr. Barlow," I said stiffly, "it's my father who has arranged it all."

"Very good, miss," he said, pulling at his forelock again. "I've but done my duty, which is what I'm deputized to do." And before I could speak further he scurried off.

I wanted to run after him, to cry, "Yes, for God's sake, get me off!" But, again, there was nothing in me that allowed for such behavior.

Indeed, I was left with a despairing resolve never to leave the cabin until we reached America. Steadfastly I shut my door. But by doing so I made the space completely dark, and I quickly moved to keep it ajar.

I was exhausted and desired greatly to sit down. But there was no place to sit! My next thought was to *lie* down. Trying to put notions of vermin out of mind, I made a move toward my bed but discovered that it was too high for me to reach easily in my skirts. Then suddenly I realized I must relieve myself! But where was I to go? I had not the slightest idea!

If you will be kind enough to recollect that during my life I had never once—not for a moment—been without the support, the guidance, the *protection* of my elders, you will accept my words as being without exaggeration when I tell you that at that moment I was certain I had been placed in a coffin. *My* coffin. It's hardly to be wondered, then, that I burst into tears of vexation, crying with fear, rage, and humiliation.

I was still stooped over, crying, when yet another knock came on my cabin door. Attempting to stifle my tears I turned about to see an old black man who, in the light of the little lantern he was holding, looked like the very imp of death in search of souls.

His clothing, what I could see of it, was even more decrepit than the previous sailor's, which is to say, mostly rags and tatters. His arms and legs were as thin as marlinspikes. His face, as wrinkled as a crumpled napkin, was flecked with the stubble of white beard. His tightly curled hair was thin. His lips were slack. Half his teeth were missing. When he smiled—for that is what I assumed he was attempting—he offered only a scattering of stumps. But his eyes seemed to glow with curiosity and were all the more menacing because of it.

"Yes?" I managed to say.

"At your service, Miss Doyle." The man spoke with a surprisingly soft, sweet voice. "And wondering if you might not like a bit of tea. I have my own special store, and I'm prepared to offer some."

It was the last thing I expected to hear. "That's very kind of you," I stammered in surprise. "Could you bring it here?"

The old man shook his head gently. "If Miss Doyle desires tea —captain's orders—she must come to the galley."

"Galley?"

"Kitchen to you, miss."

"Who are you?" I demanded faintly.

"Zachariah," he returned. "Cook, surgeon, carpenter, and preacher to man and ship. And," he added, "all those things to you too, miss, in that complete order if comes the doleful need. Now then, shall you have tea?"

In fact, the thought of tea *was* extraordinarily comforting, a reminder that the world I knew had not entirely vanished. I couldn't resist. "Very well," I said, "Would you lead me to the . . . galley?"

"Most assuredly," was the old man's reply. Stepping away from the door, he held his lantern high. I made my way out.

We proceeded to walk along the passageway to the right, then up the short flight of steps to the waist of the ship—that low deck area between fore- and quarterdeck. Here and there lanterns glowed; masts, spars, and rigging vaguely sketched the dim outlines of the net in which I felt caught. I shuddered.

The man called Zachariah led me down another flight of steps into what appeared to be a fairly large area. In the dimness I could make out piles of sails, as well as extra rigging—all chaotic and unspeakably filthy. Then, off to one side, I saw a small room. The old man went to it, started to enter, but paused and pointed to a small adjacent door that I had not noticed.

"The head, miss."

"The what?"

"Privy."

My cheeks burned. Even so, *never* have I felt—secretly—so grateful. Without a word I rushed to use it. In moments I returned. Zachariah was waiting patiently. Without further ado he went into the galley. I followed with trepidation, stopping at the threshold to look about.

From the light of his flickering lantern I could see that it was a small kitchen complete with cabinets, wood stove, even a table and a little stool. The space, though small, had considerable neatness, with utensils set in special niches and corners. Knives placed just so. An equal number of spoons and forks. Tumblers, pots, cups, pans. All that was needed.

The old man went right to the stove where a teapot was already on, hot enough to be issuing steam.

He pulled a cup from a niche, filled it with fragrant tea, and offered it. At the same time he gestured me to the stool.

Nothing, however, could have compelled me to enter further. Though stiff and weary I preferred to stand where I was. Even so, I tasted the tea and was much comforted.

As I drank Zachariah looked at me. "It may well be," he said softly, "that Miss Doyle will have use for a friend."

Finding the suggestion—from him—unpleasant, I chose to ignore it.

"I can assure you," he said with a slight smile, "Zachariah can be a fine friend."

"And I can assure you," I returned, "that the captain will have made arrangements for my social needs."

"Ah, but you and I have much in common."

"I don't think so."

"But we do. Miss Doyle is so young! I am so old! Surely there is something similar in that. And you, the sole girl, and I, the one black, are special on this ship. In short, we begin with two things in common, enough to begin a friendship."

I looked elsewhere. "I don't need a friend," I said.

"One always needs a final friend."

"*Final* friend?"

"Someone to sew the hammock," he returned.

"I do not understand you."

"When a sailor dies on voyage, miss, he goes to his resting place in the sea with his hammock sewn about him by a friend."

I swallowed my tea hastily, handed the cup back, and made a move to go.

"Miss Doyle, please," he said softly, taking the cup but holding me with his eyes, "I have something else to offer."

"No more tea, thank you."

"No, miss. It is this." He held out a knife.

With a scream I jumped back.

"No, no! Miss Doyle. Don't misunderstand! I only wish to give you the knife as protection—in case you need it." He placed a wooden sheath on the blade and held it out.

The knife was, as I came to understand, what's called a dirk, a small daggerlike blade hardly more than six inches in length from its white scrimshaw handle, where a star design was cut, to its needle-sharp point. Horrified, I was capable only of shaking my head.

"Miss Doyle doesn't know what might happen," he urged, as though suggesting it might rain on a picnic and he was offering head covering.

"I know nothing about knives," I whispered.

"A ship sails with any wind she finds," he whispered. "Take it, miss. Place it where it may be reached."

So saying, he took my hand and closed my fingers over the dirk. Cringing, I kept it.

"Yes," he said with a smile, patting my fingers. "Now Miss Doyle may return to her cabin. Do you know the way?"

"I'm not certain . . ."

"I will guide you."

He left me at my door. Once inside I hurriedly stowed the dirk under the thin mattress (resolving never to look at it again) and somehow struggled into my bed. There, fully dressed, I sought rest, fitfully dozing only to be awakened by a banging sound: my cabin door swinging back and forth—rusty hinges rasping—with the gentle sway of the ship.

Then I heard, "The only one I could get to come, sir, is the Doyle girl. And with *them* looking on, I had to put on a bit of a show about wanting to keep her off."

"Quite all right, Mr. Keetch. If there has to be only one, she's the trump. With her as witness, they'll not dare to move. I'm well satisfied."

"Thank you, sir."

The voices trailed away.

For a while I tried to grasp what I'd heard, but I gave it up as incomprehensible. Then, for what seemed forever, I lay listening as the *Seahawk*, tossed by the ceaseless swell, heaved and groaned like a sleeper beset by evil dreams.

At last I slept—only to have the ship's dreams become my own.

• • • •

IN THE WEEKS and chapters that follow, Charlotte will see more than she would like of her new weapon, as she is caught between a murderous captain and a mutinous crew, with death and intrigue lurking in every shadow.

Other books by Avi include *Bright Shadow; Captain Grey; The Fighting Ground; The Man Who Was Poe; Nothing but the Truth; Romeo and Juliet—Together (and Alive!) at Last; S.O.R. Losers; Something Upstairs: A Tale of Ghosts; "Who Was That Masked Man, Anyway?"*; and *Wolf Rider.*

Fans of *Charlotte Doyle* will also enjoy *The December Rose* by Leon Garfield (page 345) and *The Iceberg Hermit* by Arthur Roth (page 371). Mature readers will also enjoy *Mutiny on the Bounty* by Nordhoff and Hall. See also Robert Newman's novels—*The Case of the Baker Street Irregular, The Case of the Murdered Players, The Case of the Vanishing Corpse*, and *The Case of the Watching Boy.*

Paper **C**lips

• • • • • • • • •

Seven stories from the best print
bargain in the world—
the daily newspaper.

THE LAND OF WITS, SAGES, ORACLES, MUCKRAKERS, AND INSIDERS

The daily newspaper has always been and still is the greatest print bargain in the world. Packed into its two- or three-foot pages of cheap paper is something for everyone—news, sports, opinions, comics, weather, health tips, entertainment, obituaries, and the best buys in the marketplace. As if that were not enough, the text is updated every twenty-four hours!

At a penny a page, it's a whole lot cheaper than a magazine or paperback book (two cents a page) or a hardcover (five cents a page). As for giving the reader vast amounts of information, quickly and accurately, nothing comes close—not magazines, not fax machines, and not television. At the same time it gives the reader the opportunity to "eavesdrop" on a conversation that playwright Arthur Miller once described this way: "A good newspaper, I suppose, is a nation talking to itself."

Walter Cronkite liked to tell how the average evening's network newscast delivers approximately thirty-six hundred words during its twenty-two minutes. That sounds like a lot of words, he said, until you spread them out on paper. Then they would fill only the bottom half of the front page of *The New York Times*.

Despite these advantages, recent years have seen a dramatic decline in newspaper readership among American citizens—especially younger ones. Increasingly young people rely on that half-page from the anchorperson, experiencing each item as a spoken piece that lasts but a minute and then only the ones for which there is video footage.

Admittedly, I have a soft spot for newspapers. I grew up with them. My parents couldn't afford a car until I was in fourth grade and we didn't have our own home until I was in seventh grade—but we always subscribed to a newspaper. Each evening at 7:00 P.M., my father would turn off the radio and pull me onto his lap and pick up the *Newark Evening News*. He'd start by reading me a daily children's feature called "Uncle Wiggily," which ran at the top of the comics page, and then proceeded down the page to the comics. The newspaper became one of the few things in the adult world I could taste as a child.

As I grew older, I graduated from the comics page to sports, and then to news, and finally to the editorial page—which was pretty much the pattern I followed ten years later when I graduated from college and went to work for a daily newspaper in New England. Today I read three newspapers a day—not every story or even every page, just what interests me.

True newspaper readers have their favorite part or section of the paper, one they will either read first or keep to savor for last. Any newspaper editor will attest to this. Let him *dare* to drop a certain feature—comic or column—and his phone will ring for days with irate callers wanting to know "what you've done with the only reason I ever bought your paper in the first place!!"

My personal favorite—and I am far from alone in this—is that collection of opinionated wits, sages, pundits, oracles, scribes, seers, insiders, observers, muckrakers, and analysts who call themselves columnists. Their offerings range from advice for the lovelorn to suggestions on how to remove ballpoint stains, from the "inside scoop" on who made what deal to steal the election to why the manager or mayor has grass growing between his ears.

Columnists are revered or reviled—but seldom ignored (once they're ignored, they soon cease to be columnists). Most begin as reporters covering fires, board meetings, and press conferences, and checking out the dozens of rumors that float through a community each day. But of those thousands of reporters, only a few have that special talent to be local columnists—banging out nine hundred words every few days to stoke the interest of the hometown folks. And of all the local columnists, only the tiniest number of those are good enough to become syndicated columnists whose words run in newspapers throughout the nation. Any good writer can write a good story if you give him enough space, say, two or three thousand words. Those are murals. The columnist is a miniaturist; he must paint his story in just nine hundred words.

Television has tried its best to copy the idea of the columnist from the print media and has been largely unsuccessful. TV calls them commentators, but "borers" would be closer to the mark in the opinion of most viewers. The only one who has been even moderately successful in gaining any kind of following is Andy Rooney on "60 Minutes." Radio, on the other hand, had a large field of successful commentators fifty years ago, before music became its principal format. Today, only Paul Harvey remains from the dozens and dozens who once populated the national radio waves. (Talk-radio hosts don't count as commentators—they're more like referees or moderators.)

Most columnists are specialists, like the advice twins Ann Landers and Abigail Van Buren (they really *are* twin sisters). But the ones who face the biggest challenge of all are the general-interest columnists, who can take any subject—politics, sports, dog hairs, MTV, or the governor's ingrown toenail—and make it interesting or infuriating.

Following here is the work of four columnists and two non-professional writers. They are distinctly different in their styles and approaches, yet each creates pieces of contemporary art that people can buy just for pieces of change.

WRONG MOM? TOUGH!

by Mike Royko

The Boy Bartender Who Turned Watchdog

One of America's most widely read columnists began his public life as a streetwise kid tending bar for his saloon-keeping parents when he was thirteen. He quit school at fifteen, was caught and sent to pupil adjustment school, quit again at sixteen, went to a private school, graduated, and then dropped out of junior college at nineteen to join the air force. That's a pretty rough beginning for someone who would go on to win journalism's grandest prize, the Pulitzer, in 1972. His name is Mike Royko.

His column runs five days a week, forty-seven weeks a year, and each one takes anywhere from eight to ten hours to write. He's read in more than six hundred papers in four countries by nearly ten million people. If he didn't receive a sterling education in school, he certainly got one in those Chicago bars he tended for his folks. He learned how the city ran, what people did to get elected—and *stay* elected—and who paid off whom. And along the way he eavesdropped on enough boozy conversations to learn every sob story life can offer.

He also observed enough con jobs to be able to work one himself whenever he needed it—like the time the air force assigned him to be a military policeman. Rather than become an MP, Royko convinced the personnel officer that he'd once worked for the *Chicago Daily News*. He not only got the transfer to the air force paper, but he was immediately made editor. That, of course, required a marathon three-day session at the public library, where he read everything available on newspapers.

He soon made himself a "columnist" for the paper and began what would become a career-long pursuit—ruffling the feathers of those on high. (He kiddingly questioned why military personnel had to observe a strict dress code when they were on base and yet their wives were allowed to shop at the base exchange in curlers. The ensuing reaction impressed on the young scribe how much power he held under his fingers.)

It was a power he would put to better use in a few years when he finished his service time and, after a succession of reporting jobs with local weeklies, he earned a real job—and then a column in 1963—with the *Chicago Daily News*. Within a year his feather-ruffling was the talk of the town.

Those teen years tending bar had taught him the language of the city. Even in a noisy barroom, what holds people's attention is stories—funny stories, sad stories, angry stories, told in simple, declarative sentences. In short order he became the spokesman for those who had no one—the victims, the disenfranchised. In doing so, he also became the enemy of those who target the helpless—deadbeat politicians, pinky-ring crooks, and bullies. No one was too lofty for Royko—from the president of the United States to the alderman. If you did something stupid that hurt people, beware! Royko was watching and waiting.

Some people resent this concept of journalist as watchdog—and thus resent Royko. What they don't understand is that Royko follows an American tradition that is nearly four hundred years old. The first newspaper in the English language was printed in Holland in 1620 by a collection of future Americans. The English Pilgrims (the same ones who would sail the *Mayflower* to Plymouth) were forbidden by English censors to criticize the church or government of King James in their newspaper, so they slipped next door to Holland and printed their newspaper from there. A century later, there were nearly fifty colonial newspapers keeping a watchful eye on the British crown from this side of Atlantic and fanning the flames that led to the American Revolution. So you see, Mike Royko is an old story for Americans.

There have been other columnists who have played watchdog roles, but few have ever done it with Royko's style. His sharpest weapon is the same one used by another journalist of some repute—Mark Twain. Both carried a rapier wit. With it, Royko pins the culprit to the wall so all ten million readers can see the bullying meanness or foolishness spill over the page.

He seldom thinks about what he is going to write about until he arrives in the office. Until he hands in the column ten minutes before deadline, his hours are spent phoning, writing, checking and double-checking, and writing some more.

Here is a column that contains the best of all elements for a Royko column: a defenseless mother, an abandoned baby, and a nonthinking bureaucracy.

• • • •

Mrs. Fran Lasota is in real trouble. She has been formally accused of abandoning her own baby. And she has received a summons, ordering her to appear in court and to bring the neglected baby with her.

Fran's friends and neighbors in the town of Marengo will probably by shocked and dismayed to read that Fran would abandon her baby in Chicago. Especially since Fran is in her forties and hasn't had a baby for many years.

It came as a shock to Fran, too, when her phone rang a few weeks ago and a bureaucrat from the Illinois Department of Children and Family Services asked her why she had abandoned her baby.

"My what?" asked Fran.

"Your baby," the bureaucrat said.

"What are you talking about?"

The man told her that a week-old boy had been brought to a Chicago hospital to be treated for a rash.

The hospital cured the rash, but the mother never came back for the baby.

"Why do you think it is my baby?" Fran asked.

"Is your name Frances Lasota?"

"Yes."

"Well, that's the name of the mother," the bureaucrat said.

Fran told the man that he had the wrong Fran Lasota. And she asked him how she had been chosen as the errant mother.

From what he said, she gathered that he had just looked in phone books for people named Lasota until he found one named Fran.

"Well, you'll have to keep looking," she said, "because it's not my kid."

She thought that would be the end of it. But recently she received a registered letter.

It was the summons, telling her that she had to appear in court on a neglect charge. And it said she should bring her baby with her.

Naturally she was flustered. She called the Cook County state's attorney's office, which prosecutes neglectful parents, and explained her problem.

"He told me I had better show up in court," she said.

She called a lawyer in Marengo and asked him what to do.

"He told me I should get a Chicago lawyer to defend me."

She called the Marengo Police Department to see if it had any advice.

"They told me that I should probably go to court. If I didn't, I might be held in contempt of court for not showing up with the baby I don't have."

She called the Department of Children and Family Services and tried to explain her problem.

"They didn't seem to understand what I was talking about."

Now she doesn't know what to do. It's a long trip from Marengo to Chicago, and Fran doesn't see why she should have to come all that way for something she hasn't anything to do with. Nor does she want to spend money on a lawyer.

But she is afraid if she doesn't show up, she will be held in contempt and will be in even worse trouble.

So she sought my advice, which was a wise thing for her to do, since I've had a lot of experience in dealing with bureaucrats.

My advice to Fran is that she had better go to court.

And she had better bring a baby with her.

Believe me, if you show up without a baby, they'll just get suspicious. They'll think you dropped the kid on his head and don't want to admit it, and you'll be in deeper trouble.

So borrow one. Somebody must have a baby you can use for a day. Go in there, show them the kid is healthy and happy, and maybe they'll let you off with just a stern warning.

On the other hand, they might decide you are unfit and take the baby away from you. Then you'd have to go back to your friend and say: "Sorry, but your kid's in a foster home. But thanks for trying to help."

That wouldn't be good because your friend would probably be miffed. So I'll have to come up with another plan.

OK, here's what you do. Go rent a monkey. There are places you can get them.

Put the monkey in baby clothes and take it to court and say to the judge:

"OK, Your Honor. I admit it. I abandoned my baby. But look

at this kid. He looks like a monkey. It's from his father's side. If you had a kid this ugly, Your Honor, wouldn't you abandon him? I mean, he's got hair on his feet."

Chances are, the judge will be sympathetic and let you go, especially if the monkey bites him.

The worst that can happen is that they will declare you an unfit mother and take the monkey away from you and put it in a foster home.

You'll be out one monkey and the Department of Children and Family Services will be stuck with a foster baby that bites, climbs the drapes, and has hair on its feet.

And who knows—someday you might be proud. The kid could grow up to be an alderman.

• • • •

IF YOU WANT MORE ROYKO (and who, except the fat cats, doesn't?) you'll find him daily in six hundred newspapers. Almost one thousand of his past columns are collected in the following books: *Up Against It; I May Be Wrong, but I Doubt It; Slats Grobnik and Some Other Friends; Sez Who? Sez Me; Like I Was Sayin'* . . . ; and *Dr. Kookie, You're Right!*

His 1971 best-seller, *Boss: Richard J. Daley of Chicago*, is regarded by many as the finest study of the modern political machine and is still used in many college political science departments. And finally, if you check out *Continental Divide* from your local video store, the character played by John Belushi is based upon a "character" named Mike Royko (but the story line is fictitious).

NOTHING TO WORRY ABOUT
and THE TURTLE
by Jim Bishop

The Bishop Who Bided His Time

The ten-year-old boy sat at the dining room table each night and watched his father fill out his police reports. The father was a 250-pound lieutenant in Jersey City, New Jersey, and he was the man "you had to see" if you wanted anything done by the police. Night after night, the policeman's son watched his father fill in the blanks, detailing exactly when he saw the suspect, when and where he was apprehended, and when he was booked—minute by minute, hour by hour. The concept of time became a subject of frequent musing for the boy as he grew up.

Eventually the dining room lessons would lead the boy, Jim Bishop, to the attention of millions of newspaper readers, the best-seller lists, and even a contest of wills with the most powerful woman in America.

But the road from Jersey City to fame would be a painful thirty years long. A pivotal juncture on that road, he recalled later, was discovering the Clinton Avenue Public Library. "Here I could be anyone I chose, go anywhere I pleased. Among my chums, I became a storyteller. Among the teachers at St. Patrick's Elementary, I became a liar who seldom had a passing grade." Insecure because of his short stature, he adopted a cocky attitude as a cover-up. This didn't win him an abundance of friends, and he gravitated closer to books, forging a friendship that would last his entire life.

After eighth grade he spent two years at a business school to learn shorthand and typing. At sixteen he was out in the work force, beginning as an errand boy on Wall Street (thanks to his father's influence). One day he was handed an envelope containing a check for one million dollars and told to deliver it to the Corn Exchange

Bank. It wasn't the first time he'd been given one of these checks, so he didn't give it too much thought. Instead, on this glorious spring day, he detoured through a nearby graveyard. The ancient headstones prompted thoughts, not of the check in his pocket, but about time.

Everything was related to time, he thought, strolling through the cemetery. "There is a time to be at school—a precise time. There is another for church. There is one for going to bed. . . . There are birthdays and anniversaries to mark the motion of time; there are family deaths. . . . Time, not destiny, is the key to life." But books, he thought, books make time stand still, retreat, or fly into the future. These were the things he thought about that lazy afternoon, the afternoon he forgot to deliver the check. The mistake cost his employer a lot of money (more than a thousand dollars by today's standards) and cost Bishop his job. It was the first of a string he would lose or quit—factory worker, door-to-door salesman, delivery boy, meat grinder, clerk, milkman. Each lasted but a few weeks. And then, after a disapproving lecture, his father would wearily write a letter to another friend in hopes of securing a future for his aimless son.

After five years of lost opportunities, Bishop approached his father with one last request. He'd been reading the New York newspapers since he was ten years old. It was the golden age of American journalism, with New York boasting fourteen dailies (by the 1990s there would be only four), each trying to outdo the others with sensational headlines and stories. Young Bishop saw in newspapers yet another dimension of time. Apprehensively he said, "I've finally decided what I really want to do." The father lifted a suspicious eyebrow. "I want to become a writer," the boy declared.

The man stared disbelievingly at the twenty-one-year-old before him, the one who once flunked grade-school English. The boy continued: "I've been reading the New York *Daily News*. They have a columnist, Mark Hellinger, and I think I can write like that."

"You're crazy," his father stated. And yet he wanted to believe the boy. So one more time he wrote a letter, this one to a retired cop in charge of copyboys at the *News*.

Though Bishop got the job, he narrowly averted another dismissal for being too aggressive—for trying to write stories instead of sitting obediently on a bench with the copyboys. He did, however, quickly become the favorite of his hero, Hellinger, who fled the *News* for the rival *Mirror* a year later and took Bishop with him as an assistant and reporter. There he continued draining the public library, borrowing the encyclopedia volume by volume, reading the old writers as well as the new ones, trying to copy their styles—styles like the one used by a newspaper guy out of Kansas City who'd begun to make a name for himself with a terse and to-the-point writing style, Ernest Hemingway. (The Hemingway style was perfect for the columns Bishop would write twenty-five years later.)

Bishop's writing talents matured but his income did not, so he began selling articles to magazines to support his wife and family. Each step he took along the way helped him develop and refine a style of his own. Nonetheless, over the next twenty-five years, which he spent as a reporter, promoter, designer, editor, and free-lance magazine writer, the early pattern of lost jobs and restlessness continued to plague him.

And so, too, did a strange piece of American history. With the eye for detail he'd inherited from his father, he noted the historical inconsistencies in many interpretations of Abraham Lincoln's assassination—most of them dealing with time. In 1930, for no reason he could recall afterward, he began filling a notebook with scribblings about the event. Through the years it grew from one notebook to twenty-six, one for each of Lincoln's last twenty-six hours, and each fed by Bishop's obsession with time.

In 1953 he was again jobless, in debt for three thousand dollars, and borrowing money from his father. In desperation he turned to the twenty-six notebooks and began to write the story that would change his life—a minute-by-minute account entitled *The Day Lincoln Was Shot*. Five publishers turned it down before Harper took a chance and published it in 1955. The critics loved it, the public loved it, history teachers loved it, and television turned it into a drama with a wild-eyed young actor named Jack Lemmon as John Wilkes Booth. The book's you-are-there, minute-by-minute style would become Bishop's trademark, and suddenly the guy who couldn't sell a line was the hottest game in town.

Although he would write other best-selling "day" books (including *The Day Christ Died*), none would be as successful as the Lincoln book. There would, however, be one more assassination book, and it would force him to draw upon every investigative trick he'd learned from his father and the great reporters he'd worked with through the years. After President Kennedy's assassination, his widow declared that there would be one definitive book on the day's events and it would be written by someone hand-chosen by the family. That someone would *not* be Jim Bishop, who had antagonized brother Bobby Kennedy a decade earlier; instead, it would be William Manchester who would write *The Death of a President*.

When Bishop announced his intention to write his own version, Jacqueline Kennedy instructed all associated with the tragedy to avoid consulting with him. She failed, however, to consider the resourcefulness of the influential policeman's son. Knowing the bitter feelings between the Kennedys and the new president, Lyndon Johnson, Jim Bishop cultivated a friendship with LBJ, who in turn opened many of the doors the Kennedys had locked. And in the end, the critics saw the Manchester and Bishop books as a "dead heat." Twenty years later, both books are still in print.

After the Lincoln best-seller, Bishop was invited home again; that is, back to newspapers, with a three-times-a-week general-interest column—something he did effortlessly if you count only the thirty-five minutes he spent at the typewriter for each one. If you count the painful failures from 1929 to 1955, then each column took a lot longer.

He wrote about family, religion, show business, politics, race, and human interest—which was his favorite. His human-interest columns also became the favorites of his readers—especially a young teenager reading them in the Columbus, Ohio, papers. "It was the first stuff I ever read in a paper that had a heartbeat to it, that grabbed me. Suddenly I felt there was someone in the paper who *knew* me," Bob Greene told me years later when his own column was appearing in as many papers as Bishop's once had.

Bishop said each of the human-interest stories began with a true incident. He then expanded the story, changed names, filled in the missing pieces, and added a punch line. His models were the classic short-story writers Guy de Maupassant and O. Henry, along with his old boss, Mark Hellinger. Before he died at the age of seventy-nine, he wrote more than two thousand of these. Here are two of my favorites.

• • • •

Nothing to Worry About

THE HILLS looked like vanilla cupcakes in the late snow. The cars cut black scars around them and, where the road dropped steeply to the river, the bridge looked like a child's Erector set. On the far side were the town, a few church spires and some old-fashioned houses and two or three traffic lights, which were brighter in the gloom of a snowy day.

Bob ordered one more fast one. He was careful about his drinking because Ymelda worried. It wasn't that he was alcoholic. She claimed that it affected his judgment. Not much. A little. Liquor made him happier and more ebullient and more confident and less cautious.

This made Bob smile. Women, he felt, never really understand their men. They are always afraid of something that never happens. Nervous Mel, he called her. He snapped the shot glass up, tilted his head, and nodded farewell to the bartender.

The car outside was his. It was old, but it was all his. He patted it and pulled his gloves on and sat behind the wheel and ran the engine a little. A sweet-sounding baby, that engine. It had a quiet roar of authority. Bob chewed on a mint as he swung the car around, watching in both directions for traffic, and on across the bridge and up into the hills.

He thought of his happiness. He had so much of it. Not much money, but a fortune in contentment. He had come home from the war safely and Ymelda had been waiting for him as though she had not stirred since he kissed her good-by.

Both had jobs. His paid $118.50 with time and a half. He cannibalized old cars in a junk yard and he had a boss who trusted him all the way. Bob and Mel had bought a four-and-a-half-room house —he called it a bungalow—for $7,250 and little Mickey had been born in it suddenly and unexpectedly eight months ago.

Now there was another baby coming. A girl, he hoped. A real girl with a yellow pony tail and a saucy mouth and laugh-squinted eyes and big wet kisses for Daddy. Bob drove through the hills, swelling with pride. He was richer than Rockefeller and he knew it.

He looked at his watch. Mel should be almost through at the doctor's office. He started back, around the bases of the hills. He was happy. Extraordinarily happy. He moved the car up a notch or two and spun it a little on the snowy turns. There was no traffic up here. Nothing to worry about. He had promised Mel that he would not take a drink. Bob removed the glove on his right hand, dug into his pocket, and popped two more mints into his mouth.

What a woman doesn't know cannot hurt her. He came to the brow of the hill leading down to town and he knew, the instant he passed the edge of it, that he was going too fast. It is a knowledge that a good driver feels, without looking at a speedometer.

Bob knew, the moment he tapped the brakes lightly, that he would never make the bottom turn onto the steel bridge. A man full of liquor would be unintelligent and in a situation like this he would panic. But not Bob. He had thirty seconds left in which to think. So he figured all the angles.

He was glad that Mel wasn't with him. She'd scream. She'd complicate everything. The best thing to do, he knew, was not to turn the wheel. The car was going faster and faster, down the icy road. He would stay in his lane—luckily, there was nothing ahead—and, when he reached the river, he would permit the car to go through the wooden handrail. Before it left the road, he would open the door on his left and jam his foot in it so that it would not close.

The moment it hit water, he would push the door all the way, and strike out. How far would it be to the muddy bank? Thirty feet? Forty? Bob thanked God that he was a man who used his head.

The old car went down, down, faster and faster. People coming up saw it and knew what was going to happen. They held their breaths. Bob opened the door, jammed his foot in it, and swung the wheel slightly so that the vehicle, instead of crashing into the steel girders, splintered the wooden handrail and arched gracefully over the river and splashed in.

He struck out and headed for shore, shivering in the icy current. He could hear the cheers as he staggered up the bank. Then he remembered that he had left little Mickey in a basket on the rear seat . . .

• • • •

The Turtle

THERE HAD BEEN TOYS around the house before. Many of them. But little Dennis loved the twenty-five-cent turtle more than the Erector sets, the book of games, the orange scooter, or the baseball mitt. The turtle was about as big as a coin. On his brown shell was his name: Oscar.

Dennis loved him and Dennis was eight years old. He saved for a ninety-eight-cent goldfish bowl and he packed small brightly colored stones in it, so that, when water was added, Oscar had his own private beach. Then he placed Oscar and the bowl on a window ledge in his room so that the afternoon sun warmed the cold wrinkles in the turtle's legs and moved him, now and then, to slip and slide down the stones into the cool clear water.

When Dennis came in from school, he hurried to his room to see what Oscar was doing. Oscar was the first live thing that Dennis had ever owned.

One afternoon, Dennis hurried up the stairs and found Oscar on his back floating. As young as he was, Dennis understood the finality of death. His shoulders shook and his breath caught and a wail came from his lips.

His mother hurried upstairs. She saw her little boy standing, arms hanging straight down, chin on chest, and she heard the sobs. She knew the genuine sound and she stood in front of him and held him to her breast. It took her a moment to find out what the trouble was.

He was promised a new turtle if he would stop crying. It didn't help. The crying continued and no promise on her part could slow the sobs.

She phoned her husband at his office. He was irritable. He had a business to conduct. He got into his car and came home. He hurried straight up to Dennis's room and put his arm around his boy.

"You can cry as long as you like," he said softly, "but it will not bring Oscar back. When God calls us it means that He loves us so much that He cannot bear to be apart from us any longer. God must have loved Oscar a great deal."

The sobbing continued. The father kept talking quietly, insistently and inexorably. "Coming home, I kept saying to myself, 'Well, now that Oscar is dead we should be asking ourselves what we can do to show him how much we love him.' Crying isn't the answer. It won't bring him back, son. What I think we ought to do is to have a funeral service for Oscar."

The sobbing began to slow. The boy was listening. He brushed his shirt sleeve against his eyes and he tried his first few words.

"What can we do for him, Dad?"

"Personally," the father said in a tentative tone, "I think we ought to bury Oscar in the back yard. We will invite Mommy and all the children of the neighborhood and I will attend too." Dennis stopped crying. His father took a solid silver cigarette case from his pocket. "See this? This is Oscar's casket. He will be the only turtle in the world buried in solid silver."

The eyes of Dennis glistened. "Will we have a solemn procession?"

"Certainly," the father said. "And I will get a big rock and chisel Oscar's name on it so that centuries from now, everybody will know that Oscar is buried there."

Dennis was smiling. He looked at the goldfish bowl in time to see Oscar flip on his stomach and swim toward shore. Dennis looked up at his father.

"Let's kill him," he said.

• • • •

BESIDES *The Day Kennedy Was Shot*, only a few of the twenty-one books Jim Bishop wrote in his seventy-nine years are still in print—*The Day Christ Died, The Day Christ Was Born*, and *The Day Lincoln Was Shot*. Public libraries, of course, have these and others on their shelves or they can obtain them through interlibrary loan. My personal favorite is his collection of columns, *Jim Bishop: Reporter*.

HE WAS NO BUM

by Bob Greene

The Reporter Who Can Cover Anything

Bob was only a college junior and he was being given the chance most journalists would die for. He was being assigned to a national political convention—but not just *any* one. It was the soon-to-be-infamous 1968 Democratic convention in Chicago, the one that spilled protest blood over the streets of Chicago. And though he was only being loaned by his hometown paper as an errand boy to the Scripps-Howard newspaper chain during the convention, it was still the big time.

Because every hotel room in the city was booked, it first appeared he wouldn't have a bed. Finally a room reservation was found that had been made for veteran reporter Jim Lucas, who was ill. Bob was told to go to the hotel, check in as Lucas, get a good night's sleep, and be ready to work. All of this he did. He even put the "Do Not Disturb" sign on the doorknob, locked the door, and secured the chain. Just what you are supposed to do in a hotel.

What you are *not* supposed to do is what he did the next morning. He locked himself in the bathroom because of a jammed door. It was the biggest moment in his budding career and he was locked in the bathroom, with no phone and no one to hear his screams, his family unaware that he was registered under someone else's name, the hotel room double-locked, and the "Do Not Disturb" warding off even the chambermaids.

When he finally—and bloodily—extricated himself, he was too embarrassed to ever tell anyone—until fifteen years later, when another hotel door jammed for a few seconds. As his life flashed before him, it brought back the Chicago bathroom memory. For most people, it would be just that—a memory. But for Bob Greene, syndicated columnist for the *Chicago Tribune*, it was a column as well.

Greene is one of the new breed of columnists. Unlike the other columnists included here, he had a conventional childhood in an upper-middle-class community and graduated from college (Northwestern). And he might have gone into business like his father if it hadn't been for that writing bug.

It had been with him long before he joined a newspaper or even went to college. Looking back on it today, Greene credits a silver-haired syndicated columnist in the Columbus paper by the name of Jim Bishop, the first columnist he'd ever read who really "grabbed" him. So Greene was walking around with the writing bug like some inactive virus until the day he heard a teacher tell a high school journalism convention that the best way to develop the self-discipline necessary to become a writer is to keep a journal. So during his senior year, he kept a diary listing what he'd done each day, where he'd gone, the guys he'd kidded, the girls he'd kissed, and the records he'd bought. Because boys weren't supposed to keep diaries, he never told anyone, not even his best friend. But he kept the spiral-bound notebook in the bottom of his shirt drawer for twenty years—until he turned it into not just a magazine column but a best-selling book called *Be True to Your School*.

When he was seventeen, the *Columbus* (Ohio) *Citizen-Journal* hired him as a summer copyboy. "As I entered the room," he recalled years later, "I was greeted with the sound of a floorful of typewriters banging away; the smell of paste pots that sat atop every desk; the sight of men and women talking into telephones that were cradled between their shoulders and their ears. At that precise moment, I fell in love. I had not spoken to a single person in the room, but I knew for sure that this was what I wanted to do for the rest of my life: work in rooms like this room, with people like these people."

Unlike those of Mike Royko, his newsroom colleague at the *Chicago Tribune*, Greene's columns seldom fit the conventional "news" mold or deal with urban America. They're not tied to headlines; they're closer to snapshots of what he calls the "stage play of life that never ends."

Investigative reporters follow their noses; Greene follows his curiosity. For example:

- Looking at athlete–media star Frank Gifford, he wondered what it was like to have spent your entire adult life as the "coolest guy in the room." So he asked Gifford and got a column out of it.

- Thinking about the house he grew up in Bexley, Ohio, he called the people who were now living in it and moved in for the weekend—and a column.
- A few years after Watergate, when Richard Nixon was living in media exile, Greene was curious about what it must be like to hear people refer to you as "Tricky Dick." So he and Nixon sat for hours and talked about it for another column.
- What's it like to be the grandchild of one president and the son-in-law of another? That was the subject of a column he did on David Eisenhower (who is married to Julie Nixon).
- And what's it like to be Frank Sinatra's son, singing in moth-eaten nightclubs and knowing you'll never have even *one* hit record? Another column.

What separates the best writers from the pack is not the writing but recognizing a good idea when it appears. Like anyone else, a writer sooner or later has a problem spelling or subtracting something. At that point, he or she wonders for a moment, "Am I getting dumber?" But not many writers would recognize the moment for what it was: a great column. Greene decided to see if he really was "losing it." He took the SATs again, joining 1.6 million others on a Saturday morning, to see if he had become dumber or smarter since he'd taken the test as a seventeen-year-old many years earlier. The result was a column for *Esquire* magazine that showed he scored fifty points higher on the verbal and two hundred points lower in math. (Why? What had he been doing for a living for fifteen years?)

A good column not only gives you pause but illuminates corners of your life. "Yes," you think, "this is the way it is. I've seen this kind of thing for years and never stopped to think about it." This Bob Greene column is like that. I think of it often, when I pass a firehouse or see someone slouched beside a street vent.

. . . .

A BUM DIED. That's what it seemed like. They found his body in a flophouse on West Madison Street, Chicago's Skid Row. White male, approximately fifty-five years old. A bum died.

They didn't know.

He was no bum. And his story . . . well, let his story tell itself.

The man's name was Arthur Joseph Kelly. Growing up, he wanted to be a fireman. When he was a child he would go to the firehouse at Aberdeen and Washington, the home of Engine 34. His two sisters would go with him sometimes. The firemen were nice to the kids. This was back in the days when the neighborhood was all right.

Arthur Joseph Kelly became a teenager, and then a man, and he never quite had what it takes to be a fireman. He didn't make it. He did make it into the Army. He was a private in World War II, serving in the European Theater of Operations. He didn't make out too well. He suffered from shell shock. It messed him up pretty badly.

He was placed in a series of military hospitals, and then, when the war was over, in veterans' hospitals. Whatever had happened to him in the service wasn't getting any better. He would be released from a hospital, and he would go back to the old neighborhood in Chicago, and suddenly the L train would come rumbling overhead and Arthur Joseph Kelly would dive to the ground. Some people laughed at him. He didn't want to do it. A loud noise and he would drop.

He walked away from a veterans' hospital in 1954. He decided that he had to live in the real world. But he was in no condition to do that. He tried for a while, and then he went back to the only place that he remembered as being a place of happiness.

He went back to the fire station at Aberdeen and Washington.

Some of the men of Engine 34 remembered Arthur Joseph Kelly from when he was a boy. They remembered him as a bright-eyed child wanting to be a fireman. And now they saw him as a shell-shocked war veteran.

They took him in.

They fed and clothed him and gave him a place to sleep and let him be one of them. He wasn't a fireman, of course, but he lived in the firehouse, and he had the firemen as his friends. The military people didn't know what to do with his veterans benefits, so some of the firemen went to the Exchange National Bank and arranged for the benefit money to be paid to a special account. The firemen of Engine 34 took it upon themselves to become Arthur Joseph Kelly's conservator and guardian.

The years went by. Some of the firemen were transferred, and some retired, and some died. But there was always at least one fireman at the station who would take responsibility for Arthur Joseph Kelly. The firemen didn't ask for anything in return, but Kelly would stoke the furnace and clean up and help out as much as he could. There were maybe a dozen firemen over the years who became his special guardians—the ones who would deal with the bank and the military, and who would make sure that no harm came to Kelly. For a long time it was the Sullivan brothers; when they left Engine 34, another fireman willingly took over, and then another.

Once Arthur Joseph Kelly went to a Cubs game. A car backfired. He hit the ground. There was some snickering. But an older man, who had been in the service himself and was familiar with shell shock, helped Kelly up and said, "That's all right, fellow. You'll be all right." After that, Kelly stayed close to the firehouse.

His mind and his nerves were not good. The firemen had to remind him to bathe, and to change clothes, and to eat properly. They did it, for twenty years and more, without anyone asking. "He's an easygoing fellow," one of them said. "He doesn't harm anybody. It's not so hard for us to take care of him."

Then the firehouse closed down. The firemen were transferred to another station house, at Laflin and Madison. Arthur Joseph Kelly went with them, but it wasn't the same. It wasn't the firehouse he had loved as a child. He didn't want to live there.

So the last fireman to take care of him—George Grant, a fifty-one-year-old father of eight—found Arthur Joseph Kelly a place to live. It wasn't much—it was the room on Madison Street—but every month Grant would take care of the financial arrangements with the bank, and would go to Madison Street to give money to a lady who ran a tavern near Kelly's room. The understanding was that she would give Kelly his meals at the tavern. No liquor. The firemen didn't want Kelly to end up as a Madison Street wino.

"The firemen had started taking care of Art way before I even got on the force," Grant said. "I just happened to be the last in a long line of men who took care of him. I didn't mind."

When Arthur Joseph Kelly was found dead in his room, they thought he was a bum. But they should have been at the funeral.

Arthur Joseph Kelly was buried with dignity. He was carried to his grave by uniformed firemen. They were his pallbearers. Most of them were not even born when, as a boy, Kelly had started hanging around the firehouse. But they were there at the end. The firemen never let Kelly live like a bum. They didn't let him die like one, either.

• • • •

BOB GREENE'S WRITING can be found in more than two hundred papers throughout America. Hundreds of his best columns can be found in his books, including: *He Was a Midwestern Boy on His Own; Homecoming; Cheeseburgers; American Beat; Johnny Deadline, Reporter;* and *We Didn't Have None of Them Fat Funky Angels on the Wall of Heartbreak Hotel, and Other Reports from America.* Some of these are now out of print but still available from your local library.

His best-seller, *Good Morning, Merry Sunshine,* is his personal journal recounting the first year in the life of his daughter. In my estimation, it is the best book of its kind and should be required reading for all parents.

THE YELLOW HANDKERCHIEF

by Pete Hamill

An Angry Voice from Brooklyn

His first brush with national fame came in 1970 when the vice-president of the United States lumped him with American traitors and called his writings "irrational ravings." Yet one year later he wrote a column that led to one of this century's most memorable demonstrations of patriotism.

The first incident occurred at a time when America was losing ten thousand soldiers a year in Vietnam and student protests had turned college campuses into a second battleground. Then in May 1970, nervous national guard troops at Kent State University in Ohio opened fire on a field of student demonstrators, killing four.

That incident became the pivotal moment when majority sentiment began to turn against the war. Almost immediately the nation's fury boiled out of the typewriters of its columnists and commentators. No writer, however, was angrier than a Brooklyn-born son of Catholic immigrants from Northern Ireland named Pete Hamill. A Navy veteran, Hamill had already covered the war from the Vietnam front and was less than euphoric about its slaughter. When the blood spilled here as well, he was outraged.

When Vice-President Agnew read Hamill's column in the then-liberal *New York Post*, he puffed himself to full patriotic indignation and attacked all such critics as traitors to America. And the most vicious of them all, he declared, was Pete Hamill, with his "irrational ravings."

Hamill grew up as the oldest of seven children in a family so poor he didn't taste his first steak until he was seventeen, and he went to school on rainy days with cardboard stuffed in his shoes. He candidly admits that his anger didn't begin with Vietnam; he says he *grew up angry*—angry at the humiliation of his poverty, and angry at the world because it wasn't always fair. (Some of that he might have inherited from his father, who once had been an active member of the Irish revolutionary forces.)

He recalls his neighborhood as being littered with mobster hit men, youth gangs, homeless rummies, and deranged vets still fighting old wars: "I grew up in a state of rage. Sometimes I hid the rage; sometimes I displaced it in long afternoons at the public library near my house, where the books of Howard Pyle, Robert Louis Stevenson, and Kenneth Roberts took me out of the present time and put me into some other world where bearded pirates clashed on stretches of yellow beach, or young boys hid under bridges away from Blind Pew.

"The library," he remembers, "allowed me to borrow the first beautiful things I ever took home. When I was reading them, I would place them on tables, on the mantelpiece, against a window, just to be able to see them, to turn from dinner and glance at them in the next room. I hated to bring them back, and often borrowed some books three or four times a year, just to have them around."

At the time, America was witnessing a new phenomenon called comic books, and Hamill was enchanted by them. His reading had given birth to a desire to write stories of his own, and when he discovered he could draw better than most kids, comics seemed a natural outlet. The comic books, in turn, led him to newspaper comics, which led him to the rest of the paper.

By the time he quit school at sixteen to work in the Brooklyn Navy Yard, he was a daily newspaper reader. A year later he joined the navy and met the first person he'd ever known who'd gone to college. Through this friendship, he began to read his way through the base library, absorbing a different brand of writer than he'd known as a teenager.

After the navy, he thought about college—but Columbia University told him to consider community college and become a dental technician. Three New York newspapers refused to consider him for copyboy. Although the navy yard was beckoning again, Hamill was dreaming of more important things than paychecks. Finally he landed a job as a messenger for an advertising agency. There his eagerness to learn caught the eye of the agency. His bosses promoted him and urged him to study art at the Pratt Institute at night.

In an English composition class at Pratt he met a professor who would spend the next five years teaching him how to read with his head and not just his heart. He taught him how to write by picking

Hemingway and Aristotle apart—line by line. Hamill was still reading newspapers every day, especially the *New York Post*, which at that time had the best columnists in town. By 1960, at age twenty-five, he was a partner in an advertising agency when he read that the *Post*'s editor had just published a book. After finishing it, he impulsively wrote the editor "a long, impassioned letter about the book, the world, and the state of American journalism." A few days later—and ten years after walking to school with cardboard in his shoes—Pete Hamill was a reporter with his favorite newspaper. Five years after that he was a columnist, covering the ready-to-burst rage of America at war with itself.

(Hamill's combative style has not been dulled with age. At one point in 1993, the near-bankrupt *New York Post* had three different owners, and the first one named Hamill editor-in-chief. The second one fired Hamill the day he took possession of the paper. But Hamill was held in such high esteem and his replacement held in such contempt by the *Post*'s writers and editors, they refused to accept the firing and kept his name on the masthead as editor, an event that gained national headlines for the paper founded by Alexander Hamilton 192 years before. The owner then agreed to rescind the firing, but when he continued to intrude on Hamill's editorial domain, the latter moved his office into a nearby diner and in public protest worked from there. The second owner soon thereafter sold out to a third buyer, and Hamill, knowing the paper was finally in secure financial hands, preferred to respectfully resign in order for the new management to bring back a previous editor of the paper.)

Hamill once said that all he could hope for with a column was to present the fragment of an event or idea and move readers, or remind them of the gathering darkness before they moved on to the comics page. And perhaps that is all that does happen most of the time. There was, however, at least one column that did more than that. On October 14, 1971, with the Vietnam War showing no signs of abating, Hamill offered not a grim reminder of darkness and body bags but a nine-hundred-word ray of hope.

The idea came one night while he was in the Lion's Head, a New York writers' pub, talking with a woman friend. She shared an anecdote that gave him an idea for the ending of a column (he was then doing four a week and most of his days were spent looking for column ideas). After hearing the anecdote, he recalls going into the men's room and writing the ending on a small index card. "There's a column in there someplace," he thought to himself.

A few weeks later, when one of his news-oriented columns fell through, out came the index card. All he had to do was invent a beginning for the anecdote with the wonderful ending. He used it in "The Eight Million," a continuing series of semifictional columns relating to the eight million people who live in New York City. Soon after it appeared, *Reader's Digest* published it for its nearly fifty million American readers. PBS made it into a television special and Japanese filmmakers turned it into a full-length movie. And then, when the hostages were released from Iran, Americans turned it into a national demonstration.

• • • •

THEY WERE GOING to Fort Lauderdale, the girl remembered later. There were six of them, three boys and three girls, and they picked up the bus at the old terminal on 34th St., carrying sandwiches and wine in paper bags, dreaming of golden beaches and the tides of the sea as the gray cold spring of New York vanished behind them. Vingo was on board from the beginning.

As the bus passed through Jersey and into Philly, they began to notice that Vingo never moved. He sat in front of the young people, his dusty face masking his age, dressed in a plain brown ill-fitting suit. His fingers were stained from cigarettes and he chewed the inside of his lip a lot, frozen into some personal cocoon of silence.

Somewhere outside of Washington, deep into the night, the bus pulled into a Howard Johnson's and everybody got off except Vingo. He sat rooted in his seat and the young people began to wonder about him, trying to imagine his life: perhaps he was a sea captain, maybe he had run away from his wife, he could be an old soldier going home. When they went back to the bus, the girl sat beside him and introduced herself.

"We're going to Florida," the girl said brightly. "You going that far?"

"I don't know," Vingo said.

"I've never been there," she said. "I hear it's beautiful."

"It is," he said quietly, as if remembering something he had tried to forget.

"You live there?"

"I did some time there in the Navy. Jacksonville."

"Want some wine?" she said. He smiled and took the bottle of Chianti, and took a swig. He thanked her and retreated again into his silence. After a while, she went back to the others, as Vingo nodded in sleep.

In the morning they awoke outside another Howard Johnson's and this time Vingo went in. The girl insisted that he join them. He seemed very shy, and ordered some black coffee and smoked nervously, as the young people chattered about sleeping on beaches.

When they went back on the bus, the girl sat with Vingo again and after a while, slowly and painfully and with great hesitation, he began to tell his story. He had been in jail in New York for the last four years, and now he was going home.

"Four years!" the girl said. "What did you do?"

"It doesn't matter," he said with quiet bluntness. "I did it and I went to jail. If you can't do the time, don't do the crime. That's what they say and they're right."

"Are you married?"

"I don't know."

"You don't know?" she said.

"Well, when I was in the can I wrote to my wife," he said. "I told her, I said, Martha, I *understand* if you can't stay married to me. I told her that. I said I was gonna be away a long time, and that if she couldn't stand it, if the kids kept askin' questions, if it hurt her too much, well, she could just forget me. Get a new guy—she's a wonderful woman, really something—and forget about me. I told her she didn't have to write me or nothing. And she didn't. Not for 3½ years."

"And you're going home, not *knowing*?"

"Yeah," he said shyly. "Well, last week, when I was sure the parole was coming through I wrote her. I told her that if she had a new guy, I understood. But if she didn't, if she would take me back she should let me know. We used to live in this town, Brunswick, just before Jacksonville, and there's a great big oak tree just as you come into town, a very famous tree, *huge*. I told her if she would take me back, she should put a yellow handkerchief on the tree, and I would get off and come home. If she didn't want me, forget the handkerchief and I'd keep going on through."

"Wow," the girl said. "Wow."

She told the others, and soon all of them were in it, caught up in the approach of Brunswick, looking at the pictures Vingo showed

422 • READ ALL ABOUT IT!

them of his wife and three children, the young woman handsome in a plain way, the children still unformed in the cracked, much-handled snapshot.

Now they were 20 miles from Brunswick, and the young people took over the window seats on the right side, waiting for the approach of the great oak tree. Vingo stopped looking, tightening his face into the ex-con's mask, as if fortifying it against still another disappointment.

Then it was 10 miles, and then five, and the bus acquired a dark hushed mood, full of silence, of absence, of lost years, of the woman's plain face, of the sudden letter on the breakfast table, of the wonder of children, of the iron bars of solitude.

Then suddenly all of the young people were up out of their seats, screaming and shouting and crying, doing small dances, shaking clenched fists in triumph and exaltation. All except Vingo.

Vingo sat there stunned, looking at the oak tree. It was covered with yellow handkerchiefs, 20 of them, 30 of them, maybe hundreds, a tree that stood like a banner of welcome, blowing and billowing in the wind, turned into a gorgeous yellow blur by the passing bus. As the young people shouted, the old con slowly rose from his seat, holding himself tightly, and made his way to the front of the bus to go home.

• • • •

A s you may have noticed, this 1971 column by Hamill bears a striking resemblance to a 1973 song written by Irwin Levine and L. Russell Brown, a blockbuster hit for Tony Orlando and Dawn—"Tie a Yellow Ribbon 'Round the Old Oak Tree." Indeed, the column and song were so similar it took a civil court judge to decide that it was just a coincidence, and that historical documents showed such legendary events involving returning men and their lovers as far back as the Crusades. Further, during the years after the Civil War, it was customary for an army wife to wear a colored ribbon corresponding to her husband's branch insignia—red for field artillery, blue for infantry, yellow for cavalry, and so on. When the husband was away on duty the ribbon was attached to the front door. There was also a hit song in the 1950s based upon an old cavalry tune, "She Wore a Yellow Ribbon," that had been revived in the 1949 John Wayne–John Ford movie of the same name.

Be that as it may, the Hamill story in print and the song on the airwaves ignited a remarkable national movement in the form of yellow ribbons hanging from trees, streetlights, mailboxes, and doorways welcoming home the fifty-two American hostages from Iran in 1981. Ten years later it happened again when American soldiers came home from the Gulf War with Iraq. So great was the mania for yellow ribbon by this time that one major ribbon manufacturer had to go to a six-day, twenty-four-hour operation to meet the demand and increased its production to thirty million yards, ten times more than in a normal year.

Through both of these events, a Hamill enemy and one of America's former grand patriots—Spiro T. Agnew—was strangely silent. When last seen publicly he was tiptoeing out the back door of the Nixon White House after resigning in a bribery and kickback scandal. Hamill, it turned out, would have the last word between them: He used Agnew's words to name his first collection of newspaper columns: *Irrational Ravings*.

Related reading: There is a cultural phenomenon in which someone repeats a farfetched story he or she has heard, believing it is absolutely true. When it has passed through enough mouths and minds, it becomes what is called an "urban legend." Jan Harold Brunvand has compiled a book of such stories, *The Vanishing Hitchhiker: American Urban Legends and Their Meanings*.

I'VE GOT YOUR NUMBER

by Robe Imbriano

All the Views
Fit to Print

The next time you pass the letters-to-the-editor section of your newspaper and rush to the entertainment or sports section, consider this: One of the most important writers, politicians, scientists, and figures in American history made his public debut in such a spot—as a *female impersonator*!

For almost as long as there have been newspapers, letters to the editor have been an important part of the process. They have served as an opportunity for readers to voice their own views as well as for the newspaper's editors to camouflage some of their more radical views under pen names. The term *correspondent*, now used so freely by television and radio as well the print media, comes from the days when those who regularly wrote letters to the editor were called correspondents. In England during the 1700s, many of the day's most brilliant essays first appeared in newspapers. But the same essayists, using pen names, also wrote letters *against* their own essays. This served to create controversy (which sold more newspapers) and to keep the essayists and their work in the news. If they were alive today, they might be doing the talk shows or writing for the grocery-store tabloids.

Thus it was that a bright, sixteen-year-old apprentice printer sat and watched his older brother begin to publish a newspaper in Boston in 1721 that was politically radical and often irreverent toward religion. He watched as his brother's friends mischievously created fictitious characters for their satirical letters to the editor, and his palms began to itch. And before long, a series of anonymous letters began to appear at the press, penned by a female correspondent named Silence Dogood. No one doubted for a moment their genuineness or originality. The good lady was quickly promoted from the back page to the front, as she aired her views on religious hypocrisy, freedom of speech, censorship, drunkenness, and equal education for women. After fourteen letters, the lad ran out of ideas and revealed himself to his astonished brother. Soon thereafter, the older brother was jailed and censored for the paper's insubordinate views and the liberated younger brother headed for New York and eventual fame and fortune under his real name—Benjamin Franklin.

Satire and controversy continue to be the mainstay of letters to the editor. They are so eagerly read and so well regarded in England that major political figures have resigned their offices through the letters department of *The Times* of London. In America today, *The New York Times* has the best letters department. For many years, however, *The New York Times* was known in the trade as "the Gray Lady" because of its monotonous gray-print appearance and stingy use of photographs throughout the paper. Finally, in 1970, with the nation's cities in ferment with racial strife, college campuses bursting with political and social protest, and the United States losing its first war in two hundred years, "the Gray Lady" decided it was time for a change. It seemed minor at the time, but the *Times*'s idea would eventually be adopted by many of the major and minor papers throughout North America. And no doubt it would have been firmly endorsed by the Franklin brothers.

The *Times*'s motto is "All the news that's fit to print." With the nation engulfed in a whirlwind of ideas and controversy, the editors reasoned, "Why not a page where you would have 'all the *views* fit to print'?" The page, while an extension of letters to the editor, would contain essays and articles that were longer than letters and that often expressed views boldly opposed to those the *Times* expressed in its editorials. The articles would be both solicited and unsolicited, and illustrated with unconventional artwork. Since the articles were going to appear on the page *opposite* the editorial page, the editors decided to call it the op-ed page—a title that is used throughout the newspaper business today. Since then, newspapers have customarily added many of their most controversial columnists to the page as well.

In the more than twenty years since the *Times* began its op-ed page, more than four hundred thousand manuscripts have been received and nearly twenty-five thousand used. Their authors include the rich, the famous, the infamous, and the anonymous—from ex-presidents, Nobel Prize winners, novelists, generals, convicts, and radicals to conservatives, liberals, foreigners, actresses, and athletes. All—regardless of fame or importance—received the same fee. Richard Nixon got the same as Casey Stengel and Roseanne Barr Arnold—$150.

The trademark of a good op-ed piece is its power and importance to the moment we are living in and what we are as a culture. The best articles are not long-winded but always opinionated. I have selected two of my favorites, both in the tradition of America's rebellious and noncompliant founders. Neither author is famous, both wrote them unsolicited, and both pieces stayed in my mind long after I finished reading them.

This first one appeared on Sunday, March 4, 1990. It was written by Robe Imbriano (Im-bree-AH-no), a resident of New York City and a producer at ABC News in Manhattan. He wrote it immediately upon arriving home after the incident, submitted it unsolicited, and it was accepted immediately.

• • • •

Last Sunday night, sometime after 10:30 p.m., I put an end to my seventh straight day of work. I left behind the stress of my office to confront another set of pressures—finding transportation home on the coldest day of the year.

I didn't have the right change for a bus, nor had I any tokens. So when I found both booths at the 66th Street subway station closed, I re-emerged to ground level—flustered, a shade more than tired and a hair less than frostbitten—and began to search for a yellow cab with a light on top.

That's where we met.

Remember me?

I was the fairly well-dressed man on the corner of 66th Street and Broadway, facing uptown. Surely you must; I was the only one there. I was waving to you as I'd imagine a refugee in a wartorn country would wave to his would-be savior.

Any recollection?

You slowed, your cab clearly empty, its back seat filled only with warmth. You looked at me—turned your head in my direction. Was that a smile that played on your lips?

Just as people on foot nod their heads in recognition at those they find vaguely familiar, cabbies, too, signal pedestrian acquaintances, particularly those of my stripe.

You accelerated.

Now, you weren't off duty. If perhaps I had been mistaken, my doubts were soon resolved when, at the next block, you stopped for the fairly well-dressed man at the corner of 67th Street and Broadway.

The white man at the corner of 67th Street and Broadway.

Through the tears that the sub-zero wind brought to and blew from my eyes, I saw two more of your colleagues pass underneath my raised arm.

My raised black arm.

Until we meet again, Mr. T57030T.

Until we meet again.

• • • •

D ID IMBRIANO and the cabdriver ever have that promised meeting? In preparing this anthology, I talked with Imbriano and asked that question. He said, "Soon after the article appeared, I received a package from the Taxi and Limousine Commission that contained instructions on filing a formal complaint. I filled it out and eventually was asked to testify before the commission, facing the driver." The driver was fined fifty dollars and a negative citation was placed in his permanent file.

WHY ALI LOVED FLAG BURNINGS

by Craig Nelsen

Burned Up over Old Glory

Though this op-ed article is one of the shortest pieces in this book, it is also one of the more complicated and controversial. For those reasons, it might be helpful to set the "stage" on which the article made its debut.

The core of the article had its origins in the revolutionary 1960s, the same time the phrase "Different strokes for different folks" debuted on the American scene. That saying was intended to pacify citizens who were repulsed by the sweeping, though less than neat, changes in dress and hairstyles of the young and the countercultural. It also served as an abbreviation of what American democracy is all about.

What sets our form of democracy apart from others is not the *power* of our citizens but the *amount* of their power and how well protected our citizens are when they dare to differ. Our Founding Fathers knew it would be natural for humans to disagree (indeed, some of those founders were among the most disagreeable). Thus the Bill of Rights was annexed to the Constitution to protect American citizens—Christian or Hindu, liberal or conservative, rich, well dressed, and influential or poor, ill-clad, and disenfranchised—as they pursued their "different strokes." All of which looks lovely on paper. Putting it into practice is another thing. Consider, if you will, two citizens looking at a museum painting:

"That's the most beautiful thing I ever saw," says the first.

"It's the ugliest *I* ever saw!" says the other.

There's no problem—until the first says, "My daughter painted that. And if you don't take back what you just said I'm going to punch your lights out!"

If you substitute politics or government policy for the painting, you can see how difficult it is for true democracy to function. Although the First Amendment guarantees our freedom to disagree, to criticize, even to demean the government, from its very beginning there has been ongoing debate over what the amendment actually means. How *much* freedom to disagree? What's fair game for criticism?

America's most heated disagreements in recent years came during the Vietnam War. While Presidents Lyndon Johnson and Richard Nixon poured more and more troops into the war zone of Southeast Asia, the death toll mounted, and Americans divided into two camps: prowar and antiwar. When their cries went unheeded, protesters reached for increasingly dramatic means for getting the attention of their fellow citizens, as well as the government and media. On college campuses, new and creative protests evolved. You might say the war's opponents turned protest into an art form—one that would be mimicked twenty years later by oppressed Soviet, European, and Asian citizens.

Peace marches led to demonstrations that tied up traffic in major cities. Speeches intensified to chants and four-letter graffiti. Since the military draft was the principal means by which the government maintained its forces, protesters began to burn their draft cards in protest. When that didn't draw enough reaction, they turned to burning the American flag.

Of course, the prowar camp was far from silent about all of this. From pulpits and public podiums, the protesters were labeled "unpatriotic," "un-American," and "Communists." Some sought old or new laws to restrict the protests. Eventually the demonstrations were so loud and numerous—and the war's death toll so high—that America ended the war and withdrew its forces.

Some states adopted laws that limited certain demonstrations of protest—such as flag burning—and a decade later, when a political protester in Texas was arrested for burning a U.S. flag, the old emotions were rekindled. His case ultimately reached to the Supreme Court, which ruled five to four that the Texas law violated the protester's right to free speech—as much as we might disagree with what he was saying, he had a right to say it, explained the court.

A wave of patriotic indignation immediately swept the land. With religious fervor, politicians, veterans, and ordinary citizens declared, "If the Constitution will not protect our most treasured and sacred symbol, then we will create a twenty-seventh amendment that *will*!"

An interesting and heated eighteen-month debate followed between the conservative Right and the free-speechers. Indeed, before the issue died a natural death of exhaustion and lack of interest, a broad cross section of American society declared its positions on "Old Glory." One of the most original positions was posed by this article from the *New York Times* op-ed page. It is one of the most *American* stories I know. It also exemplifies perfectly the meaning of the phrase "It depends on your frame of reference."

• • • •

M Y FRIEND ALI TOLD ME that when he was a young boy growing up in Jordan during the 1960's, he used to like to go to the movies. But before the film could start, he is embarrassed to say, a huge likeness of King Hussein would appear on the screen, and everyone had to stand and sing along while a military band played the Jordanian national anthem.

Armed guards stood in the back of the theater to insure participation. If you didn't sing along, they would arrest you, charge you with disrespect for the symbol of the country—King Hussein—and haul you off to jail.

Then Ali remembers going home and watching the news on TV. Thanks to America's free press, there was always plenty of American news footage. Night after night, he watched Americans protesting the policies of their Government in Vietnam. On many nights, he watched Americans burn the American flag.

No doubt the Jordanian Government allowed these pictures on their state-controlled television with the intention of showing the population how rotten things were in America. They wanted to demonstrate to their own horribly repressed people just how good they really had it.

The effect, naturally, on young Ali was just the opposite.

It was the Americans who had it good. Here were citizens burning the American flag and, unbelievably, the armed soldiers in the background just stood and watched.

What freedom! What glorious, unyielding, sacred freedom! Ali learned to love that burning flag. Oh, he still stood and sang King Hussein's praises at the movies but, in his heart, where it counted, he cursed King Hussein and sang the praises of Old Glory. He knew that a flag you could so openly and freely disrespect was a flag worth respecting.

Ali decided he would come to America and live in such freedom. He saved and saved until that day finally arrived. It was very difficult when he got to America but he worked hard and soon he was a productive member of society.

He fell in love with America and vowed never to return to Jordan where you could go to jail for not singing the national anthem. He married and now has a son and, today, he talks eagerly of his boy's future in America, the land of the free.

• • • •

ONE OF THE HEALTHY ASPECTS of open debate is the enlightenment that occurs when issues are examined. During the flag controversy, for example, participants learned that many of our patriotic symbols were newly honored, not historically time-honored. For example:

- While there is a public law that prescribes a code of etiquette for the flag, it didn't become law until 1976—199 years *after* the flag design was approved, but in time for the bicentennial celebration
- The story of Betsy Ross and the first flag is mythical, not historical
- It wasn't until 1890 that states (New Jersey and North Dakota) first required the flag to be displayed in the classroom
- Only in 1892, when large numbers of immigrants began to arrive in America, did we conceive of the idea of a "pledge of allegiance" in order to Americanize foreigners
- The words *under God* were not included in the pledge until 1954
- "The Star-Spangled Banner," written in 1814, didn't begin as a song—it started as a poem, and didn't become our national anthem until 1931

One of the most riveting and original books on the subject of patriotism and free speech is Avi's novel *Nothing but the Truth*. It is subtitled *A Documentary Novel* because the text consists entirely of letters, memos, newspaper articles, and scripted dialogue about a high school student who uses the national anthem to antagonize and unnerve his teacher. As talk radio and the media impel the issue of free speech to new limits, Avi's novel is both thought-provoking and frightening.

Nonfiction

As

Literature

• • • • • • • • • • •

In the home, the kitchen,
in the family, or out in the woods,
fact can be as interesting as fiction.

HELPING HANDS

by Brent Ashabranner

A Dream Deferred

It took almost sixty years and more than a hundred thousand miles of traveling, but Brent Ashabranner finally achieved his dream and became a full-time writer. And for his readers it has been worth the wait, for he has given us some of the finest nonfiction books for children in the last decade.

Not all authors travel as long a path to success, but many start the same way Ashabranner did. To begin with, he was a reader as a child growing up in Oklahoma during the Great Depression. Before hard times hit, his family purchased a set of encyclopedias for him and his brother. There was also a set of leather-bound books about travel in exotic lands called *Stoddard's Lectures*; these were too difficult for him to read, but he loved thumbing through their pages and daydreaming over the illustrations. All of these books would portend things to come in his life—his writing success would be in nonfiction, like the encyclopedia, and he would live in some of the most exotic corners of the world.

As it was for many of the other writers or figures in this volume—Ray Bradbury, Robert W. Service, Langston Hughes, Jim Bishop, Gary Paulsen, Pete Hamill, and Ellery Queen—the local library was a cornerstone of Ashabranner's childhood. There were weekly trips to the Carnegie Public Library with his mother, where he loved to read books such as those in the Oz, Tarzan, and Tom Swift series. One that left him particularly ravenous for more was *Bomba the Jungle Boy*, a popular Tarzan imitation. When Ashabranner discovered there were no more books in the series, he decided to write his own sequel—*Barbara of the Jungle*. It lasted but a few pages before he grew discouraged and went on to other things.

His father recognized the boy's writing interests, however, and scrimped to buy a cheap typewriter for him when he was in junior high school. Its impact had him feeling very much a professional, and he promptly dug out one of his handwritten stories about jewel smugglers in Bangkok. He had already learned from *Writer's Digest* about how a professional manuscript should look, so when it was properly typed, he sent it off to a men's adventure magazine. It promptly came back rejected, as did the others he sent on the heels of the first. Eventually he tired of the retyping and ceased sending them—but he continued his dream of becoming a writer.

By the time Ashabranner was in high school, his teachers recognized his talent, and one of them, Mrs. Covey, gave him one memorable piece of advice: "Write about what you know about." Though his heart was set on fiction, he applied the advice to a class assignment. His brother had been doing some professional boxing, and Ashabranner took the knowledge he'd gained from watching his brother and wrote a story around it. The assignment won a fourth place award in the national Scholastic story competition. Mrs. Covey's advice would never be forgotten, and it would play an essential part in his future career.

At Oklahoma A & M, he came under the influence of a great writing professor, Thomas Uzzell, who had sold his work to many of the best magazines in the country. When Ashabranner told him of his ambitions to sell his writings, Uzzell advised him to start with the "pulps"—the sports, detective, western, and science-fiction magazines that were printed on cheap paper instead of the "slick" pages used by more expensive magazines such as *The Saturday Evening Post*. The pulps' standards weren't as high and they were willing to take chances on unknown writers. The advice paid off, and Ashabranner was selling regularly by the time he graduated—but not enough to support a wife and someday a family. So he accepted an offer to teach in the college's English department and settled down to writing in his spare time.

That routine was quickly interrupted when he received an offer that would dramatically alter his life's plans. He was asked to go to Ethiopia in North Africa for two years to develop reading materials for primary and secondary students. After Ethiopia, he and his family were asked to take on similar responsibilities in two more emerging African countries, Libya and Nigeria. Through these years, Ashabranner was working primarily with children's stories he learned from the natives—cultural fairy and folk tales, as well as nonfiction. This would slowly shift the focus for his own writing in the future.

In March 1961, Ashabranner's future took another turn, this time steered by someone he had never met. The new president, John F.

Kennedy, signed a bill to create the Peace Corps, a civilian volunteer force that would fan across the globe to teach practical skills to the people in developing nations. Kennedy had appointed his brother-in-law, Robert Sargent Shriver, to head the Peace Corps and make sure it worked. When Shriver arrived in Nigeria a few months later, Ashabranner was in charge of his local itinerary. The two hit it off quickly, and Ashabranner was recruited to help run the Nigerian program.

For the next eight and a half years, Ashabranner's responsibilities grew with the size of the Peace Corps. By the time he resigned as its deputy director, it had grown to fifteen thousand volunteers in sixty countries, the largest and most successful program of its kind in the world. His next eight years were spent in Southeast Asia with the Ford Foundation, awarding education grants.

Finally, with his children grown and a retirement income to serve as a cushion, Ashabranner set about resuming that deferred dream he had begun so many years before with *Barbara of the Jungle*. He was no longer interested in writing fiction, however. Nearly twenty-five years of living in dozens of cities and countries had convinced him that fact could be as interesting as fiction. So, following Mrs. Covey's advice, he began to write what he knew about. Since there were only a handful of magazines for children, he focused on the broader market of children's *books*.

I might add that he wrote like a man trying to make up for all those years away from the typewriter—fifteen books in almost as many years. He had also come back to writing at just the right time. By the 1980s, librarians and teachers were discovering the need for good nonfiction books. Educators were trying to move students away from dry textbooks and toward *real* books called trade books. Too much of the previous nonfiction material had been written in a style that bored the reader. If writers would write interesting books, students would read them. Into that void stepped outstanding nonfiction authors such as Brent Ashabranner, Russell Freedman, and Seymour Simon.

Ashabranner had learned from his experiences here and abroad that heroes are everywhere, not just in the history books. In his mind, a hero is anyone who uses determination and hard work to do extraordinary things that change a piece of the world—even if that piece is just a couple of blocks in Pasadena, California. And those were the kinds of men, women, and children he used as subjects for his book *People Who Make a Difference*. In this selection, we meet a woman and her friends who have done the impossible—at least what we used to think was impossible. And they did it by borrowing one of Bomba the Jungle Boy's helpers.

• • • •

Helping Hands

YOU ARE THIRSTY. A cold drink is in the refrigerator ten feet away, but it might as well be ten miles away. You can't move a muscle to reach it. Your nose itches until your eyes water, but you can't lift a hand to scratch. You want to watch a videotape, but all you can do is look helplessly at your VCR across the room and wait until someone comes to put in the cassette.

Your name is Mitch Coffman, and you are a prisoner in your own body. Your mind is clear and sharp; you can talk and move your head, but you can't move any other part of your body. Like almost a hundred thousand other men and women in the United States, you are a quadriplegic, totally paralyzed from the neck down.

Mitch Coffman's entry into the world of the quadriplegic came on a day that should have been a happy one. He was returning from a party to celebrate his thirtieth birthday when his car skidded on a bridge and went into a spin. Mitch was thrown out with an impact that broke his neck.

When Mitch regained consciousness, he came instantly face-to-face with a terrible reality: he had suffered permanent damage to his spine between the third and fifth cervical vertebrae. He would be paralyzed for the rest of his life.

After months of physical therapy, Mitch regained enough movement in his left hand to operate the control for an electric wheelchair. And he was more fortunate than most quadriplegics because he was able to move into a government-subsidized apartment building especially equipped for people with severe physical disabilities. The building has ramps instead of stairs, roll-in showers, light switches and other electrical and kitchen equipment that are easy to reach and operate. Attendants are also on duty at all times. Still, there were endless hours every day and night when Mitch was alone in his apartment waiting, waiting for the simplest tasks to be performed for him.

And then one day a stranger arrived in Mitch's little apartment. She was only eighteen inches tall, weighed but a furry six pounds, and communicated in excited squeaks and endless trills. But she could open the refrigerator door and bring Mitch a cold drink or a sandwich. She could scratch his nose with a soft cloth when it itched. She could put a videotape in the VCR. She could do dozens of other things for him that he could not do for himself.

The stranger was a black and brown capuchin monkey, and her improbable name was Peepers. Almost as important as what she could do for him was the fact that she was there, a companion, a constant presence in the apartment where, for most of the long hours of long days, there had been only Mitch.

"It took us months to learn to live together," Mitch explains as Peepers sits quietly in his lap. "Now I can't imagine living without her."

THE MODEST QUARTERS of Helping Hands: Simian Aides for the Disabled are on the fourth floor of an office building on Commonwealth Avenue in Boston. On my first visit there I could hear monkeys chattering in the training room. I was eager to watch the training, but before that I wanted to talk to Mary Joan Willard, the educational psychologist who started and is director of Helping Hands.

Quantum leaps of the imagination have always fascinated me, and I opened our conversation on that point. "How did you get the idea that monkeys might be trained to do things for paralyzed human beings?" I asked. "What made you think it was possible?"

Mary Joan explained that after receiving her doctorate in educational psychology from Boston University, she began a postdoctoral fellowship in 1977 at Tufts New England Medical Center in Boston. The fellowship was for rehabilitative study and work with persons who had suffered severe physical injury. In her daily rounds she soon came to know Joe, a patient at the center. One minute he had been a happy, healthy twenty-three year old. The next minute, because of a diving accident, he was a quadriplegic, paralyzed from the neck down. His story was an all-too-familiar one, but he was the first quadriplegic Mary Joan had ever known.

"I was shocked," she said. "I found it inconceivable that someone so young, so full of life was going to spend the rest of his days completely dependent on other people, dependent for a drink of water, for a bite of food, dependent on someone to bring him a book or turn out a light. I am a psychologist, and I kept thinking, There has to be some way to make him more independent.

"I couldn't get him out of my mind. I would sit in my room and think about him lying there in his room, helpless. And then one night it hit me out of the blue. Chimps! Why couldn't chimpanzees be trained to do things for quadriplegics like Joe? I kept thinking about it, and I didn't get much sleep that night."

The next day Mary Joan went to see B. F. Skinner, the famous Harvard psychologist who has done extensive pioneering research with animals, using reward and punishment techniques to alter their behavior. Mary Joan had worked three years for Skinner as a parttime assistant. He might not think her idea was workable, but she knew he would not scoff at it.

Skinner was amused at his assistant's excitement over her new idea; he pointed out that chimpanzees grow to be almost as big as humans, are stronger than humans, and often are bad-tempered. Chimpanzees would be too risky. But Mary Joan was right; Skinner did not laugh. The idea intrigued him.

Why not, he asked, think about using capuchins, the little creatures traditionally known as organ-grinder monkeys? They are small, usually no more than six or seven pounds and seldom more than eighteen inches tall. They are intelligent, easy to train, and form strong bonds of loyalty to their human masters. Furthermore, they have a long life expectancy, an average of about thirty years.

That was all the encouragement Mary Joan needed. She did some reading about capuchins, found out where they could be purchased, then went to the director of postdoctoral programs at Tufts and asked for money to start an experimental capuchin training program.

"He nearly fell off his chair laughing," Mary Joan said, remembering the director's first reaction to her proposal.

But Mary Joan was persistent and persuasive. When the director stopped laughing, he came through with a grant and some training space. The grant was just two thousand dollars, but it was enough for Mary Joan to buy four monkeys, some cages, and hire student trainers at one dollar an hour.

"I thought we could train them in eight weeks," Mary Joan recalled. "I had never touched a monkey! It took us eight weeks just to coax them out of their cages. The monkeys I was able to buy had had some pretty hard treatment. They weren't in a mood to trust any human being."

But a beginning had been made, and patience and dedication paid off in training the monkeys in an astonishing variety of tasks: taking food from a refrigerator and putting it in a microwave oven; turning lights on and off; doing the same with a television set, stereo, heater, air conditioner; opening and closing curtains; setting up books, magazines, and computer printouts on a reading stand.

One piece of equipment essential to most quadriplegics is a mouthstick which is used for turning pages, dialing a phone, typing, working a computer, and many other actions which improve the quality of a quadriplegic's life. One problem is that the mouthstick often falls to the floor or onto the wheelchair tray. The monkey helper is quickly taught to pick up the stick and replace it correctly in its master's mouth.

"The capuchins have great manual dexterity, greater than a human adult's," Mary Joan said, "and they're very bright. But we don't try to train them to do tasks where they have to think."

Judi Zazula, an occupational therapist, has been with Helping Hands almost from the beginning. Her title is program director, but Mary Joan describes her as a partner. Judi makes the same point about not putting a monkey in a situation where it has to think about the right way to do something. "Everything," she says, "is planned so that the monkey has just one way to respond if it does the task right."

The basic motivation for a monkey to perform a task correctly is a simple reward system. When it carries out a command as it is supposed to—turning on a VCR or bringing a drink—the trainer, and later the quadriplegic owner, praises the monkey for doing a good job and at the same time gives it a treat, usually a few drops of strawberry-flavored syrup. The quadriplegic releases the syrup by means of a wheelchair control.

There is also a system of punishment because capuchins are endlessly curious and occasionally mischievous. One monkey, for example, began dimming the lights when its owner was reading so that it would get a reward when it was told to turn them up again. More often, however, misbehavior is likely to be opening a drawer without being asked to or throwing paper out of a wastebasket in the hope of finding something interesting.

The monkeys are taught that anything with a white circular sticker pasted on it—such as a medicine cabinet—is off limits. If a monkey violates the off-limits rule, it is warned with a buzz from a small battery-operated device that it wears on a belt around its waist. If it doesn't obey the warning, the quadriplegic master can use remote controls to give the monkey a tiny electric shock. The warning buzz is usually sufficient, and most owners report that they almost never have to use the shock treatment. Judi Zazula points out that buzz-shock collars are also used in dog training.

LATE IN 1979 Robert Foster, a twenty-five-year-old quadriplegic living near Boston, became the first person to take part in a pilot project to test the feasibility of using a capuchin monkey aide. Robert, paralyzed from the shoulders down as the result of an automobile accident at the age of eighteen, had been living by himself for several years with the help of a personal care attendant. The attendant lived in the apartment with Robert but worked full time in a nearby hospital. That meant that Robert was alone in the apartment for nine hours or more at least five days a week.

Robert's new helper, a six-pound capuchin female named Hellion, helped to fill the long hours and continues to do so eight years after the experiment began. Robert communicates with Hellion—who deserves a nicer name—by aiming a small laser pointer at what he wants the monkey to bring or do. The laser is mounted on the chin control mechanism of his wheelchair. He also gives her a voice command such as "Bring" or "Open."

Hellion feeds Robert, brushes his hair, tidies up his wheelchair tray, brings him books, and carries out a whole range of other helpful tasks. For his part Robert dispenses strawberry-syrup rewards and tells Hellion how nice she is. Hellion is close by Robert's wheelchair all day, but when he tells her it is time for bed, she will go into her cage and lock the door.

As publicity about simian aides has spread across the country, Helping Hands has been swamped with requests for monkeys. Mary Joan and Judi are proceeding slowly with placements, however, still treating each case as an experiment. A number of additional capuchins have been placed with quadriplegics, and there have been no failures.

Mary Joan has had to spend an increasing amount of her time in fund raising and in administrative details of making Helping Hands a smoothly functioning nonprofit organization. "For the first two years we had to get along on three thousand dollars a year," Mary Joan said. "Fortunately, we don't have to pay student trainers much, and they love the experience."

Several major organizations and agencies concerned with severely disabled persons were interested, but all were skeptical. In the early stages Mary Joan wrote thirty-nine grant proposals and sent them to philanthropic foundations and government agencies, but not one was approved. But she persisted and, as evidence mounted that the capuchins could do the job, a trickle of financial support began. Now the Veterans Administration, National Medical Enterprises, the Educational Foundation of America, and the Paralyzed Veterans of

America give some financial help to Helping Hands. Money is also received through private contributions, but fund raising still requires time that Mary Joan would rather be giving to other parts of the program.

Lack of money was not the only problem in the early days of the program. Some critics said that the idea of monkeys serving as helpers was demeaning to the quadriplegics as human beings. Some medical authorities said that mechanical equipment—robotics is the technical term—could be developed to do a better job than monkeys.

To the first criticism, Mary Joan points out that no one thinks it is beneath the dignity of a blind person to have a dog serve as a guide. As to robotic equipment, she agrees that for some quadriplegics mechanical tools may be best. But she points out that no piece of equipment can provide the companionship and sheer pleasure that an affectionate capuchin can.

"A robot won't sit in your lap and put its arms around you," Mary Joan said.

Developing a reliable supply of trainable monkeys was a problem that Helping Hands solved through the cooperation of Walt Disney World in Florida. A capuchin breeding colony has been established on Discovery Island in this world-famous recreational-educational center, and it will produce most of the monkeys needed in the quadriplegic program. Other monkeys are received through private donation, and Helping Hands has become a safe haven for monkeys that have been confiscated by government agencies because of mistreatment or having been brought into the country illegally.

Trial-and-error testing proved to the Helping Hands crew that early socialization was necessary to train a monkey that would be affectionate and happy when it became part of a human household. The answer has been the creation of a foster home program. When the monkeys from Walt Disney World are young babies, six to eight weeks old, they are placed with foster families. These volunteer families agree to raise the monkeys in their homes for about three years and then turn them over to Helping Hands to be trained as aides to quadriplegics.

The carefully selected volunteer families agree to spend ten hours a day with their primate babies for the first six months—ten hours with the monkey outside its cage. This means that the foster mother and father and older children are actually carrying the baby monkey as they go about their household routines. Older monkeys require less time, but members of the household still must spend at least four hours daily with the young capuchin if it is to become a truly "humanized" primate.

Being a foster parent to a young monkey may sound like fun, and in many ways it can be a delightful experience. But it is time-consuming and demanding, and the time inevitably comes when the monkey must be given over to Helping Hands. "Everyone knows this moment of parting is coming, and most people handle it well," Mary Joan said, "but for some it is very hard. We have been offered as much as five thousand dollars to let a family keep a monkey. But, of course, we can't do that."

If for any reason a monkey does not successfully complete its training at Helping Hands, it is offered to its foster care family as a pet. Should the foster care family be unable to take it, Helping Hands maintains a carefully screened list of other families who have applied for a monkey pet. The "unsuccessful" monkey will be placed in the kind of human home environment to which it is accustomed.

Over sixty-five monkeys are now living with foster families. More than a hundred additional families have passed the screening test and are waiting to receive their foster "children."

Judi Zazula is a rehabilitation engineer. Together with Doug Ely, a solar research specialist for Arthur D. Little, Inc., she has designed most of the special equipment needed in the Helping Hands program: the laser pointer, chin and other wheelchair controls, and equipment that the capuchin's tiny hands can hold and manipulate.

"One of the first things I was asked to design was the nose scratcher," Judi told me and added, "The monkeys helped design a lot of the equipment."

She explained that by watching the monkeys as they carried out their tasks, she and Doug Ely could tell when a piece of equipment needed changing or when some new device was necessary.

Almost all of the monkeys selected for training are females because they tend to be gentler and more affectionate than males. Even so, to preclude the possibility of a capuchin aide hurting anyone, the teeth are extracted from the trainee monkeys when they reach maturity at about three-and-a-half to four years.

This operation has no harmful effects on the monkey or on her ability to eat and digest her food. All Helping Hands monkeys, from soon after they go into foster care, have a diet which is 85 percent commercial monkey food (Purina Monkey Chow). After teeth extraction the food pellets are softened a bit with water, and the monkey can eat them with no difficulty. The rest of the diet usually is fruit—

bananas, apple slices, peaches—which the monkey, even without teeth, can eat easily, especially as her gums harden.

The training of a monkey usually takes about eight months. A session with the student trainer may last from half an hour to an hour, but it might be as short as ten minutes depending upon the monkey's personality. There may be several training sessions a day.

"Every monkey is different," Judi said. "Every one has her own personality and her own strengths and weaknesses."

Judi's biggest job within Helping Hands is to match the right monkey with the right quadriplegic who is being considered to receive one. A training log is kept on each monkey, and Judi pores over every page until she knows everything that can be known about a particular capuchin's personality and about her strengths and weaknesses.

Then Judi visits the quadriplegic. She stays at least two days and gets to know as much about the person as she can and about the environment where the monkey is going to live and work for the rest of her life. Judi even makes a video of the quadriplegic's living quarters so that they can be duplicated in the final training of the monkey the quadriplegic will receive.

"I am totally consumed with getting the right monkey in the right place," Judi said to me. "By the time they leave this training room, they are my children. I always think, what kind of life will they have out there? I want to make sure it will be the best and most useful life possible."

Judi has come to know dozens of quadriplegics very well, and she has thought a great deal about the total loss of hope that they suffer. "A spinal cord injury is an especially terrible thing," Judi said, "because it usually happens to young people, and it usually occurs at a happy moment in life—a car accident after a junior-senior prom or having fun diving into a swimming pool or playing football. Then everything is lost in a split second. The person comes to and his or her world has collapsed and a nightmare begins.

"Most people thinking about something like that happening to them say, 'I wouldn't want to live; I'd rather be dead.' But these people aren't dead. Slowly, if they begin to believe that they can do things and affect things, they begin to think that it is worth hanging around."

Both Mary Joan and Judi know very well that the success of Helping Hands depends upon how effective simian aides are in performing tasks that help quadriplegics lead better and more productive lives. But they also believe passionately that having a capuchin helper adds an interest and spice to quadriplegics' lives that can make a huge psychological difference. The companionship is important, but beyond that their ability to control the monkey makes them special. They can do something few other people can do.

As part of her master's degree work, Judi made a study of how people react to a quadriplegic with and without a monkey helper. When one quadriplegic she was using in her study was at a shopping center without his monkey, only two strangers stopped to talk with him in the course of an hour. When the monkey was sitting beside him on the wheelchair, seventy-one people took time from their shopping to speak to the quadriplegic during about the same amount of time.

"The quadriplegic who can control a monkey is an expert in a very unusual way," Judi said, "and that makes him interesting to other people."

One quadriplegic had this to say: "When I go outdoors in my wheelchair, all that people see is the wheelchair. But when I go out with my monkey, the only thing they see is the monkey. Nobody notices the chair at all."

Mary Joan Willard has a sense of history and a vision of the future. In terms of need and demand, Helping Hands may seem slow in getting trained monkeys to the thousands of quadriplegics who want them. But she points out that the possibility of training dogs to guide the blind had been debated and advocated for a century before the Seeing Eye program began early in this century.

"Compared to that, we are doing all right," Mary Joan said to me.

Mary Joan's immediate goal for Helping Hands is to place forty simian aides a year and to move beyond that as fast as the job can be done properly. Costs for training, equipment, and placement are approximately nine thousand dollars for each Helping Hands monkey. If a recipient is able to meet these costs from insurance payments or other personal resources, he or she is expected to do so; however, no one selected to receive a monkey is refused for inability to pay. For most quadriplegics, costs are met from U.S. Veterans Administration and state rehabilitation program funds or from private research or charitable organizations.

Of one thing Mary Joan Willard is sure. "I see this as a life's work," she told me.

Judi Zazula feels the same way. "I can't imagine getting the satisfaction out of anything else that I get from this work," she said.

Judi was recently married to Doug Ely, her long-time partner in equipment development. Instead of a flower girl, Judi decided to have a flower primate. Hellion, the first monkey to become a simian aide in the Helping Hands program, carried a little bouquet of flowers.

• • • •

ASHABRANNER'S OTHER BOOKS include *Always to Remember: The Story of the Vietnam Veterans Memorial; An Ancient Heritage: The Arab-American Minority; Born to the Land: An American Portrait; Children of the Maya; Counting America: The Story of the United States Census; A Grateful Nation: The Story of Arlington National Cemetery; Into a Strange Land; A Memorial for Mr. Lincoln; Morning Star, Black Sun; The New Americans; The Times of My Life: A Memoir*; and *To Live in Two Worlds: American Indian Youth Today.*

If the selection included here sparked your interest, check out *Helping Hands: How Monkeys Assist People Who Are Disabled* by Suzanne Haldane.

I also recommend *Extraordinary People*, a study of three former thalidomide babies who have grown up to lead extraordinary lives (sixty-minute video).

IN THE PANTRY

by Charles Panati

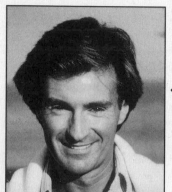

Food for Thought and Interesting Reading

Any school librarian will confirm that the most popular book in any junior or senior high school over the last twenty years was one that had two thousand characters, was set in more than a hundred countries and states, and had no plot.

Of course I am talking about the *Guinness Book of World Records*. The very people who would never tolerate a plotless movie or novel will devour record books. Why? Well, first of all, you won't have to do a book report on it. Second, it doesn't require a very long attention span. And third, since there's no plot, you can start and finish wherever you wish.

Unfortunately, many teenagers never journey beyond *Guinness* and into anything more interesting. One reason for that could be found in the old story about the fourth-grader who read a book about whales and wrote a book report that began, "This book has more about whales than I needed to know. . . ." Most of us believe the whales should be saved but we have neither the desire nor the time to read 250 pages explaining why. Which brings us to another reason. Too often the nonfiction students encounter is less than the best, and often it is less interesting than fiction. Writing good nonfiction is an art—but not every author is an artist. The number of boring-boring-boring textbooks in this world proves that. (There are legitimate reasons why you've never seen anyone reading a textbook on the beach!)

It's true that an author writing a book on whales needs to know a lot about whales, but he also must recognize that his readers don't need to know that much. The author-expert may have spent years accumulating background knowledge and may possess complicated ideas, but his success as a writer will be determined by two things:

(1) how well he translates complicated ideas into images and concepts the reader can understand, and (2) how interesting he makes the subject. (Interest is the universal sticky-glue that holds the reader.)

This section offers four diverse selections that demonstrate nonfiction can be as interesting or powerful as fiction when the author is an artist with words and ideas.

An excellent example of this kind of writer is Charles Panati (Puh-KNOTTY), the author of four books on what he calls "general information," his publisher calls "trivia," and I call "*readable* reference books."

Panati came to his writing in a circuitous fashion. He'd been trained in college as a scientist and eventually became head physicist for RCA. While at RCA he wrote a textbook with another physicist, and over lunch one day his editor complimented him on his ability to take complex scientific ideas and reduce them to a language the nonprofessional could easily understand. "Have you ever thought about writing for magazines like *Scientific American* or *Newsweek*?" he asked.

No, Panati hadn't thought of such a thing—until then. That afternoon, returning from lunch, he happened to pass the headquarters for *Newsweek*. Impulse—or was it fate?—pulled him inside and up to the personnel department, where he learned that the magazine had fired its second-string science writer the day before and was determined to hire a scientist for the position. Panati left with the job that afternoon.

Mealtime, it turns out, was an important spawning ground for Panati's career. One morning a few years later, he was having breakfast with a woman friend in a Manhattan café when she mischievously challenged him with a trivia question. Holding aloft the croissant she was eating, she asked, "Do you know where this comes from?"

His response was what most people would have said, "France," and he was wrong. The crescent-shaped croissant was created by a Vienna baker to celebrate his city's liberation from the Turks, who had a crescent on their flag. Viennese citizens thereafter took great pride in "devouring" their enemy whenever they ate a croissant.

For the rest of the day, Panati and his friend played a game of "origins and beginnings" with various items they encountered. When they came up empty on the origins of many, he thought they might have a book idea. Thus was born a book of origins called *Panati's Browser's Book of Beginnings*, followed by *Extraordinary Origins of Every-*

day Things; Panati's Extraordinary Endings of Practically Everything and Everybody; and *Panati's Parade of Fads, Follies, and Manias: The Origins of Our Most Cherished Obsessions.*

The difficult part of writing this kind of book, Panati explains, is the research. It is also the best part. Each volume consists of hundreds of mini-essays or stories, which must be both interesting and accurate. "I don't want my book to tell the reader what he *already* knows. I want to tell him what he *doesn't* know."

This requires a certain amount of detective work on Panati's part, ferreting out the unknown from reference books, journals, magazines, newspapers, and phone calls to experts. His writing style is that of the obsessed scientist: from early morning to bleary-eyed night, seven days a week, for the year it takes to complete a book.

One of Panati's strengths is that he doesn't fall into the "overkill" trap that captures so many nonfiction authors. He correctly senses how much most people really care to know about his subjects. He rejects the "trivia" label for his books because his subjects are usually more essential than that. In *Extraordinary Origins of Everyday Things,* he chose five hundred everyday items—such as Kleenex, Barbie dolls, the can opener, the bikini, Mother Goose, and Uncle Sam—and related the stories of their origins.

From that same book, here are four of his origin stories. Before reading them, however, consider how much time and money you have spent in eating the following items: potato chips, pretzels, popcorn, and peanuts. Now ask yourself how much you really know about them. Where did they come from?

• • • •

CHAPTER 16
In the Pantry

POTATO CHIP: 1853, SARATOGA SPRINGS, NEW YORK

As a world food, potatoes are second in human consumption only to rice. And as thin, salted, crisp chips, they are America's favorite snack food. Potato chips originated in New England as one man's variation on the French-fried potato, and their production was the result not of a sudden stroke of culinary invention but of a fit of pique.

In the summer of 1853, American Indian George Crum was

employed as a chef at an elegant resort in Saratoga Springs, New York. On Moon Lake Lodge's restaurant menu were **French-fried potatoes**, prepared by Crum in the standard, thick-cut French style that was popularized in France in the 1700s and enjoyed by Thomas Jefferson as ambassador to that country. Ever since Jefferson brought the recipe to America and served French fries to guests at Monticello, the dish was popular and serious dinner fare.

At Moon Lake Lodge, one dinner guest found chef Crum's French fries too thick for his liking and rejected the order. Crum cut and fried a thinner batch, but these, too, met with disapproval. Exasperated, Crum decided to rile the guest by producing French fries too thin and crisp to skewer with a fork.

The plan backfired. The guest was ecstatic over the browned, paper-thin potatoes, and other diners requested Crum's potato chips, which began to appear on the menu as Saratoga Chips, a house specialty. Soon they were packaged and sold, first locally, then throughout the New England area. Crum eventually opened his own restaurant, featuring chips. At that time, potatoes were tediously peeled and sliced by hand. It was the invention of the mechanical potato peeler in the 1920s that paved the way for potato chips to soar from a small specialty item to a top-selling snack food.

For several decades after their creation, potato chips were largely a Northern dinner dish. In the 1920s, Herman Lay, a traveling salesman in the South, helped popularize the food from Atlanta to Tennessee. Lay peddled potato chips to Southern grocers out of the trunk of his car, building a business and a name that would become synonymous with the thin, salty snack. Lay's potato chips became the first successfully marketed national brand, and in 1961 Herman Lay, to increase his line of goods, merged his company with Frito, the Dallas-based producer of such snack foods as Fritos Corn Chips.

Americans today consume more potato chips (and Fritos and French fries) than any other people in the world; a reversal from colonial times, when New Englanders consigned potatoes largely to pigs as fodder and believed that eating the tubers shortened a person's life.

PRETZEL: A.D. 610, NORTHERN ITALY

The crisscross-shaped pretzel was the creation of a medieval Italian monk, who awarded pretzels to children as an incentive for memorizing prayers. He derived the shape of his confection from the folded arms of children in prayer. That origin, as popular folklore has it, is supported by the original Latin and Italian words for "pretzel": the Latin *pretiole* means "little gift," and the Italian *bracciatelli* means "small arms." Thus, pretzels were gifts in the shape of praying arms.

From numerous references in art and literature, as well as extant recipes, we know that the pretzel was widely appreciated in the Middle Ages, and that it was not always baked firm and crisp but was frequently chewy. A recipe for moist, soft pretzels traveled in the thirteenth century from Italy to Germany, where the baked good was first called, in Old High German, *bretzitella*, then *brezel*—the immediate predecessor of our word.

The pretzel is one of the few foods to have played a role in the history of warfare. Early in the sixteenth century, Asian armies under the Turkish-Mongol emperor Babar swept into India and parts of Europe. A wave of Turkish forces encountered resistance at the high stone wall surrounding the city of Vienna. Following several unsuccessful attempts to scale the wall, the Turks planned to tunnel secretly beneath it, and to avoid detection, they dug at night.

Turkish generals, however, were unfamiliar with the working hours of Viennese pretzel makers, who to ensure the freshness of their specialty, baked from midnight to daybreak. A group of bakers, toiling in kitchen cellars, heard suspicious digging and alerted the town council; the local military thwarted the invasion. Viennese pretzel bakers were honored for their part in the victory with an official coat of arms that displays a pretzel, still the bakers' emblem today.

POPCORN: 3000 B.C., AMERICAS

Not all corn pops. Ideally, a corn kernel should have at least 14 percent water content so that under heat, the water expands to steam, causing the nugget to explode into a puffy white mass.

The art involved in popping corn is at least five thousand years old, perfected by the American Indians. They clearly appreciated the difference between sweet corn (for immediate eating), field corn (as cattle feed), and so-called Indian corn, which has sufficient water content for popping.

Popped corn was a native Indian dish and a novelty to the early explorers of the New World. Columbus and his men purchased popcorn necklaces from natives in the West Indies, and in the 1510s, when Hernán Cortés invaded the territory that today is Mexico City, he discovered the Aztecs wearing amulets of stringed popcorn in religious ceremonies. The dish derives its echoic name "popcorn" from the Middle English word *poppe*, meaning "explosive sound."

The Indians developed three methods for popping high-moisture corn. They might skewer an ear of popping corn on a stick and roast it over a fire, gathering up kernels that popped free of the flames. Alternatively, the kernels were first scraped from the cob, then thrown directly into a low fire; again, those that jumped free were eaten. The third method was the most sophisticated. A shallow clay cooking vessel containing coarse sand was heated, and when the sand reached a high temperature, corn kernels were stirred in; cooking, they popped up to the surface of the sand.

Legend has it that the Plymouth Pilgrims enjoyed popcorn at the first Thanksgiving dinner in 1621. It is known that Indian chief Massasoit of the Wampanoag tribe arrived with ninety of his braves bearing various foods. Massasoit's brother, Quadequina, is supposed to have contributed several deerskin bags of corn already popped.

Popping corn was simplified in the 1880s with the introduction of specially designed home and store popping machines. But at the time, corn could be purchased only in enormous quantities, and often still on the cob. The 1897 Sears, Roebuck catalogue, for instance, advertised a twenty-five-pound sack of popping corn, on cobs, for one dollar. The problem with buying popping corn in quantity was that storage depleted the kernels of their essential water content. Today food scientists know that if the internal moisture falls below about 12 percent, kernels open only partially or not at all. Charred, unpopped kernels are now called "duds" and are rare, which was not the case in the nineteenth century, when they were cursed as "old maids."

The first electric corn popper in America appeared in 1907, at a time when electrical appliances were new, often large, and not always safe. A magazine advertisement for the device pointedly addresses these two drawbacks: "Of the host of electrical household utensils, the new corn popper is the daintiest of them all," and "children can pop corn on the parlor table all day without the slightest danger or harm."

The advent of electric popping machines, and the realization during the Depression that popcorn went a long way in stretching the family food budget, heightened the food's popularity. But it was in the lobbies of movie theaters that popcorn became big business. By 1947, 85 percent of the nation's theaters sold the snack, and 300,000 acres of Midwestern farmland were planted annually with Indian popping corn.

The arrival of television in the '50s only increased Americans' demands for corn, to pop in the kitchen between programs. A mid-decade poll showed that two out of three television watchers munched popcorn as often as four nights a week. Not all brands, though, were of equivalent quality; some yielded an annoyingly high number of duds. It was the quest to produce a high-quality popcorn that led Orville Redenbacher, a graduate in agronomy from Purdue University, to experiment with new hybrids of Indian popcorn.

Agronomy, the science and economics of crop production, was an established field of study by the 1950s, having contributed to improved management of America's farmlands. In 1952, Redenbacher and a college friend, Charles Bowman, produced a corn whose kernels seldom failed to pop—and popped into larger, puffier morsels. But the quality hybrid was comparatively expensive, and popcorn companies that Redenbacher approached declined to sell his product, believing that snack food had to be low-priced. Convinced that popcorn lovers hated duds as much as he did, Redenbacher began packaging his corn and selling it to retail grocers. Its quality proved worth the price, for it became America's best-selling popcorn, contributing substantially to the 192 million pounds of corn popped annually in electric poppers, in fireplaces, and atop stoves. Today the average American consumes almost two pounds of popcorn a year.

PEANUTS: 1800s, UNITED STATES

As a plant, the peanut is prehistoric; as a snack food, it is comparatively modern. And its name is a misnomer, for the nugget is not a nut (which grows aboveground on trees) but a legume, a member of the bean family, and one whose seed pods grow underground.

Native to South America, peanut plants were brought from Brazil to North America—to the area that today is Virginia—centuries before Columbus's arrival. They flourished throughout the Southeast, where they were grown mainly for feeding pigs, chickens, and turkeys. Only poor Southern families and slaves ate peanuts, which were commonly known as "goobers," from the Bantu word *nguba*. By the 1850s, "goober" was also a derisive term for any backwoodsman from Virginia, Alabama, or Georgia, and the latter state, for its prodigious peanut crop, became known as the Goober State. It was not until the American Civil War that Northerners really got to taste peanuts.

In the 1860s, when Union forces converged on the South, thousands of hungry soldiers found themselves gladly eating a new kind of pea-size bean from an unfamiliar vine. Soldiers brought the vine, *Arachis hypogaea*, which bears yellow flowers and brittle pods, home with them, but the peanut remained little more than a culinary curiosity in the North. In the 1880s, showman P. T. Barnum began marketing peanuts in nickel-size bags at his circuses, and as Americans took to the circus, they also took to peanuts; as popcorn would become the quintessential movie snack, peanuts became part of the three-ring experience.

Peanut, as a word and a food, entered our lives in other ways. At public entertainments throughout the 1880s and 1890s, the euphemism "peanut gallery" gained currency to designate the remote seats reserved for blacks at circuses, theaters, and fairs. Not until the 1940s would the phrase, reiterated on television's *Howdy Doody* show, gain wide recognition simply as a grandstand for children. And peanut butter was an 1890s "health food" invention of a St. Louis physician; etymologists do not find the term linked with "jelly" until the 1920s, when the classic sandwich became a national dietary mainstay.

• • • •

FANS OF PANATI'S BOOKS will also enjoy *They All Laughed . . . From Light Bulbs to Lasers: The Fascinating Stories Behind the Great Inventions That Have Changed Our Lives* by Ira Flatow.

Nonfiction of a different nature can also be found in "Escape Reading," beginning on page 291.

POWER OF THE POWERLESS: A BROTHER'S LESSON

by Christopher de Vinck

A Story of Brotherly Love

One of the most powerful teams I ever knew practiced in private for thirty-five years before the public finally saw them. Afterward, anyone who experienced them always used one word: *unforgettable*.

In the traditional sense, Chris and his brother Oliver weren't the best athletes. Oliver, in fact, wasn't *any* kind of athlete, and Chris lasted only one day on his high school soccer team. They didn't "shoot hoop" together, didn't play catch or even tag. But as a team, they could teach world champions everything there is to know about courage, about coming from behind or overcoming odds. Most of all, they could teach them—and the rest of us—something about teamwork.

In the beginning, they never teamed in public. They always worked together in private, at home. Oh, the family saw them, along with relatives and sometimes neighbors, but no one else for almost thirty-four years. And then one day in 1985, Chris de Vinck was talking with some editors from the best-selling magazine in the world—*Reader's Digest*—and he mentioned his brother. At the time, Chris was teaching high school English in New Jersey and doing some free-lance writing. The *Digest* editors were picking his brain for story ideas he might contribute to them, and when they heard about Oliver, they said his story was the one they were most interested in.

So Chris wrote it out for the first time. For three weeks he wrote and rewrote, until, on his fourth draft, he had what he wanted. Unfortunately, it wasn't quite what the *Digest* editors wanted—though they said they'd consider printing it if he made certain revisions.

Chris was disappointed but not offended. He thanked them for considering the piece, then he sent it, unsolicited, to the op-ed page of *The Wall Street Journal,* the largest newspaper in America. Except for some trimming to fit the available space, the *Journal* took it just the way he wrote it.

It wasn't the kind of story most people expected to find in the business-oriented *Journal,* but when they did, the phones began ringing and the mail poured in. Two brothers who would never play in the Olympics or in the Super Bowl had teamed up to move some of the most powerful people in American society. No one could remember President Ronald Reagan ever calling the *Journal* about an op-ed piece before—but he did for this one. In another rare move, the *New York Post* called immediately to ask permission to reprint the article the next day. Eventually, *Reader's Digest* would call, hat in hand, requesting permission as well.

The letters came from clergy, politicians, doctors, lawyers, and CEOs. But more important, letters arrived from people who had brothers or sons or sisters like Oliver. Here is the essay that started it all.

• • • •

I GREW UP IN THE HOUSE where my brother was on his back in his bed for almost 33 years, in the same corner of his room, under the same window, beside the same yellow walls. Oliver was blind, mute. His legs were twisted. He didn't have the strength to lift his head nor the intelligence to learn anything.

Today I am an English teacher, and each time I introduce my class to the play about Helen Keller, "The Miracle Worker," I tell my students about Oliver. One day, during my first year teaching, a boy in the last row raised his hand and said, "Oh, Mr. de Vinck. You mean he was a vegetable."

I stammered for a few seconds. My family and I fed Oliver. We changed his diapers, hung his clothes and bed linen on the basement line in winter, and spread them out white and clean on the lawn in the summer. I always liked to watch the grasshoppers jump on the pillowcases.

We bathed Oliver. Tickled his chest to make him laugh. Sometimes we left the radio on in his room. We pulled the shade down over his bed in the morning to keep the sun from burning his tender skin. We listened to him laugh as we watched television downstairs. We listened to him rock his arms up and down to make the bed squeak. We listened to him cough in the middle of the night.

"Well, I guess you could call him a vegetable. I called him Oliver, my brother. You would have liked him."

One October day in 1946, when my mother was pregnant with Oliver, her second son, she was overcome by fumes from a leaking coal-burning stove. My oldest brother was sleeping in his crib, which was quite high off the ground so the gas didn't affect him. My father pulled them outside, where my mother revived quickly.

On April 20, 1947, Oliver was born. A healthy looking, plump, beautiful boy.

One afternoon, a few months later, my mother brought Oliver to a window. She held him there in the sun, the bright good sun, and there Oliver looked and looked directly into the sunlight, which was the first moment my mother realized that Oliver was blind. My parents, the true heroes of this story, learned, with the passing months, that blindness was only part of the problem. So they brought Oliver to Mt. Sinai Hospital in New York for tests to determine the extent of his condition.

The doctor said that he wanted to make it very clear to both my mother and father that there was absolutely nothing that could be done for Oliver. He didn't want my parents to grasp at false hope. "You could place him in an institution," he said. "But," my parents replied, "he is our son. We will take Oliver home of course." The good doctor answered, "Then take him home and love him."

Oliver grew to the size of a 10-year-old. He had a big chest, a large head. His hands and feet were those of a five-year-old, small and soft. We'd wrap a box of baby cereal for him at Christmas and place it under the tree; pat his head with a damp cloth in the middle of a July heat wave. His baptismal certificate hung on the wall above his head. A bishop came to the house and confirmed him.

Even now, five years after his death from pneumonia on March 12, 1980, Oliver still remains the weakest, most helpless human being I ever met, and yet he was one of the most powerful human beings I ever met. He could do absolutely nothing except breathe, sleep, eat, and yet he was responsible for action, love, courage, insight. When I was small my mother would say, "Isn't it wonderful that you can see?" And once she said, "When you go to heaven, Oliver will run to you, embrace you, and the first thing he will say is 'Thank you.' "

I remember, too, my mother explaining to me that we were blessed with Oliver in ways that were not clear to her at first.

So often parents are faced with a child who is severely retarded, but who is also hyperactive, demanding or wild, who needs constant care. So many people have little choice but to place their child in an institution. We were fortunate that Oliver didn't need us to be in his room all day. He never knew what his condition was. We were blessed with his presence, a true presence of peace.

When I was in my early 20s I met a girl and fell in love. After a few months I brought her home to meet my family. When my mother went to the kitchen to prepare dinner, I asked the girl, "Would you like to see Oliver?" for I had told her about my brother. "No," she answered.

Soon after, I met Roe, a lovely girl. She asked me the names of my brothers and sisters. She loved children. I thought she was wonderful. I brought her home after a few months to meet my family. Soon it was time for me to feed Oliver. I remember sheepishly asking Roe if she'd like to see him. "Sure," she said.

I sat at Oliver's bedside as Roe watched over my shoulder. I gave him his first spoonful, his second. "Can I do that?" Roe asked with ease, with freedom, with compassion, so I gave her the bowl and she fed Oliver one spoonful at a time.

The power of the powerless. Which girl would you marry? Today Roe and I have three children.

· · · ·

IN OPENING THE PRIVATE CHAMBERS in his family's life, Chris de Vinck gave shelter and hope to the thousands who have Olivers in their lives. After reading their letters and receiving their calls, de Vinck packed his suitcase and went to visit and interview many of them for the book *The Power of the Powerless: A Brother's Legacy of Love.*

Shortly after Oliver died, Chris's mother gave him the thick, blood-red, inexpensive dinner bowl that had been Oliver's through much of his life. It has resided ever since on the shelf next to the books in the cellar room where Chris writes.

Today, Dr. de Vinck teaches high school in New Jersey. He also consults for the U.S. Department of Education, where he is not averse to reminding his colleagues that his high school verbal SAT score was only 380 out of a possible 800. His essays regularly appear in Catholic newspapers, as well as the *New York Times* and *Wall Street Journal* op-ed pages. Many of his best essays and columns have been collected in *Only the Heart Knows How to Find Them: Precious Memories for a Faithless Time* (also available from Penguin Highbridge Audio). And de Vinck's all-time favorite book—in the classroom or out—is Harper Lee's *To Kill a Mockingbird*, a chapter from which can be found on page 67.

In conjunction with this selection, I recommend *Extraordinary People*, a study of three former thalidomide babies who have grown up to lead extraordinary lives (sixty-minute video from PBS).

from **W**OODSONG

by Gary Paulsen

His First Survival Story
Was His Childhood

Gary Paulsen writes award-winning survival stories and he does it as well as anyone in the business. But the best of his survival tales is his own, the one you find spread through his books. All the abandonments, the runaways, the drunks, the bitter days and nights, the lonely, split-lip searchings and gropings, and, yes, the weary fist-in-the-air gasp of "I made it!"—they're all Gary Paulsen's story.

Paulsen, you must understand, is not one of those make-it-up-as-you-go-along writers. Not that there is anything wrong with writers like that. Lord knows, the world could do with more Ray Bradburys or J. R. R. Tolkiens. But there are those who *invent* it and those who *live* it—Paulsen lived it. He never had a choice.

His father was a professional soldier who spent most of World War II away from home, and his mother did likewise, working in a munitions factory. They could also be abusive drunks. When the war was over, the family marched from one base to the next, and Paulsen never spent more than five months in any one school. "I was an 'army brat,' " he recalls, "and it was a miserable life. School was a nightmare because I was unbelievably shy, and terrible at sports. I had no friends, and teachers ridiculed me." His high school grades were mostly C's and D's, and his schoolyard fighting wasn't rated much better.

There was never enough money for clothes, so Paulsen began working at an early age—setting pins in a bowling alley, or selling newspapers in hospitals and bars. When family life became intolerable, like the one he describes in *The Foxman*, he either ran away or was shipped to live with his grandmother and aunts, whose homes of warm support were his "safety nets."

And then, in the midst of his pain and tumult, he discovered a beacon in the darkness—the same one that had rescued such writers as Robert W. Service, Ray Bradbury, Jim Bishop, and Cynthia Rylant (to name but a few). "One night, in a small Minnesota town where I was selling newspapers, as I was walking past the public library in twenty-below temperatures, I could see the reading room bathed in beautiful golden light. I went in to get warm and to my absolute astonishment the librarian walked up to me and said, 'Would you like a book?'

"I said, 'Sure.' And she said, 'Bring it back when you're done and you can get another one.' This went on for a long time. The librarian kept giving me things to take home and read—westerns, science fiction, and every once in a while a classic. She didn't care if I wore the right clothes, dated the right girls—none of those prejudices existed in the library. When she handed me a library card, she handed me the world. I roared through everything she gave me. It was as though I had been dying of thirst and the librarian had handed me a five-gallon bucket of water." Hiding from his parents' arguments, Paulsen would retreat to their apartment-building basement, snuggle beside the furnace with a book, a quart of milk, and some peanut butter sandwiches, and read into the winter nights.

While books gave him an anchor in the storm, the tempest was a long way from over. He ran trap lines to pay his way through one year of college, then quit to join the army. There he worked with missiles, thought his future lay in electronics, and took enough correspondence courses to land a job in the aerospace industry when he finished with the service.

But the long hours behind a computer console in a darkened tracking station in California convinced him that there must be better ways to spend a life. In fact, he thought writing would be an *ideal* way to live. So, faking an impressive résumé, he landed an associate editor's job with a men's magazine. His bosses soon discovered he didn't know much about writing or editing, but he was certainly a willing and hungry student. For the next year, every night after work, he wrote something and brought it to them for criticism the next morning. After eleven months, he sold his first article.

From there he returned to Minnesota to write full-time, which left little money for food and other necessities, but he struggled through—producing a handful of articles and two forgettable books. Thinking he was now an "author," he moved to an artists' colony in New Mexico to write the great American novel. What he did instead was to become a drunk. He spent the next six years drinking, fighting, ruining his marriage, and letting his talents rust.

Finally, in 1973, he quit drinking, came back to earth and to Minnesota with a new wife, and began writing again—this time not looking for greatness as much as money for food and clothing. When his readers meet characters who live off the land, they should know Paulsen has been there. Living in a converted chicken coop with make-shift electricity and no indoor plumbing, surrounded by chickens and goats, he and his family planted three gardens and lived off them—making their own ketchup, butter, and cheese. They were so deep in the woods, his son spent nearly five hours a day on a bus going back and forth to school. Paulsen averaged three thousand dollars a year writing books whose titles would make impossible author-trivia questions—*Dribbling, Shooting, and Scoring Sometimes; The Building a New, Buying an Old, Remodeling a Used Comprehensive Home and Shelter Book*; and *Careers in an Airport*.

When he turned to fiction, however, he not only opened a vein to his heart and ultimately success, he also opened a Pandora's box. In 1977 he published what is still one of his most important and powerful books, an antiwar novel called *The Foxman*. That year he also published *Winterkill*, about an alcoholic family. Unfortunately, some people thought they recognized themselves in the book and sued him for libel. Already on the edge of poverty, he looked up and saw a team of high-powered lawyers bearing down on him from one direction, and in the other direction he saw the retreating back of his publisher, who wanted no part of the problem. Taking the case to state supreme court, Paulsen eventually won, but the suit left him nearly bankrupt and bitter beyond reason. If this is what writing did to people, he wanted out, and he quit.

To support his family, he ran a beaver trap line. He worked a twenty-mile line on skis until someone gave him some dogs and a sled, which allowed him to expand the line to sixty miles. Although it was not written during those years, the excerpt printed here from *Woodsong* is based upon those days and nights running his dogs—first for trapping and then, when he quit hunting for good, for the most grueling race in the world, the Iditarod, a twelve-hundred-mile sled-dog race near the Arctic Circle.

The Iditarod is both intensive and expensive, with an entry fee and expenses running into thousands of dollars. Paulsen didn't know how he was going to afford it until he received a phone call one day from Richard Jackson, then editor in chief at Bradbury Press and now head of Orchard Books. Jackson, who had read Paulsen's work but never met him, wanted to know what he was writing. Paulsen told him, "I'm not writing anything. I'm running dogs and I don't have the money for the Iditarod!" Jackson saw an opportunity and promised to send Paulsen the money if he could get first shot at the next thing Paulsen wrote. It was a deal.

Eventually, age and the eighteen-hour days of running dogs would catch up with Paulsen. But by then he had resumed writing and, under Jackson's guidance, was writing from the heart and from his years of experience. He wrote three young-adult novels before the Zenlike *Dogsong* won a 1986 Newbery Honor Medal. All of a sudden, librarians and teachers were "discovering" a guy who had already published fifty books. On the heels of this came his most popular book to date, *Hatchet*, which won another Newbery Honor Medal. This story of a thirteen-year-old from a broken home who survives fifty-four days in the northern wilderness was so believable that *National Geographic* called Paulsen looking for the boy's name and address for a feature. It's just a story, Paulsen explained, fiction—except for the lonely heartache and pain, that is.

Today, health problems have driven a sober Paulsen, who has passed age fifty, back to the climate of New Mexico. His more than thirty dogs are gone, alive only in his books. He sees the only race left to him now as the one between himself and death. He has so much to say, yet fears he has little time left to say it in. His wife scoffs at this but he races on, trying to make up for lost time, averaging more than a book a year, and talking with teachers and classes of schoolchildren. Movie offers arrive regularly for his books, and he can take his pick from a dozen publishers standing in line at his door.

Success, though, hasn't spoiled him. None of his nearly one hundred books is in sight, nor are any of the awards he has won. "That's dangerous," he says, "if you start looking at that stuff. You become corrupt." Instead, what he chooses to look at and write about is the precious human struggle to survive, drawing upon his life as an alcoholic, field engineer, soldier, actor, farmer, carpenter, demolition worker, rancher, truck driver, trapper, migrant farm worker, sailor, and professional writer.

Here is a chapter from *Woodsong*, a nonfiction account of his years as a woodsman-husband-father-dogsledder. Using the vivid, short sentences that are not that far removed from Hemingway's but still distinctive enough to be his own, Paulsen writes with great realism. Therefore, his stories are not for the faint of heart or weak stomachs.

The world of dog and man, and the world of hearth or woods, can be violently painful places, tempered only by the blessed peace of kindness.

• • • •

CHAPTER 4

THE ADVENTURE really begins in differences—the great differences between people and animals, between the way we live now and the way we once lived, between the Mall and the Woods.

Primarily the difference between people and animals is that people use fire. People create fire, and animals don't. Oh, there are minor things—like cars and planes and all the other inventions we seem to have come up with. But in a wild state, the real difference is that we use controlled fire.

And it was in the business of fire that I came to the first of many amazements inside the woods.

It started with a campfire.

I was on a hundred-mile run in deep winter with new dogs— pups, really, just over a year old. I had gone beyond the trapping stage and was training new dogs for a possible attempt on the Iditarod. The pups had lived in kennels, mostly. They had only been on short training runs so that almost everything they saw on this run was new to them. They had to learn to understand as they ran.

A cow in a field was a marvel and had to be investigated; it took me half an hour to get untangled from the fence. A ruffed grouse that flew down the trail ahead of us had to be chased. A red squirrel took the whole team off the trail into the woods, piling into deep drifts and leaving us all upside down and packed with snow.

It was, in short, a day full of wonders for them and when night came and it was time to stop—you can really only do about twenty miles a day with young dogs—we found a soft little clearing in the spruce trees. I made beds for them and when they were fed and settled, or as settled as young dogs can get, I made a fire hole in the snow in the center of the clearing, next to the sled, and started a small fire with some dead popple. It was not a cold night so the fire was very small, just enough to melt some snow and make tea. The flames didn't get over a foot high—but the effect was immediate and dramatic.

The dogs went crazy with fear. They lunged against their chains, slamming and screaming. I went to them and petted them and soothed them and at length they accepted the fire. I put their frozen blocks of meat around the edges of the flames to soften, and fed them warm meat. Then they sat and stared at the flames, the whole ring of them.

Of course they had never seen fire, or flame, in the kennel—it was all completely new to them. But the mystery was why they would automatically fear it. They had seen many new things that day, and they didn't fear anything but the fire.

And when they were over the fear of it, they were fascinated with it. I stretched my foam pad and sleeping bag out in the sled to settle in for the night. This is a complicated process. The felt liners for my shoepacs had to be taken off and put down inside the bag so my body heat could dry them for the next day. My parka had to be turned inside out so all the sweat from the day could freeze and be scraped off in the morning. Any wet clothing had to be flattened and worked down into the bag to dry as well. While I was doing all this in the light from my head lamp, I let the fire die down.

Just as I started to slide into the bag one of the dogs started to sing. It was the sad song.

They have many songs and I don't know them all. There is a happy song they sing when the moon is full on the snow and they are fed and there is a rain song, which is melancholy—they don't like rain very much—and there is a song they sing when you have been with them in the kennel and start to walk away, a come-back-and-don't-go-away sad song.

That was the song one dog had started to sing. When I turned to look at him he was staring where the fire had died down into a cup in the snow, and in a moment the rest of them had picked up the song and were wailing and moaning for the lost fire, all staring where the flames had been.

In an hour they had gone from some coded, genetic fear of fire, to understanding fire, to missing it when it went away.

Cave people must have gone through this same process. I wondered how long it had taken us to understand and know fire. The pups had done it in an hour and I thought as I pulled the mummy bag up over my head and went to sleep how smart they were or perhaps how smart we weren't and thought we were.

SOMETIMES when they run it is not believable. And even when the run is done and obviously happened it is still not believable.

On a run once when it was the perfect temperature for running, twenty below—cold enough for the dogs to run cool, but not so bitterly cold as to freeze anything exposed—I thought I would just let them go and see what they wanted to do. I wouldn't say a word, wouldn't do anything but stand on the back of the sled—unless a bootie or a quick snack was needed. I'd let them run at an easy lope. I thought I would let them go until they wanted to stop and then only run that way from then on, and they ran to some primitive instinct, coursed and ran for seventeen hours without letup.

One hundred and seventy-five miles.

And they didn't pant, weren't tired, could have done it again. I nearly froze—just a piece of meat on the back of the sled—but they ran and ran in a kind of glory and even now I can't quite believe it.

The second incident with fire was much the same—something from another world, another time. It happened, but is not quite believable.

We had run long in a day—a hundred and fifty miles—with an adult team in good shape. The terrain had been rough, with many moguls (mounds of snow) that made the sled bounce in the trail. I had taken a beating all day and I was whipped. I made beds and fed the dogs and built up a large fire. It had been a classic run but I was ready for sleep. It was nearly thirty below when I crawled into the sleeping bag.

I was just going to sleep, with my eyes heavy and the warmth from the fire in my face, when the dogs started an incredible uproar.

I opened my eyes and there was a deer standing right across the fire from me.

A doe. Fairly large—more than a year old—standing rigid, staring at me straight on in the face across the fire. She was absolutely petrified with terror.

At first I thought she had somehow stupidly blundered into the camp and run past the dogs to the fire.

But she hung there, staring at me, her ears rotating with the noise of the dogs around her. She did not run and still did not run and I thought she must be a medicine doe sent to me; a spirit doe come in a dream to tell me something.

Then I saw the others.

Out, perhaps thirty yards or more beyond the camp area, but close enough for the fire to shine in their eyes—the others. The wolves. There was a pack of brush wolves and they had been chasing her. I couldn't tell the number, maybe five or six; they kept moving in agitation and it was hard to pin them down, but they were clearly reluctant to let her go, although they were also clearly afraid of me and being close to me. Unlike timber wolves, brush wolves are not endangered, not protected, and are trapped heavily. We are most definitely the enemy, and they worried at seeing me.

And when I saw them I looked back at the doe and could see that she was blown. Her mouth hung open and spit smeared down both sides with some blood in it. They must have been close to getting her when she ran to the camp.

And the fire.

She must have smelled her death to make the decision she made. To run through the circle of dogs, toward the fire and the man was a mad gamble—a gamble that I wasn't a deer hunter, that the dogs weren't loose or they would have been on her like the wolves, that somehow it would be better here.

All those choices to make at a dead, frantic run with wolves pulling at her.

This time it had worked.

I sat up, half raised, afraid to move fast lest she panic and run back into the wolves. I had more wood next to the sled and I slowly put a couple of pieces on the fire and leaned back again. The wolves were very nervous now and they moved away when I put the wood on the fire, but the doe stayed nearby for a long time, so long that some of the dogs actually went back to lying down and sleeping.

She didn't relax. Her body was locked in fear and ready to fly at the slightest wrong move, but she stayed and watched me, watched the fire until the wolves were well gone and her sides were no longer heaving with hard breathing. She kept her eye on me, her ears on the dogs. Her nostrils flared as she smelled me and the fire and when she was ready—perhaps in half an hour but it seemed like much more— she wheeled, flashed her white tail at me, and disappeared.

The dogs exploded into noise again when she ran away, then we settled back to watching the fire until sleep took us. I would have thought it all a dream except that her tracks and the tracks of the wolves were there in the morning.

FEAR COMES in many forms but perhaps the worst scare is the one that isn't anticipated; the one that isn't really known about until it's there. A sudden fear. The unexpected.

And again, fire played a role in it.

We have bear trouble. Because we feed processed meat to the

dogs there is always the smell of meat over the kennel. In the summer it can be a bit high because the dogs like to "save" their food sometimes for a day or two or four—burying it to dig up later. We live on the edge of wilderness and consequently the meat smell brings any number of visitors from the woods.

Skunks abound, and foxes and coyotes and wolves and weasels —all predators. We once had an eagle live over the kennel for more than a week, scavenging from the dogs, and a crazy group of ravens has pretty much taken over the puppy pen. Ravens are protected by the state and they seem to know it. When I walk toward the puppy pen with the buckets of meat it's a toss-up to see who gets it—the pups or the birds. They have actually pecked the puppies away from the food pans until they have gone through and taken what they want.

Spring, when the bears come, is the worst. They have been in hibernation through the winter, and they are hungry beyond caution. The meat smell draws them like flies, and we frequently have two or three around the kennel at the same time. Typically they do not bother us much—although my wife had a bear chase her from the garden to the house one morning—but they do bother the dogs.

They are so big and strong that the dogs fear them, and the bears trade on this fear to get their food. It's common to see them scare a dog into his house and take his food. Twice we have had dogs killed by rough bear swats that broke their necks—and the bears took their food.

We have evolved an uneasy peace with them but there is the problem of familiarity. The first time you see a bear in the kennel it is a novelty, but when the same ones are there day after day, you wind up naming some of them (old Notch-Ear, Billy-Jo, etc.). There gets to be a too relaxed attitude. We started to treat them like pets.

A major mistake.

There was a large male around the kennel for a week or so. He had a white streak across his head which I guessed was a wound scar from some hunter—bear hunting is allowed here. He wasn't all that bad so we didn't mind him. He would frighten the dogs and take their hidden stashes now and then, but he didn't harm them and we became accustomed to him hanging around. We called him Scarhead and now and again we would joke about him as if he were one of the yard animals.

At this time we had three cats, forty-two dogs, fifteen or twenty chickens, eight ducks, nineteen large white geese, a few banty hens

—one called Hawk which will come up again later in the book—ten fryers which we'd raised from chicks and couldn't (as my wife put it) "snuff and eat," and six woods-wise goats.

The bears, strangely, didn't bother any of the yard animals. There must have been a rule, or some order to the way they lived because they would hit the kennel and steal from the dogs but leave the chickens and goats and other yard stock completely alone—although you would have had a hard time convincing the goats of this fact. The goats spent a great deal of time with their back hair up, whuffing and blowing snot at the bears—and at the dogs who would *gladly* have eaten them. The goats never really believed in the truce.

There is not a dump or landfill to take our trash to and so we separate it—organic, inorganic—and deal with it ourselves. We burn the paper in a screened enclosure and it is fairly efficient, but it's impossible to get all the food particles off wrapping paper, so when it's burned the food particles burn with it.

And give off a burnt food smell.

And nothing draws bears like burning food. It must be that they have learned to understand human dumps—where they spend a great deal of time foraging. And they learn amazingly fast. In Alaska, for instance, the bears already know that the sound of a moose hunter's gun means there will be a fresh gut pile when the hunter cleans the moose. They come at a run when they hear the shot. It's often a close race to see if the hunter will get to the moose before the bears take it away. . . .

Because we're on the south edge of the wilderness area we try to wait until there is a northerly breeze before we burn so the food smell will carry south, but it doesn't always help. Sometimes bears, wolves, and other predators are already south, working the sheep farms down where it is more settled—they take a terrible toll of sheep—and we catch them on the way back through.

That's what happened one July morning.

Scarhead had been gone for two or three days and the breeze was right, so I went to burn the trash. I fired it off and went back into the house for a moment—not more than two minutes. When I came back out Scarhead was in the burn area. His tracks (directly through the tomatoes in the garden) showed he'd come from the south.

He was having a grand time. The fire didn't bother him. He was trying to reach a paw in around the edges of flame to get at whatever smelled so good. He had torn things apart quite a bit—ripped one side off the burn enclosure—and I was having a bad day and it made me mad.

I was standing across the burning fire from him and without thinking—because I was so used to him—I picked up a stick, threw it at him, and yelled, "Get out of here."

I have made many mistakes in my life, and will probably make many more, but I hope never to throw a stick at a bear again.

In one rolling motion—the muscles seemed to move within the skin so fast that I couldn't take half a breath—he turned and came for me. Close. I could smell his breath and see the red around the sides of his eyes. Close on me he stopped and raised on his back legs and hung over me, his forelegs and paws hanging down, weaving back and forth gently as he took his time and decided whether or not to tear my head off.

I could not move, would not have time to react. I knew I had nothing to say about it. One blow would break my neck. Whether I lived or died depended on him, on his thinking, on his ideas about me—whether I was worth the bother or not.

I did not think then.

Looking back on it I don't remember having one coherent thought when it was happening. All I knew was terrible menace. His eyes looked very small as he studied me. He looked down on me for what seemed hours. I did not move, did not breathe, did not think or do anything.

And he lowered.

Perhaps I was not worth the trouble. He lowered slowly and turned back to the trash and I walked backward halfway to the house and then ran—anger growing now—and took the rifle from the gun rack by the door and came back out.

He was still there, rummaging through the trash. I worked the bolt and fed a cartridge in and aimed at the place where you kill bears and began to squeeze. In raw anger, I began to take up the four pounds of pull necessary to send death into him.

And stopped.

Kill him for what?

That thought crept in.

Kill him for what?

For not killing me? For letting me know it is wrong to throw sticks at four-hundred-pound bears? For not hurting me, for not killing me, I should kill him? I lowered the rifle and ejected the shell and put the gun away. I hope Scarhead is still alive. For what he taught me, I hope he lives long and is very happy because I learned then—looking up at him while he made up his mind whether or not to end me—that when it is all boiled down I am nothing more and nothing less than any other animal in the woods.

• • • •

ENSUING CHAPTERS focus on further adventures with his dogs as they train for and finally run the grueling Iditarod.

Other Paulsen books include *Canyons, The Cookcamp, The Crossing, Dancing Carl, The Island, The River* (sequel to *Hatchet*), *Sentries, Tracker*, and *The Voyage of the Frog*. He is also the author of a poignant, season-by-season portrait of farm life, *Clabbered Dirt, Sweet Grass*.

Those who enjoy *Woodsong* will also enjoy Sterling North's *Rascal* and *The Wolfling*, and these dog books: *The Call of the Wild* and *White Fang*, both by Jack London; *Kavik, the Wolf Dog* by Walt Morey; *Lassie Come-Home* by Eric Knight; and *Where the Red Fern Grows* by Wilson Rawls. For the names of survival stories, see the listing at the end of the excerpt from *The Iceberg Hermit* in this book (page 380).

Surprise Endings

• • • • • • • • • • •

A sidewalk story and a subway story,
one fictional and the other true.

THOSE THREE WISHES
by Judith Gorog

A Wishful Cautionary Tale

Riddle: What is one of the richest gifts we have and yet, the poorer we are, the more abundant it is? Answer: A wish.

From the very beginning, long before there were such things as novels and movies, wishing was a fundamental part of our stories—the things we use to make sense of our lives. Even the oldest of stories begins with a wish. What would the story of Adam and Eve be without the wish for eternal knowledge contained in that apple?

Ancient and medieval stories were inhabited by heroes and heroines, princes and princesses, witches and goblins, and were plotted around wishes wished, wishes granted, and wishes denied. Centuries before the Grimms collected their woodland wish-tales, Arabs in the desert were telling stories of mighty genies granting wishes in return for freedom from their bottles.

One need look no further than the nursery to understand how naturally wishing comes to us. No one has to teach a child to wish. All of us spend an important part of our childhoods wishing—wishing for something to eat or drink, wishing for toys, wishing for Mommy and Daddy. As we grow older, we wish to be bigger, stronger, prettier, smarter, richer, and happier. Wishing stops only when life stops.

By the same token, wishing can get out of hand. Social scientists suggest that modern society has taken wishing to new extremes. In fact, whole industries have risen to support our wish-worlds. Where a century ago people walked along Main Street and window-shopped by wishing for the clothes in the store windows, today's citizens don't even have to leave their homes to do the same, if they have the Home Shopping Network on their cable system. The largest field of wishers ever assembled is probably the hundred million Americans lined up daily or weekly to play their lucky lottery numbers.

In this next selection, Judith Gorog takes the ancient wish-tale and mixes it with "grandmother wisdom"—that is, "Be careful what you wish for; it's liable to come true."

The idea for the tale was planted when Gorog was a youngster at Campfire Camp and the cook warned her about one of her childish exclamations. Gorog, who grew up to become first a technical writer and eventually a children's author after her three children were born, never forgot the cook's words. I, in turn, will never forget the response of my two children the first time I read this story to them back in 1982. It was a school day morning. Elizabeth was seventeen, combing her hair in the bathroom, and Jamie was thirteen, eating his cereal in the kitchen. I was positioned halfway between the bathroom and kitchen, reading aloud this story from Judith Gorog's collection *A Taste for Quiet: And Other Disquieting Tales*. When I reached the last line, there was a collective groan of surprise from Elizabeth and Jamie—a short-story writer's highest praise.

• • • •

No ONE EVER SAID that Melinda Alice was nice. That wasn't the word used. No, she was clever, even witty. She was called— never to her face, however—Melinda Malice. Melinda Alice was clever and cruel. Her mother, when she thought about it at all, hoped Melinda would grow out of it. To her father, Melinda's very good grades mattered.

It was Melinda Alice, back in the eighth grade, who had labeled the shy, myopic new girl "Contamination" and was the first to pretend that anything or anyone touched by the new girl had to be cleaned, inoculated, or avoided. High school had merely given Melinda Alice greater scope for her talents.

The surprising thing about Melinda Alice was her power; no one trusted her, but no one avoided her either. She was always included, always in the middle. If you had seen her, pretty and witty, in the center of a group of students walking past your house, you'd have thought, "There goes a natural leader."

Melinda Alice had left for school early. She wanted to study alone in a quiet spot she had because there was going to be a big math test, and Melinda Alice was not prepared. That A mattered; so Melinda

Alice walked to school alone, planning her studies. She didn't usually notice nature much, so she nearly stepped on a beautiful snail that was making its way across the sidewalk.

"Ugh. Yucky thing," thought Melinda Alice, then stopped. Not wanting to step on the snail accidentally was one thing, but now she lifted her shoe to crush it.

"Please don't," said the snail.

"Why not?" retorted Melinda Alice.

"I'll give you three wishes," replied the snail evenly.

"Agreed," said Melinda Alice. "My first wish is that my next," she paused a split second, "my next thousand wishes come true." She smiled triumphantly and opened her bag to take out a small notebook and pencil to keep track.

Melinda Alice was sure she heard the snail say, "What a clever girl," as it made it to the safety of an ivy bed beside the sidewalk.

During the rest of the walk to school, Melinda was occupied with wonderful ideas. She would have beautiful clothes. "Wish number two, that I will always be perfectly dressed," and she was just that. True, her new outfit was not a lot different from the one she had worn leaving the house, but that only meant Melinda Alice liked her own taste.

After thinking awhile, she wrote, "Wish number three. I wish for pierced ears and small gold earrings." Her father had not allowed Melinda to have pierced ears, but now she had them anyway. She felt her new earrings and shook her beautiful hair in delight. "I can have anything: stereo, tapes, TV, videodisc, moped, car, anything! All my life!" She hugged her books to herself in delight.

By the time she reached school, Melinda was almost an altruist; she could wish for peace. Then she wondered, "Is the snail that powerful?" She felt her ears, looked at her perfect blouse, skirt, jacket, shoes. "I could make ugly people beautiful, cure cripples . . ." She stopped. The wave of altruism had washed past. "I could pay people back who deserve it!" Melinda Alice looked at the school, at all the kids. She had an enormous sense of power. "They all have to do what *I* want now." She walked down the crowded halls to her locker. Melinda Alice could be sweet; she could be witty. She could—The bell rang for homeroom. Melinda Alice stashed her books, slammed the locker shut, and just made it to her seat.

"Hey, Melinda Alice," whispered Fred. "You know that big math test next period?"

"Oh, no," grimaced Melinda Alice. Her thoughts raced; "That damned snail made me late, and I forgot to study."

"I'll blow it," she groaned aloud. "I wish I were dead."

• • • •

JUDITH GOROG's first short-story collection, *A Taste for Quiet: And Other Disquieting Tales*, is presently out of print. Your public library, however, can probably locate a copy for you through interlibrary loan. Gorog's strength is taking the routine acts of everyday life—such as feeding a baby, getting a bump on the head, baby-sitting, taking a trip to the mall—and giving them a "weird" or "kooky" surprise ending.

While her first collection was aimed at young adults, her other books focus on middle-grade readers and include *In a Messy, Messy Room: And Other Strange Stories; No Swimming in Dark Pond and Other Stories; On Meeting Witches at Wells*; and *Three Dreams and a Nightmare: And Other Tales of the Dark.*

The next story here is also about wishes. It is as strange and improbable as Judith Gorog's, but it is absolutely true.

IT HAPPENED ON THE BROOKLYN SUBWAY

by Paul Deutschman

Lila and DeWitt Wallace

The Little Magazine That Could

Wally would someday become the greatest publishing success in American history, but you couldn't convince his father, the college president, of that. Not after the boy became obsessed with sports and practical jokes (like smuggling a cow up to the third-floor chapel). His older brother Benjamin, who became Minnesota's first Rhodes scholar, wasn't all that impressed either. All he ever saw his kid brother reading was magazines, instead of books like himself. And you would have been hard pressed to convince his Massachusetts prep school teachers after he ran away to California before they could discipline him for pranks. Or the professors at two colleges he dropped out of, colleges where he billed himself to fraternity brothers as "the Playboy of the Western World."

Older brother Benjamin had been an excellent example, however, and Wally Wallace had watched him studiously. Benjamin read large volumes and reduced the knowledge in them to easily referenced note cards. In 1911, at age nineteen, Wally spent the summer selling maps door-to-door in rural Oregon, sometimes walking twenty-five miles a day. The traveling salesmen and strangers he met along the road made a big impression on him. It seemed that each had some nugget of knowledge to impart, and he began to jot down their ideas on index cards.

It should also be noted that, in those days, books and magazines often were written in a more descriptive and flowery style than today's standard. Many authors and editors felt two words were better than one. So through the long evenings on the road, Wally the salesman waded through his magazines, reducing various articles to note size.

He wrote his father: "I have 3 × 5 inch slips of paper, and when I read an article I place all the facts I wish to preserve or remember on one of these slips. Before going to sleep at night I mentally review what I've read during the day, and from time to time I go through the file recalling articles from memory. I do not see why time thus spent is not as beneficial as if spent studying books."

One day on his map-selling route, Wally stopped to observe a courtroom trial and marveled at the jousting between the two attorneys. Their verbal contest before the jury reminded him of the challenge facing every salesman. "If there is a book in the library on courtroom cross-examination," he thought to himself, "it might be worth reading and applying." Through the rain he marched two miles to the Medford (Oregon) Carnegie Library, one of two thousand such places constructed with Andrew Carnegie's sixty-million-dollar trust fund for curious Americans such as Wally. Not only did he find a book on cross-examination, he also discovered the purpose of a library—to be a free "people's university" and fountain of knowledge, just like his note cards.

Wally was sensing as a young man what American industry had begun to surmise. Mechanization was at hand and Americans were no longer going to spend sixty-hour weeks in the factories and fields. Americans were demanding an easier life. Machines were about to be invented that would speed us through the workday—such "time-savers" for the home as dishwashers, automatic toasters, and coffee makers. How long would it be before someone did the same thing for reading?

In the ensuing years, as he worked a variety of jobs in printing and sales, Wallace toyed with the idea of publishing some of what he'd collected on the note cards. And then in 1918, during World War I, while recuperating in Europe from near-fatal wounds, he came up with the idea of a general-interest magazine condensed from lengthy magazine articles. For the next few months he read and condensed every magazine in the hospital library. Returning home to St. Paul, Minnesota, he spent another six months doing the same. With thirty-one of the best articles in hand, each two pages long, he had several hundred sample copies printed. The size, by the way, would be comfortable enough to stick into a pocketbook or back pocket, almost palm size, and just the right weight for reading in bed.

Benjamin loaned him three hundred dollars and, after much deliberation, his father reluctantly advanced another three hundred dollars, but they were the only ones interested in financing the project.

Major publishing houses ignored his pitch, claiming it was "naive, or too serious and educational in intent." Finally, after Wally lost his job with Westinghouse during a cutback in 1921, he took up the project full-time. A friend had suggested he try selling the magazine directly through the mail instead of through newsstands or the major publishers' subscription lists. Day after day and into the night, Wally sat at the typewriter in his rented room and copied the names and addresses of people he'd collected from lists given to him by hospitals, schools, colleges, churches, and civic clubs. Each person would receive a hand-typed invitation to subscribe, along with a description of the publication (no ads, no fiction, no pictures, but lots of informative articles), and a money-back guarantee if the subscriber was not satisfied with the first edition.

By the winter of 1922, Wally had moved to New York City, and one morning he and his fiancée, Lila, along with a few patrons hired from a Greenwich Village speakeasy, mailed off the first five thousand copies of what would soon become America's greatest publishing success—*Reader's Digest*. One year later, Henry Luce would attempt a similar "digest" formula for news and call it *Time*, and almost three quarters of a century later similar digests would be born in newspapers (*USA Today*) and television (CNN–Headline News). None, however, would know the success of the original.

Today the Reader's Digest Association, which began with just DeWitt "Wally" Wallace and his new bride, employs more than ten thousand people in fifty locations across the globe. The *Digest*'s U.S. subscription rolls are now at seventeen million, with more than half of its readers between the ages of eighteen and forty-four. Worldwide figures expand the total to twenty-eight million subscriptions with forty-one editions in seventeen languages, and, when you consider the second and third parties who read each issue in a home, office, or library, you may safely say each issue has more than one hundred million readers.

Wally's "get-to-the-point" approach is still evident: *Reader's Digest* is the only popular magazine in America that puts its table of contents on the cover and its artwork on the back. His respect for the common man he met while selling maps is evident as well: While most magazines charge the readers to read the magazine, *Reader's Digest* works a strange twist on that routine—it employs and pays its readers. Each issue features more than a hundred articles, jokes, inspirations, and anecdotes that have been sent to the *Digest* by its readers throughout the world, and for which they are handsomely paid.

Wallace's conservative, flag-waving, Middle America recipe of inspiration, information, and self-help is still the magazine's working formula, though slightly expanded. The *Digest* has a passion for making everyone's love life better, thighs thinner, wallet thicker, prayers more effective, and hospital bills lower. Its basic premise, often laughed at by sophisticates, is still the one most often espoused by ministers, generals, psychologists, and football coaches: God helps those who help themselves! So get off your duff and help someone— starting with yourself.

The magazine has stayed more a heartland than a headline publication. It lets other publications spend the money and time chasing the story, and when the dust settles a month later, the *Digest* leisurely pays both the author and the original publication to use the story, boils it down to its own size, and prints it. For the vast majority of its readers, it is a brand-new story.

Anyone who complains that the American media never focus on the good news obviously doesn't subscribe to *Reader's Digest*. Critics often label the *Digest*'s readers as "middlebrow," and rightly so. But they also could be labeled religious and community "activists," and, as such, they are more apt to pick up a phone or pen in response to reading an article. When the *Digest* ran a story about a black family's struggle to find a bone-marrow donor for their dying daughter, it generated more than two thousand inquiries from interested donors.

The *Digest*'s formula, however, is not foolproof. You should have heard the howls from various quarters when they dared to produce a condensed Bible a few years ago!

To generate the articles for each month's issue, staff members still do what their old boss did—they read five hundred monthly magazines and journals looking for material. In addition, dozens of books are read by other editors looking for condensation prospects, and a host of editors and staffers process the thirty thousand reader contributions that arrive monthly. All of this is in addition to the dozen original articles the *Digest*'s editors assign monthly to its freelancers. Incidentally, readers will find very few "correction" notices in *Reader's Digest*. Each issue's thirty-four hundred or so facts are checked through fourteen hundred various sources throughout the world.

One of Wally Wallace's favorite sayings was "The dead carry with them to the grave in their clutched hands only that which they have given away." As a consequence, the Wallaces, who had no children, gave away the *Digest*. They drew up one of the most generous wills in this century, donating all the magazine's profits to such causes as the Metropolitan Museum of Art, Lincoln Center, the Sloan-Kettering Cancer Center, the New York Zoological Society, and a charitable trust called The Lila Wallace–Reader's Digest Fund. Ironically, the ultraconservative Wallaces' fortune is now the leading private support fund for some unconservative arts projects in the United States, and is often the principal economic brace for new and experimental projects by ethnic-minority artists. In 1992, its fifty-two-million-dollar donation to Spelman College was the largest single donation to a predominantly black college in U.S. history.

If there was ever a typical *Reader's Digest* article, this is it. Originally published in 1949, it exemplifies the generous heart of the American people and the courage of its immigrants. Whatever else it says, I leave to the reader to discover. Its author, Paul Deutschman, was one of the first soldiers to land in the European theater during World War II, and, wanting to preserve what he saw upon landing, he wrote out his initial impressions. By luck, the piece came into the hands of *Life* magazine, which not only ran it as a prediction of what American troops would be meeting overseas but also offered Deutschman a job when the war was over.

During the postwar period at *Life*, he did a story on the travails and determination of displaced persons arriving in the United States. While he was researching the story, someone in one of the agencies set up to handle family case histories told Deutschman about a certain New York photographer's experience. When his *Life* article was completed, he tracked down the photographer and his story. The subsequent article was sold as an original to *Reader's Digest*, and while it is a testimonial to the American spirit, if not other kinds as well, it is also appropriate that its author should be the son of two Russian immigrants who worked their way through American night schools and medical schools to become a successful doctor and dentist, respectively.

If ever there was a case to substantiate the claim "Truth is stranger than fiction," this is it, and Wally Wallace must have loved it.

• • • •

T HERE ARE TWO DIFFERENT EXPLANATIONS of what happened as the result of a subway ride taken by Hungarian-born Marcel Sternberger on the afternoon of January 10, 1948.

Some people will say that Sternberger's sudden impulse to visit a sick friend in Brooklyn—and the bright world of dramatic events that followed—was part of a string of lucky coincidences. Others will see the guiding hand of Divine Providence in everything that happened that day.

But whatever the explanation, here are the facts:

STERNBERGER, a New York portrait photographer living in a Long Island suburb, has followed for years an unchanging routine in going from his home to his office on Fifth Avenue. A methodical man of nearly 50, with bushy white hair, guileless brown eyes and the bouncing enthusiasm of a *czardas* dancer of his native Hungary, Sternberger always takes the 9:09 Long Island Railroad train to Woodside, at which station he catches a subway train to the city.

On the morning of January 10, he boarded the 9:09 as usual. En route he suddenly decided to visit Laszlo Victor, a Hungarian friend who lived in Brooklyn and who was ill.

"I don't know why I decided to go to see him that morning," Sternberger told me some weeks afterward. "I could have done it after office hours. But I kept thinking that he could stand a little cheering up."

Accordingly, at Ozone Park Sternberger changed to the subway for Brooklyn, went to his friend's house and stayed until midafternoon. He then boarded a Manhattan-bound subway for his office.

"The car was crowded," Sternberger told me, "and there seemed to be no chance of a seat. But just as I entered, a man sitting by the door suddenly jumped up to leave and I slipped into the empty place.

"I've been living in New York long enough not to be in the habit of starting conversations with strangers. But, being a photographer, I have the peculiar habit of analyzing people's faces, and I was struck by the features of the passenger on my left. He was probably in his late 30s and his eyes seemed to have a hurt expression in them. He was reading a Hungarian-language newspaper and something prompted me to turn to him and say in Hungarian, 'I hope you don't mind if I glance at your paper.'

"The man seemed surprised to be addressed in his native language but he answered politely, 'You may read it now. I'll have time later on.'

"During the half-hour ride to town we had quite a conversation. He said his name was Paskin. A law student when the war started, he had been put into a labor battalion and sent to the Ukraine. Later he was captured by the Russians and put to work burying the German dead. After the war he had covered hundreds of miles on foot, until he reached his home in Debrecen, a large city in eastern Hungary.

"I myself knew Debrecen quite well, and we talked about it for a while. Then he told me the rest of his story. When he went to the apartment once occupied by his father, mother, brothers and sisters, he found strangers living there. Then he went upstairs to the apartment he and his wife had once had. It also was occupied by strangers. None of them had ever heard of his family.

"As he was leaving, full of sadness, a boy ran after him, calling: '*Paskin bacsi! Paskin bacsi!*' That means 'Uncle Paskin.' The child was the son of some old neighbors of his. He went to the boy's home and talked to his parents. 'Your whole family is dead,' they told him. 'The Nazis took them and your wife to Auschwitz.'

"Auschwitz was one of the worst concentration camps. Paskin thought of the Nazi gas chambers, and gave up all hope. A few days later, too heartsick to remain longer in Hungary, which to him was a funeral land, he set out again on foot, stealing across border after border until he reached Paris. He had managed to emigrate to the United States in October 1947, just three months before I met him.

"All the time he had been talking, I kept thinking that somehow his story seemed familiar. Suddenly I knew why. A young woman whom I had met recently at the home of friends had also been from Debrecen; she had been sent to Auschwitz; from there she had been transferred to work in a German munitions factory. Her relatives had been killed in the gas chambers. Later, she was liberated by the Americans and was brought here in the first boatload of Displaced Persons in 1946. Her story had moved me so much that I had written down her address and phone number, intending to invite her to meet my family and thus help relieve the terrible emptiness in her present life.

"It seemed impossible that there could be any connection between these two people, but when I reached my station I stayed on the train and asked in what I hoped was a casual voice, 'Is your first name Bela?'

"He turned pale. 'Yes!' he answered. 'How did you know?'

"I fumbled anxiously in my address book. 'Was your wife's name Marya?'

"He looked as if he were about to faint. 'Yes! Yes!' he said.

"I said, 'Let's get off the train.' I took him by the arm at the next station and led him to a phone booth. He stood there like a man in a trance while I searched for the number in my address book. It seemed hours before I had the woman called Marya Paskin on the other end. (Later, I learned her room was alongside the telephone but she was in the habit of never answering it because she had so few friends and the calls were always for someone else. This time, however, there was no one else at home and, after letting it ring for a while, she answered it.)

"When I heard her voice, at last, I told her who I was and asked her to describe her husband. She seemed surprised at the question but gave me a description. Then I asked her where she had lived in Debrecen and she told me the address.

"Asking her to hold the wire, I turned to Paskin and said, 'Did you and your wife live on such-and-such a street?'

" 'Yes!' Bela exclaimed. He was white as a sheet, and trembling.

" 'Try to be calm,' I urged him. 'Something miraculous is about to happen to you. Here, take this telephone and talk to your wife!'

"He nodded his head in mute bewilderment, his eyes bright with tears. He took the receiver, listened a moment to his wife's voice, then suddenly cried, 'This is Bela! This is Bela!' and began to mumble hysterically. Seeing that the poor fellow was so excited he couldn't talk coherently, I took the receiver from his shaking hands.

"I began talking to Marya, who also sounded hysterical. 'Stay where you are,' I told her. 'I am sending your husband to you. He will be there in a few minutes.'

"Bela was crying like a baby and saying over and over again, 'It is my wife. I go to my wife!'

"At first I thought I had better accompany Paskin lest the man should faint from excitement, but decided that this was a moment in which no stranger should intrude. Putting Paskin into a taxicab, I directed the driver to take him to Marya's address, paid the fare and said good-by."

Bela Paskin's reunion with his wife was a moment so poignant, so electric with suddenly released emotion, that afterward neither he nor Marya could recall anything about it.

"I remember only that when I left the phone I walked to the mirror like in a dream to see maybe if my hair had turned gray," she said later. "The next thing I know a taxi stops in front of the house and it is my husband who comes toward me. Details I cannot remember; only this I know—that I was happy for the first time in many years.

"Even now it is difficult to believe that it happened. We have both suffered so much; I have almost lost the capability to be not afraid. Each time my husband goes from the house I say to myself, 'Will anything happen to take him from me again?' "

Her husband is confident that no overwhelming misfortune will ever again befall them. "Providence has brought us together," he says simply. "It was meant to be."

Skeptical persons would no doubt attribute the events of that memorable afternoon to mere chance. But was it chance that made Sternberger suddenly decide to visit his sick friend, and hence take a subway line that he had never been on before? Was it chance that caused the man sitting by the door of the car to rush out just as Sternberger came in? Was it chance that caused Bela Paskin to be sitting beside Sternberger, reading a Hungarian newspaper?

Was it chance—or did God ride the Brooklyn subway that afternoon?

• • • •

AUTHOR PAUL DEUTSCHMAN went on to work for the U.S. State Department, then became a free-lance writer and novelist.

A extensive personal portrait of DeWitt Wallace can be found in the February 1987 issue of *Reader's Digest*, and many of its facts were incorporated into the introduction of this article.

Audio- and Videocassette Production Companies

(Your local bookstore may not carry any or all of the audio- or videocassettes recommended with the stories in this book. Should you wish to contact the production companies, here is a reference list.)

Books on Tape
P.O. Box 7900
Newport Beach, CA 92658
(800) 626-3333

Dercum Press
P.O. Box 1425
West Chester, PA 19380
(215) 430-8889

G. K. Hall
P.O. Box 159
Thorndike, ME 04986
(800) 223-6121

Harper-Caedmon Audio
10 East 53rd Street
New York, NY 10022-5299
(800) 242-7737

JimCin Recordings
P.O. Box 536
Portsmouth, RI 02871
(401) 847-5148 (in Rhode Island)
(800) 538-3034 (outside Rhode Island)

Listening Library
One Park Avenue
Old Greenwich, CT 06870
(800) 243-4504

The Mind's Eye
P.O. Box 1060
Petaluma, CA 94953
(800) 227-2020

PBS Video
Public Broadcasting Service
1320 Braddock Place
Alexandria, VA 22314-1698
(800) 344-3337

Penguin Highbridge Audio
P.O. Box 999
Bergenfield, NJ 07621
(800) 526-0275

Random Audio
Random Inc. Distribution Center
400 Hahn Road
Westminster, MD 21157
(800) 733-3000

Recorded Books
270 Skipjack Road
Prince Frederick, MD 20678
(800) 638-1304

Photograph credits: Jerry Spinelli: Chuck Cully; Mary Steele: Courtesy of Penguin Books Australia Ltd; Gary Soto: Carolyn Soto; Jon F. Hassler: Pete Crouser; Patricia Pendergraft: Courtesy of the author; Frederick Dannay: The Bettmann Archive; Manfred B. Lee: The Bettmann Archive; Harper Lee: G. D. Hackett, from the Special Collections Library, University of Alabama; Langston Hughes: Library of Congress; Cynthia Rylant: Courtesy of Orchard Books; Robert Newton Peck: Jim Trelease; Willie Morris: Alen MacWeeney; Allan Eckert: Jay Paris; John Christopher: A. Vaughan Kimber, used by permission of Dutton Children's Books, a division of Penguin Books USA Inc.; Roald Dahl: Mark Gerson; Rudyard Kipling: Library of Congress; Howard Pyle: Delaware Art Museum, Wilmington, DE; Walter de la Mare: Library of Congess; Ernest L. Thayer: Harvard University Archives; Robert W. Service: The National Archives of Canada; Rhys Davies: Harry Ransom Humanities Research Center, University of Texas at Austin; Philippa Pearce: Adam Pearce; William Sleator: Nancy Goldring; David Braly: Edwin L. Braly; Ray Bradbury: The Bettmann Archive; Andy Strasberg and Roger Maris: Arnold Cardillo; Frederick Douglass: Leib Image Archives, York, PA; Moss Hart: The Bettmann Archive; Loren Eiseley: The Bettmann Archive; Alexander Dolgun: © Charmian Reading; Maya Angelou: Courtesy of the author; Leon Garfield: Courtesy of Penguin Books USA Inc.; Scott O'Dell: Photo by Jim Kalett, used by permission of Houghton Mifflin Co.; Anne Holm: Courtesy of the author; Arthur Roth: Muffin Gifford, East Hampton *Star*; Avi: Coppella Kahn; Mike Royko: Tribune Media Services; Jim Bishop: Courtesy of Elizabeth Kelly Bishop; Bob Greene: Tribune Media Services; Pete Hamill: Deirdre Hamill; Brent Ashabranner: Jennifer Ashabranner; Charles Panati: Courtesy of HarperCollins Publishers; Christopher de Vinck: Jim Trelease; Gary Paulsen: © Ruth Wright Paulsen; Judith Gorog: Alison Speckman; DeWitt and Lila Wallace: Courtesy of The Reader's Digest Association, Inc.

FOR THE BEST IN PAPERBACKS, LOOK FOR THE

In every corner of the world, on every subject under the sun, Penguin represents quality and variety—the very best in publishing today.

For complete information about books available from Penguin—including Pelicans, Puffins, Peregrines, and Penguin Classics—and how to order them, write to us at the appropriate address below. Please note that for copyright reasons the selection of books varies from country to country.

In the United Kingdom: For a complete list of books available from Penguin in the U.K., please write to *Dept E.P., Penguin Books Ltd, Harmondsworth, Middlesex, UB7 0DA.*

In the United States: For a complete list of books available from Penguin in the U.S., please write to *Consumer Sales, Penguin USA, P.O. Box 999— Dept. 17109, Bergenfield, New Jersey 07621-0120.* Visa and MasterCard holders call 1-800-253-6476 to order all Penguin titles.

In Canada: For a complete list of books available from Penguin in Canada, please write to *Penguin Books Canada Ltd, 10 Alcorn Avenue, Suite 300, Toronto, Ontario, Canada M4V 3B2.*

In Australia: For a complete list of books available from Penguin in Australia, please write to the *Marketing Department, Penguin Books Ltd, P.O. Box 257, Ringwood, Victoria 3134.*

In New Zealand: For a complete list of books available from Penguin in New Zealand, please write to the *Marketing Department, Penguin Books (NZ) Ltd, Private Bag, Takapuna, Auckland 9.*

In India: For a complete list of books available from Penguin, please write to *Penguin Overseas Ltd, 706 Eros Apartments, 56 Nehru Place, New Delhi, 110019.*

In Holland: For a complete list of books available from Penguin in Holland, please write to *Penguin Books Nederland B.V., Postbus 195, NL-1380AD Weesp, Netherlands.*

In Germany: For a complete list of books available from Penguin, please write to *Penguin Books Ltd, Friedrichstrasse 10-12, D-6000 Frankfurt Main 1, Federal Republic of Germany.*

In Spain: For a complete list of books available from Penguin in Spain, please write to *Longman, Penguin España, Calle San Nicolas 15, E-28013 Madrid, Spain.*

In Japan: For a complete list of books available from Penguin in Japan, please write to *Longman Penguin Japan Co Ltd, Yamaguchi Building, 2-12-9 Kanda Jimbocho, Chiyoda-Ku, Tokyo 101, Japan.*